POLITICAL PARTIES AND THE
CANADIAN SOCIAL STRUCTURE

POLITICAL PARTIES

AND THE

CANADIAN SOCIAL STRUCTURE

by

FREDERICK C. ENGELMANN

Department of Political Science
University of Alberta

and

MILDRED A. SCHWARTZ

Department of Sociology
University of Illinois at Chicago Circle

p
PRENTICE-HALL ♣ OF CANADA LTD.
h

Library of Congress Catalog Card No. 67-18898
    68473——Pa.
    68474——Cl.
1 2 3 4 5 71 70 69 68 67
    PRINTED IN CANADA

243293
Politics.

Contents

●

Contents

Preface

•

This book constitutes a first attempt to present an account of Canadian parties as forces operating within Canada's political system. We draw together existing information on the origin of parties, forms of party organization, leadership, patterns of support, issues, and the relation of parties to the electoral system and government. In dealing with these materials, we have been handicapped by the lack of comprehensive empirical treatment of the subject; hence our analysis is necessarily less than complete. Hopefully, our present efforts will encourage others to help us fill in those areas which remain in urgent need of more systematic treatment.

We have drawn together a number of approaches to the study of parties, used by political scientists of various schools and by political sociologists. In order to integrate these approaches, we focused on those influences on and effects of political parties which we considered to be significant. The strategy we adopted made it necessary to abandon both the topic headings and the descriptive approach customarily associated with the study of parties. Yet our method still allows us to account for all those aspects of parties normally considered pertinent. The reader then has two alternatives. He may, if he chooses, follow our order of presentation. But if he prefers a more traditional approach, he can still find all the material he would expect in a book on parties, aided by an index prepared specifically with a view to accommodating such a reader.

That we followed what some may consider an unorthodox approach to the study of parties is not surprising when seen in relation to our own characteristics. One of us, Fred Engelmann, is a political scientist and the other, Mildred Schwartz, a sociologist. We began by dividing responsibility for writing this book according to our areas of interest and competence. In the process of collaboration, we both broadened our intellectual horizons and sharpened our arguments in meeting each other's criticisms. The final result is then truly a partnership, where we both contributed equally to the effort and hence take equal responsibility for everything in the book. We hope that the reader too will share with us the excitement of subjecting a particular body of data to the scrutiny of more than one discipline.

As a first venture, it should be apparent that we could not have completed this book without help from numerous sources. It is not a very effective form of thanks, but the public acknowledgement we give here is a sincere expression of our appreciation.

We owe a special debt to those colleagues who took the time to offer detailed criticism and advice. These include John Meisel, Peter Regenstreif, Robert Alford, Robert Gilsdorf, Helen Jones Dawson, Frank Munger, Donald Gordon, and Frank Peers. They are, of course, in no way responsible for any shortcomings of the book.

Several people generously supplied us with previously unpublished materials. These are Robert Alford, Helen Jones Dawson, William F. Dawson, Jean Laponce, Maurice Pinard, John Porter, Peter Regenstreif, and Irwin Shulman.

Within the political parties, we were able to call on help from Keith Davey, Paul Lafond, Richard O'Hagan, Gordon Edick, David Greenspan, John Carstairs, Nicholas Ediger, Dalton Camp, Alvin Hamilton, Flora MacDonald, C. Joseph Clark, David Allin, Terence Grier, Donald C. MacDonald, and Ruth Cook. Others in public life who were of assistance are David Archer, Nelson Castonguay, and Peter C. Newman.

Students at the Universities of Calgary, Alberta, and Chicago contributed research assistance, term papers, and general critical acumen. These were Carolyn Bond, Wallace Gagne, Martin Westmacott, Hans Brown, Brian Coulter, Eileen Ellinson Kaul, Heinz Kaul, David Surplis, Linda Gurevitch, Ken Johnson, Michael Alcorn, Steven Davison, J. Alex Jupp, A. T. Chernushenko, Anthony Martin, Kenneth McRoberts, Lynda Erickson, Lynda Hodges, Sandra Hendrickson, Donald Blake, Neil Bullough, Colin Campbell, Jacklin Andrews. Mary Engelmann gave editorial assistance.

Grants to both writers, at Calgary and Edmonton, by the General Research Committee of the University of Alberta aided in the writing of the book. Coauthorship necessitated the typing of more than the usual number of drafts, and for this we thank particularly Mrs. Elise Wittig and the secretarial pool, and Mrs. E. T. Turek, at the University of Calgary; Mrs. M. Brooks, Mrs. D. Stachniak, Mrs. I. Badger, Miss M. Jabs, and Miss G. Baldwin, at the Department of Political Science of the University of Alberta. The final version of the manuscript was typed, in Chicago, by Ruth Howard and Judy Krysko, and in Edmonton, by Myrna MacSorley.

F.C.E.

M.A.S.

POLITICAL PARTIES AND THE
CANADIAN SOCIAL STRUCTURE

Section I

INTRODUCTION

1

The Role of Political Parties in a Democratic State

To the layman, political parties are the most obvious feature of political life. Whether born a little Liberal, a little Conservative, or neither, we are likely to equate "parties" and "politics." To many, the role of parties in modern competitive politics appears as dominant as the role of the corporation in modern competitive economics.

What is a political party, as we encounter it in the political life of a modern democracy? We are confident that most academic experts, professional politicians, and laymen would agree on the following: (1) Parties are organizations, (2) Parties concern themselves with providing governmental leaders, (3) Parties concern themselves with providing public policies, (4) Parties are most conspicuously active during elections, (5) Parties play a continuous part in political life.

It is difficult for us to conceive of democratic politics without organized political parties. Their activities permeate much of our lives. But the modern political party as we know it has not always been with us. It is not easy to place the time of its origin.[1] In many political systems, parties predate the establishment of universal suffrage and of responsible executives. In the political life of Britain, parties played a prominent role as early as the 18th Century, in the United States by 1800, and in Canada in the decade preceding Confederation. With the appearance of parliamentary groups in 17th Century England there was discussion about the desirability of such groups, variously referred to as "factions" or "parties." Initially, most attitudes toward Party were negative. To Royalist Tories, parties were divisive and unpatriotic. James Madison felt that factions would be so harmful to the polity that a federal government, immune to their influence, would have to be created. Ostrogorski and Michels, both intensive students of party at the turn of the century, were wary of its harmful influence. Ostrogorski considered party the triumph of private over public interest; Michels believed parties to be the bane of democracy. In North America, municipal reformers right up to the present tend to consider parties as inevitable vehicles of graft and corruption and as enemies of good government, at least on the local level.

Gradually, however, the party's unique position as a bridge between a society and its government began to be recognized. Some of the "early greats" of political science, among them Bagehot, Maine, Bryce, Wilson, and Lowell, acknowledged the prominent place parties were beginning to occupy in the modern polity. Today, most political philosophers and analysts agree that parties are vital connectors between the people and the organs of government, and that they are instrumental in providing the political system with leadership and decisions in the authoritative public domain.

Although they recognize the crucial importance of political parties, political scientists have not developed a unified and generally recognized way of viewing them. This contrasts with their much more generally accepted view of aspects of the governmental structure, such as legislatures and chief magistracies.

In the following section, we will characterize parties along five dimensions: origin, support, organization, appeal, and relation to government, and use these to construct a typology of parties.

•

THE STUDY OF POLITICAL PARTIES: FIVE DIMENSIONS

Circumstances of Party Origin

Parties may be classified into two broad categories of origin: parliamentary and extra-governmental. Those of parliamentary origin form where parliamentary bodies exist prior to the development of a broad suffrage. The foremost example is the two traditional British parties. Tories and Whigs developed in an age (1688 - 1832) in which Parliament was an important part of the governmental structure, but when parliamentary elections were the business of the few and, in some boroughs, of the landlord only. In Sweden, "Caps" and "Hats" developed in the 18th Century, when there was a functioning parliament, but highly restrictive suffrage within the four estates of the realm. The last famous example of the parliamentary origin of parties was the convening of the Estates General during the French Revolution. Here again, a legislature had been assuming almost total power, while the members represented only a small proportion of the population.

---

[1] For a useful account of the development of parties see Austin Ranney and Willmoore Kendall, *Democracy and the American Party System* (New York: Harcourt, Brace and Company, Inc., 1956), Part II.

Parties are said to have an extra-governmental origin when the rise of parliamentary institutions is accompanied by a significant expansion of the electorate, or when the party develops from a particular interest, ideology, or distinct population grouping. The former phenomenon was seen in France during the early Third Republic, where the expansion of the suffrage accounted for the electoral origin of the Radical Socialist Party. The latter is found frequently when a particular segment of the population seeks representation within the governmental structure. Notable examples are labour, socialist, communist, fascist, agrarian, Catholic, and Protestant parties.

Until recently, totalitarian parties have been the only ones whose origins were subjected to close study. In general, traditional historians have subordinated the study of the rise of groups to that of the actions of persons and governments. The systematic study of party origins dates only from the post-war period.[2]

Breadth of Party Support

The functioning of parties in a political system is affected by the nature of their support. This support may be evidenced through militant or ordinary membership, or regular or casual adherence. In some parties, members and supporters may be drawn from a narrow segment of the population only. In others, members and supporters will come from most or all walks of life. The extent of the sources of support is often called the social base of the party. The first mentioned type of party has a restricted social base; the latter has a broad social base.

Most parties do not restrict themselves to a completely homogeneous social base, but some must be classified as narrowly based. Their narrow base may be one of a number of types. The party may have developed, as did the older Swedish parties, from one of the historical estates. It may be, as was the *Zentrum*, the Catholic party of imperial Germany, the political organization of a particular religion. It may, as was the *Action française*, be restricted to those espousing a particular set of ideas. As did the Party of the Middle Estate of the Weimar Republic, it may represent a particular economic interest. It may, as does the *Suedtiroler Volkspartei* of present-day Italy, represent a particular ethnic minority. Finally—and here we have the most celebrated type of a restrictively-based party—it may be the political exponent of a social class, as were the early, class-conscious Marxist parties.

In contrast to these parties with a restricted base, we have parties whose social base is broad. Ideally, such a party will be based on at least minority elements of every significant segment of the society. The Democratic Party of the United States, particularly in the present decade, and the Liberal Party of Canada, certainly between 1896 and 1956, come close to this ideal. Less pure examples would be the Conservative parties of the United Kingdom and Canada, the Republican Party of the United States, the Christian Democratic parties of Germany and Italy, and the present-day British Labour Party.

Party support has been the subject of many studies, making use of various approaches. The oldest empirical study of party support is André Siegfried's *Tableau politique de la France de l'Ouest dans la troisième République*.[3] This study is an example of electoral geography, that is, it is concerned with tracing the geographic distribution of party support. In studies of this type inferences are drawn from statistical correlations between political and other characteristics, such as urban or rural residence, occupation, religion, and native or foreign birth. The strength of electoral support for a party in a region and the characteristics of that region, for instance a preponderance of Catholics, are interpreted as indicating that there is a particular association between religion and party. Frequently such analyses of regional voting patterns are extended over a period of time.

While in many of these studies the nature of the party preference associated with a particular region is inferred to be in some non-political characteristic of that region, others argue that political factors such as party loyalty may be the persistent ones. This latter emphasis characterizes the work of V. O. Key, the foremost exponent of electoral geography in the United States, and of his followers.[4]

Studies in political geography have pointed out bellweather areas of changes in voting patterns. They have revealed the extent of political sectionalism and of the political competitiveness of regions. Social influences on voting behaviour have also been examined in such studies as, for instance, the increase of voting for a class-oriented party accompanying the increase of the numerical strength of that class in a particular area.

The social bases of party support have also been studied through sample surveys, of which *The People's Choice* by Lazarsfeld, Berelson, and Gaudet[5] is an early example. Such voting studies may be based on single or repeated interviewing of community or country-wide samples of voters, giving us detailed pictures of the characteristics of party supporters. They determine directly such attributes as social class, ethnic origin, age, and sex. They also examine party indentification and partisan loyalty, relating these to voters' perceptions of parties, leaders, candidates, and issues.

Voting studies, then, inform us not only on the kinds of party supporters, but also on such matters as the stability of party support, the results

---

[2] Except for the account in Ranney and Kendall, the literature remains sparse. See also Maurice Duverger, *Political Parties*, trs. Barbara and Robert North (New York: John Wiley & Sons, Inc., 1954), pp. xxiii-xxxvi.

[3] André Siegfried, *Tableau politique de la France de l'Ouest dans la troisième République* (Paris: Armand Colin, 1913).

[4] See for example V. O. Key, Jr., *American State Politics: An Introduction* (New York: Alfred A. Knopf, Inc., 1956), and V. O. Key, Jr., and Frank Munger, "Social Determinism and Electoral Decision: The Case of Indiana," in *American Voting Behavior*, eds. Eugene Burdick and Arthur J. Brodbeck, (Glencoe: The Free Press, 1959), pp. 281-99.

[5] P. F. Lazarsfeld, B. Berelson and H. Gaudet, *The People's Choice*, 2nd ed., (New York: Columbia University Press, 1948). Four major works in this genre are discussed by Peter H. Rossi, "Four Landmarks in Voting Research," in *American Voting Behavior*, eds., Burdick and Brodbeck, pp. 5-54.

of party efforts to increase the numbers or kinds of supporters, and the strengths and weaknesses of political parties as these are seen by the electorate. One area they do not illuminate fully is the influence on party support of the activities of political parties and of those who act within the structure of government.

Party Organization and Leadership

In regard to organization, political parties fall into two broad categories. The first tends to have a loose structure, few dues-paying members, orientation primarily toward electoral activity, and domination by the party's governmental leaders. The second, in contrast, tends to have a tight structure, mass membership, constant party activity involving the members, and organizational leaders who vie for power with the party's governmental leaders. Duverger, stressing structure, calls the former a "cadre," the latter a "mass," party.[6] Neumann, stressing the involvement of the individual, calls the former "party of representation," the latter, "party of integration."[7] While we combine the emphasis of Duverger and Neumann, we adopt Duverger's terminology, and apply it to the nature of basic organizational units, nature of membership, involvement of members, nature of leadership, and participation in organizational policy making.

The normal site of the basic organizational unit of the cadre party is an electoral unit, such as the poll or the constituency. In the mass party, the basic unit is normally a local section or branch. It may also be a workplace cell or a basic formation of the party militia. The member of the cadre party is usually one of three kinds: a party notable (a prominent figure within the party organization), a financial supporter, or an election worker. The member of the mass party often has an ideological commitment to party doctrine. The involvement of the cadre party member is tied to his organizational or electoral role, while the run-of-the-mill party supporter participates at election time only, if at all. In the mass party, the daily life of the member is frequently tied to the party. Many of his social activities may take place in ancillary organizations of the party, such as women's, youth, or athletic groups. The important national leaders of the cadre party are governmental leaders; bureaucrats in the electoral organization normally hold a subordinate power position. In the mass parties, in contrast, there is usually coordinate power for governmental and organizational leaders, and foremost among the latter are permanent secretaries. Organizational policy in the cadre party normally is determined by governmental leaders, professional experts and bureaucrats, and some amateur notables. In the mass party, the first two groups are also of great importance, but the place of the amateur notable is taken by the participating segment of the dues-paying mass membership. In view of the latter's involvement, constitutional arrangements within the party tend to be important.

The study of parties as organizations began with M. I. Ostrogorski[8] and Robert Michels,[9] who wrote between 1900 and 1920. They felt that parties as they were organized did not further the cause of self-government, and their studies of party organization had the primary purpose of demonstrating the non- or anti-democratic effects of party. The substantive content of their studies, however, gives detailed pictures of party organization in the United Kingdom and the United States (Ostrogorski), and of the structure, including bureaucracy and leadership, of the socialist parties of the European continent (Michels). Both writers searched for the actual as distinguished from the formal structure of political parties. During the next two decades, the works of Ostrogorski and Michels were all but forgotten.

A generation after Ostrogorski, E. E. Schattschneider[10] attempted a realistic organizational analysis of parties in the United States. Unlike Ostrogorski and Michels, Schattschneider began with the assumption that the internal democratic control of political parties was impossible and, at any rate, unnecessary for the working of democracy in general. Paradoxically, Schattschneider's work did not lead to further organizational analysis, but to a protracted and largely normative squabble over the very same intraparty democracy he had initially found to be impossible.

In 1951, Maurice Duverger published the first integrated volume dealing with party structure and party systems. His organizational typology classifies party structure in general, basic units of party organization, relations between these and higher units of party organization, and party leadership.[11] Duverger attempts to correlate the various other characteristics of political parties with organizational elements. The internal power structure of parties, not one of Duverger's central concerns, forms the main subject of R. T. McKenzie's work on British parties.[12] McKenzie's main thesis is that the power structure of British parties is adapted to the function of these parties within the governmental structure of the United Kingdom.

All the writers named concentrate on mass parties, though one half of McKenzie's emphasis is on a major cadre party, the British Conservatives. All the major writers on party organization study organization because they are concerned—normatively, empirically, or both—with the place of the individual in party decision making.

---

[6] Duverger, *Political Parties*, pp. 63-71.

[7] Sigmund Neumann, "Toward a Comparative Study of Political Parties," in *Modern Political Parties*, ed. S. Neumann (Chicago: The University of Chicago Press, 1956), pp. 403-5.

[8] M. I. Ostrogorski, *Democracy and the Organization of Political Parties*, 2 vols., tr. Frederick Clarke (New York: The Macmillan Company, 1902).

[9] Robert Michels, *Political Parties: A Sociological Study of the Oligarchical Tendencies of Modern Democracy*, trs. Eden and Cedar Paul (London: Jarrold and Sons, 1915).

[10] E. E. Schattschneider, *Party Government* (New York: Rinehart & Company, Inc., 1942).

[11] Duverger, *Political Parties*, Part I.

[12] R. T. McKenzie, *British Political Parties*, 2nd ed. (New York: Frederick A. Praeger, Publisher, 1963).

Focus of Appeal

All political parties worth their salt want to be successful, but they differ in how they measure success and in the steps they will take to achieve it. These differences in orientation are frequently not extreme, but are rather differences of degree. There is enough differentiation in parties' orientation, however, to permit a further order of classification that divides them into parties of electoral success and parties of principle. Parties oriented to electoral success are highly pragmatic in their approach to voters. Examples of such parties are the national Republican and Democratic parties in the United States. There are, in contrast, parties oriented to principles based on special interests, issues, groups, or ideology.

In the party oriented toward electoral success, any principle (other than the maintenance of freedom, democracy, and legality) is subordinated to the requirement of winning elections or at least of maximizing electoral gains. Such parties attempt to fashion winning coalitions by appealing to as many interests and demographic groups as possible. They do so by taking flexible stands on salient issues, and by avoiding restrictive ideological commitments. Not only in their electoral appeal, but also in their activities within the governmental structure, they attempt to act as brokers for the maximum number of interests and demographic groups.

Parties of principle need not be strongly ideological in character. It is true that we would place traditional Marxist parties in this category, but we would also so classify parties with a less consistent and elaborate political philosophy, as long as their focus of appeal continues to be narrow. Examples would be prohibition, free trade, farmers', and ethnic parties. In all such cases, the significant fact is that the party leadership has decided that it is more important to retain the distinctive character of the party than to increase its share of the electorate. Of course, this may not always be a conscious decision at each point in time, but the historical continuity of a narrow appeal will in itself be sufficient to enable us to characterize parties on the basis of principle.

While this typology was derived independently, it is based on observations about the nature of parties which have been recognized by others. The terminology differs, but the basic distinctions remain the same. For example, Sigmund Neumann draws attention to the difference between what he terms the all inclusive faith movement (*Weltanschauungs-* or *Glaubens-Parteien*) and expediency interests.[13] The former is an example of our parties of principle and the latter concept captures the pragmatic nature of success-oriented parties. Gabriel Almond has made a related, but three-fold, distinction among parties. He terms these: "secular, 'pragmatic,' bargaining parties; absolute value-oriented, *Weltanschauung* or ideological parties; and particularistic or traditional parties."[14] It seems reasonable to compare the appeal of the secular party to that of the success-oriented party, and to consider the value-oriented and the particularistic parties as belonging in the category of the parties of principle.

INTRODUCTION

The study of party appeals for votes is of considerable interest in contemporary political science. Notable examples of such studies are the Nuffield studies of British and Continental elections,[15] and John Meisel's work on elections in Canada.[16] In the United States, there has been, in addition, strong interest in the impact of party appeals on the individual voter. U.S. voting studies frequently conclude that voters are not affected strongly by the issue positions taken by the two major parties. However, V. O. Key's posthumous volume, *The Responsible Electorate*,[17] directly challenges those commentators who state that, as far as voters are concerned, issues are less important than partisan loyalty and candidate appeal.

Relation to Government

Our final method of categorizing parties stems from the nature of their legislative experiences. Examining the history of any country with a competitive party system, we can readily find parties with four kinds of legislative experience. Most prominent are those whose fortunes have led them to assume the role of government. Other parties have taken the role of major opposition. In contrast to the major opposition are those parties which, while never forming the government, nevertheless continue to have some of their members elected. Sometimes no more than a handful of representatives attain elected office; at other times, sizable numbers are elected, yet their status remains as members of minor or third parties. Finally we have those parties which field candidates without attracting sufficient support from the voters to elect even one representative. Normally, such discouraging experiences contribute to the demise of the parties, but some seem able to survive for decades without achieving even a modicum of electoral success.

We are interested primarily in the contrast between those parties which govern and those parties which do not, whether or not the latter constitute the official opposition. A party which governs is called upon to provide leadership and decisions on a day-to-day basis. In other words, the governing party must be prepared to deal with routine matters normally associated with the conduct of government and, at the same time, must be responsive to unanticipated crises and demands whenever these arise. Responsibility for both the routine and the unexpected means

---

[13] Neumann, "Toward a Comparative Study. . . ," in *Modern Political Parties*, ed., Neumann, p. 400.

[14] Gabriel A. Almond, "Introduction: A Functional Approach to Comparative Politics," in *The Politics of Developing Areas*, eds. G. A. Almond and J. S. Coleman (Princeton: Princeton University Press, 1960), p. 43.

[15] The most recent of the British studies is David E. Butler and Anthony King, *The British General Election of 1964* (London, Macmillan and Company Limited, 1965); the foremost Continental Nuffield study is U. W. Kitzinger, *German Electoral Politics* (London: Oxford University Press, 1960).

[16] John Meisel, *The Canadian General Election of 1957* (Toronto: University of Toronto Press, 1962), and John Meisel, ed., *Papers on the 1962 Election* (Toronto: University of Toronto Press, 1964).

[17] V. O. Key, *The Responsible Electorate* (Cambridge: Belknap Press of Harvard University Press, 1966).

that decision making must primarily be made within the governing councils—that is, within the Cabinet and the party caucus. No matter how elaborately organized the extra-parliamentary party structure, nor how concerned its party membership is with formulating policy guidelines, the members are usually precluded from having much influence on the parliamentary structure once their party gains power. The demands placed on government for operating with reasonable efficiency and speed require that the governing party must govern, without waiting to activate the party structure which exists outside the legislature. Moreover, the kinds of policy directives which come from outside the legislature, no matter how impressive in content or how praiseworthy in principle, are now viewed by the party in power in a new light. While situations vary, it is quite customary that the governing party takes on a pragmatic bent. The legislators are concerned with which policies will work, with how to retain support from the voters, and with similar practical matters.

Parties outside the government, in contrast, need not be worried either by daily exigencies or by finding solutions to new problems, at least not as soon as these arise. As a result, they can and frequently do permit their extra-parliamentary party organization considerable control over the pronouncements of their legislative members. It is this contrast in the amount of authority exercised by the extra-parliamentary party structure which concerns us. For example, in the British Labour Party, the extra-governmental structure has always been of crucial importance. That is, elected members were expected to be guided in their parliamentary activities by the directives coming from outside Parliament, from the National Executive Committee. But when the Labour Party achieved power after World War II, this pattern was drastically modified, as the parliamentary structure gained ascendancy. Defeat, and a lengthy period from 1951 to 1964 out of power, again increased the impact of the extra-parliamentary structure. Yet the experience of government was itself critical, and served to permanently decrease the influence of the extra-parliamentary body.

The important differences between parties that govern and parties that do not, should not blind us to important role differentiations, brought on by specific systems of government or party systems, which may cut across our classification. Let us list some examples. In some federal systems, and the Canadian in particular, parties that have never attained even major opposition status have governed and do govern provinces. The arrangements for executive tenure in the German Federal Republic seemed to lessen the chances of the major opposition party, the Social Democrats, ever to form the government. In a multi-party system, regardless of the number of major parties, minor parties may attain governmental experience in coalitions, though hardly as leading and therefore principally responsible members of such governments. Finally, should there be several major parties, as in France, no single party can be spoken of as the major opposition party.

We would have liked to conclude this section with references to important literature on the relation of party to government, but such literature does not exist. At the present, discussion is limited to minor sections in the few comparative works on political parties, dealing with the interaction of parties with the governmental structure.[18]

•

A SCHEME FOR CLASSIFYING POLITICAL PARTIES

The dimensions we have just discussed enable us to classify political parties. Individually, they aid us in the analysis of parties. Taken together, they make possible the kind of description that has validity beyond the individual party. A classification scheme based on our dimensions helps us to arrive at a meaningful, unified way of viewing parties—something the literature does not offer us at present.

We will omit consideration of one of the dimensions, circumstances of party origin. We do this because, of present parties known to us, all parties with intra-governmental origins have a wide base of support, a cadre type of organization, an orientation toward electoral success, and a present or past governmental role. Thus, they all belong in the same category. We are left, therefore, with the four dimensions of breadth of support, organizational type, focus of appeal, and relation to government.

The significance of breadth of support in the analysis of parties lies in the interaction of party and society. A broadly based party is a microcosm of the society. A party with a restricted base draws support from one or more segments of the society only; in its initial stages at least, the most it can hope for is to represent this support base in the governmental structure. Organizational type is important in party analysis because it tells us something about role differentiation within the party. A cadre party enlists the aid of individuals primarily in order to win elections; in a mass party, ideally at least, each party supporter has an active role within the party structure. Focus of appeal affects the way in which the party interacts with the interest structure of society. The success-oriented party will attempt to aggregate—to bring together—as many interests as it can, and in this process it will tend to accept the interests as they present themselves. The party of principle, on the other hand, while not necessarily spurning most of the interests represented in society, expects these interests to accept an aggregation on terms of an overriding party principle or principles. The party's relation to government, finally, is important to party analysis because a party which has formed a government is likely to act in the light of present or past governmental experience, while other parties tend to behave, vis-à-vis the government, as outsiders.

Before introducing our scheme, we want to present two sets of cautions. We confront these as we move from the theoretical realm of our classification to the empirical world of actual parties. The first set refers to the interdependence of the dimensions. There is a tendency for a broad support base, cadre-type organization, orientation toward electoral

---

[18] Duverger, *Political Parties*, pp. 392-421.

success, and governmental experience, to go together. Broad-based and success-oriented parties tend to go with a social system without serious, dominant fissures, and cadre-type parties with voters whose party support tends to have at least some flexibility. We may find that parties show this association between the four characteristics because of some order of causal connection. Let us present a few likely linkages of categories. A success-oriented party with a restricted base may try to widen its base to achieve electoral success, or a broad-based party of principle may become success oriented. In either case, the party may at some later date attain a governmental role. Once that role is attained, the party may change its mass-type organization in the direction of a cadre-type organization, in order to permit greater freedom of action to its governmental leadership. Possibly a party with a restricted base but orientation to success may also attain governmental experience and then proceed to widen its base in order to continue to govern, or at least to compete on fairly equal terms with other contenders for a major governmental role. In any of these cases, a party—or usually its elite—will have *acted* in such a way as to change its character along one or more dimensions. The adaptive behaviour of parties may thus over the years bring about changes in their place in our classification scheme.

The second set of cautions refers to the lack of clear dichotomies along the dimensions. They are continous rather than neatly divided. Also, the place of a particular party along a dimension may depend on more than one criterion. A party may have a rather broad base, but its modal support may come from only one or two segments of the population. A party may have a loosely constituted cadre-type organization, and many dues-paying members, while another may have strict constitutional provisions laying down the parts to be played by the members, yet rather few members (in terms of their percentage of electoral supporters) to play these parts. A party may insist on one or more principles even when its campaigns are clearly geared to electoral success. Finally, the assessment of parties' governmental role is extremely difficult in countries with multi-party systems and frequent or constant coalition governments. All these circumstances disturb the neatness of a classification scheme. Yet we submit that parties do tend to occupy meaningfully discernible places along our four dimensions.

As Chart 1-1 shows, our four dimensions give us sixteen possible categories. Not all of them contain important parties, and some, only parties in systems that are not both mature and competitive. As we will show later, Canadian parties cluster in but a few of the categories.

Broad-based, success-oriented cadre parties with governmental experience make up many of the major parties in mature, competitive political systems, especially in those with a lengthy tradition of an executive whose tenure depends on the expressed will of the legislature or the electorate. This includes all parties with intra-governmental origin now in existence: the major parties of the United States and Canada, and the Conservative Party of the United Kingdom. Also included in this group are

CHART 1-1

PARADIGM FOR THE CLASSIFICATION OF POLITICAL PARTIES

		Cadre		Mass	
		Non-		*Non-*	
		Government	*Government*	*Government*	*Government*
Broad	*Success*	Democratic Party (U.S.)	Freedom Party (Austria)	British Labour Party (post-1945)	Social Democratic Party (Germany: 1945-66)
	Principle	Radical Party (France)	*Action Française*	Communist Party of the Soviet Union	Communist Party of Italy
Restricted	*Success*	Country Party (Australia)	Refugee Party (Germany)	*Zentrum* (Germany: Pre-1933)	
	Principle		Prohibition Party (U.S.)		Communist Party (U.S.)

such recently established parties as Germany's Christian Democratic Union and the French Independents. As most broad-based, success-oriented cadre parties are wont to govern, only a few of them are in the category lacking governmental experience.

Mass parties that have a broad base and an orientation to electoral success include such of the grand socialist parties as have "de-ideologized," i.e., abandoned a significant orientation to principle, during recent decades. Among those with governmental experience are the Labour parties of the United Kingdom, Australia, and New Zealand. An important party in this category, but without governmental experience, is the federal Social Democratic Party of West Germany.

Broad-based cadre parties tend to be oriented toward electoral success, and thus we do not find many important broad-based parties of principle; this applies to parties in either category of governmental experience. There are, however, important mass parties in these categories. Prominent among those with governmental experience are the Communist Party of the Soviet Union, and the now defunct parties of the interwar fascist dictatorships. Prominent in the non-governmental category are the Communist parties of Italy and France.

The remaining categories differ from those already discussed in that the parties have a restricted base. Such a base is not one which a competitive party admits to readily, and, lacking demographic data, we are forced to place parties in these categories on the basis of observation and judgment. We do not know of any important cadre party with a restricted base that has governed a political system with a wide suffrage. Among mass parties with a restricted base, there are important Catholic parties; of these, the French *Mouvement Républicain Populaire* and the *Zentrum* of Weimar Germany have formed governments.

We do not know of a narrowly based party of principle, cadre or mass, that has played a major governmental role under conditions of wide suffrage. Mass parties of this kind, without governmental experience, include many Communist parties, among them, those of America north of the Rio Grande, and ethnic minority parties that restrict their appeal to the minority they represent.

We have now presented what we consider to be the significant dimensions in the descriptive and analytical study of political parties, and a scheme for classifying parties which utilizes these dimensions. However, our task in this opening chapter goes further. In order to account significantly for the role of political parties in democratic states in general, we must place parties functionally within the context of the political and the wider social systems. We will now introduce the theoretical perspective in which we do so.

•

A NOTE ON OUR THEORETICAL PERSPECTIVE

A Model For Viewing Political Parties

The perspective we bring to our study of parties is basically simple. It is based on the premise that, with varying degrees of closeness, the different parts of the social system are interrelated. Parties are of course part of society. Hence we presume that in their origins, organizational structure, and functioning, parties will be affected by the social setting in which they are found. In turn, parties can be expected to have an effect on their social setting.

This approach is hardly unique. It is, for example, current in most of contemporary sociology.[19] At the same time, it has a long tradition in political science. Writing forty years ago on the nature and function of party, Merriam said:

. . . what looks like a vast power of a party leader, or boss, will upon more careful analysis be found to be the visible part of a larger process not at first seen because of its being below the surface of things. Deep down in the social and economic interests of the society, hidden in its social and political psychology, lie the habits, tendencies and forces which condition the action of the party. . . .[20]

Yet the statement of perspective we have presented provides little guidance to the selection and analysis of data if we leave it as is. Fortunately, we find a way of explicating our approach to the relationship between the political and non-political through the work of writers such as David Easton, Gabriel Almond, and Talcott Parsons.[21] Easton, for example, focuses on the political system, relating it to the broader milieu through the concepts of inputs and outputs. Most generally, he sees inputs to the political system as demands and support, and outputs from it as decisions and actions. The nature of this circular relationship is brought out graphically in Chart 1-2. It is the political system which is the central unit in this model, not political parties. Yet the model can also be utilized for our purposes by placing parties in its centre. In so doing, our intention is not to detract from the overriding significance of the political system, but rather to draw attention to the place of parties as part of the larger system.

It is obviously still necessary to spell out some of the details of the model. In doing this, we will frequently sacrifice theoretical rigour to the requirements of what we know to be necessary for an adequate description of Canadian parties. Our specification will cover the nature of the environment, differentiation of the political system, a definition of political parties, distinctions among political outputs, and distinctions among party outputs.

The Environment

The operation of political parties takes place within a particular political context and also a broader social one. In the analysis which follows we will deliberately limit ourselves to those features of the environment which general knowledge about the operation of party systems, and the Canadian scene in particular, lead us to believe are most relevant. At the same time, this selection is closely linked to the availability of information, so that we unfortunately have had to ignore some aspects of social existence which present inputs to the political system. For example, it would be useful to know about family life and the school system since both of these provide important avenues for the political socialization of future voters.[22] However, the sketchiness of available data and the importance of other environmental factors have precluded their consideration in this book.

To begin with, it is important to have some understanding of the total social system in which the parties under study are to be found. Through

[19] In a presidential address given to the American Sociological Association several years ago, Kingsley Davis affirmed that this approach, generally termed functionalism, has become almost synonomous with sociological analysis. Kingsley Davis, "The Myth of Functional Analysis as a Special Method in Sociology and Anthropology," *American Sociological Review*, XXIV (December 1959), 757-772.

[20] Charles E. Merriam and Harold F. Gosnell, *The American Party System* (New York: The Macmillan Company, 1922), p. 386.

[21] David Easton, "An Approach to the Analysis of Political Systems," *World Politics*, IX (1956-57), 383-400; David Easton, *A Systems Analysis of Political Life* (New York: John Wiley & Sons, Inc. 1965); Gabriel Almond, "Introduction," in *The Politics of Developing Areas*, eds., Almond and Coleman; Talcott Parsons, " 'Voting' and the Equilibrium of the American Political System," in *American Voting Behavior*, eds., Burdick and Brodbeck, pp. 83-85.

[22] For some data on the United States, see *The Annals*, 361, (September 1965), a special issue edited by Roberta Sigel, entitled "Political Socialization: Its Role in the Political Process."

CHART 1-2

A MODEL OF THE POLITICAL SYSTEM

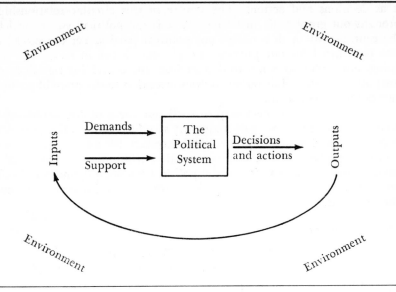

Source: David Easton, *A Systems Analysis of Political Life* (New York: Wiley, 1965), p. 32.

an examination of the nature and distribution of human and non-human resources and rewards available in a particular society, it becomes possible to assign some relative importance to particular subsystems and their elements insofar as these influence the party system. For example, as we will go on to argue, in the case of Canada, the social structure has developed in such a way that two critical dimensions have emerged, with great significance for political parties. These dimensions are regional-ethnic and regional-economic. In this book we use ethnicity to refer to "descent from ancestors who shared a common culture based on national origin, language, religion, or race, or a combination of these."[23] The regional-ethnic dimension hence takes into account the division of Canada into regions, whose identity has been reinforced by their settlement by different ethnic groups. The regional-economic dimension derives its significance from the strengthening of regional cleavages by differences in economic resources and development. In our consideration of the major subsystems which have influenced the emergence and development of Canadian parties, we will look at the religious and economic systems. While religion is certainly not synonomous with ethnic origin, there is enough overlap to make dealing with religion a convenient means of handling the institutional manifestations of this primary social characteristic. We will also deal with the communications system, looking at it in relation to interest groups, elites, and the mass media.

INTRODUCTION

The economy will interest us in terms of what people do to earn their livelihood and where they do it. The impact of the economy on political parties may be through beliefs and values associated with it, as in the case of free enterprise as a value; through the activities of organized interest groups such as Chambers of Commerce or trade unions; or through the efforts of a special elite, such as the president of a large corporation.

Religion is less closely allied with the political system than is the economy. Yet historically it has been a major influence on political development and, for reasons specific to Canada, continues to be an important political force. As in the case of the economy, the institutions and organizations associated with religion may have their effect on parties through beliefs, organized interest groups, or the activities of elites.

The communications system is closely connected with other parts of the social system and generally represents the interests of other subsystems. For example, a newspaper such as the *Wall Street Journal* quite obviously expresses the viewpoints of certain sectors of American big business. But we contend that the system of communication also has some independent influence on parties through, for example, the publicity it provides for candidates.

The Political System

The most obvious parts of the environment affecting political parties are other aspects of the political system in which they are located. In addition to the party system, the total political system is made up of other relevant parts. In Canada, the most pertinent are the parliamentary and federal systems. The effects of these on parties will be examined in Chapter 6. In turn, parties influence the structure and operation of other parts of the political environment, and these will concern us in Chapters 8 and 9.

Political Parties Defined

Political parties are political organizations performing political functions. Yet they are not the only political organizations. There are, for instance, political organizations closer to the points at which demands from individuals and groups are originally raised; these are interest groups. Interest groups are formed so that demands from various publics may be politicized, that is, shaped in such a manner that they can be formulated as public policy demands. In other words, organized interest groups serve to translate the needs and requirements of some segment of the public into pressure on the political machinery, in the form of support for new programs, rewards for past favours, or requests for specific actions.

---

[23] Frank G. Vallee, Mildred Schwartz, and Frank Darknell, "Ethnic Assimilation and Differentiation in Canada," *Canadian Journal of Economics and Political Science,* XXIII (November 1957), 541.

There are also political organizations closer to the level at which public policy is administered and made effective, such as a Crown prosecutor's office, a court of law, or an administrative agency. Because this type of political organization is itself instituted by constitution or law (which interest groups and, incidentally, political parties are not, in most parts of the Western World), political scientists have been in the habit of calling it an institution. Such terminology would of course be confusing to students of sociology, and to modern social scientists in general. In order to avoid confusing them, and also those students of political science who are not accustomed to calling these "instituted" organizations by the term organization, we will follow a path indicated by several contemporary political scientists and refer to political organizations such as legislatures, public magistracies, and courts of law, as governmental structures.

But, clearly, political life is not made up merely of interest groups that articulate demands, and of governmental structures that actually implement public policy. There must be some transitional stages between these two. For one thing, demands need to be aggregated, that is, decisions are required as to which demands will actually be proposed as objects of public policy. For another, it is necessary that individuals be selected who will give leadership to the public policy-making process and who will direct the implementation of public policy. Much of the bridging between the articulation of interests on the one side and public administration on the other is done through (1) interests which exert regular and well-organized public pressure, such as the Canadian Labour Congress and the Royal Canadian Legion, and (2) decision-making governmental structures such as the House of Commons and the Cabinet. But the master agency linking society, in terms of politicized demands, and government, is the political party. Ideally, the political party integrates the activities of aggregating demands and of turning these into public policy. In so doing it contributes to the provision of leadership and decisions in the authoritative public domain. In a real sense then, political parties are the grand connectors of people and the organs of government.[24]

Political Outputs

According to Easton, political outputs consist of decisions and actions. To Almond, they are made up of rule making, application, and adjudication. To Parsons, they consist of effective leadership and binding decisions. Since political sociology and systematic political science are essentially still pioneering ventures, this difference in emphasis on the part of leading theorists should not surprise us. The common element among all of them is the emphasis on the authoritative nature of the outputs. These outputs of course vary in kind; they range from the drafting of constitutions and basic laws (a highly infrequent event in a stable polity), to such frequent decisions as the enactment of statutes, the application of legislated rules to specific cases, and the selection (election or appointment) of public officials. In the case of the latter function, we may correctly say that what is being provided is either leadership or decisions.

Party outputs differ from more general political outputs in several respects. Primarily, the difference lies in the site where inputs are converted into outputs—where demands for policy become actual policy. For the political system generally, the conversion takes place within the structure of government: in legislative committees, legislatures, administrative agencies, and so on. But for parties, some inputs become converted into party policy before they are converted into authoritative public policy. For instance, a party nominates a candidate, but he does not become a public official until he is successful in his electoral competition with the candidates of other parties. Similarly, a party may decide on a certain policy: again, this policy decision is not enacted authoritatively unless it receives the sanction of the appropriate segment of the governmental structure. Party outputs may or may not become political outputs eventually, but they precede political outputs. At the same time, political outputs are by no means always preceded by party outputs. Hence the difference between party and political outputs generally is both analytically and actually distinct. The party is more frequently and more fully involved in supplying leadership than in supplying policy decisions.

Party Outputs

In a democratic state, outputs from political parties involve essentially two activities. These are the organization of popular consultation and the direction of the operation of government. These outputs in turn have an impact on the broader social setting and contribute to the emergence of new inputs.

POPULAR CONSULTATION   The extension of the suffrage to mass electorates made necessary the presence of continuous party organizations for organizing political life. The role of the party in the process of popular consultation centres on the institution of voting. It is, however, not restricted to the electoral situation.

The central electoral role of the party system is the organization of the entire process of popular consultation. It is here that demands are brought to bear on the political system in an institutionalized fashion. The process has at least four distinct activities, each of them involving the political party. The first is the setting of the electoral calendar wherever this is not done by a written constitution or an organic law. The responsibility for calling an election, usually referred to as the power of dissolution, is normally vested in the governing party or the governing party coalition. The second activity is the nomination, for each party, of candidates who will then be called upon to stand for election. This process, for reasons of law as well as of political ethos, is particularly significant in the United

---

[24] Sigmund Neumann called party ". . . the great intermediary which links social forces and ideologies to official governmental institutions and relates them to political action within the larger political community," in *Modern Political Parties*, ed., Neumann, p. 396.

States. The third activity in the election process, sometimes preceding the second in point of time, is the fashioning of the party's electoral program. The fourth activity is the electoral campaign itself, conducted by the various political parties.

Discussions of the party system in the United States tend to emphasize parties' role in the nomination of personnel; discussions of the British party system and of that of the "old" Commonwealth tend to stress parties' role in the formation of governmental policy. Neither party system, of course, engages in one activity to the exclusion of the other. It is clear, however, that the political system of the United States, with its separation of powers into three branches, and the internal separation of the legislative branch, discourages parties from presenting clear-cut alternatives to voters. The British-type parliamentary system, on the other hand, permits parties to seek, ostensibly at least, an election "mandate" for policies. In the selection of personnel, the role played by the British party system is simple, as the parties themselves take care of the business of nominating candidates. In the United States, the nomination of candidates is highly complex. It involves not only the parties, but most of the voters as well. The latter participate in the nomination process in primary elections, which are in turn regulated by vastly differing laws in most of the individual states.

While the party's role in the process of popular consultation focuses on the electoral institution, it is in evidence at other times. A party is engaged in organizing popular consultation whenever it expresses articulated interests or demands. It does so whenever it issues propaganda and whenever it organizes discussion. As Leiserson states, a political party maintains ". . . continuing channels of mutual influence and communication with [the party's] sources of electoral support."[25]

OPERATION OF GOVERNMENT   In a competitive political system, political parties play vital roles in the operation of the government, and in the conduct of opposition to the government. These intra-governmental roles of parties vary from country to country. They are most clearly in evidence in a British-type parliamentary system, but they are present also in the United States, despite the low degree of party cohesion in the country.

In operating the government, parties take ". . . political responsibility for organizing the legislature and conducting the Executive business of government."[26] In so doing, they must coordinate the activities of their organizations outside the government with those of their government leaders. A party may govern by itself or in coalition with one or more other parties. In either case, it is concerned with determining the business of the major governmental structures, and with intra- and extra-governmental party coordination.

The conduct of the opposition is also a party role wherever there is a competitive party system. Opposition roles, long neglected in the literature of political science, have recently been analysed in studies under the editorship of Robert Dahl.[27] Where there is an alternative two-party system, the main role of the second major party is to attempt to replace the government. In a multi-party system, the role of an opposition party is likely to be more modest: an attempt to displace at least part of the personnel of government. In any case, a minor party, in order to be functioning as a party at all, must at least attempt to influence the government with a view to some displacement of governmental personnel in the future. If it does not even seek this minimal displacement, its role is indistinguishable from that of an interest group.

Applying Our Model

We have briefly explained all parts of the model we have adapted, primarily from the work of David Easton. We will now apply it to a description and analysis of Canadian parties. In essence, the model provides the theoretical rationale for the organization of this book. Section II represents significant inputs to parties and Section III, outputs from parties. In Section II, after reviewing in Chapter 2 some important aspects of Canadian society and a description of Canadian political parties, we turn directly to influences on parties. First, we deal with more general societal influences, and then work to the specifically political inputs. In Section III, our ordering is just the reverse. There we begin with the effects of parties on the specifically political environment, and move to the broader social environment.

---

[25] Avery Leiserson, *Parties and Politics* (New York: Alfred A. Knopf, Inc., 1958), p. 274.

[26] *Ibid.*, p. 80.

[27] Robert Dahl, ed., *Political Oppositions in Western Democracies* (New Haven: Yale University Press, 1966).

Section II

THE SHAPING OF POLITICAL PARTIES

2

The Roots of Canadian
Political Parties

●

It is possible to take one of several approaches in considering the roots of Canadian parties. We could, for example, begin with the experiences of party government in Britain, a course which we have deliberately eschewed. We could also trace the history of popular government in Canada, with a view to establishing the points at which political parties emerged. This too is not our intention, although we will certainly pay considerable attention to the system of government in later chapters. The perspective which we bring to an examination of political parties begins with the consideration of political parties within the broader context of the society in which they operate. For us, the roots of Canadian parties are in Canadian society and our understanding of parties is dependent on an appreciation of the nature of that society. This chapter, in its first section, will have little to say about parties as such. Instead it will provide the setting against which our subsequent discussion will unfold. But if it does not deal with parties directly, it is still directly relevant to the development of our presentation and, more important, to a fuller comprehension of how these parties came into being and how they have taken their present shape.

The second section of this chapter will focus directly on political parties. But there will be no attempt at tying in with what has gone before. In keeping with the general purpose of this chapter, to provide the context and background for the remainder of the book, the section on parties will be confined to a detailed description of parties and their fortunes.

THE SOCIAL STRUCTURE OF CANADA

It would be impossible, in the few pages we have allotted to this topic, to describe with any richness of detail the present nature of Canadian society or its historical development.[1] We will instead concentrate on only a few of the features of Canadian society which our own research experiences and critical reading have led us to select as especially pertinent to an understanding of the origins and operation of political parties. These include the nature and distribution of the population, the available physical resources, and the distribution of material and non-material rewards.

Population

From a handful of permanent settlers who followed the explorers three hundred years ago, the population of Canada has expanded to about twenty million. During these three centuries certain patterns have emerged. One is the continued settlement of the bulk of the population along the southern boundary of the country. While this ribbon-like pattern has been largely conditioned by climatic factors, it has had consequences for the close contact between the United States and Canada. Long before Canadian nationalists began worrying about the penetration of American mass media into Canada, border communities, especially in sparsely populated areas, had closer ties with their foreign neighbours than with their countrymen.

But even the southern border area has not been evenly settled. Concentrations of population have always been in pockets, with relatively empty expanses between them, again hindering the establishment of ties which could result from geographic closeness. The location of these population concentrations has altered over the years. For example, while Prince Edward Island, Nova Scotia, and New Brunswick had among them almost one-quarter of the population of Canada at the time of Confederation, their share of the greatly expanded population began declining after the provinces were united, so that by 1961, the Atlantic provinces, now including Newfoundland, had only 10 per cent of the total population. While the central provinces of Quebec and Ontario have continued to be the home of the majority of Canadians, their proportionate share of the population has declined with the westward expansion which began early in this century.

---

[1] The reader who requires additional background about Canada has many written sources from which to draw. As an introduction, we would suggest the following discussions of the history, economy, and social structure of Canada. J. B. Brebner, *Canada, A Modern History* (Ann Arbor: University of Michigan Press, 1960); Donald G. Creighton, *Dominion of the North*, 2nd ed. (Toronto: Macmillan Company of Canada, 1957); Mason Wade, *The French Canadians, 1760-1945* (Toronto: Macmillan Company of Canada, 1955); Marcel Rioux and Yves Martin, *French-Canadian Society*, I (Toronto: McClelland & Stewart Ltd., Carleton Library No. 18, 1964) ; John Porter, *The Vertical Mosaic* (Toronto: University of Toronto Press, 1965); Bernard R. Blishen, Frank E. Jones, Kaspar D. Naegele, John Porter, *Canadian Society*, rev. ed. (Toronto: Macmillan Company of Canada, 1964); W. T. Easterbrook and Hugh G. J. Aitken, *Canadian Economic History* (Toronto: Macmillan Company of Canada, 1956).

This continuous redistribution of population has come about in several ways. It has been, for one thing, an accompaniment of the shift from a rural, agricultural society to an urban, industrialized one. Several indicators of these changes are available. For example, in 1911, 39 per cent of the male labour force fifteen years of age and older were employed in agriculture. At the time of the 1961 census, only 12 per cent were so employed. While the contraction of the agricultural labour force has taken place in all provinces, it has been least prominent in Prince Edward Island and the Prairies. Saskatchewan, in fact, had 43 per cent of its male labour force in agriculture at the time of the 1961 census.

Changes in farm production and marketing have meant a more efficient use of land by a smaller labour force. The dispossessed have then moved to cities to find new types of employment. While World War II provided the impetus for the mechanization of agriculture, there was a time lag before its impact was felt in growing urbanization. In 1951, 54 per cent lived in urban centres; by 1961, it was 71 per cent. While the definition of urban centres used by the Dominion Bureau of Statistics (centres with 1,000 population or more), may not appear to tap the numbers of people actually living in cities, it can be supplemented with other information. In 1871, at the time of the first census after Confederation, there was not one city with a population of 100,000. By 1961 there were twelve such cities and more than half the population of Canada resided within their metropolitan areas. However we choose to measure the extent of urbanization, the relation between it and industrialization is great. That is, those provinces which are most highly urbanized are also most industrialized.

The urban growth which has been so marked since the end of World War II has taken place, not in city centres, but in suburbs. These areas are predominantly the home of families with young children. They have often expanded so rapidly that unusually large population concentrations are represented by only one electoral district.

"We must think of our population as in motion, with tides of people flowing this way and that, often filling new stretches, sometimes retreating from long-settled countrysides."[2] We have considered some of the directions of this movement—from rural to urban and suburban centres and from the eastern provinces westward. In recent years the major beneficiaries of interprovincial movements have been Ontario, Alberta, and British Columbia. Not only has the population not been stationary, but it has also expanded greatly in size. Growth has come about from a high birth rate and from immigration. While the birth rate had been higher in rural areas and among French-speaking Canadians, one recent phenomenon has been the leveling of birth rate differences among various population groups. Growth through immigration has also been important. While providing more Canadians, it also brought about a basic alteration in the ethnic composition of the country. Not including the indigenous inhabitants, the original settlers of Canada came first from

France and then the British Isles, the latter often by way of the American colonies. The census of 1871 found only 7 per cent of those of European origin to be neither British nor French. By 1961 persons neither British nor French (for the sake of brevity, we will call them other Europeans) had increased to 27 per cent. Since the turn of the century, when settlement agencies were eager to recruit homesteaders for the then empty western territories, other Europeans were welcomed to Canada. Often settling in ethnically homogeneous areas, their origins are revealed by an examination of place-names in western Canada. While the English-speaking population has continued to be reinforced by immigrants from the British Isles, other European origins make up half the population of the prairie provinces. Since the heavy immigration of the 1950's, their proportion has risen to 30 per cent in Ontario and 37 per cent in British Columbia.

With the differences in ethnic origin and the uneven dispersion of origin groups across the country are related differences for religions. The largest religious community is Roman Catholic. But because of their historical alliance with French origin, four-fifths of those in Quebec are of this religion, compared to under half of all Canadians. The two largest Protestant denominations are the United and Anglican churches, but their representation in the western provinces is considerably reduced both by the presence of churches more closely connected with other European origins and by fundamentalist groups which found a congenial climate in the newer communities of the west.[3]

We have digressed from the theme of growth through immigration to a consideration of the ethnic and religious composition of immigrants and their settlement patterns. Looking again at population growth, it becomes clear that if Canada had retained all its immigrants along with those accruing through natural increase, its population would have been vastly in excess of the present twenty million. What has happened to these ghost-Canadians? In some cases they were foreign-born and, disillusioned with the conditions they found, decided to move on, or perhaps as they became older, preferred to spend their last years in the surroundings of their youth. But most of the movement out of the country has been to the United States, and most of these emigrants have been native born. Whenever employment opportunities appear better in the United States, those with the requisite skills have crossed the border, often in large numbers. For example, between 1921 and 1930, 925,000 Canadians moved to the United States, the equivalent of losing the entire province of Saskatchewan. For the individual leaving the country, there may be regrets, but these are subordinated to the expectation of richer rewards. For the country suffering the loss, there is no such compensation and we now

---

[2] Nathan Keyfitz, "The Changing Canadian Population," in *Canadian Society*, ed. Blishen, *et al.*, p. 24.

[3] For information on the latter, see S. D. Clark, *Church and Sect in Canada* (Toronto: University of Toronto Press, 1948).

read frequent worried comments about the "brain drain."[4] It is, of course, not only the highly skilled who emigrate, but when they do, it is the occasion for soul-searching about the Canadian opportunity structure.

Here then are the highlights of Canadian demography: an ethnically and religiously heterogeneous population distributed in ways which could only reinforce diversity; population expansion in some areas and relative shrinkage in others; movement from a rural, farming society to an urban, industrialized one, but where not all provinces have shared equally in these changes; the influx of large numbers of immigrants not sharing either of the official cultural traditions; the strong attraction of the United States to many Canadians, particularly those with a high level of training. These provide some of the conditions out of which Canadian political parties emerged and upon which their continuity is dependent.[5]

Physical Resources

The economic history of Canada is the history of dependence on a small number of staples. Fur, fish, lumber, grain, and minerals all had their period of dominance. The consequences of a relatively undifferentiated economy, highly dependent on export markets, have meant vulnerability to the fluctuations of world trade. This has been accentuated by development of industries closely tied to these staples, such as ship building, mining and refining, and pulp and paper. The location of these products and related industries varies. Ship building, for example, was an important source of wealth for the maritime provinces, but by Confederation, it had been superseded by other forms of transportation and technological innovations in sea transportation, foreshadowing the economic depression which has continued to plague that area. Grain growing is concentrated in the prairie provinces, and dependence on one crop has meant that its residents are subject to a "boom or bust" economy. Ontario and, less clearly, British Columbia, have the most diversified economies and should be best able to weather temporary dislocations. But they too are closely tied to export markets. Quebec's situation appears to be one of a late starter on the road to industrialization and the movement away from unprofitable small farms. Lacking adequate coal reserves important for industrializing at an earlier period, Quebec can now expect to catch up to its more prosperous neighbour, Ontario, as it begins to develop large reserves of hydroelectric power.

In considering physical resources, some word is necessary about how these have been developed. While resources are rich, the population has always been relatively small, with limited capital of its own. As a result, Canadians have looked to foreign capital to provide the means of developing their resources. Citizens of the United States and Britain have been the major sources of this capital, with those from the United States providing increasingly larger shares since the end of World War I. American companies have also been prominent in setting up subsidiary manufacturing in Canada. The share of the total investment in Canadian resources and industries owned by Americans is constantly shifting, but

THE SHAPING OF POLITICAL PARTIES

by 1961 was close to eighteen billion dollars, compared to over three billion in 1926. In that same time span, total investments by residents of the United Kingdom have risen from 2,637,000,000 dollars to 3,385,000,000 dollars. The extent of foreign ownership and control varies by industry, with the largest proportion in manufacturing, mining and smelting, and petroleum and natural gas. In all these industries, United States investment is heaviest of all foreign investments.[6] Whether we consider this good or bad is irrelevant here: it is one of the facts of Canadian existence.

Our summary of the main features of Canada's resource and industrial development has been even briefer than that on population, but we do not mean to underestimate the importance of the kinds of opportunities the land itself makes available to its inhabitants. Resources are rich, but they are not often readily available without the outlay of considerable capital, and this has led to a dependence on the wealth of outsiders. At the same time, an economy based on a few items is highly vulnerable to dislocation, through the depletion of resources, fluctuations in world demand, and the obsolescence of products and the materials from which they are produced. The resources themselves and the wealth they bring are not equally distributed among the provinces.

Distribution of Rewards

To put it in the simplest terms, some places in Canada are wealthier than others in resources, have greater potential for industrial development, and are more conveniently located in relation to markets both inside and outside the country. The people who live in these areas are thus able to enjoy a higher income and more of the amenities of life. The relative advantage of provinces has shifted over time, but since Confederation, Ontario has been the most prosperous. In recent years, with increased settlement and economic diversification, British Columbia has come to approach Ontario in per capita disposable income. Since about 1954, Alberta has come to rank third in this respect with the opening of its rich reserves of oil and gas, which has supplanted the previous dependence on ranching. By 1961, the remaining order of provinces according to per capita disposal income was Manitoba, Quebec, Nova Scotia, Saskatchewan, and the other Atlantic provinces.

---

[4] See the details cited by the report of the Economics and Research Branch, Department of Labour of Canada, *Skilled and Professional Manpower in Canada, 1945-55*, Royal Commission on Canada's Economic Prospects, (Ottawa: July 1957). An unusually positive evalution of this phenomenon is given by Harry G. Johnson, "The Economics of the 'Brain Drain': The Canadian Case," *Minerva*, III (Spring 1965), 299-311.

[5] The conditions which we present as underlying the emergence and operation of Canadian parties also provided the background for the Royal Commission on Bilingualism and Biculturalism. While we did not have benefit of the Commission's findings in writing this book, its reports and studies will provide an important new source for understanding Canadian politics.

[6] Canada, Dominion Bureau of Statistics, *The Canadian Balance of International Payments, 1961 and 1962 and the International Investment Position* (Ottawa: Queen's Printer, August 1964), pp. 70 and 80.

The kinds of enterprises associated with a province do not, however, give a complete answer as to how income differences are maintained. Regional inequalities exist for income from the same kind of work. For example, median earnings in manufacturing are highest in Ontario and British Columbia and lowest in the Atlantic provinces. The continuation of these differences reflects not only the lack of a truly national economy but also the unevenness of industrialization across the country, the limits of federal jurisdiction over labour matters, the vulnerability of the economy to seasonal and other fluctuations, the lack of a unified trade union movement, and the general absence of militancy of trade union political action.[7] These features have increased the attractiveness of the central provinces and British Columbia for workers able to move, and also contribute to the likelihood that such inequalities will continue for the less mobile part of the labour force.

Other indications of the nature of inequalities appear from data on employment. The proportion of the labour force unemployed rose sharply from 1951 to 1961. While all regions were affected, the most seriously affected were the Atlantic provinces followed by Quebec and British Columbia. More diversified Ontario and the less industrialized prairie provinces were both able to weather this period with below average rates of unemployment. Industrialization, or the lack of it, in itself was no guarantee that high levels of employment could be maintained; what presumably is important is the ability to absorb manpower in pursuits for which the market at least remains stable.

We could go on to regard a variety of indicators of regional differences in living standards, such as the per capita share of physicians or dentists, the quality of educational facilities, or the availability of cultural amenities. These have and continue to differ in a manner similar to the other kinds of rewards we have considered. Let us then take only one further indicator of living standards, that of infant mortality, which is correlated throughout the world with general economic conditions. In Canada, differences among regions in this respect were much greater than they are at present, as Table 2-1 indicates. While differences have not disappeared, the leveling which has occurred does indicate that at least some of the advances of modern medicine are being more equitably shared across the country.

A final word is in order here about the kind of social class hierarchy which has emerged in Canada. Some research has been done on social class but little on the stratification of ethnic groups in Canada. From information available it seems clear that, at least until very recently, the highest social class positions and the positions of greatest influence and power in the economic sphere have been held by those of British origin in proportions vastly greater than their share of the total population.[8] In politics, the mass media, the civil service, and the universities, this overrepresentation at the upper echelons exists as well, although not to as great an extent.[9]

Out of these circumstances of a heterogeneous population distributed

THE SHAPING OF POLITICAL PARTIES

in such a way as to encourage diversity, further accentuated by inequalities in rewards, Canadian political parties have emerged. While these parties operate in a political system primarily adopted from the political experiences of other nations, the social context in which they must oper-

TABLE 2-1

INFANT MORTALITY PER 1,000 LIVE BIRTHS

Region	1941	1961
Canada	61	27
Atlantic (including Newfoundland)	71	31
Quebec	76	31
Ontario	46	23
Prairies	52	26
British Columbia	37	24

Source: Canada, Dominion Bureau of Statistics, *Vital Statistics* (Ottawa: 1963).

ate is in many ways unique. Before turning, in the following chapter, to the impact of this social structure on parties, we must briefly survey the parties with which we will be concerned. The questions we seek to answer at this point are simple: What are the party names? When did the parties begin? Are they represented federally and provincially? If they contest federal elections, is their strength concentrated in particular regions? We will avoid here an exposition of what parties stand for or the interests they may represent, since these will be treated in detail from Chapter 3 onward.

•

CANADIAN POLITICAL PARTIES

The entire century of Canadian nationhood has been dominated by two parties whose organizational identity was clearly discernible at least since the 1870's—the Conservative and Liberal parties. The former dates back to 1854; the latter emerged later but was able to replace the Macdonald Government by 1873. Two-party competition was clearly established by 1878, the year of the first election by secret ballot in Canada,

[7] H. D. Woods and Sylvia Ostry, *Labour Policy and Labour Economics in Canada* (Toronto: Macmillan Company of Canada, 1962); George W. Wilson, Scott Gordon, Stanislaw Judek, Albert Breton, *Canada: An Appraisal of its Needs and Resources* (Toronto: University of Toronto Press, The Twentieth Century Fund, 1965), pp. 101-153.

[8] Porter, *The Vertical Mosaic*; Bernard R. Blishen, "The Construction and Use of an Occupational Class Scale," in *Canadian Society*, ed. Blishen, *et al.*, pp. 449-458; E. C. Hughes, *French Canada in Transition* (Chicago: University of Chicago Press, 1943).

[9] Porter, *The Vertical Mosaic.*

though many independent candidates continued to compete for parliamentary seats until 1891. Since then, independents have come mainly from Quebec.

From Confederation through the First World War, Conservatives and Liberals almost preempted the political scene of Canada. Very few candidates of minor parties appeared during the period, and only in 1896 were Members of Parliament elected as representatives of third parties, which soon disappeared, however. Those elected were four McCarthyites and two Patrons of Industry. Workers' parties did compete on the federal level from 1900 on, but their showing was insignificant. The two-party monopoly was broken after the end of the First World War. Instances of this breakup and the tide of party fortunes generally are closely interwoven with the responses of individual provinces. The discussion which follows will proceed by examining provincial voting behaviour in federal elections.

Federal Party Representation

Between 1878 and 1965 there have been twenty-four general elections. During that time, the number of instances in which a province has hit on the winning party has been greatest in eastern Canada, including Quebec. Part at least of the record of the eastern provinces in picking the winner can be attributed to the weakness of third parties in the Atlantic provinces. Quebec has given a considerable share of the popular vote to third parties. In the 1945 election 41 per cent of the Quebec popular vote was given to third parties, of which 34 per cent went to Bloc Populaire Canadien. But when third party voting is high in Quebec, the main loser of the two older parties has been the Conservative. Since 1917, the first serious instance of Quebec dissatisfaction with the two-party system, the Conservatives have formed the national government in only five out of fourteen instances and thus third party voting has detracted little from the likelihood that Quebec would also support the winning party. Among the unique responses of Quebec voters has been the new strength of Social Credit in the election of 1962, and to a lesser extent, 1963. After the latter election, most of the Quebec contingent split with the national party and formed Le Ralliement des Créditistes.

From Ontario westward, voters have displayed greater variation in selecting the winning party. For one thing, Ontarians have been more likely to favour the Conservative Party compared to the nation as a whole, giving a plurality of their votes to that party in five more general elections from 1878 to 1965 than did other Canadians. Third party support in Ontario first attained significant proportions in the election of 1896, when 15 per cent of the popular vote was given to third parties, electing three McCarthyites, two Patrons of Industry, and one Independent candidate. Competition to the two older parties appeared again in 1921, when 28 per cent voted for Progressive candidates. While the Progressives had also made some inroads in provinces to the east of Ontario, it was only in Ontario that they were able to attain such a large share of the vote in addition to their stronghold in the prairie provinces. As in other prov-

THE SHAPING OF POLITICAL PARTIES

inces, the 1935 election brought support for the Reconstruction Party, formed by disgruntled Conservatives. Finally, Ontarians have, since 1945, voted for the CCF/NDP, giving that party from 11 to 22 per cent of their vote.

It has been the prairie provinces and British Columbia which have been the real centre of third party voting. In Manitoba, the first move in this direction occurred in 1896, with 18 per cent of the third party vote divided between the McCarthyites and the Patrons of Industry. In 1921, the Progressives gained more votes than the Conservatives and Liberals combined. That year also saw a small amount of support, yet sufficient to elect one member, going to the Labour Party. Meanwhile the Progressives were reabsorbed into the Liberal Party and virtually disappeared as an independent party in Manitoba by 1926. From that year until 1940, a declining number of candidates were elected under the heading of Liberal-Progressives. The potency of the Progressive label in western Canada led the Conservatives, as late as 1942, to add Progressive to their party label, as they accepted the national leadership of John Bracken, former Progressive Party Premier of Manitoba. Other third party appeals resulted in support, starting in 1935, for the CCF/NDP. Finally, a small and shifting minority favoured the Social Credit Party.

The Progressives had their greatest initial strength in Saskatchewan, winning 61 per cent of the vote in 1921. Progressive strength soon waned, however, even more so than in Manitoba, with little effect on the Saskatchewan Liberal Party. While the founding convention of the CCF took place in Alberta, in 1932, we associate the flowering of that party with Saskatchewan. Yet in 1935, in the first election contested by the CCF, a greater proportion of the vote was gained in British Columbia. But residents of Sakatchewan did support the CCF with over 40 per cent of their votes for three elections between 1945 and 1953. Since then, both the CCF and the Liberals have declined in strength and have been replaced as first choice by the Conservatives. As in Manitoba, a small group of voters prefer the Social Credit Party.

In the ten elections intervening between those of 1917 and 1958, a third party has been the major electoral force in Alberta, even though the Conservatives tied the Progressives for popular support in 1925 and exceeded them slightly in 1930. Despite the integration of the Progressives into the Liberal Party elsewhere in Canada, in Alberta they remained relatively strong until 1930. 1935 marks the emergence of the Social Credit Party, which, in the first election contested, was able to win 48 per cent of the votes. Its appeal declined somewhat with time, as the Liberals recouped some of their losses, but the Conservatives remained especially weak. The federal election of 1958 produced a dramatic change, giving the Conservatives 60 per cent of the vote, and reducing the other two parties to their weakest position. A slight shift back occurred in 1962, but in that election, proportionately more voters in Quebec chose Social Credit than did those in Alberta. Only minor support has been attained by the CCF/NDP in Alberta.

Third parties have dominated Alberta politics; they have fragmented those in British Columbia. Socialist and Labour Party candidates, as well as those of the Progressive and Reconstructionist parties, and numerous Independents, have attracted from more than 20 per cent of the vote (in 1921) to only one per cent (in 1962). Numerically, the most important third parties have been the CCF/NDP and the Social Credit. The CCF since 1935 and Social Credit since 1953 have shared the popular vote almost equally with the two older parties. Indeed, since the entry of the CCF into federal politics, there has been only one election, in 1958, when a major party attained a decisive victory.

This brief survey of political parties contesting federal elections has covered all the main contenders. One remaining party with a national organization which has offered candidates in all provinces except Newfoundland, Prince Edward Island, and New Brunswick is the Communist Party. Founded in 1921, but initially operating as an underground organization, it remained relatively unmolested by the law until 1931, at which time eight Communist leaders were tried and imprisoned for five years for advocating the forceful overthrow of the government. The Communist Party, however, continued to exist despite some legal harassment, although it was formally outlawed in 1940 by the Defence of Canada Regulations. When Hitler invaded the Soviet Union, Canadian Communists, like those elsewhere, changed their attitudes toward the war effort. In 1943 the still illegal Communist Party was disbanded and formed anew as the Labour Progressive Party. It was known by this name until 1959, when it reverted back to its old name. During these years, it has elected one Member of Parliament, from Quebec, who had the dubious distinction of being the sole MP ever to be convicted of conspiracy to violate the Offical Secrets Act, after evidence that he had been involved in an espionage ring.

The proliferation of parties should not deflect from the fact that even after World War I, the Liberal and Conservative parties retained a dominant position in Canadian political life. With the exception of the Progressives in 1921, no third party has ever obtained the second largest number of seats in the federal parliament. After 1917, the proportion of the popular vote shared by the two major parties has ranged from 87 per cent (in 1958) to 69 per cent (in 1935). The largest number of members elected since 1921 outside the fold of the major parties was 53 (of a total of 245) in 1945, but of those, seven were Independents and one an Independent Liberal. The Parliament elected in 1962 had, out of a total of 265, 49 third party members. Only 8 third party members were elected in 1958, the low point of post-1917 third party strength.

Provincial Party Representation

The greatest strength of third parties has been in provincial politics. Since a federal system of government divides responsibilities among various levels of government, it is not surprising that parties unique to a province should spring up in response to local needs. Such was the case of the farm parties, which first emerged in the 1919 provincial election in

THE SHAPING OF POLITICAL PARTIES

Ontario as a significant electoral force, forming a Farmer-Labour Government. The basis of the Farmer-Labour Party, like that of earlier farm parties such as the Patrons of Industry, was the protection of farmers' interests, which were considered to be neglected by the two main national parties. The United Farmers of Manitoba formed the government of that province in 1922 and the United Farmers of Alberta did the same in the elections of 1921, 1926, and 1930. In addition, farm parties picked up varying degrees of support in the 1920's in Nova Scotia and New Brunswick. Their strength in Saskatchewan, however, did not come until later. Since farm interests were strong in so many provinces, it is not surprising that they should seek some unity at the national level, and this occurred with the formation of the Progressive Party. This party then began to offer candidates in provincial elections from 1925 on, but its appeal was mainly in Manitoba.

The Labour Party label has been used successfully, at one time or another, in every province except Newfoundland and Prince Edward Island. Labour candidates attained success in Quebec, Ontario, Manitoba, and Alberta in the 1920's. In British Columbia, provincial Labour Party candidates were elected until as recently as 1960. In addition to the four main parties and the ones we have already discussed, other parties electing provincial members in one or more elections were L'Action Liberal Nationale, Bloc Populaire Canadien, and Nationalists (all in Quebec); Workers, a Communist front party (Manitoba); Independent Party and Unity (Saskatchewan); Veterans (Alberta); and People's Party, Provincial Party and Unionists (British Columbia). Of the minor national parties, the Labour Progressive or Communist Party has had its greatest success at the provincial level. Communist candidates were elected in Ontario in 1943, 1945, 1948, and 1951, and in Manitoba in 1936, 1945, 1949, and 1953, while they managed to get some electoral support in several other provinces. In addition, the number of party labels used unsuccessfully in provincial elections is legion. Among the more unusual labels are the United Newfoundland Party, Capital Familial (Quebec); White Canada (Ontario); Sound Money (Manitoba); and Financial Justice, Victory Without Debt, and Religious Political Brotherhood, all in British Columbia.

Looking at specific provinces, Quebec stands out as one with its own political makeup. Provincially, the Conservative Party disappeared in Quebec in 1936, and was replaced organizationally by Union Nationale, when it became the governing party. Losing to the Liberals in 1939, it won power again in 1944 and held it until displaced by the Liberals in 1960, but returned to office in 1966. While this may appear as a normal struggle between the two major parties, it is in truth difficult to see Union Nationale as merely an extension of the Conservative Party. In Quebec, it wagged the dog, following programs and policies divergent from Conservatives in neighbouring provinces and attracting voters who would not, on principle, vote for the Conservatives nationally. Other features specific to that province include the activities of L'Action Liberal Nationale, a dissident Liberal group which won 29 per cent of the popular vote in 1935. In 1944, the major third party was Bloc Populaire, which ran eighty candidates, of which four were elected. Other third parties also vied for support, along with a proliferation of Independent candidates, some of whom were loosely attached to an established party. That year 332 candidates contested 92 seats. The following election in 1948 was also one of high political activity, with 311 candidates running. Meanwhile, Bloc Populaire had disappeared from the scene. The main third party at this time was L'Union des Electeurs (as the Quebec version of Social Credit was then known) although none of its 92 candidates were elected. -

Quebec illustrates the case of an electoral battle between the two major parties, although one has been seriously transformed in the process. Third parties, though active, normally have little success, even when they represent interests peculiar to that province. Provincial elections in Alberta and British Columbia show instead the eclipse of the major parties. In Alberta, this has come about in such a way that all opposition to the government has become minimal. For example, after the United Farmers of Alberta were defeated by Social Credit in 1935, they passed from the electoral scene. Since that time, there has been virtually one-party government, with the exception of the elections of 1940, when Independent candidates received substantial support, and 1955, when the Liberals did so. In British Columbia, the weakness of the old parties led to the formation of a coalition government of the Liberals and Conservatives after the 1941 election and it continued to govern through the elections of 1945 and 1949. The CCF meanwhile had been able to gain about 30 per cent of the vote since 1933 and, from 1952 on, when Social Credit came to power, has been the major opposition.

Obviously then, on the provincial scene, the dominant position of Liberals and Conservatives has been less clear. In two provinces where government by major parties has existed, it has been so in greatly modified form for extended periods. Thus Quebec has had its Union Nationale governments and Manitoba has been governed by a coalition of major party and third party elements. For a brief period in Ontario, in Alberta since 1921, British Columbia since 1952, and Saskatchewan between 1944 and 1964, third parties have formed the government. Alberta remains as the only province which has not been governed by a major party during the greater part of its history. In contrast to experiences westward, no maritime province has ever been governed by a third party. Yet looking at the full range of provincial governments, it can be seen that provincially as well as federally, there are no recent signs of an eclipse of either the major parties or the two-party system. As of 1965, eight provinces had major party governments, eight had major party oppositions (if Union Nationale is included as a major party, and the two Liberal members in Alberta are recognized as an official opposition), and only in British Columbia were both principal positions occupied by third parties. In ten provincial elections held between 1959 and 1960, the total share of the popular vote received by the major parties was 76 per cent. If Union

THE SHAPING OF POLITICAL PARTIES

Nationale is counted as a third party, the major party share of the popular vote was 63 per cent.

•

SUMMARY: THE POLITICAL SETTING

The stage is now set for us to begin looking at the way in which Canadian political parties have been shaped. The details of Canadian existence which we have outlined have been necessarily brief, but they are among the critical aspects of Canadian society. To repeat, a population heterogeneous by reason of ethnic and religious origin and period of settlement, spread out in a country in which each region differs greatly in its resources and other potential, has meant that regional-economic and social diversity has been continuously reinforced. Canadian society is inexplicable without a knowledge of these factors; Canadian political parties too can be understood only against this background. This background information will be important for reference purposes for the remainder of the book.

The history of Canadian parties is also one of great diversity, despite the dominance of the two major parties, the Conservative and Liberal. While the details we have supplied above may appear confusing at this point in the discussion, they too will provide their greatest usefulness as reference points for our future discussion.

3

Social Structure and the
Formation of Parties

•

There is no formal provision for political parties in the Government of Canada, any more than there is in the Government of Britain. But in the political maturation of Canada, and certainly prior to Confederation, two major parties emerged, patterned after their British namesakes. Yet the context in which they, their successors, and additional rivals were to operate was considerably different from that of Britain. Our understanding of Canadian parties is best served by a consideration of the Canadian situation rather than of non-Canadian origins. The social forces shaping Canadian parties is the theme of this entire Section II, but in this chapter we will concentrate only on those social structural elements outlined in the previous chapter.

•

STRUCTURAL DIFFERENTIATION AS THE
BASIS FOR PARTY FORMATION

A variety of sociological variables may have a bearing on the emergence of political parties and their subsequent operation. For example, where people live, what kind of work they do, what they believe in, have all been related to party origins and activities. But our resumé of Canadian society has been deliberately geared to emphasize those characteristics which we believe to be of critical importance in shaping Canadian parties. The development factors involved can be compressed into two dimensions: regional-economic and regional-ethnic.

When we say we believe these to be important, we do not expect the reader to accept this on faith. It should be clear, even from our brief description, that the objective conditions of life, as these are determined by population composition, activities, and rewards, differ by region, if not by individual province. In the political context, this means that in facing problems shaped to some extent by conditions specific to regions, political organizations will adapt to these and thus will be visibly differentiated according to region. We will seek evidence of the influence of regionally-based ethnic and economic factors on Canadian political life from two perspectives. One of these concerns their implications for the attitudes and behaviour of voters. The other is their influence on the party system. We will treat evidence of regional influences on voters briefly, and on the party system in more detail, in keeping with the subject matter of this book.

In this largely interpretative analysis of Canadian parties, we are assuming that regional differences in conditions of life can be adequately demonstrated. We are not assuming, however, that these differences *necessarily* lead to political differences, any more than the existence of social classes necessarily leads to class-based behavioural differences. But it is our contention that such political consequences have occurred in Canada and we shall attempt to document these.

In documenting the significance of regional factors in Canadian politics we are presuming that these derived from the conditions of life. We cannot, however, with available information, account for the durability of these differences. It would be interesting to know, for example, the nature and strength of regional self-identifications. Are there many who see themselves, for example, as Quebeckers or Maritimers first, and then as Canadians? Are major problems perceived as local or national in scope? If regional identities are strong, we would have a further basis for the persistence of regional factors in political life. It would be of equal value to have information on the values which Canadians uphold, in particular, insofar as these serve to buttress diversity. But for the time being, we must proceed without such empirical aids to understanding the social forces which shape parties.

Effects on Voters

The two dimensions of regionalism have implications for the attitudes and behaviour of voters in such respects as turnout at elections, partisan choices, and the creation of regional climates of opinion.

TURNOUT The student of politics is interested in rates of turnout at elections because voting is one of the elemental forms of political participation available to citizens. The choice of voting or not is an important indicator of the extent to which the ordinary citizen feels involved in the politics of his nation, sees meaningful alternatives available to him, and considers himself able to influence the course of politics. We see the act of voting as a critical means whereby citizens give support to the regime and express demands of it. The symbolic, if not the actual, significance of voting is not lost to those governments who make voting compulsory, even when voters can express no other choice than approval. Here, however, we will not be concerned with the meaning of voting, but only with showing how voting participation is affected by region.[1]

Voting eligibility in federal elections has been variously determined by provincial and federal legislation, but since 1920, the federal government has decided who has the right to vote. From that time, we have reasonably comparable data for all provinces—that is, there has been almost total adult suffrage for those twenty-one and over. This will be the time span in which to make comparisons of turnout.

For those provinces where this information is available, we see marked differences in the extent to which their residents exercise the franchise during provincial elections. As Table 3-1 shows, this varies from a high in Saskatchewan, where an average of 83 per cent of those eligible voted in eight elections, to a low in Manitoba and Ontario, where only 63 per cent voted. Part of this differential may have been due to the election years considered, with data on Saskatchewan unavailable prior to 1929. It was this earlier time period, however, when turnout was lower in that province during federal elections, and this may also have been true for provincial ones. Yet even if this were the case, an inspection of turnout figures for each year indicates that Saskatchewan has consistently had a higher rate.

TABLE 3-1

RATES OF TURNOUT DURING PROVINCIAL ELECTIONS

Province	Time Span	Number of Elections	Average Per Cent Turnout
Saskatchewan	1929-60	8	83%
Quebec	1923-60	11	76
Nova Scotia	1925-60	10	75
British Columbia	1920-60	12	70
Alberta	1930-63	9	67
Ontario	1923-59	11	63
Manitoba	1920-59	11	63

Figures are not available for Prince Edward Island, New Brunswick, or Newfoundland.

Source: Data compiled by Hans Brown and G. Alex Jupp.

Related but identical results appear for federal elections (Table 3-2). In twelve general elections from 1921 to 1962, Prince Edward Island emerged as the province with the highest rate of turnout, 83 per cent. Saskatchewan, in second place, lagged behind by 7 percentage points, but

THE SHAPING OF POLITICAL PARTIES

TABLE 3-2

RATES OF TURNOUT DURING TWELVE GENERAL
ELECTIONS BETWEEN 1921 AND 1962

Province	Average Per Cent Turnout
Prince Edward Island	83%
Saskatchewan	76
Nova Scotia	76
New Brunswick	75
British Columbia	74
Quebec	73
Manitoba	73
Ontario	71
Alberta	66
Newfoundland*	63

*Results based on five elections from 1949 to 1962.

Source: Data compiled by Hans Brown from Howard Scarrow, Canada Votes (New Orleans: Hauser, 1961).

the difference would have been reduced to only three points if the elections of 1921, 1925, and 1926 had been omitted for Saskatchewan. In these earlier years, turnout in Saskatchewan was under 70 per cent, but the advent of the depression marked the beginning of a high level of political activism.[2] Turnout declined to 66 per cent for Alberta and 63 per cent for Newfoundland. For the latter province, these results are based on only five elections beginning with its admission to Confederation. Data on the remaining provinces are reported in Table 3-2. These results also reveal that circumstances in each province affect its residents in such a manner as to increase or decrease the likelihood of their voting.

PARTISAN CHOICE   A second indicator of the effects of region on voters (in this case more obviously relevant to the operation of the party system), concerns the nature of partisan choice. In our presentation of Canadian political parties in the previous chapter, our concern was to show how party fortunes were related to electoral behaviour in each of the provinces in both federal and provincial elections. There is no need to duplicate this discussion. It should be sufficient to recall that the main

---

[1] For a discussion of factors affecting rates of turnout, see S. Peter Regenstreif, The Diefenbaker Interlude (Toronto: Longmans Canada Ltd., 1965), pp. 68-70; Howard A. Scarrow, "Patterns of Voter Turn-Out in Canada," Midwest Journal of Political Science, V (November 1961), 351-364; J. A. Laponce, "Non-Voting and Non-Voters: a Typology," Canadian Journal of Economics and Political Science, XXXIII (February 1967), 75-87.

[2] S. M. Lipset, Agrarian Socialism (Berkeley and Los Angeles: University of California Press, 1950), pp. 199-219.

contests have been between the Conservatives and Liberals. Since World War I, however, the two-party system has been considerably modified by the emergence of third parties, generally more attuned to local rather than national problems. At the federal level, there certainly is a national party system—no province alone could elect enough members to form a government. But what Chapter 2 demonstrated is that voters in each province have both different parties to choose from and choose them differently. The availability of parties unique to a province is even more pronounced in provincial elections and consequently the regional bias of provincial politics is more evident.

OPINION CLIMATES Further evidence of the consequences of regional-ethnic and regional-economic differences is reflected in the climates of opinion prevailing in each region. In a secondary analysis of public opinion polls collected by the Canadian Institute of Public Opinion (the Canadian affiliate of the Gallup organization) from 1941 to 1963, region was found to be the prime differentiator of opinions. The subject of these polls, collectively giving us one way of viewing Canadian identity, covered such topics as Canada's relations with Britain, the Commonwealth, the United States, and international bodies; preferences on the nature of Canadian society with respect to population, French-English interests, and the distribution of influence among interest groups and federal and provincial authorities; and desired alternatives for the symbolic representation of the country.[3] About 225 questions were examined, but it was not possible, for all of them, to break down opinions according to population characteristics. However, in every instance where this information was available, some distinction in viewpoints was present by region. The greatest differences were between Quebec and the rest of Canada—evidence of the importance of our regional-ethnic dimension. Less pronounced but still visible were differences among the remaining regions. In the latter, the dominant climate of opinion was shaped more strongly by economic factors, although ethnic ones still played a part. It is true, as well, that Quebec residents were responding to their economic conditions of life, and these circumstances have a bearing on the continued strength of their ethnic identity. As far as the opinion data were able to reveal, there did not seem to be any lessening of differences in regional viewpoints. The one exception, perhaps surprising, is that there has been some decline in the separateness of perspectives on political symbols in recent years. This has been an instance where other Canadians have come to share Quebec views on the desirability of new or uniquely Canadian symbols. Be that as it may, at least in terms of the questions asked by the polling agency, it is reasonably clear that region continues to exert an important influence on the formation of opinions relevant to national political issues. Whether this extends to the individual province is difficult to say. The problem of analysing small cases led us to combine the provinces into five regions: Atlantic, Quebec, Ontario, Prairies, and British Columbia. However, on the basis of other evidence of provincial

THE SHAPING OF POLITICAL PARTIES

political differences, it is not unlikely that there exist provincial as well as regional climates of opinion.

Effects on Party System

Nowhere is the existence of regional cleavages more pervasive than in the party system. Their influence is reflected in a variety of responses ranging from overt conflict, leading to the breakdown of parties, to mechanisms for suppressing and accommodating differences. Here we will look in some detail at regional effects on the accommodative policies of national parties, the sustaining of differences within major parties, and the emergence of splinter parties. The accommodative policies of national parties are also related to the accommodative policies of government, but the latter will be treated in the following chapter.

ACCOMMODATIVE POLICIES   A striking feature of national politics, which has it roots in pre-Confederation struggles for responsible government, has been the practice of having the national party leader aided by a lieutenant of the other major language group. In an example set by the partnership of Baldwin and LaFontaine in their struggles with Lord Sydenham, both major parties and one of the minor ones have tried this solution to the problem of knitting together the political interests of English- and French-speaking Canada. Apparently, the most astute political leaders have been most successful in using this arrangement. Such was the case of John A. Macdonald and Georges Cartier, and of Mackenzie King and Ernest Lapointe and Louis St. Laurent. By this means, the special interests of each official language group could be represented by a man who was, if not the Prime Minister, then his trusted second-in-command. Whether the best interests of each group were served in this way is probably not as important as the visibility which French and English received for the legitimacy of their claims for recognition. As a technique for attaining and holding power, this arrangement is not, however, foolproof. It is strongly related to the person of the leader; in the case of the Macdonald-Cartier coalition, when one of the partners was no longer on the scene, the party was torn apart by ethnic and religious differences. Conservative handling of the Riel Rebellion in 1885 and the Catholic school question in Manitoba alienated large segments of French Canada and led to defections to the Liberal Party, despite the opposition of the Roman Catholic hierarchy in Quebec to the Liberals. In 1917, appeals to patriotism couched in terms of loyalty to Britain were too strong to retain the support of long-standing Liberals for their party. Laurier, who had personally been instrumental in welding together French and English into a national party but who had never been able to recruit an effective English-speaking lieutenant, could not overcome the overriding importance of national issues raised by the question of conscription and was left to end his political career in his own provincial enclave. A similar crisis in the

---

[3] Mildred A. Schwartz, *Public Opinion and Canadian Identity* (Berkeley and Los Angeles: University of California Press, 1967).

1940's was avoided by Mackenzie King. According to King's assessment, he was faced with the same situation which Laurier had confronted, but, he said, with one exception. "The only difference was that Sir Wilfrid unhappily had been in the minority in race and religion and was handicapped to that extent; that I had a following infinitely larger than the one he had."[4] There was, of course, more to it than this. Among the political strategies King adopted with the outbreak of war was the position that young men could be called to serve in defence of Canada, but not for overseas duty. While eventually this position had to be modified, it helped to bind to him the personal loyalty of many Quebec Liberals, who were of course also patriotic Canadians. At the same time they did not forget how, during the crisis of 1917, King had remained loyal to Laurier. And finally, and this is our main point, King was immeasurably aided by his lieutenants from Quebec in dealing with that province and in retaining the general support of Liberal Members of Parliament from Quebec when conscription for overseas duty became necessary. First Ernest Lapointe and then Louis St. Laurent served nobly in presenting the national cause to Quebec and at least some form of the Quebec perspective to their colleagues in Parliament. While many Quebec Members of Parliament on the Liberal side were unsympathetic to the conscription solution adopted in 1944, they generally remained steadfast to the Liberal cause.

Unlike Laurier, St. Laurent had no difficulty in finding eminent English-speaking Liberals to represent the party's interests. Moreover, St. Laurent was himself more readily identified as the leader of an undivided country, with the war over and the development of the postwar economic boom. His reputation as a lawyer had earned him respect outside of Quebec before his entry into politics. In addition to his legal distinction, his fluent English, touched with an Irish accent, and his grandfatherly manner were all considerable assets outside of French Canada. But also of major importance were the stature of the men in his Cabinet from English-speaking Canada.

Future historians will no doubt be interested in the manner in which John Diefenbaker represented himself and the Conservative cause in Quebec. In 1957, the Conservatives won only nine out of seventy-five seats in Quebec and therefore could hardly be expected to have a strong leadership potential in the House of Commons from that province. But in 1958, fifty Conservatives were returned from Quebec. Whatever the relative merits of these individuals, those who were appointed to the Diefenbaker Cabinet, were, according to some observers, hardly of the calibre needed for the role of lieutenant.[5] André Laurendeau is quoted as saying, "Not since the days of R. B. Bennett have French-Canadians felt themselves so absent from the affairs of state, as under Mr. Diefenbaker."[6] Most promising was Léon Balcer, but having opposed Diefenbaker's bid for leadership at the 1956 Conservative convention, he was never given a job commensurate with his apparent abilities or his potential as the Quebec lieutenant. While it is difficult to assess events still fluid, Balcer's open break with Diefenbaker in 1964 is at least partly a reflection of the latter's competence as a national leader who, within the limits imposed by the social and political environment, must find some way of dealing honourably with the French-speaking minority.

Another example of the partnership of ethnic opposites, but one quickly dissolved, was the national leadership of the Social Credit Party. Robert Thompson, the national leader from Alberta represented English-speaking Canada; his deputy leader, Réal Caouette, represented French Canada. While this arrangement was worked out at a convention in 1961, conflicting viewpoints brought its dissolution by June, 1963. Caouette, and most Members of Parliament elected under the Social Credit ticket in Quebec, formed their own party, Le Ralliement des Créditistes. The leader-lieutenant plan is one possible way of accommodating regional-ethnic cleavages, but it is a difficult one to keep in operation. It is strongly personality oriented, yet the lieutenant must be willing to play a second-ary role while wielding great power. And being tied so intimately to the person of the leader, the arrangement is vulnerable to the sweep of events.

Policies designed to accommodate differences stemming from the regional nature of the economy are more often directed to the *substance* of regional grievances rather than merely to their representation. One source of Macdonald's strength in French Canada lay precisely in his ability to present a promised solution to economic problems existing in that province as well as elsewhere in Canada. This was through his "national policy" of protective tariffs, westward expansion, and railroad building.

While the centralizing policies of the Conservatives were initially in-strumental in promoting national unity, they were also a source of ten-sion with the provinces. The issue of Catholic schools in Manitoba presents an interesting case in point. The school question provided a focus for religious-ethnic cleavages, with Catholics (and French) presum-ably attracted by the federal government's move to protect their rights. But paradoxically it also aroused fears in these same people that the federal government would begin a policy of intruding on provincial responsibilities otherwise protected by the provincial legislature in Quebec. Provincial rights found their champion in Wilfrid Laurier and the Liberal Party, and Laurier was then able to extend his appeal to bring about his election in 1896.

The reconciliation of sectional demands, basically economic in nature, is illustrated by the absorption of the Progressive Party into the federal Liberal Party. The election of 1921 gave the Progressives 65 out of a total of 235 seats, 15 more than the Conservatives, and appeared to seriously

---

[4] J. W. Pickersgill, *The Mackenzie King Record*, I, *1939-1944*, (Toronto: University of Toronto Press, 1960), p. 283.

[5] Regenstreif, *The Diefenbaker Interlude*, p. 41.

[6] Peter Newman, *Renegade in Power: The Diefenbaker Years* (Toronto: McClelland & Stewart Ltd., 1963), pp. 283-284.

threaten the continuity of the two-party system. Without a clear majority in the House, the Liberals under Mackenzie King began the task of incorporating outsiders into the party. After the short-lived Conservative victory in 1925, the Liberals were able to bring an end to the Progressives as a national electoral force through the eventual introduction of measures desired by the interests the Progressives represented. Western Canada was thus able to attain the re-imposition of the Crow's Nest Pass rates, preferential rates for the eastward shipment of wheat and flour, and the expansion of railroad communication.

With the population centres, industry, and wealth concentrated in central Canada, politics have tended, at least in the eyes of many western Canadians, to have a similar regional bias. We will go on to look at this more directly in our discussion of the emergence of splinter parties. Here, however, some comment can be made about the way in which western interests are given a voice in the major parties, although more attention will be given to this in our later treatment of party organization. The technique, analogous to the ethnic lieutenant, has been to have an important spokesman for western agriculture in the upper echelons of the party hierarchy. This was the role of James Gardiner in King's Cabinet and of Alvin Hamilton in Diefenbaker's Cabinet. After 1962, when the Conservatives revealed their loss of support by a decline of fourteen percentage points in the popular vote, they still either kept proportionately more support in the prairie provinces or lost it to other parties rather than to the Liberals. In other words, Hamilton's personal following remained strong (as did that of Diefenbaker), and the success of his policies remained evident. It was the failure of the Liberals in neither formulating an effective agricultural policy nor attracting support from respected spokesmen in western Canada that contributed to their weak position in that region.

INTRAPARTY CLEAVAGES In the foregoing paragraphs we have considered the possibilities of accommodating the various interests represented in Canadian society within the major parties, giving some illustrations of both successful and unsuccessful attempts. Here we will be concerned with the impact of the Canadian social structure on the character of the major parties, insofar as it permits the continuity of differences within these parties. We will look at evidence from two sources: the social composition of parties in different provinces; and the viewpoints, programs, and policies of parties with the same name but with a different geographic locus or sphere of operation.

It would hardly be surprising if great variation was found in the characteristics of a party's supporters in different provinces. From what we already know of the nature of Canadian society, any party with a sizable body of supporters will necessarily attract more Roman Catholics than Protestants in Quebec, and the opposite will be the case in British Columbia. The same would be true, for example, in terms of the attraction of farmers in Saskatchewan and industrial workers in Ontario. Even if these attributes of provinces were the sole source of difference in the composition of party support, this would be an important political fact. As we have and will continue to demonstrate, social and economic, as well as political divisions, provide the basis for political demands, and any party which seeks to attract a broad base of support must also contend with the problem of controlling tensions among divergent interests. In some cases, problems may be handled by the accommodative policies we have discussed. In others, differing viewpoints may be reconciled by the development of some integrating principles or ideology which override group ties. This is not a solution normally available to the major parties, however, although it has had some success with the minor ones, notably the CCF/NDP. Without these integrating principles, parties are left with a diversified and disunified body of supporters as at least a latent source of tension.

The existence of provincial differences with respect to the nature of their population is the limiting condition on the possible homogeneity of supporters of any broad-based party. But in addition, Canadian parties have historically found disproportionate shares of their supporters among some groups rather than others. This means that when minorities do give their vote to a party in unaccustomed proportions or when their minority status is somehow accentuated by the nature of provincial differences, the latent tensions become more volatile. It would be interesting to examine this thesis over some period of time, and the necessary data for this task are available in the collection of Canadian Institute of Public Opinion surveys conducted prior to a number of general elections. For the time being, however, we will confine ourselves to an examination of within-party differences at only one time, immediately prior to the 1962 federal election. In Table 3-3, data are reported for provinces west of the Maritimes, since the eastern ones were insufficiently sampled to allow for intensive analysis. While we are concerned here only with intraparty differences, it is instructive to compare the two major parties. For example, while both Liberal and Conservative voters in Quebec were overwhelmingly Catholic, a quick comparison of the two parties points up the relatively more pronounced minority status of Catholics among Conservatives. While the existence of a large body of Catholics among Liberals is a source of strain for that party, we would argue that it also leads to concern for their special interests and demands for representation, concerns which the relative absence of Catholics allows the Conservatives to ignore. For those Catholics who do vote Conservative, their place in the party may only be tenuous, as the 1965 defection of Conservative Members of Parliament from Quebec indicated.

Table 3-3 also reveals the manner in which voting preferences associated with social class are confounded by the provincial milieu. This is true for both the Liberal and Conservative parties, where the proportions in different occupational categories vary considerably from one province to the next.[7] The extent of within-party differences across provincial

---

[7] Robert R. Alford, "The Social Bases of Political Cleavage in 1962," in *Papers on the 1962 Election*, ed. John Meisel (Toronto: University of Toronto Press, 1964), pp. 203-234.

TABLE 3-3

SELECTED CHARACTERISTICS OF MAJOR PARTY SUPPORTERS IN
SIX PROVINCES PRIOR TO THE 1962 GENERAL ELECTION

Characteristics	Those Intending to Vote Conservative					
	Quebec	*Ontario*	*Manitoba*	*Saskatchewan*	*Alberta*	*British Columbia*
Religion:	%	%	%	%	%	%
Protestant	14	91	56	80	76	86
Catholic	84	6	35	16	24	7
Other	2	3	9	4	0	7
Occupation of household head:						
White-collar	29	38	35	21	14	23
Blue-collar	42	34	21	16	41	39
Farm	12	11	35	49	29	9
Other	17	17	9	14	16	29
Residence in union household:						
Union household	15	28	10	11	21	18
Non-union	85	72	90	89	79	82
N	(138)	(322)	(48)	(61)	(63)	(44)

Characteristics	Those Intending to Vote Liberal					
	Quebec	*Ontario*	*Manitoba*	*Saskatchewan*	*Alberta*	*British Columbia*
Religion:	%	%	%	%	%	%
Protestant	7	54	35	59	54	66
Catholic	86	42	65	34	46	32
Other	7	4	0	7	0	2
Occupation of household head:						
White-collar	31	29	22	28	39	27
Blue-collar	42	48	47	17	25	53
Farm	16	10	15	41	21	13
Other	11	13	16	14	15	17
Residence in union household:						
Union household	23	31	28	7	7	39
Non-union	77	69	72	93	93	61
N	(245)	(322)	(40)	(29)	(28)	(62)

Source: Data are derived from Canadian Institute of Public Opinion Survey #297, conducted immediately prior to the June 18, 1962, election. The results of this survey were supplied by Robert R. Alford. The above tabulations, previously unpublished, were prepared by the authors. Since the sample size varies considerably from one province to another, results should only be treated as suggestive in the more lightly sampled areas.

lines with respect to occupational-social class composition is further indicated by the proportions residing in union households. These differences are partially accounted for by regional variations in industrialization and consequently in unionization. Yet also contributing to these results are the differential attractiveness of the two parties to the working class. In this respect it is interesting to look at Alberta. While the case bases are small, it still appears that the two parties have reversed their traditional roles, with the Conservatives in Alberta currently having greater appeal to the working class than the Liberals. In general, the consequences of these interprovincial differences in party supporters are again to present the two major parties with interests at least potentially at odds with each other.

The impact of Canadian society, making for parties as groups of highly varied supporters, is not confined to the major parties. Prior to the 1962 election, the Canadian Institute of Public Opinion found relatively sizable numbers of Social Credit supporters in Quebec, Alberta, and British Columbia. While in Quebec they were all Catholic, about 80 per cent were Protestant in the two western provinces. Quebec support was also largely working class, evidenced by the large proportions living in blue-collar and union households and having only elementary schooling. In all these respects they contrasted with western Social Crediters, who were characteristically better educated and more likely to be in farm households in Alberta and in either white-collar households or outside the labour force entirely in British Columbia. For a minor party, which by definition can be expected to have a special appeal, Social Credit at this time at least, displayed a singular lack of homogeneity among its supporters.

In the three provinces, Ontario, Saskatchewan, and British Columbia, where they obtained sufficient support to permit any sort of comparisons, the NDP displayed the greatest degree of uniformity of all four parties. However, in comparing these provinces, there are two noteworthy differences. One is the almost solely Protestant social base of the NDP in Saskatchewan, and, as we would anticipate, the preponderance of farmers in that province. In addition, Saskatchewan had a relatively large share of support where the head of the household was outside the labour force, either through lack of a male head, retirement, or more rarely, unemployment. We did not comment on a similar finding among Social Crediters in British Columbia, but in both provinces and parties it is a reflection of support from those in the older age groups. In British Columbia this is difficult to explain, but in Saskatchewan it is indicative of the disenchantment of the young with the CCF/NDP.

It would be useful to present similar data on the social composition of provincial parties, but the materials available at present do not permit adequate comparisons. However, on the basis of what we have seen from empirical studies, we would conclude that the evidence supports conclusions similar to those we arrived at for federal parties.[8] That is, in the

---

[8] Sources of information include unpublished studies on Alberta, Ontario (the latter from a study by S. Peter Regenstreif for the Toronto *Daily Star*), and Le Groupe de recherches sociales, *Les Electeurs québécois* (Montréal: mimeo., 1960).

case of provincial parties, supporters of varied characteristics are subsumed under the same party heading, separated only by provincial boundaries.

Differences in the social composition of parties across provincial lines remain as latent tensions within the parties at the national and provincial levels. These tensions become manifest on many occasions when they are translated into programs and policies. Evidence of the creation and maintenance of differing approaches to political problems by the same party is much more difficult to come by than are compositional differences, but even the anecdotal accounts we are able to provide are at least suggestive of how within-party differences develop out of, and persist because of, the conditions of Canadian existence.

It is possible to distinguish between two kinds of intraparty differences in orientation. The first of these is revealed in comparing provincial and federal parties of the same name, the second, in comparing the same party across provincial boundaries. Despite the existence of such differences, previous writers have paid scant attention to this topic. One of the few instances given any sizable coverage concerns the dispute between Premier Mitchell Hepburn of Ontario and Prime Minister Mackenzie King.[9] Part of the lack of written material is no doubt due, not to the fact that others have not recognized the phenomena we are talking about, but rather that they have frequently interpreted them as evidence of the lack of ideological consistency in Canadian parties and hence not worth careful consideration. Such an interpretation may be valid, but we would argue that it is a gross over-simplification. In addition, and more important, looking at intraparty differences as these stem from the nature of Canadian society directs us to an important *source* of inconsistency, and thus helps to explain why Canadian parties are the way they are.

Differences of the kind we are discussing assume many different forms. They may involve specific policies. For example, in the 1963 provincial election in Alberta, the Liberals had planned to campaign on the issue of public ownership of electric power. Despite the fact that telephones are publicly owned in this province, this proposal aroused so much opposition within the party that it was given only minor place in the campaign. An unpublished public opinion survey conducted at this time found, in fact, greater opposition to provincial ownership from among Liberal supporters than from the supporters of any other party. Yet at about this same time, the Quebec Liberal Government was negotiating for the purchase of all major electric producers in that province. In Ontario, and at the federal leadership level as well, Liberals were mystified by the position taken by Alberta Liberals on this issue.

Differences may be related to more general policies. The Liberals, for instance, are not usually considered the party of sound finance. At least until the Diefenbaker era, this was much more the image of the Conservatives, provincially as well as federally. But in recent years, Liberals in Manitoba had emphasized fiscal orthodoxy at the expense of economic expansion, in contrast to the Liberal governments in Quebec and New

THE SHAPING OF POLITICAL PARTIES

Brunswick. Since the election of Duff Roblin's Conservative Government in Manitoba, that party has been expansionist, willing to rely on government participation in the economy if this appears necessary for economic advancement.

In some cases the differences are stylistic in nature, although they need not be confined to this dimension. While we have mainly been concerned with intraprovincial differences in the major parties, the minor ones too provide instructive examples. For instance, one of the sharpest contrasts is between the Social Credit governments in British Columbia and Alberta. A British observer writes, "Bennett's government is spectacular, unorthodox and it delivers in plenty." In contrast, Mr. Manning's Government is cautious, inclined to the austere and conventional.[10] Perhaps Social Credit is especially prone to such differences in political style, as witness the flamboyance of former deputy-leader Réal Caouette and the sober, business-like manner of Robert Thompson.

Finally, differences may assume an ideological content. While we are cautious about using a Left-Right distinction in speaking of the major parties, it is a useful distinction at times, at least in treating differences within the parties. Thus, among Liberals, Mitchell Hepburn and Ross Thatcher could be considered at the Right, at least in comparison with Mackenzie King, Jean Lesage, and Andrew Thompson, the former Liberal leader in Ontario. Joey Smallwood is difficult to classify, but in terms of his disputes with the International Wood Workers of America Union in Newfoundland,[11] his position puts him clearly to the right of many of his fellow Liberals.[12] Factionalism within the Quebec Liberal Party is at least partly attributable to ideological differences, in that the old guard prefer the status quo and the old political ways (unfortunately sometimes prone to venality) while the young Turks are committed to major social change and a rejection of the old procedures. In the Conservative Party, such ideological differences emerged in the contrast between the fiscal orthodoxy represented by Bay Street interests in Toronto and the prairie radicalism of Diefenbaker.[13]

Now, at first glance, these differences could be due to nothing more than the characteristics of the party leader who happened to be in office at a particular time. Certainly, there are individual approaches to political problems. But more careful scrutiny of these examples, and we would

---

[9] See for example H. McD. Clokie, *Canadian Government and Politics* (Toronto: Longmans, Green Ltd., 1946), p. 200.

[10] "Report on Canada," *The Economist*, CCXVI (July 10, 1965), xiv-xviii.

[11] D. A. Schmeiser, *Civil Liberties in Canada* (London: Oxford University Press, 1964), p. 222.

[12] At the 1960 Kingston Study Conference, Smallwood's policies were publicly repudiated by those active in the Liberal Party and this repudiation was openly applauded by party influentials.

[13] For a fascinating discussion of the sources of such ideological differences within parties, which focuses on ideology *per se* rather than on the impact of regionalism, see G. Horowitz, "Conservatism, Liberalism, and Socialism in Canada: An Interpretation," *Canadian Journal of Economics and Political Science*, XXXII (May, 1966), 143-171.

hypothesize, more detailed empirical evidence, should indicate that many of these differences stem from the nature of the political setting which these leaders find and the political problems with which they are faced. Each province, we repeat, has its own problems and its own economic and social characteristics. It is these which have a critical bearing on how political parties come to terms with the problems faced, to some extent independently of the specific parties involved.

THE EMERGENCE OF SPLINTER PARTIES We have already made extensive reference to the existence of third parties at the national and provincial levels. We now turn to some of the conditions for the emergence of such parties, along with the implications that these same conditions have for their future. In general it can be said that new parties have been formed at the junctures of the critical cleavages in Canadian society. Factors instrumental in promoting the growth of third parties, which in fact have been operative in the United States as well as Canada, include, in the west, the influence of the frontier. Without indulging in any mythology about the "frontier spirit," it still seems fair to conclude that life on the frontier both attracts and promotes attitudes of enterprise, experimentation, but correlatively, a suspicion of ousiders, and a concern wih the morality of traditional government. "The dominant urge of frontier populations was to be left alone, to escape the exactions and restrictions of outside political authority."[14]

More specific objections of western frontier communities, shared with older settled areas, relate to feelings of economic exploitation. To them, economic domination by Bay Street and St. James Street, or by big business, extended to political domination by the two older parties. But some regional differences emerge. While similar objections have been voiced by spokesmen in the Maritimes, Quebec, and the western provinces, it is only in the west that movements of economic protest have taken a political direction. In the Maritimes, disaffected interests have preferred to shape their destinies within the older parties. Quebec, while often combining an element of economic dissatisfaction with other grievances, has been more likely, nationally at least, to adhere to the major parties or to form third parties of nationalist (i.e., French-Canadian) protest. But splinter parties which grew up in the west—the United Farmers, Progressives, Social Credit, and CCF—all derived from the conviction that the interests of a rural population dependent on agriculture were not best served by traditional political parties dominated by "city slickers" in central Canada.

A further factor related to the emergence of third parties is the political philosophy upholding the two-party system. It is traditional to think of a parliamentary system of government, and indeed a congressional one as well, as operating most effectively when there are two main political parties involved—the governing party and the opposition party. But while a two-party system is purported to be a necessary condition of effective government, even leading political parties to campaign on this theme, as in the elections of 1958 and 1962, there is no evidence that it is

THE SHAPING OF POLITICAL PARTIES

TABLE 3-4

OPINIONS OF WHETHER OR NOT CANADA IS RETURNING
TO A TWO-PARTY SYSTEM

	1958	1962	1963
Returning	46%	42%	38%
Not returning	33	36	41
No opinion	21	22	21

Source: Canadian Institute of Public Opinion release, October 5, 1963.

a major concern to voters. A number of Canadian Gallup Poll surveys, which have asked voters their opinions of whether or not Canada is returning to a two-party system, indicate a trend toward increasing disbelief in this state, as Table 3-4 shows. Moreover, there has been an increase in the proportions feeling that it would be better for Canada if there were a two-party system. According to two Gallup Poll surveys, preference for a two-party system has increased from 38 per cent in 1956 to 53 per cent in 1966.[15] It may be of some significance that the two-party system, which owes much for its existence and justification to British parliamentary experiences, has also been weakest in those areas where the proportions of British origin are lowest—the Prairies and Quebec. While this may be related to an ineffective political socialization of non-British groups (although, in rural areas at least, those of British origin in the Prairies have been the strongest supporters of third parties), it reflects more critically the difficulty of transposing institutions from one cultural setting to another, quite different one.

These are some of the non-political factors involved in the formation of third parties. Political factors are obviously important as well. Most prominent is a parliamentary system of government. We have already indicated how this has been attached to a two-party system, and would appear to detract from the appeal of third parties. But even traditions associated with the two-party system have not been irrevocable, and given the political realities of the post-war period, recognition of the place of third parties was given in 1963, when parliamentary leaders of parties with more than eleven seats in the House of Commons were given formal acknowledgement through an extra allowance of $4,000. A more critical aspect of the parliamentary system is the requirement of caucus solidarity, upon which we shall elaborate in following chapters. Despite the lack of a strong ideological orientation within the two major parties, they do take relatively consistent positions over time, and when individuals or groups find themselves at variance with these positions, no alternative is left, because of the demands for party solidarity, but to form political

[14] S. D. Clark, The Developing Canadian Community (Toronto: University of Toronto Press, 1962), p. 210.
[15] Canadian Institute of Public Opinion release, April 2, 1966.

parties better expressing the interests of dissident groups. For some groups, such as farmers, grievances have been formulated and expressed outside the major parties. For others, protest parties derived from the major ones. One example is the Reconstructionist Party, formed by Henry H. Stevens, a former Cabinet Minister in the Bennett government. Reconstructionists contested the 1935 election in all provinces and thus had a nationwide movement, unlike that of most third parties. Another example is the Bloc Populaire, a nationalist party in Quebec formed mainly from dissident Liberals, displeased with the handling of the conscription issue.

Third parties have also been more likely to emerge where there is a history of one-party dominance. Maurice Pinard has recently developed this argument in relation to the emergence of Social Credit strength in Quebec. In general, he feels, where the second major party is very weak, opponents of the status quo have no political channels open to them except to create a new party. Pinard demonstrates the existence of this pattern with evidence from Quebec in the elections of 1958 and 1962. There, in most cases where Social Credit was successful, the Conservative Party was traditionally weak.[16]

Some of the same conditions associated with the formation of third parties also affect their continued growth and influence. If regional-ethnic and regional-economic interests contribute to the emergence of splinter parties, they also curtail their widespread appeal. Third parties have had their greatest strength in provincial politics. Attempts to branch out into the federal field by building a national party have been short-lived and of limited success. Issues which have great appeal locally and organizations well adapted to transmitting that appeal, may not be applicable elsewhere. Splinter parties may always have a place in Canadian politics at the national level, but the likelihood of building a program and organization which can capture the support of a majority, or even a plurality, much of it necessarily resident in the central provinces, is unlikely. The two older parties, to varying degrees, continue to appeal to the broad spectrum of voters. The strength of the splinter parties lies in their appeal to localized special interests.

One weakness of third parties is their frequent dependence on a strong leader. With his death or retirement, the party may disintegrate. This is more likely to occur when the party is a genuine splinter of another. Then, when the leader is gone, as occurred with Stevens and the Reconstructionists and Henri Bourassa and the Nationalists, the weakened party is especially vulnerable to reincorporation into the mainstream. Because of the weak power position of third parties, where there is so much to be gained and so little to lose, warring contenders for leadership are difficult to control, with the result that such parties are frequently fragmented. It seemed inevitable then that the election of twenty-six Social Credit members from Quebec in the 1962 election, compared to four from western Canada, would be a strong temptation for the party's deputy-leader, Réal Caouette, to challenge the national leadership of

Robert Thompson. This challenge resulted in a formal break after the 1963 election. Caouette had previously revealed his differences with national policies and viewpoints and his volatility could not be controlled by Thompson's conciliatory attempts.

Conversely, the final strength of the major parties lies in their ability to assimilate deviants. On the national scene at least, the major parties can "pay off." Government contracts, judgeships, appointments to the Senate and the office of Lieutenant Governor, and so on, are available to active party supporters when that party is in power federally, even though it is weak provincially. Parliamentary candidates must weigh the lure of a Cabinet post against righteous, but ineffectual, opposition. They must consider the possibility of being able to influence programs of the governing party so that these can become the law of the land in the foreseeable, rather than in the remote, future. Thus the Liberals in the 1920's were able to reconcile the Progressives and bring them within the party orbit. Similarly, the Conservatives from 1958 to the mid 1960's were able to attract the support of prairie farmers who otherwise voted for third parties, and presumably continued to do so in provincial elections.

Regionally-based ethnic and economic cleavages are the critical (non-political) dimensions accounting for the emergence of third parties. Given the strains attendant on these cleavages, the demands of a parliamentary system also assist the growth of such parties. At the same time, these cleavages, aided by a federal system of government (where responsibilities are divided among levels of government so that local interests are frequently served by provincial or municipal legislatures), ensure that third parties will remain weak and localized in nature.

•

FEATURES WITH LESSER IMPACT ON PARTIES

Canadian society can be characterized in ways other than those emphasizing its regional nature. Our description of the social structure was determined by a knowledge of the tie-in between regionalism and party formation. But two related omissions remain. These are the significant features of Canadian society which have never had a clear connection with identifiable parties, but which have often led to party formation in other countries. These structural features can be divided into two categories: those related to characteristics of the population and those related to the circumstances of Canadian existence.

Population Characteristics

In Canada, there has been no instance where social class, religion, or urban or rural residence has been a predominant influence on a major party.

---

[16] Maurice Pinard, "Political Factors in the Rise of Social Credit in Quebec," paper delivered to the Canadian Political Science Association, Charlottetown, 1964.

SOCIAL CLASS   Since the working classes have been enfranchised and permitted to organize, political parties specifically representing their interests have been a feature of all industrialized societies. While it is only in the United States that they have played a minor role, a compensatory tendency emerged there through the influence of organized labour on the major parties, particularly the Democratic Party. Of earlier origin than workers' parties are those representing other class interests, such as those of landowners or the bourgeoisie. The relation between class interests and parties in Canada, however, is ambiguous. Despite differences in the kinds of supporters which each party attracts, neither the Liberals nor the Conservatives are organized to represent the interests of one social class to the exclusion of others, nor are the policies of either consistently class-oriented on such issues as public ownership and social welfare. Working class parties have long existed. The striking feature about them, however, is their long-run instability, which is related to an apparent inability to convince workers that their interests can best be served through their own party. While working class parties need not be synonomous with the political parties of organized labour, the two are closely connected and the latter at least are viewed with disapproval by most Canadians. This last conclusion derives from a series of questions asked by the Gallup Poll from 1948 to 1962 on opinions toward having organized labour support its own party. While disapproval is modified by residence in a household where one or more members belong to a trade union, as Chart 3-1 shows, this in itself is not sufficient to swing a majority in favour of the proposal.

At first glance, these results may appear paradoxical. At a Canadian Labour Congress convention it was decided to form a new party deriving from the CCF, but involving greater organizational support from trade unions than had been the case with the earlier party. Along with this decision went the hopes of the founders of the NDP, despite, or perhaps because of, their connection with the trade union movement, of keeping it from being merely a workers' party.[17] Even before the advent of the NDP, there had occurred a drastic reorientation in the political philosophy of the CCF. Included in that party's Regina Manifesto of 1933 was a vow to eliminate capitalism; its Winnipeg Declaration of 1956 is notably lacking such doctrinaire socialism. Thus, while the CCF/NDP is the closest approach to a national class party, and one which has had the relatively greatest success of all Canadian labour parties, its own spokesmen have come to avoid strong emphasis on its class nature.

The weakness of working class parties in Canadian politics is no doubt related to some general North American characteristics. Among those often mentioned are the absence of feudal traditions, a belief in unlimited opportunities to those willing to work for them, and the availability of land in the west. This land provided an outlet for what otherwise might have been a dissatisfied proletariat and also contributed to the loss of social distinctions in the face of an equalizing need for hard work.[18] Hence some aspects of North American egalitarianism are at work here, although probably not as strongly in Canada as in the United States.[19]

CHART 3-1

PER CENT WHO FEEL THAT FORMATION OF A PARTY SUPPORTED BY
ORGANIZED LABOUR WOULD BE BAD FOR CANADA

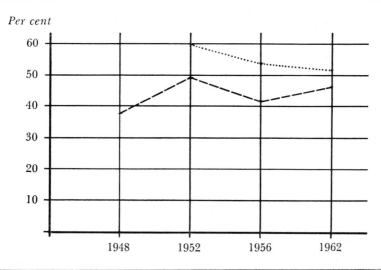

Legend: ———— Union householders
.... Non-union householders

Sources: Derived from Canadian Institute of Public Opinion releases for November 27, 1948; December 3, 1952; July 25, 1956. The 1962 figures come from CIPO Survey 293, conducted in January of that year, for which the percentages were computed by the authors.

Directly reflecting Canadian experiences as these bear on the formation and continuity of working class parties are two items. One concerns the nature of the trade union movement in Canada, the other, the opinions and behaviour of voters.

The unique aspects of trade unionism in Canada are well presented in Stuart Jamieson's *Industrial Relations in Canada*[20] and we will rely on his interpretations. Essentially, many of the circumstances already discussed, on the nature of the Canadian population and economy leading to particular political consequences, also have a bearing on the slow-

---

[17] Stanley Knowles, *The New Party* (Toronto: McClelland & Stewart, Ltd., 1961).

[18] Lipset, *Agrarian Socialism*, p. 2.

[19] S. M. Lipset, *The First New Nation* (New York: Basic Books, 1964), contains a discussion of the differences in values between the United States and Canada.

[20] Stuart Jamieson, *Industrial Relations in Canada* (Toronto: Macmillan Company of Canada, 1957), pp. 93-100. For a recent discussion of the impact of American ties on Canadian unionism, see John H. G. Crispo, *International Unionism in Canada: A Canadian-American Experiment* (Toronto: McGraw-Hill Canada, 1966).

SOCIAL STRUCTURE AND THE FORMATION OF PARTIES   57

ness of trade union development. They include an economy vulnerable to seasonal and trade fluctuations, which leaves the worker in a relatively weak bargaining position; a recently urbanized and often recently immigrated working class difficult to unionize; and limited federal jurisdiction on matters relating to labour, which allows the perpetuation of pronounced regional differences in working conditions. Individual unions have often been torn by internal dissension, with the difficulty of achieving a united outlook compounded by the existence, in Quebec, of a Catholic labour movement only recently secularized. Like many other social institutions, trade unionism was brought to Canada from Britain and the United States, and for many of the Canadian unions affiliated with the AFL-CIO, there is some question of their policy-making autonomy. Perhaps related to all of these points has been a reluctance on the part of unions to engage directly in political action. The Trades and Labour Congress never officially supported the CCF, although some of its member unions did, in contrast to the Canadian Congress of Labour which gave the CCF open support beginning in 1943. The merger of the TLC and CCL negotiated in 1956 did not commit the new organization to follow the CCL's political lead. The changes which took place with the formation of the NDP still leave union organizations at any level the option of not supporting that party. If, in most countries, workers' parties derive their strength from a tie-in with organized labour, we can now see some of the reasons for the weakness of such parties in Canada.

Another indicator of the weakness of social class factors in Canadian politics, despite the importance of economic issues *per se*, is manifested in the behaviour of voters. Considering voting intention as this was given to Gallup Poll interviewers from 1940 to 1961, Robert Alford, in his comparative study of class-based voting, concluded that this was lowest in Canada in contrast to Britain, Australia, and the United States.[21] Similarly, his analysis of voting intentions prior to the 1962 election did not find class voting high.[22] His interpretation, compatible with our own view of Canadian society, is that regional-ethnic and regional-economic interests and loyalties are so strong, that even in the case of economic interests, they work against the emergence of national class-oriented behaviour. Further support for these conclusions comes from an examination of a variety of Gallup Poll surveys, in which questions were asked about different aspects of Canada's identity. There it was found that differences based on social class played a secondary, though not an unimportant, role in shaping Canadians' perceptions of their country.[23] While social class factors have been important in leading to the emergence of some minor parties, they do not provide a critical dimension for differentiating between the two major parties.

RELIGION In some ways, the relatively lesser impact of religion on political parties is more difficult to account for than that of social class. Of all the factors dividing Canadians in their political outlook and behaviour, religion is uppermost in importance.[24] Yet there has never been a specifically religious party in Canada, such as the Christian Democrats, nor one dominated by anti-religious sentiments. The closest approaches to either kind of party were Le Parti Rouge in pre-Confederation Canada and the early period of Social Credit. Les Rouges, influenced by the European revolutionary fervour of 1848, were outspokenly anti-clerical in orientation. But they were no match for the Catholic Church in Quebec and their arguments were eventually toned down, aided by Laurier's placatory efforts in later years. Social Credit, on the other hand, in addition to the secular teachings of a British engineer, Major Douglas, who first promulgated its radical economic principles, owed much of its early success to its connection with religion. William Aberhart, its first Canadian leader and Premier of Alberta, found it easy to transfer the evangelical message of the Calgary Prophetic Bible Institute, where he was a lay preacher, to the political arena. However, despite the fact that Aberhart, and after him Ernest Manning, were able to utilize their religious authority to political advantage, Social Credit was never specifically a religious party.

The above examples have been of provincial parties, and this in itself is instructive. Religious issues do not normally become national, since the areas in which they are most likely to arise, child welfare, the solemnization of marriage, divorce, and education, are all under provincial jurisdiction. The most famous and divisive religious issue concerned the existence of state-supported parochial schools in Manitoba. While this had been provided for in the British North America Act when Manitoba was a territory, the Manitoba Government felt free to reinterpret its responsibilities on becoming a province. The subsequent actions of the Conservative government in Ottawa helped to further divide Canadians according to their religion. But as we argued in our earlier discussion on the importance of regionalism, the issue of provincial rights was even more important to Catholics in Quebec, as interpreted by the Liberals under Laurier. Since that time, educational rights for Catholics have become solely provincial issues, though of continuing relevance. Yet even at the provincial level, neither this nor related issues have led to the emergence of religious parties.

In effect, no major party has had to take on a particular religious

---

[21] Robert R. Alford, *Party and Society* (Chicago: Rand McNally, 1963). Alford computes his index of class voting for Canada by combining votes for the CCF and Liberal parties. But as we describe them, the Liberals do not make up a consistent part of the Left. The limitations of Alford's method, which may be serious in some contexts, are of little consequence here. His point, in substantiation of our argument, is that there is an absence of large-scale, class-based voting in Canada.

[22] Alford, "The Social Bases of Political Cleavage . . . ," in *Papers on the 1962 Election*, ed. Meisel. In this case, Alford treats each of the four parties separately.

[23] Schwartz, *Public Opinion and Canadian Identity*, pp. 172-186.

[24] Alford, "The Social Bases of Political Cleavage. . . ," in *Papers on the 1962 Election*, ed. Meisel; Mildred A. Schwartz, "Political Behaviour and Ethnic Origin," *ibid.*; John Meisel, "Religious Affiliation and Electoral Behaviour: A Case Study," *Canadian Journal of Economics and Political Science*, XXII (November 1956), 481-496; Grace Anderson, "Voting Behaviour and the Ethnic-Religious Variable: A Study of a Federal Election in Hamilton, Ontario," *Canadian Journal of Economics and Political Science*, XXXII (February 1966), 27-37.

orientation since the conciliation of all religious bodies is a general aim. Of considerable importance is the fact that no major religious denomination has been excluded from political participation. Canada was the first member of the British Empire to elect a Jew to public office. This was Ezekial Hart, elected from Trois Rivières to the Quebec (Lower Canada) Assembly in 1807 but not allowed to take his seat. As a result of the ensuing controversy, the oath was changed and full political and civil rights were granted to Jews in 1832, 25 years before they were to receive similar treatment in Great Britain. While Roman Catholics in the United States had to wait until 1960 before one of their communicants attained the highest office in the land, in Canada, John Thompson, a convert to Catholicism, preceded Laurier by four years as Prime Minister. In addition, all parties take heed of the pronouncements of the main religious bodies. Thus the major parties at least have been reluctant to change either the procedures whereby persons in Quebec and Newfoundland may obtain a divorce or the grounds for such action.

COMMUNITY OF RESIDENCE   While farm parties have existed, and have in fact been more successful than labour parties, they have been more short-lived, and, except for a very short period in the case of the Progressives, have never united into a national party. An interesting contrast here is the Australian Country Party which, although it too is a third party, remains a stable representative of agricultural, rural interests. Part of the explanation for the Country Party's comparative durability is no doubt connected with its social base of prosperous farmers. This is reflected in the conservative policies it propounds. Neither its social base not its policies are then subject to the same pressures toward social change felt by radical farm parties in Canada. In the case of the latter, times of prosperity or lack of political impact made them vulnerable to inroads from other parties.

While farm parties, even if local in nature, have represented rural interests, urban parties have been absent from the political scene. Labour parties have of course stood for urban workers, but the crucial aspect of their organization was not that they were urban dwellers, but that they were workers. Cleavages between town and country currently manifest themselves in the political choices which voters make among the existing parties. As we reported in Table 3-5, voters in communities of different types differed in their likelihood of selecting the four main political parties in the elections of 1962 and 1963. As a result, candidates elected for the Liberals and NDP have come mainly from the big cities and those for the Conservatives and Social Credit, from smaller towns and rural communities. If Table 3-5 does not reflect this too clearly, it is because the proportions refer to popular vote and this is imperfectly aligned with electoral districts. What we mean is that rural areas are at present, in terms of population, over-represented.

Further support for our contention that rural-urban differences are relatively weakly reflected in the political system comes from an analysis of opinions on national problems. Without regard to the particular con-

THE SHAPING OF POLITICAL PARTIES

TABLE 3-5

CHOICE OF PARTY, BY SIZE OF COMMUNITY, FOR ELECTIONS OF
1962 AND 1963

Choice of Party for Elections of 1962 and 1963	Community Size			
	Over 100,000	10,000 to 100,000	1,000 10,000	Rural
1962 Election:				
Conservative	31%	36%	38%	44%
Liberal	40	37	35	33
NDP	15	13	9	9
Social Credit	12	12	18	12

Source: Canadian Institute of Public Opinion release, July 25, 1962. Votes for other parties have been omitted from the table so that percentages do not add to 100.

1963 Election:				
Conservative	25%	39%	32%	41%
Liberal	46	40	40	35
NDP	16	11	10	8
Social Credit	13	10	18	16

Source: Canadian Institute of Public Opinion release, May 4, 1963.

tent of these opinions, differences between residents in urban or rural communities were, in total, not especially pronounced. When these opinions were compared within parties, they were often found to be identical. In fact, rural-urban differences were most frequently found in the CCF/ NDP, apparently a reflection of the strains inherent in attempting to reconcile two groups who each regarded that party as the spokesman of its own interests.[25]

While farmers do see their interests as distinctive, and urban dwellers characteristically are unconcerned about farmers' problems, it is only the former who have, from time to time, acquired a self-conscious identity of interest leading to the formation of parties. And these parties have normally been provincial. Urban residents, in contrast, are so heterogeneous that it is unlikely that they will ever form their own parties. Although labour parties are generally made up of urban workers, such parties tend to differentiate, rather than to unite, those in cities.

Existential Circumstances

Two critical aspects of Canada's existence are pertinent here. The first concerns Canada's traditional ties with Britain, the second, ties with the United States. While both these facts present crucial political issues with

---

[25] Schwartz, *Public Opinion and Canadian Identity*, pp. 140-145.

which all political parties must contend, they have neither formed the basis out of which viable political parties have emerged, nor have they resulted in consistent orientations clearly differentiating among existing parties.

TIES WITH BRITAIN   The nature of Canada's ties with Britain have frequently been troublesome. With the British conquest of New France, two questions were raised. How quickly, and in what respects, should the weaning of this colony from the mother country take place? What should be the nature of the relationship between the British and the French, between what those of French origin persist in seeing, in this connection quite correctly, as the conquerors and the conquered? These are questions to which time has not yet brought satisfactory solutions. On the occasion of the Boer and the two World Wars, and in other times of crisis, these British ties have been the source of bitter quarrels among fellow Canadians. Tension was greatest between English and French over the decision to proceed with conscription in 1917, a decision which the French saw as reflecting a commitment primarily to Britain rather than to Canada. But even the idea of being a Canadian has been a difficult one to formulate. John A. Macdonald, whom Canadians rightly see as one of the major architects of their country, expressed his loyalty in terms of, "A British subject I was born, a British subject I will die." It was only after World War II that a legal concept of the Canadian citizen evolved, in distinction from the previous characterization as a British subject with Canadian domicile. And the symbols of nationhood, those emotionally-laden objects, ideas, and ceremonials which serve to evoke the patriotic fire of other nations, have usually been expressed in Canada through primary or adapted British symbols. Up until 1952, the office of Governor General was occupied by a man born in Britain and, only in 1964, was a uniquely Canadian flag adopted. In a country made up of diverse ethnic groups, whose loyalty to the nation is presumably desired, it is noteworthy how weak have been the attempts to forge a unifying set of political goals. Yet while the retention of various ethnic identities has been permitted, and even encouraged, the image of Canada's political identity has been essentially British.

We are adumbrating here the two hundred years of history since the British conquest. During that time there have been both valiant and petty episodes in the demonstration of Canadian ties with Britain. If we have singled out just a few, and those which were bound to exacerbate relations between English and French, it would be misleading if we did not also point out that there have been occasions when those of British origin have regarded their ties with the mother country with less than favour. Here we shall consider only the impact of British ties, as these have been perceived by French and English, on the party system. Most noteworthy is the fact that Britain herself has rarely been the object of French-Canadian hostility. After all, it was the British who, in the Quebec Act, initially ensured the continuity of French existence on this continent. The conscription crises were reflections of French indifference not only to Britain, but to all events occurring beyond the confines of their province. Their anger was directed at English Canadians for involving them in what they persisted in seeing as none of their concern. And it is the result of their quarrels with their English-speaking compatriots which has led to the contemporary response of separatist movements. Disapproval of the Queen's 1964 visit to Quebec and her unfriendly reception there was again a manifestation of these sentiments. If the Queen symbolizes important political values to English Canadians, they seem to reason, she must, therefore, be rejected.

It is in English-speaking Canada that a more directly critical evaluation of British ties arose. Seven years after Confederation, a group of young men in Toronto formed the "Canada First" movement in response to what they felt was a lack of both unified purpose in the country and stable party politics. What alternatives they proposed were never clear. The young men of "Canada First" were never quite sure whether or not their watchword meant political independence, and whether their function was to liberalize the Liberal party, or to found a new third party, or merely to help in creating a deeper consciousness of the implications of the new nationality among the community at large.[26] They soon invited the aid of Goldwin Smith, a recent immigrant but one who had long been an advocate of Canadian nationhood. Politically their closest ties were with Edward Blake, leader of the Liberals. The movement aroused considerable alarm, and Goldwin Smith's editorials on political independence provided the occasion for bitter personal attacks from the Toronto newspapers, such that Blake abandoned his dealings with the movement, and it quickly collapsed. It was an episode of short-lived significance. Since that time, the problematic nature of Canada's ties with Britain have subsided. English Canada too has, except in time of crisis, come to see Britain in less immediate, pressing terms. From the study already cited on public perceptions of national problems, there was evidence of an increasing trend toward lack of awareness, and presumably of concern, on questions pertaining to Britain.[27]

Hence, relations with Britain have played only a minor role in the formation of parties. They have not been unimportant, however, in shaping the outlooks of the two older parties. Traditionally, it has been the Conservatives who have held most steadfastly to the British connection; this was reflected in recent years by support for British action in the 1956 Suez campaign, and the 1958 campaign promise to divert trade from the United States to Britain. The Liberals, as we shall discuss, have been oriented more to the United States. Still, it was a Liberal Government which permitted Canadian participation in the Boer War and which stood by Britain in 1939 and after, profferring economic as well as military aid in times of distress. The Conservatives as well have not been

---

[26] Frank H. Underhill, *In Search of Canadian Liberalism* (Toronto: Macmillan of Canada, 1961), pp. 93 and 172-175.

[27] Schwartz, *Public Opinion and Canadian Identity*, pp. 220.

entirely consistent in their policies when they have formed the government. Macdonald refused to send Canadian troops to the Sudan in 1884
(although volunteers did go later), and the Diefenbaker Government introduced discriminatory legislation against British immigrants during a
time of high unemployment in Canada. Yet whatever the basis in fact,
the Conservatives and Liberals are often described as differing in their
orientation to Britain.

TIES WITH THE UNITED STATES   However we may wish to evaluate the
significance of Britain in contemporary Canada and its politics, there is
no gainsaying the increasingly powerful role which is played by the
United States. Never has this pervasive influence given rise to party formation, although a para-political annexationist movement existed in
Canada East long before separatists blew up Wolfe's statue in Quebec
City. More important have been the ways in which American influence
has been felt in Canada and the responses of existing parties. We will treat
these in terms of economic, military, and cultural relations.

Regardless of the political utility of proposing to divert trade from the
United States to Britain, the Conservatives, following their election in
1958, found they were unable to do this. Contrary trading patterns had
long been established, the pull of geography could only be stopped by
impossibly high tariffs that simply could not be instituted in the modern
world, and the two neighbours share enough of a common life to find
each other's products and resources impossible to do without.[28] Trade
across the border has long been attractive to both countries; this was
manifested in the pre-Confederation Reciprocity Treaty of 1854. Free
trade had ceased by 1890, when it became the campaign promise of the
Liberal Party. Historians differ in their interpretation of the events surrounding the election of 1891.[29] But it is clear that while the Conservative government had reluctantly considered the merits of reciprocity,
revelation of its connection with outright annexationists in both the
United States and Canada discredited the movement. This contributed to
the defeat of the Liberals, tarnished by their advocacy of what had become a treasonous policy. Free trade rose as an issue again in 1911, this
time instigated by the Americans while the Liberals were in power. In
response to pressure from farmers, who would benefit from the free movement of products, the Liberals concurred to negotiate an agreement. But
reciprocity was not so attractive to other interests in the country, which
would only suffer from the admission of cheaper American products and
the encouragement of an economy based on the export of raw materials.
Conservative opposition was strong, especially following ill-timed pronouncements from the American Government that the trade agreement
heralded the absorption of Canada. Other issues contributed to the defeat
of the Liberals in the general election that year, but the emotionalism of
"No Truck or Trade with the Yankees" was a potent factor. While the
fervour of that anti-Americanism soon subsided, the sentiment itself has
remained as a latent current in Canadian politics. As our earlier discussion
revealed, the economic influence of the United States on Canada has

64   THE SHAPING OF POLITICAL PARTIES

increased vastly. With increased influence have come increased sources of friction. For example, one aspect of the 1956 pipeline crisis was opposition to the Liberal Government's proposal to have a trans-Canada pipeline financed and administered through government and private resources, the private resources being both Canadian and American. American involvement in a program so intimately related to the total economic development of the country appeared to many as distasteful, if not actually unpatriotic. Along with this ready-made issue, the Conservatives devoted their campaign in the election of 1957 to documenting other areas of American control through widespread ownership of Canadian businesses and through farm and other trade policies. It was an approach that paid off with a plurality for the Conservatives in that election and a strong majority the following year.

Economic relations thus have implications for continued tensions between the two countries and have, traditionally, served to align the two older parties at opposite sides, with the Conservatives more often taking an anti-American stance. The Social Credit Party has not been so intimately involved in these controversies, both because of the recency of its origin and its locus in provincial politics. The CCF/NDP, on the other hand, has displayed considerable ambivalence in relation to the United States. While one segment of the party, including university-centred intellectuals and some westerners, has looked with suspicion at all things American, in particular its "economic imperialism," the party itself has been restrained in its anti-Americanism by the more continentalist trade union officials, who are themselves sometimes victims and sometimes beneficiaries of this imperialism.

Military relations between the two countries have ranged from open conflict to unified defence measures. In the former case, where the countries have been on opposite sides, there is no cause for disagreement among political parties—all must stand united in the face of the enemy. It is amity, however, which has brought new and vexing problems. In World War II, American troops in Canada, unlike the troops of other allies, served under American law.[30] Some of the heavy-handedness of the war years has disappeared from Canadian-American relations, but grievances inevitably recur as the two countries work more closely in their joint defence, although one partner is disproportionately weaker. Issues of defence were another dimension of anti-Americanism in the Conservative campaigns of 1957 and 1958. Less successful was the Conservative approach to military problems in the campaigns of 1962 and

---

[28] For an overview, from a particular perspective, see Harry G. Johnson, *The Canadian Quandry* (Toronto: McGraw-Hill Canada, 1963).

[29] Donald G. Creighton, *John A. Macdonald: The Old Chieftain* (Toronto: Macmillan Company of Canada, 1955), pp. 548-553; C. C. Tansill, *Canadian American Relations, 1875-1903* (Toronto: Ryerson Press, 1943), pp. 424-480; W. L. Morton, *The Canadian Identity* (Madison: University of Wisconsin Press, 1961), pp. 62-64.

[30] Stanley Dziuban, *Military Relations Between the United States and Canada, 1939-1945* (Washington: Office of the Chief of Military History, Department of the Army, 1959).

1963. At those times the Conservative Government was under pressure from military advisers in both Canada and the United States to acquire nuclear warheads from the United States for the manned missiles purchased from that country. The Conservatives were themselves divided on the issue, with a Cabinet crisis resulting in the resignation of the Minister of Defence, Douglas Harkness, an advocate of nuclear arms, and two other Ministers. The Liberals too had their doubts about Canada joining the "nuclear club," but the official view was that Canada was committed to the purchase of nuclear warheads, without which the existing weapons were of only limited effectiveness, and they fulfilled these commitments upon election in 1963. Throughout the controversy, the NDP displayed considerable equivocation. That segment of the party which is identified most strongly with anti-Americanism also has isolationist tendencies. Spokesmen for it did not want nuclear arms, and previously had expressed a desire to withdraw from NORAD and, under some circumstances, from NATO. They were countered by others who stressed the importance of Canada's international commitments, including its military commitments, for the continuity of Western democracy. The party was united only in its oppposition to nuclear weapons. The Social Credit Party was also divided on the issue of arms, with the wing led by Mr. Thompson favouring them under limited conditions and Mr. Caouette's wing opposing them.

Questions of defence raise serious problems for the maintenance of national sovereignty. In the age of overkill, no nation can stand alone, and in the partnerships of pygmies with giants, it is not unusual that the smaller and weaker receive cavalier treatment. Perhaps what is most surprising under the circumstances is that the expression of grievances against American policies has been so mild and the potential for partisan dissension so infrequently exploited.

The one aspect of Canadian-American relations about which there is most consensus among parties is that pertaining to cultural matters. All unite in deploring the overwhelming influence of American produced or imitated television, movies, magazines, and popular literature. Other countries watch Hollywood movies, model their television shows after American ones, read foreign editions of American magazines and best sellers, but the Canadian situation is in many ways unique. The materials which originate in the United States do so in English and the Canadian who would compete with them has no insulating wall of language or geography. Meanwhile the Canadian is handicapped by a smaller population, fewer financial resources, and a market already accustomed to technical standards set by the neighbouring country. In a very real sense, Canadian popular culture is North American culture. This is true even in French Canada, where the barriers of language have not prevented the importation of American movies and television, although French dialogue is dubbed in. Under these circumstances, Canadian intellectuals and those involved in the mass media have looked to government protection for the continuity of their enterprises.

In response to the inroads of American culture, several Royal Commissions have been set up. Some, like the Royal Commission on the Arts, Letters and Sciences (the Massey Commission), and the Royal Commission on Publications (the O'Leary Commission), have been specifically concerned with countering American influences. Others, such as the Royal Commission on Broadcasting (the Fowler Commission), or the Royal Commission on Bilingualism and Biculturalism (the Dunton-Laurendeau Commission), have centred on different problems, but have had at the same time secondary concerns stemming from American cultural hegemony. In all these cases, the dominance of the United States has been seen as a problem by all political parties. Despite the proliferation of Royal Commissions (a typically Canadian response to difficult problems which frequently provide a cooling-off period before changes are introduced), and the institution of such cultural buffers as the Canadian Broadcasting Corporation, the National Film Board, and Canada Council, Canadian identity at this level is impossible to create through government decree and difficult to protect. The emotional appeal of this issue, however, makes it an attractive focus for anti-Americanism, unhampered by the painful realities restraining economic or military nationalism. It has brought forth no new party, but it has provided all existing parties with political ammunition.

•

SUMMARY

This chapter has covered a large number of topics, as benefits the diffuse nature of the subject matter treated—social structure and the formation of parties. Let us briefly recapitulate some of the highlights. Paramount importance has been assigned to the existence of regionally-based ethnic and economic cleavages. The political consequences of these cleavages were viewed from two perspectives: the behaviour of voters and the party system. In the case of the former, the significance of region was reflected in rates of turnout, partisan choice, and climates of opinion. The tensions created by regional differences have had their impact on the party system in a number of ways. For one thing, the major parties have responded with deliberately accommodative policies in order to attract and reconcile divergent interests. In some cases, parties have been successful in doing this by giving high level representation to these interests. In others, accommodation has been sought through policies aimed at the problems of special groups. Regional differences have not always been accommodated to the extent of becoming permanently suppressed. Instead, they remain as a potential source of conflict. This is seen through the diversified social composition of parties when the same party is compared across provincial lines. The potential becomes manifest in two ways—through the formation of opposing policies and programs by the same parties separated by provincial boundaries, and through the creation of splinter parties. Both of these responses, in their own way, confirm the pervasive influence of the regional-ethnic and regional-economic cleavages.

It has also been of interest to consider other features of Canadian society which, while important sources of party formation in other countries, have had relatively lesser impact in Canada. Of the features related to population characteristics—religion, social class, and urban or rural residence—only class and rural interests have influenced the creation of parties. But even these have been minor parties, frequently short-lived, and where most successful, provincial rather than national in scope. Those features related to the nature of Canada's existence have had even less influence on the formation of parties than have population characteristics. Yet, while not nearly as critical as the two dimensions of regionalism, relations with Britain and the United States, like those of religion, class, and urban-rural residence, all have considerable influence on the actions of existing parties.

4

The Mass Media and Elites

•

In this and the following chapter on interest groups, we will direct our attention to how the active force of public opinion affects Canadian political parties. Here the stress is on *active* public opinion, manifested in the mass media, elite and interest groups, rather than in the undifferentiated public opinion measure by Gallup Polls which may have limited relevance to political action.

•

THE MASS MEDIA

The systems of communication found in a society are largely dependent on the state of technological innovations to which it has access. Currently, communication takes place in many ways, with varying degrees of control by governmental agencies, and with differing repercussions on the life of the people. Our interest in the communications systems does not extend to the whole range of communication media, their organization and effects, but to some restricted aspects of communication in Canada. Specifically, we shall explore the influences which the mass media of radio, television, press, and magazines have on the operation of political parties.

The political ramifications of the mass media have been poorly documented for Canada. As a result, we have been forced to organize our subject according to what has been learned about the mass media in other countries, using the data we do have on Canada to illustrate our major points.[1]

---

[1] A useful overview of the field is contained in Kurt Lang and Gladys Engel Lang, *Collective Dynamics* (New York: Thomas Y. Crowell & Co., 1961), pp. 423-461. Canadian information was supplied by Frank Peers and Irwin Shulman.

The mass media have an impact on political parties and their fortunes in three ways: informational, stylistic, and electoral.

The Informational Role of the Mass Media

In their capacity to inform large numbers of people of events as they occur, the modern media of communication have no parallel. Of all the publics responsive to the messages of the media, there is probably none so attentive as that of politicians. Through the media, current happenings throughout the country and in foreign lands are quickly communicated to all those concerned. The media are indispensable sources of news on political events, especially to those who do not have ready access to the channels of information provided by the civil service. This includes those in parties not forming the government and often those, even in the governing party, who are low in the party echelon. But keeping party activists informed of day-to-day political occurrences does not exhaust the media's informational role in relation to the parties. The media may themselves generate the news rather than passively transmitting it. For example, a television program by the CBC in 1961 had direct consequences for the actions of the Conservative Government in Ontario. The program was concerned with divorce procedures, and while it may have been intended to have other effects, it nonetheless did have some impact on the Government. Adultery is the sole grounds for divorce in Ontario, and while such behaviour is in fact associated with marital discord, it is often not easy to provide legal evidence of its occurrence. It is also true that many couples find it difficult to continue to live together even when there has been no infidelity. As a result, some couples have entered into collusive agreements in order to "prove" adultery. The CBC show in question involved interviews with a so-called "shady lady" who purportedly acted as a professional co-respondent in divorce suits. While many officials may have suspected the existence of such techniques for obtaining divorces, their public disclosure required that some action be taken. With several alternatives available, the Conservatives responded to TV's newsmaking role by appointing a Queen's Proctor to investigate the legality of divorces already granted.

The media also provide the whole gambit of national, international, and local news to the public generally, including information on the actions of the various legislative bodies. During the famous pipeline debate in 1956, all the media helped publicize what was essentially a highly complex and technical issue, and a Gallup Poll survey taken at the time found that 73 per cent of those interviewed were aware of the debate.[2] The unfavourable evaluation of the Liberal Government's handling of the pipeline issue with respect to parliamentary traditions, propagated in large measure by the media, undoubtedly contributed to the defeat of the Liberals in 1957.[3]

There are differences in the media's informational role, depending on whether it is played during an election or between elections. Elections naturally increase the sheer volume of political news which the media

THE SHAPING OF POLITICAL PARTIES

must handle. In addition, they alter the relative coverage given to partisan policies and political leaders, as distinct from more general political issues. At election times, most of the political news transmitted is received not only by political activists but also by a broader spectrum of the electorate.

Influences on the Style of Politics

High speed methods for transmitting information over great distances have had a revolutionary impact on the media, and through them, the peoples of the world. We already take for granted that an event such as the funeral of Sir Winston Churchill can be witnessed simultaneously by hundreds of millions of people all over the world. Yet it is not thirty years since North Americans have begun to view televised events as they occur even in their own city. Perhaps less dramatic but equally far-reaching have been the technological changes in other media. In the realm of politics, these have given new immediacy to events with a political content. That is, the very informational role we discussed in the preceding paragraphs now has additional implications for the style in which politics is conducted. If we can imagine what campaigning was like during the time of John A. Macdonald, we can appreciate more fully how the media have affected changes. In the early years of Confederation, it took weeks or even months for interested constituents far from the capital to learn what had taken place in the House of Commons. Today, debates in the House are truly public, liable to be picked up at any time by the correspondents in constant attendance in the Press Gallery and immediately made the subject of widespread distribution. Formerly, if a politician representing the governing party were to make a speech in a Quebec constituency promising the people some measure relevant to their special interests, this might never come to the notice even of voters in the neighbouring riding. Today, such action must be carefully weighed against the possibility of outcries from western Canadians, quickly cognisant of what has passed, about "concessions to Quebec."

The 265 Members of Parliament who now are elected to govern the country could make their programs and ideals known to only limited numbers of people if they had to rely on personal appearances. But the technical improvements throughout the communications system have opened up vast new audiences for the parties. The media, in particular, provide a forum in which the parties can present their case to the electorate. Not all parties, however, share equally in the coverage the media allow them. This is especially noteworthy in the case of the press.[4] The existence of partisan newspapers is of long duration in many countries,

---

[2] Canadian Institute of Public Opinion, Survey #247, March 1956.

[3] John Meisel, *The Canadian General Election of 1957* (Toronto: University of Toronto Press, 1962), p. 179.

[4] An entertaining and equally informative account of the prejudices of the press, particularly in the United States, is contained in A. J. Liebling, *The Press*, rev. ed. (New York: Ballantine Books Inc., 1964).

where in many cases, those closely connected with one party are directly involved in running the paper. Even when there are not such direct tie-ins with a party, editorial support is common. While these forms of partisanship are easily recognized and understood for what they are, less readily discernible are more subtle ways of giving the favoured party more advantageous treatment. If, as the old-time party bosses in the big American cities used to feel, even bad publicity is better than no publicity at all, newspapers differentially reward the parties according to the amount of coverage they are given, *outside the editorial pages*. That is, the ordinary reporting on party platforms, candidates, and meetings is affected primarily by the newspaper's partisan viewpoints, with the party the newspaper favours receiving the greatest amount of coverage. In addition, in national elections at least, it is unusual for the two minor parties to be given the same amount of space which is given to the two older parties.[5] Evidence of partisanship in news reporting used to assume even more blatant forms than merely extent of coverage. For instance, in the early years of the Press Gallery in Ottawa, reporting slanted to favour one or another party was quite prevalent.[6]

Similar biases in reporting on radio and television are not as pronounced, if they occur at all. Since these media come under some governmental regulation, provision is made for air time to be made available to the parties without cost to them. This amount of time is naturally limited and does not fulfill what the parties feel is adequate. The free air time is, additionally, allocated on the basis of each party's representation in the previous Parliament, so that again the smaller parties are penalized. These arrangements apply to federal elections, but similar policies are followed for provincial ones.

For those parties who wish to supplement their use of radio and television beyond that provided without cost, it is possible to purchase additional time from private stations, subject to the regulations of the controlling body, now the Board of Broadcast Governors. But such time is expensive. Political parties buying time are treated no differently than other commercial interests and are charged the going rate. Finding funds for publicity, whether for the media, tours and personal appearances, mailings or handouts, is increasingly a problem as the population expands and the potential for contacting the electorate increases. Without a ceiling on election costs, those parties with the financial resources are free to spend as much as they choose on advertising. The biggest spenders are the Liberals and Conservatives, whose financial burdens have increased commensurately as they respond to the temptations of utilizing the media for more and more publicity. Since neither of these parties has a stable membership base from which to obtain funds, they are increasingly dependent on large-scale donations, mainly from business.[7] The extent to which this in turn affects party organization and policies is a topic we shall return to later in this chapter and again in Chapter 8.

The full exploitation of the broadcast media have had a new bearing on the way in which candidates for political office are evaluated. Television, and radio as well, offer unique means for entering the homes of millions who might otherwise never have direct contact with political candidates. Such skillful users of radio as Franklin Delano Roosevelt in his presentation of measures to deal with the depression, and Sir Winston Churchill in his appeal to the British during the war, have provided standards against which other political leaders have been judged. Not many have been as dramatically effective, but William Aberhart, first Social Credit Premier of Alberta, was probably the most notable radio personality in Canada. Both as a lay preacher for the Calgary Bible Institute and as a politician, Aberhart made regular use of radio. He was quick to realize its capacity for vivid communication and, in the election campaign of 1935, used dramatized programs, featuring "Mr. Orthodox Anonymous." This was the first year that radio became important in campaigning and the Conservatives as well used dramatized broadcasts, where their character was "Mr. Sage." The Conservatives, however, had no one with the histrionic skills of Aberhart. But the use of dramatization worried the Liberals, now in office, because of the attempts to hide the party sponsorship of "Mr. Sage" and of its libelous overtones with respect to Mackenzie King. As a result legislation was passed preventing dramatized political broadcasts, including "any device which would be considered unnecessarily theatrical."[8] Aberhart managed nevertheless to continue to exploit the potential of radio in appealing to voters, and he found a worthy successor in this respect in the next Alberta Premier, Ernest Manning.

Television appears to be an even more intimate medium than radio and, as such, allows a more personalized appeal to voters. Because of its expensiveness and broad coverage, it is the one medium most exclusively for the use of leaders. But while there is growing self-consciousness on the part of party personnel concerning such concepts as the projection of personality and the building of an appealing leadership image, to date at least, no political leader in Canada has been selected primarily on the basis of his radio or television "personality." The one possible exception is Réal Caouette, but his is more a case, analogous to that of Aberhart, of a man with a sense of mission and flair for attracting attention and then devoted support, who made good use of television and then created a party. That is, he was not so much the choice of members of a party

[5] T. H. Qualter and K. A. MacKirdy, "The Press of Ontario and the Election," in *Papers on the 1962 Election*, ed. John Meisel (Toronto: University of Toronto Press, 1964), pp. 145-168; Léon Dion, "The Election in the Province of Quebec," *ibid.*, pp. 109-128; Pierre Berton, "The Election Coverage of Three Toronto Papers," in *Politics: Canada*, ed. Paul W. Fox (Toronto: McGraw-Hill Company of Canada Ltd., 1962), pp. 18-20; J. H. Aitchiscn, ed., *The Political Process in Canada: Essays in Honour of R. MacGregor Dawson* (Toronto: University of Toronto Press, 1963).
[6] C. K. Seymour-Ure, *An Inquiry into the Position and Workings of the Parliamentary Press Gallery* (Unpublished master's thesis, Carleton University, Ottawa, April 1962), p. 25.
[7] E. E. Harrill, "Money in Canadian Politics," in *Party Politics in Canada*, ed. Hugh G. Thorburn (Toronto: Prentice-Hall of Canada, Ltd., 1963), pp. 60-69.
[8] Board of Broadcast Governors, *Guiding Principles and Policies for Information of Broadcasters, Speakers and Agencies, Federal Election Campaign—1963* (Ottawa), p. 3. The original legislation is the Broadcasting Act of 1936.

organization as the moulder of that organization. Of the present national leaders of the two older parties, Mr. Diefenbaker is ranked more highly in his usage of television. Mr. Pearson, on the contrary, despite the concern of his advisers, has not yet come to terms with the newer media in presenting his message to large audiences.

The impact of the mass media on party politics has been felt in yet another way—through the hiring of advisers, not only because of their political experience and knowledge, but also because of their experience in handling publicity. For example, on the election of the Conservative Government in 1957, the appointment of new parliamentary assistants was notably in the direction of those who had worked in public relations. Such personnel also have a place in the highest echelons of the two older parties. Those with media experience at the upper levels of the Conservative Party include Senator Allister Grosart, formerly of McKim Advertising, and Dalton Camp, elected president of the National Conservative Association in 1964, head of his own public relations firm. Within the Liberal Party, Mr. Pearson's special assistant has been Richard O'Hagan, who came from an advertising and public relations background; Senator Keith Davey, past National Organizer of the National Liberal Federation, was formerly employed by a Toronto radio station; and Tom Kent, one of Mr. Pearson's chief advisers before appointment as Deputy Minister of Manpower, was once editor of the *Winnipeg Free Press*. To some extent this tendency to make use of experts is present in provincial politics as well. Probably the most notable example is that of former Premier Lesage of Quebec, who prior to winning office in 1960, was considered stiff and unattractive in television appearances (this according to some of his closest supporters). But he learned to make effective use of this medium under the tutelage of René Lévesque, a television commentator who was himself a master at using television and who was to become a member of Lesage's Cabinet. In effect, this move toward the political involvement of those skilled in the communicative arts is a further step toward the rationalization of politics. This has meant the recruitment of those with the technical qualifications to ensure the most effective use of the media in order to get a party's candidates elected and retain the support of the electorate.[9]

Many of the stylistic issues we have dealt with here have caused concern to the traditionalists, who deplore what they see as a move toward the "Americanization of Canadian politics." As apparent ammunition for them, we can cite a study commissioned by the Canadian Broadcasting Corporation to ascertain audience response to the Kennedy-Nixon debates before the 1960 presidential election. The study found both large audiences and a favourable evaluation of the debates.[10] Moveover, a large majority in seven large urban centres across the country agreed that "heads of the Canadian political parties should debate on television." Agreement ranged from 63 per cent in Ottawa to 75 per cent in Vancouver, Winnipeg, and English-speaking Montreal.[11] Comparable debates prior to federal elections did not take place, however, Mr. Diefen-

THE SHAPING OF POLITICAL PARTIES

baker as Prime Minister being particularly adamant about not appearing with other party leaders and allowing them to benefit from his ability to attract large audiences. Yet a majority of a national sample interviewed prior to the 1962 election would have welcomed a debate between Mr. Diefenbaker and Mr. Pearson.[12] Closest to the American format was a debate between Premier Lesage and the then opposition leader Daniel Johnson, broadcast on radio and television in the fall of 1962. True to the reactions predicted during the Kennedy-Nixon debates, audience for the native variety was large and interest widespread.[13] Whether or not we like what is happening to Canadian politics as a result of the media, we cannot, however, blame it on the Yankees. It is the nature of the media themselves which gives them the capacity to revolutionize the style of politics, no matter what the prior political traditions. Naturally, existing traditions will set limits to and shape the ways in which the media are used, and all governments exert some measure of control over political uses of the media. But the speed with which news can travel, the sense of immediacy the media convey, the lack of dependence on literacy of radio and television, lead to techniques for mobilizing the electorate which never existed before and which have the potential for affecting political parties and their leadership.

Impact on the Electorate

Political parties have always been concerned with their treatment by the media for one overwhelming reason—the influence which the media hold to shape party fortunes through their impact on the electorate. For example, the Liberals were very disturbed by the media's coverage of the pipeline issue, and in particular, the number of critical broadcasts carried by the CBC. They were quick then to attribute their defeat in 1957 to the concerted attacks by the media.[14] Even more sensitive to criticisms were the Conservatives during their 1957-1963 term of office. Mr. Diefenbaker, highly conscious of his image as Prime Minister and ever anxious that it be communicated with full respect to his office and to the sense of mission he brought to it, was by 1963 at the point of seeing the

---

[9] Richard Gwyn, "Ad-men and Scientists Run This Election," in *Party Politics in Canada*, 2nd ed., ed. Thorburn, (Toronto: Prentice-Hall of Canada, Ltd., 1967), pp. 21-23.

[10] Canadian Broadcasting Corporation, Audience Research Division, "Canadian Audiences to the 1960 U.S. Election Night Telecast" (Ottawa: January 1961); Canadian Broadcasting Corporation, Audience Research Division, "Canadian Reactions to the 4th Nixon-Kennedy Television Debate of 21st October 1960 and to Certain Other Features of the U.S. Presidential Campaign" (Ottawa: December 1960).

[11] Canadian Broadcasting Corporation, "Canadian Reactions to the 4th . . . Debate . . . ," p. 8.

[12] Canadian Institute of Public Opinion release, June 30, 1962. Fifty-seven per cent thought TV debates were a good thing, 28 per cent not a good thing, and the remainder gave qualified answers or were undecided.

[13] Société Radio-Canada, Service des recherches, "Réactions du public de la région métropolitaine de Montréal au débat 'Johnson-Lesage' télédiffusé le 11 novembre 1962" (Montréal: avril, 1963).

[14] For some observations from a journalist, see John Bird, "When the Liberals Lost the Press," *Canadian Commentator*, I June 1957), 3.

media as part of an organized conspiracy to drive him from power. Whether or not history will agree with his evaluation, Newman's indictment of Diefenbaker is especially pointed concerning his attacks on the nation's press, which was a major part of his 1963 election campaign.

It was typical of the man from Prince Albert that his strongest political testament in these final days of power was not the defence of some principle, but a quarrel with the projection of his image.[15]

But a pioneering study of voting behaviour, designed to trace the influences of the media on electoral decisions, had to shift focus because of the limited effects found.[16] A number of studies have continued to examine the influence of the media, with similar results. From an intensive survey of the literature examining the persuasive effects of the media in settings additional to elections, Klapper concluded that it is not correct "to say that major changes and conversions do not occur, nor that under particular conditions they may not be widespread. It is rather to say that by comparison they are rare, and that persuasive mass communication normally tends to serve far more heavily in the interests of reinforcement and of minor change."[17] Canadian studies are rare, but the CBC did enquire whether the Lesage-Johnson debate resulted in party switching. Considering the techniques of obtaining information, findings should be treated with caution. Yet it is instructive that only 3 per cent of those interviewed stated that they intended voting for a party other than that selected prior to the debate.[18] One reason for the great concern with how the media present party leaders and election issues is likely an inability to accept that the media, so pervasive and apparently so powerful, can do so little to change the minds of voters. The media do have significant consequences, however, even though they do not bring about radical shifts in the distribution of party supporters. Encouraging party loyalty, strengthening loyalty with reason, rapidly spreading information about new parties and appeals, and aiding undecided voters to come to a decision, are all consequences of considerable importance. We cannot document directly the effects of the media on party success in Canada, but we can assume that there is some connection, although not particularly in the direction of affecting partisan conversions.

•

THE ROLE OF ELITES

We owe the widespread usage of the concept of elites to the economist-sociologist Vilfredo Pareto.[19] According to his definition, elites are those most eminent, those who fulfill the requirements of their roles best, no matter what the field of activity. A somewhat different definition stresses that elites are the holders of positions highly evaluated with respect to their access to and control of significant values.[20] We will lean more to the latter approach, since it better emphasizes the power position of elites with regard to the society generally. However, we will consider elites as those most eminent in the economic, political, administrative, and ideological subsystems.[21]

In distinguishing among subsystems we are spilling over into the next chapter, where we deal with interest groups—the formally organized representatives of these subsystems. There is some difficulty in separating our concern here with elites by virtue of their skills from elites by virtue of their representation of special interests. Yet keeping this distinction in mind, we will deal with some particular aspects of elites separate from the questions we will raise in the following chapter.

Two approaches are possible in treating the influence of elites on parties. We could begin by surveying the contribution made by each set of elites associated with a particular subsystem, or we could deal with the nature of the influences on parties, illustrating these from the behaviour of each subsystem's elite. Since our interest is primarily in the influences, we will follow the second procedure. We have isolated five areas of influence. (1) Elites may serve as important sources of party support. (2) They may provide information and ideas to party leaders. (3) They may directly participate in the formulation of policy. (4) They may play a role in directing electoral strategy. (5) Finally, they may serve as candidates for elected office.

Sources of Support

The importance of support from elites, as distinct from that from other individuals or groups, lies in the role of elites as opinion leaders. Through occupancy of positions which give them access to special knowledge and through the esteem in which they are held, they hold a great potential for persuading others of the rightness of causes which they espouse. For example, in a study which attempted to evaluate the relative influence on women of personal contact compared to the mass media, with respect to selection of movies, purchase of food, fashions, and opinions on public issues, it was found that personal influence was most important.[22] We cannot equate these "influentials" with our elites, since they often do not possess characteristics definitive of elites. The findings, however, provide empirical evidence of how those most eminent in their field act as influentials, in the sense of being looked to for leadership in decision making.

---

[15] Peter C. Newman, *Renegade in Power: The Diefenbaker Years* (Toronto: McClelland and Stewart Ltd., 1963), p. 248.

[16] Paul F. Lazarsfeld, Bernard Berelson, Hazel Gaudet, *The People's Choice*, 2nd ed. (New York: Columbia University Press, 1948).

[17] Joseph T. Klapper, *The Effects of Mass Communication* (Glencoe: Free Press, 1960), pp. 15-16.

[18] Société Radio-Canada, "Réactions du public . . . ," 43.

[19] Vilfredo Pareto, *The Mind and Society*, ed. and tr. A. Livingston (London: Cape, 1935), II, pp. 1423-4.

[20] H. D. Lasswell, D. Lerner, C. E. Rothwell, *The Comparative Study of Elites* (Stanford: Stanford University Press, 1952), p. 6.

[21] This selection is borrowed from John Porter, "Elite Groups: A Scheme for the Study of Power in Canada," *Canadian Journal of Economics and Political Science*, XXI (November 1955), 501.

[22] Elihu Katz and Paul F. Lazarsfeld, *Personal Influence* (Glencoe: Free Press, 1955), Chapter 5.

We infer from this, and from numerous other studies, especially of small groups, that elites have a natural advantage in influencing opinions and providing leadership.[23]

The opinion leadership of Canadian elites, whether actual or potential, is manifested in a number of ways, partly dependent on the subsystem involved. The economic elite, for example, makes its influence felt through its open advocacy of parties and policies. Those who look to the economic elite for leadership can then take their actions as guideposts for their own behaviour. This is true of trade union leaders with respect to the CCF/NDP and business and industrial leaders with respect to the two older parties. Such support is of course welcomed by all parties, although the frontier tradition is sufficiently strong that overwhelming support from Bay Street or St. James Street would be feared. The economic elite, both as labour and industrial leaders, is able to give support in a way almost as welcome as votes—money. In the case of the Liberals and Conservatives, fees from members make up a small part of the financial requirements and characteristically they both rely on large donations from business. It is customary for businesses to give money to both parties in an election, on the principle that it is better to hedge one's bets. On the provincial level, Union Nationale and Social Credit share in the same largesse. However, Social Credit did originally rely on contributions from individual members. The CCF/NDP does have a mass membership base which has provided the major part of its funds, but the main significance of the formation of the NDP with trade union assistance was that the new party would have a larger, more stable supply of money through the automatic contributions of union members in locals which chose to affiliate with it. (Union members unwilling to contribute may opt out.) Here the actions of an elite, the national trade union leadership, were instrumental in providing one party with considerable financial resources.

According to Max Weber's classical analysis, a fully rational bureaucracy, including the administrative elite, faithfully carries out the directives deriving from leaders who are outside the bureaucracy. In the political sphere, it is the politicians who decide on policies, the civil servants who carry them out. The origins of a basically non-partisan civil service, selected and promoted on merit, date, on the federal level, to 1918. At the highest levels, administrators are appointed through Order-in Council and this leaves the way open for political appointments, although considerations of efficiency are usually uppermost in their selection. Whatever the remaining weaknesses of an independent civil service, active support from administrators is expressly forbidden. The administrative elite as a source of support for parties is therefore unimportant in Canada, although high administrative posts still remain as *rewards* for judicious support for those initially outside the bureaucratic framework. Provincially, the civil service has been less free of political involvement but there too the movement has been to non-partisanship.

Porter considers members of the ideological elite to be those involved in "the creation and articulation of myths, formulas, and derivations which aid in orienting the individuals in the system to super-empirical goals such as the Kingdom of God, the classless society, or Canada's century."[24] Specifically, Porter relates these elites to the mass media, higher learning, and religion.[25] We would like to extend this definition to encompass the leadership of ethnic groups insofar as these are concerned with ideological issues of group identity and survival. As with the economic elite, concern is with their influence as voters and persons able to mobilize the electorate. We can now account for some of the phenomena previously noted with respect to the influence of the elite associated with the mass media. The partisanship of the press has come about, not through direct ownership of newspapers by political parties, as is the case in some European countries, but primarily through the personal loyalties of owners and managers. In some cases, most conspicuously that of George Brown, the newspaper owner uses the editorial pages to wage his own campaign.[26] Other publishers have entered politics, but normally they take their place with other candidates in the amount of space given their personal campaign.[27] More usually, the partisan inclinations of newspaper owners, managers, and leading columnists and correspondents—radio and television personnel have these inclinations as well but regulations on political broadcasting make them relatively unimportant in this context—exist independently of party sponsorship or electoral ambitions. Remembering the importance which parties attach to their media coverage, we can expect that support will be actively sought and newspapermen, at all levels, assiduously courted by the parties.[28] But such support is often tenuous, as witnessed by the widespread desertion of the Diefenbaker cause by usually Conservative newspapers in 1963.

In the evolution of the modern state, the participation of religious leaders in secular politics has been tendentious. Its occurrence has not been uncommon in Canada, nor is it looked upon consistently with disfavour. The political activities of the clergy are usually directed toward the enactment of new legislation or the protection of existing laws or habits with a moral content. More direct partisan support is generally reserved for those opposed to atheistic Communism. Yet as we have already mentioned in Chapter 3, the major parties have not been free from religious

---

[23] See for example Sidney Verba, *Small Groups and Political Behavior* (Princeton: Princeton University Press, 1961).

[24] Porter, "Elite Groups . . . ," 501-502.

[25] John Porter, *The Vertical Mosaic* (Toronto: University of Toronto Press, 1965).

[26] J. M. S. Careless, *Brown of the Globe*, Vol. I, *The Voice of Upper Canada, 1818-1859* (Toronto: Macmillan Company of Canada, Ltd., 1959).

[27] This was the procedure, for example, of John Bassett, publisher of the Toronto *Telegram* and a Conservative candidate in 1962. Despite the resources available to him, he was beaten by a relatively unknown Liberal.

[28] Seymour-Ure, *An Inquiry into the . . . Parliamentary Press Gallery*. See also T. Joseph Scanlon, *Promoting the Government of Canada; A Study of the Information, Explanation and Promotional Activities of the Federal Government Departments* (Unpublished M. A. thesis, Department of Political Science, Queen's University, April 1964), p. 46.

controversies. Before Laurier had consolidated his leadership position in the Liberal Party, he had to overcome suspicion by the Catholic clergy toward the anti-clericalism of Les Rouges, heightened by the even stronger anti-clericalism of Continental European liberal parties. Direct intervention by the clergy through their sermons did not halt until Laurier had prevailed on the Vatican to send a Papal legate, followed by a proclamation that the Canadian Liberal Party was in the tradition of the British Liberals rather than of its Continental namesakes.

It is not meaningful to separate the leadership of the major ethnic groups in Canada, which Porter has termed the charter groups, from their positions as elites in other subsystems. Those who can be identified as prominent members and spokesmen of the English- or French-speaking community have achieved this position through their eminence in areas such as the political or economic; or where it is ideological, through intellectual or religious activities. In the case of other ethnic groups, elite status may derive mainly from the ability to speak for an ethnic group, distinct from subsystem commitments. It is the leaders of such non-British, non-French groups with which we are concerned. Specifically, the question is whether ethnic elites are identified as partisan supporters and whether this then has an effect on the political behaviour of the remainder of their group. A full scale investigation of the politics of ethnic leaders is still to be conducted, but some propositions about the connection between ethnic origin and political behaviour, along with a number of illustrations drawn from experiences in the 1962 federal election, are available. These suggest that ethnic leaders as party supporters do have some influence in affecting the votes of other ethnic members, although this is probably not as great as imagined, and that party officials in turn perceive this influence as a force deserving their courtship.[29]

In considering the intellectual elite, we are concerned mainly with those in universities. Intellectuals are of course present in the arts and in the mass media. The political interests of artists are not sufficiently developed in Canada to merit attention here, although they are not irrelevant in other contexts. Journalists and commentators are important agents for communicating political information, affecting the style of politics, and in some instances, influencing electoral decisions. We should recall that those attached to the CBC are restrained from voicing partisan support through the media's channels. With some variations according to local conditions, such restraints do not ordinarily operate for university personnel. It would appear, however, that this intellectual elite, although certainly not disinterested in political issues or parties, is least significant of all the elites we have discussed in terms of an opinion leadership role. There is little evidence that they, through their political activities and support for parties, have much impact on how any sizable group of people vote.

THE CONSEQUENCES OF ELITE SUPPORT   In recounting these instances of elite partisanship, we have emphasized the positive functions which support from elites gives to parties. These advantages stem from the emi-

THE SHAPING OF POLITICAL PARTIES

nence of elites, allowing them to be opinion leaders and role models for those not in such privileged positions.

Elite support may not be an unmixed blessing and may bring with it perverse influences. The very act of support can be accompanied by new demands, providing the opportunity for elites to ask a price for their open support. This was recognized, for example, by some of the farm leaders of the CCF who feared that new and added support from trade union officials for the NDP, along with the money which they would provide, could only alter the policies of their party. Similarly, the support given by the business elite to the two older parties, especially as the need for money increases, makes the parties vulnerable to increased demands from these interests.[30]

On the positive side, political parties have much to gain from the activities of elites. But their contributions may not be available to parties for a variety of reasons. Elites may be excluded by law or custom from participation in politics, as is frequently the case of the military or civil service. Secular values with respect to the separation of church and state may preclude the political activities of the religious elite; the same end result would stem from religious values which forbade involvement in wordly affairs. Excluding the intellectual elites associated with the mass media, support from other intellectuals, mainly those in universities, has minimal impact on the voting behaviour of major population groups. Lack of support from them may then be dismissed as irrelevant. However, in other areas in which elites may exert influence, they have the ability to make unique contributions.

Informational Role

Because of their specialized knowledge, elites often have information and ideas valuable to parties in formulating their programs. Assistance from elites does not usually require any partisan commitment but only a willingness to communicate their information and a responsiveness to this information on the part of the parties. Often it is the governing party which makes the most concerted efforts to establish bonds with various elites in order to benefit by their information, but opposition parties too can find this a useful means of gaining knowledge necessary to make a meaningful appeal to the electorate. Channels of communication are established through personal contacts, informal meetings, conferences, and writing—letters, scholarly and journalistic articles, books, and briefs. The Government, in addition, has recourse to the establishment of Royal Commissions. Such commissions are set up in response to pressing problems, and while those created by the federal government are most widely known, there are also many instances of provincial commissions. Through this device, elites have the opportunity

---

[29] Mildred A. Schwartz, "Political Behaviour and Ethnic Origin," in *Papers on the 1962 Election*, ed. Meisel, pp. 253-271.

[30] Hugh G. Thorburn, "Politics and Business in Canada: Some Questions," in *Party Politics*, ed. Thorburn, p. 152.

to pass on their expert opinions through direct employment by the Commission or through public hearings and presentations. To appreciate the extent of elite participation in this respect, it is only necessary to glance at the names and occupations of those appearing before the hearings of any Royal Commission.

Through each of the devices mentioned, Canadian elites representing all of the pertinent subsystems have the opportunity to influence the political parties. Of special interest are several instances in which parties have encouraged exchanges of information, especially with intellectual elites. In September 1960, the Liberals held a Study Conference on National Problems in Kingston, Ontario. To it were invited representatives of business, the professions, universities, trade unions, and the mass media. The avowed purpose of the conference was to provide an open forum for liberally-minded people to discuss national problems in an atmosphere relatively free from partisan controversy. For some spokesmen of the Liberal Party, it meant the provision of a sounding board for future policies. From the prepared papers and discussions by those not connected with the party, party officials were exposed to the opinions and advice of those expert in their fields, and were provided with new ideas for party programs. The Conservatives, presumably impressed by the invigorating effect of the Kingston conference on the Liberals, held their own "thinkers" conference in Fredericton in September of 1964. They were more exclusive and confined it mainly to Conservative supporters, although a few outsiders were invited. The CCF/NDP, which has always been attractive to Canadian intellectuals, was the party to which many prominent Canadian scholars directed their writing on national problems in the publication *Social Purpose for Canada*.[31] It is difficult to say where Social Credit fits with respect to the intellectual elite. The party tends to discourage the support of intellectuals by its presumed dedication to economic principles which hardly bear analysis. Intellectuals, it fears, would subject its ideological orientation and economic principles to critical scrutiny. This is not to deny that the party does pay attention to the counsel of experts, much of which is freely given, as it is to the other parties.

A new step toward better communication among some segments of the political and intellectual elite was undertaken in 1964 with the formation of Exchange for Political Ideas in Canada (EPIC). EPIC was made up of politicians and intellectuals representing the "democratic left," and concerned with the "study, discussion and propagation of ideas which might foster change and reform of Canadian political life." In addition to reflecting the natural interest of politicians in the revitalizing role of ideas in political life, it also reflected the rejection of a disengaged intellectual elite as the Canadian ideal. According to the then Forestry Minister, Maurice Sauvé, one of the directors of EPIC, "I'm sick and tired of people who solve problems in the beer parlors. . . . We have to work through political parties."[32] It is questionable, however, whether it is possible for these goals to be achieved in a context which assumes some

THE SHAPING OF POLITICAL PARTIES

cooperation between two competing political parties, the Liberal and NDP.

The governmental bureaucracy is the one group with most to give the political parties of an informational nature. Because it is an arm of government, many of its skills are reserved for the leaders of the governing party. These it must serve impartially, regardless of political affiliation. But considerable bodies of information collected and compiled by the civil service are available to the public, and these can be utilized by the opposition parties. Because of the increasing needs for expert knowledge, there are pleas, from time to time, that some portion of the public bureaucracy be devoted to the informational needs of the opposition. No one has, however, been able to convince the government, of whatever political label, of the expediency of such a move.

Elites as Policy Formulators

Elites, whether inside or outside the party structure, not only give information and ideas, but also participate directly in the formulation of policy. In some cases, they represent interests such as business or trade unions while at the same time they are also members of the party hierarchy. In others, they are called in by the parties to give their expert advice on the solution to some vexing problem.

Of greatest interest is the role of the administrative elite. Analyses of bureaucracy, beginning with the work of Max Weber, have frequently stressed the impersonal, non-partisan nature of governmental bureaucracies where hiring and promotion are based on technical qualifications. Politicians, however, have always been suspicious of this system, whether out of a desire for the means to reward their own supporters or from skepticism that anyone can serve a political master without being shaped by his orientation. In any event, the positions held by government administrators, who have access to information essential for policy making and whose continuity of careers is not based on political favour, make them uniquely equipped to develop policy. This elite corps of administrators is not easy to replace, and any party coming into office, especially for the first time, is understandably hesitant about assuming that its bureaucracy will be opposed to carrying out policy directives on partisan grounds. Such was the case of the CCF Government when it first took office in Saskatchewan in 1944. The Liberal Government had previously been in power for a total of thirty-four years, with a gap of five years between 1929 and 1934 when they were defeated, and the top ranking civil servants had been trained in a Liberal milieu. For their new political leaders, many without parliamentary experience, the top level administrators contributed not only their administrative skills but the

---

[31] Michael Oliver, ed., *Social Purpose for Canada* (Toronto: University of Toronto Press, 1961).

[32] Don McGillivray, "'Thinkers' Exchange' Launched," *Calgary Herald* (May 25, 1964).

acumen gained through experience in judging the feasibility of new policy measures. If their judgments were so well appreciated by Cabinet Ministers that some CCF programs were shelved as impractical, the covert policy-making role of the civil service went unrecognized by both groups involved. According to Lipset's study of the CCF in the early years of its rule, it was not until CCF supporters outside the government pointed out what was happening that the political leaders became aware of how they had been moved from their original policies.[33] This lesson has not been forgotten in Saskatchewan. The election of a Liberal Government in 1964 heralded the resignation of some top civil servants, either on their own initiative or through considered opinions of how they would be regarded by their new leaders. An example of one of the curiosities of politics in Saskatchewan, the resignations included that of Thomas K. Shoyama, the major economic advisor to the former government. He left to take a civil service post in Ottawa, where presumably the federal Liberal Government would be more compatible than the provincial one.

Our discussion of this topic would not be complete without the inclusion of the Coyne affair. James Coyne, as Governor of the Bank of Canada was not an ordinary civil servant, yet this affair indicates the limits of bureaucratic involvement in policy making.[34] Donald Fleming, then Minister of Finance in the Conservative Cabinet, chose to view Governor James Coyne's tight money policies as quite independent of the wishes of the Government. When Coyne proceeded to flout the traditional anonymity of governmental bureaucrats by a number of public speeches defending his monetary policies, and even more, by presenting his policies as a way of achieving solutions to Canada's social and political problems, he could no longer be permitted to behave as though there was no one to whom he was responsible.

Other protagonists, who were in our terms elites, entered the controversy with a detailed attack against Coyne. Among these were representatives of the intellectual elite—twenty-nine economists employed in Canadian universities. Their communications to the Government were met with silence.[35]

To complete the issue, yet a third elite entered the arena. When it appeared from a speech by Prime Minister Diefenbaker that Fleming would soon be removed from office, a group of prominent businessmen, fearful of the Prime Minister's fiscal unorthodoxy, urged him to retain Fleming as "the only remaining link between the federal government and the country's investment community."[36] It is not certain whether Fleming was left as Minister of Finance because of this pressure or because of policy concessions he made to his chief.

The preceding two illustrations were instances in which the influence of elites on the formation of party policy was debatable. But these were instances in which elites attempted to participate in policy making in relation to the party in power. They tried, by their uninvited activities, to usurp the prerogatives of the Government. The free counsel of elites is generally welcomed by parties, but attempts at policy making are suspect

THE SHAPING OF POLITICAL PARTIES

unless such advice is asked for or the elites are part of the party hierarchy.

The Direction of Electoral Strategy

We have chosen to regard the participation of elites in designing electoral strategy from two approaches: pragmatic and theoretical. On the pragmatic side we include the day-to-day tactics of electioneering and decisions on the allocation of scarce electoral resources. The theoretical side of electoral strategy manifests itself in the political principles outlined by party theorists.

One indication of the place of elites in guiding electoral tactics emerged from our discussion of the mass media. In the course of rationalizing politics, increasing numbers of those with prior training and experience in the exploitation of the mass media are included among party advisers. With the help of advertising agency personnel, public relations experts, and to some extent, those skilled in surveying and interpreting public opinion, election campaigns are being planned with an eye to obtaining greatest coverage from the mass media, most effective communication of party promises, added depth to the creation of a favourable image for the party leader, and maximization of the party's appeal to as great a variety of voters as possible. The old-fashioned party worker has increasingly less influence on the planning of overall strategy. But with his intimate knowledge of the political habits of his neighbours, he continues to play a considerable role in delivering the vote at the local level. In an age of mass communication and of deference to the expert, the political views of French-speaking dock workers in Montreal, Italian construction workers in Toronto, and German wheat farmers in Saskatchewan must be converted into grosser occupational, regional, social class, and ethnic categories in order to be meaningful to them at the national or provincial level. This task has fallen to the elites in the communications systems. In fulfilling their responsibilities, these elites direct themselves to such practical questions as, "What are my opponents' weaknesses and my party's strengths?" and "What can we do to capitalize on these strengths and weaknesses in order to obtain the greatest measure of electoral support?"

Such strategists are not recent phenomena, even though the substance of their skills is new. Successful election campaigns have always required forethought to the most effective procedures. Now, however, these involve

---

[33] S. M. Lipset, *Agrarian Socialism* (Berkeley & Los Angeles: University of California Press, 1950), pp. 255-275.

[34] A complete history of this *cause célèbre* must await the passage of time, when all the documents involved are made public and when distance allows us to judge the events dispassionately. In the interim, Newman's report of the affair seems fair and objective. Newman, *Renegade in Power*, pp. 295-321.

[35] Scott Gordon, *The Economists Versus the Bank of Canada* (Toronto; Ryerson Press, 1961).

[36] Newman, *Renegade in Power*, p. 131.

skills not casually resurrected just prior to an election, but ones constantly being exercised in readiness for election campaigns.

In contrast to these strategists are those who devote themselves to developing and communicating a political philosophy for their party. Such ideologists are an important part of most political systems, but what is notable in Canada is their absence. Underhill states:

When we compare ourselves with Britain and the United States there is one striking contrast. Those two countries, since the end of the eighteenth century, have abounded in prophets and philosophers who have made articulate the idea of a liberal and equalitarian society. Their political history displays also a succession of practical politicians who have not merely performed the functions of manipulating and manoeuvring masses of men and groups which every politician performs, but whose careers have struck the imagination of both contemporaries and descendants as symbolizing certain great inspiring ideas. We in Canada have produced few such figures. Where are the classics in our political literature which embody our Canadian versions of liberalism and democracy? Our party struggles have never been raised to the higher intellectual plane at which they become of universal interest by the presence of a Canadian Jefferson and a Canadian Hamilton in opposing parties. We have had no Canadian Burke or Mill to perform the social function of the political philosopher in action. We have had no Canadian Carlyle or Ruskin or Arnold to ask searching questions about the ultimate values embodied in our political or economic practice.[37]

While we have not had party ideologists of the stature which Underhill enumerates, there have been some minor exceptions. They are exceptions in that they involve some positive attempt to formulate party philosophies, but they are minor in that they nowhere approach the intellectual quality nor the historical significance of comparable ideologies in other lands. Our exceptional political theorists are found in the minor parties and in Quebec.

Political theorists in Quebec have emerged out of the conditions of French-Canadian existence, taking as their prime purpose the continuity of their ethnic group. A more philosophical approach to practical problems generally, is found in French Canada for a number of reasons, one being the critical self-examination associated with the status of a defensive minority. This has contributed to a more amenable climate for intellectualizing political problems than is found in English Canada. Thus, as John Porter reminds us, newspaper editors in Quebec take their ideological role much more seriously than is true in the rest of the country.[38] Such varied people as Henri Bourassa, André Laurendeau in the days when he supported Bloc Populaire, and currently Pierre-Elliott Trudeau and the youthful contributors to *Cité Libre*, have made contributions to party politics, in the sense of developing some theoretical rationale for behaviour.[39]

THE SHAPING OF POLITICAL PARTIES

In the minor parties outside of Quebec, ideology has a more purely economic basis. The League for Social Reconstruction, an association of university professors, provided much of the intellectual content leading to the formation of the CCF.[40] Political theorists were important in the early days of Social Credit, but there they played a different role. Since, as far as they were concerned, Major Douglas had developed all the working theories required, they had only to be concerned with interpreting these and spreading their message rather than with creating new theories.

Candidates for Office

In considering elites as party candidates, we must view the relation between elites and politics as an interchange. Some of those with the characteristics and interests of elites enter politics, while some of those leaving active politics are able to then assume elite positions. We can summarize the nature of political representation in Canada by saying that the attainment of office, and to a lesser extent, recruitment as candidates, falls disproportionately to those from more privileged backgrounds and from those social groups normally accorded greatest prestige. They are better educated, employed in the most prestigeful occupations, from the dominant ethnic and religious groups, and with access to the centres of authority in all the significant subsystems. This is most true of the political elite—the Prime Minister, Cabinet members, and provincial premiers.[41]

We will confine our analysis to the political elite elected to office at the federal level. Since Confederation, Canada has had fourteen Prime Ministers, nine Conservative and five Liberal. Only two of them could be classed as "school drop-outs," with their education confined to elementary schooling, and these held office in the early years of Canada's nationhood. The remainder had a university education or its equivalent, even in those periods when higher education was far from customary. Ten of the fourteen were trained in law and two were newspaper editors. Significantly, two of the Liberal Prime Ministers had experience as senior civil servants before entering party politics. Before taking office, all had varied and impressive political experience, the bare facts of which we have summarized below.

[37] Frank H. Underhill, *In Search of Canadian Liberalism* (Toronto: Macmillan Company of Canada, Ltd., 1961), pp. 6-7.

[38] Porter, *The Vertical Mosaic*, pp. 487-490.

[39] For some discussion of the intellectual elite in French Canada see Michael Oliver, "Quebec and Canadian Democracy," *Canadian Journal of Economics and Political Science*, XXIII (November 1957), 504-515; Charles Taylor, "Nationalism and the Political Intelligentsia: A Case Study," *Queen's Quarterly*, LXXII (Spring 1965), 150-168.

[40] Research Committee, League for Social Reconstruction, *Social Planning for Canada* (Toronto: Thomas Nelson & Sons, Ltd., 1935).

[41] For documentation see Porter, *The Vertical Mosaic*, pp. 386-416.

Summary of Prior Political Experiences of Fourteen
Canadian Prime Ministers

7 were Cabinet members
4 were leaders of federal opposition
4 had served in provincial legislatures
2 were Senators
1 had been in municipal government
1 had been a Supreme Court judge
2 had experience confined to lengthy terms as MP's

There have been three Roman Catholic Prime Ministers, two of these Liberals, and one Conservative, who served briefly during the post-Macdonald interregnum. A specific denomination is known for eight of the remaining eleven, all of whom were Protestant. Of these eight, six represented churches now making up the numerically dominant United Church, one was Church of England and one Baptist. Two were of French origin, eleven of British, and one of mixed German-United Empire Loyalist heritage. With one exception, all were born and lived most of their lives in central Canada. This one exception, John Diefenbaker, has deviated from the norm in some of his other characteristics, and as a result can be seen as representing the formerly unrepresented in Canadian political life and hence as somewhat of an innovator. From this and other available information, we can derive a picture of Canadian Prime Ministers as well educated, and with the background characteristics of the groups traditionally dominant in Canadian society, yet not of great wealth nor intimately tied to aristocratic familial backgrounds or to the centres of great economic power.[42]

Cabinet members display similar characteristics, but with some differences. For one thing, they better reflect the regions of Canada than do the Prime Ministers. For another, their selection for Cabinet posts is at least partly an exercise in *Realpolitik,* where not only special talents and party loyalty, but also the groups from which they come and the interests they represent all bear on the likelihood of appointment.[43] Entry into the Cabinet should bring with it political influence over powerful elites and interests, such as trade unions, the financial community, and the military, with whom the government's decision making is closely bound up and whose support is essential for the continuity of the government. Some indication of their more varied backgrounds and experience comes if we look, in Table 4-1, at four representative Cabinets: those of Bennett, King, St. Laurent, and Diefenbaker. These were divided between the two major parties and cover years during which Canada experienced a depression, war, prosperity, and economic recession. Again we see the preponderance of those trained in law and the increasing importance of university education. The Conservatives have given fewer posts to Catholics than have the Liberals, although the Diefenbaker Cabinet was somewhat more balanced than the Bennett Cabinet. Of the Protestants, almost

TABLE 4-1

SELECTED CHARACTERISTICS OF MEMBERS,
INCLUDING PRIME MINISTERS,
OF FOUR FEDERAL CABINETS

Four Federal Cabinets	Total Members	Religion		Occupation				Education (Univ.)
		R.C.	Prot.	Law	Med.	Bus.	Farm	
Bennett, 1930	19	5	14	9	3	3	1	9
King, 1935	25	5	10	8	0	1	3	12
St. Laurent, 1948	20	7	13	9	1	3	1	15
Diefenbaker, 1961	23	7	16	9	0	2	1	19

Note: A complete breakdown of occupations and education is not given here, but we have included sufficient information to show the dominant trends. Data compiled by A. T. Chernushenko, M. Alcorn, S. Davison.

TABLE 4-2

PRIOR POLITICAL EXPERIENCE IN MUNICIPAL AND
PROVINCIAL POLITICS OF MEMBERS
IN FOUR FEDERAL CABINETS

Four Federal Cabinets	Total Members	Municipal Office	Provincial Office
Bennett, 1930	19	5	4
King, 1935	15	2	6
St. Laurent, 1948	20	1	3
Diefenbaker, 1961	23	9	4

Note: In addition, several members ran for provincial office but had been unsuccessful.

Data compiled by A. T. Chernushenko, M. Alcorn, S. Davison.

all were either United Church, Church of England, or Presbyterian. Finally, with respect to prior political experience, we again find that those with experience outside the federal house frequently become Cabinet ministers. As Table 4-2 indicates, there has been some difference between the two parties, with members of both Conservative Cabinets having considerably more experience in municipal politics. While this may be related to the whole recruitment process which these parties follow, it also has an undoubted connection with the longer history of Liberal Governments. The Liberal Party has had greater opportunity to examine the leadership

[42] The preceding data on the Prime Ministers were compiled by Carolyn Bond.
[43] See for example, Paul Fox, "The Representative Nature of the Canadian Cabinet," Politics: Canada, ed. Fox, pp. 140-143; Sir George Foster, "Getting into the Cabinet," ibid., pp. 143-144.

potential of its candidates since they are more likely to be elected to the House of Commons and to be given extra responsibilities as parliamentary assistants and committee members. The Conservatives, however, must often come by their political skills outside the federal Parliament.[44]

What does this description of the characteristics of Canada's Prime Ministers and four Cabinets tell us about the influence of elites? Thus far, we have shown that the political elite display the ethnic and religious affiliations of the majority charter groups and the educational and occupational backgrounds of the privileged minority. But this information describes only the nature of the political elite. It tells us little about the connections between the political and non-political elites, and it is the latter which concern us in considering elites as party candidates. Cabinet Ministers acquire their positions partly on the basis of their connection with significant interest groups, and are thus at least near-elites in the appropriate subsystems. For example, even though law is the most frequently represented profession among politicians, at the upper levels of the major parties at least, lawyers are often engaged in corporate law and serve as directors of major corporations as well. Also, company directorships are often rewards which Cabinet members can expect *after* completing their parliamentary service. Another connection between elites in politics and those elsewhere arises from the practice, following the pattern set by Mackenzie King, of having senior civil servants become Cabinet Ministers. This has been the policy of Liberal governments, in which, between 1940 and 1957, eight civil servants entered the Cabinet.[45]

We have demonstrated previously that the most eminent members of specified subsystems were able to influence political parties, either directly or potentially. In the case of non-political elites as political office-holders, the connection is not so clear-cut. We can show that political leaders have elite characteristics. Yet we cannot be certain what this means. It is often presumed that occupancy of common social positions makes for common problems, interests, and outlooks; this is after all a basic tenet in sociology, from theories of Marx to those of reference groups. But to assume that people act only in terms of their own interests is to take an unduly cynical view of human nature, and one which cannot be substantiated. In terms of the exercise of political power, the implications of self-interested elites becomes even more sinister when it is argued that all the major elites are interlocking, resulting in a monolithic power structure. Neither Porter's research nor our own observations lend credence to such a situation in Canada. Moreover, we feel that it is not possible to conclude from the evidence we have presented that elites holding political office are engaged in any form of conspiracy, deliberate or otherwise. Elite interpenetration is not that extensive, elites do not all represent the same interests, and the vagaries of attaining and holding elected office in a democracy force even unwilling democrats to take account of at least the political demands of their own constituents. We can only conclude then by emphasizing the characteristics of political elites—what the implications of these are, we cannot be certain.

SUMMARY

In this chapter we have considered the possible effects of two forms of active and organized public opinion—the media and elites. We have focused on three ways in which the media could influence political parties. Through the dissemination of information, they keep the electorate and party activists aware of issues which affect them. As technological innovations increase the media's capacities for spreading vast amounts of information to more people more quickly, the style in which party politics is conducted is altered. Among the consequences is a need for extensive financial resources in order to fully use the media. Parties with insufficient funds from membership contributions must thus rely on large donations from a few contributors. By doing so, they make themselves vulnerable to the pressure which such contributors are then able to exert. A further consequence has been the utilization of personnel skilled in the exploitation of the media, which tends to turn parties away from volunteer workers and party strategists concerned with issues, to highly paid experts primarily concerned with techniques for electing candidates, regardless of the issues involved. These trends further contribute to the professionalization and rationalization of politics. The great attention which politicians pay to the media is premised on the belief that the media have a great capacity for influencing electoral behaviour. Research in other countries, however, seriously challenges this assumption. While the media do help voters in deciding and in retaining their loyalty for one party, they have minimal impact in converting voters to other parties.

Elites were given more extensive treatment and their effects were seen as operative in five ways. (1) They give support to a party and, as important opinion leaders, may lead groups of voters who identify with them to follow suit. Support is also given through financial contribution, but again there may be strings attached. (2) Elites, in the sense of experts, provide the parties with information not otherwise available. (3) Elites, generally now within the party structure, contribute to the formation of policies. (4) They also have a hand in the shaping of electoral strategy. This may be of a pragmatic nature, confined to the best means to electoral success. Increasingly, these pragmatic strategists play an important role in the parties, again reflecting a move to the rationalization of party politics. Elites have historically played an important part in the development of political theories or ideologies as an aspect of party strategy. In Canada, however, with the exception of third parties, their role has been a minor one. (5) Finally, elites representing a number of important subsystems have been candidates for elective office. By examining characteristics of some of the political elite we were able to show that they came predominantly from the highest status groups in the society. It was not possible, however, to state what effects this had on their subsequent behaviour.

---

[44] For characteristics of Members of Parliament in general, see Alan Kornberg, "The Social Bases of Leadership in a Canadian House of Commons," *Australian Journal of Politics and History*, XI (1965), 324-334.

[45] Peter C. Newman, "The Ottawa Establishment," *Maclean's* (August 22, 1964), 7-9, 33-38.

5

Organized Interest Groups

•

INTRODUCTION

Organized interest groups are the vehicles through which the demands emanating from the various subsystems of the society are carried to the political system. They make these demands in order to secure favourable policies and acts of administration. As they do so on behalf of interests in various subsystems—economic, ethnic, ideological, communications, administrative—they engage in what Almond calls "interest articulation."[1] Our concern here is with the influence of these groups, and primarily the economic ones, on political parties.

This chapter will consist of four sections. The first, this introduction, deals with the nature of organized interest groups, their relevance to the political system, and their distinction from political parties. In the second section, we will present a taxonomy of Canada's interest life, and follow this with a presentation of the general characteristics of organized interest groups. The third section will be a delineation of the extent to which Canadian interests seek access to the governmental structure directly, and the extent to which they channel this access through political parties. The fourth section will present some details regarding the access of interests to parties. Our work in these final sections will be hampered by the paucity of available empirical research.

What are interest groups? What distinguishes them from other groups? In search of a definition, we go to the classic source, *The Governmental Process* by David B. Truman:

> . . . 'interest group' refers to any group that, on the basis of one or more shared attitudes, makes certain claims upon other groups in the society for the establishment, maintenance, or enhancement of forms of behavior that are implied by the shared attitudes. . . . [A]ll groups are interest groups because they are shared-attitude groups. In some groups at various points in time, however, a second kind of common response

92

emerges, in addition to the frames of reference. These are shared attitudes toward what is needed or wanted in a given situation, observable as demands or claims upon other groups in the society. The term 'interest group' will be reserved . . . for those groups that exhibit both aspects of the shared attitudes.

The shared attitudes, moreover, constitute the interests.[2]

How do these interest groups fit into the political system? What is their function? For an answer to this question, we turn to Gabriel Almond:

Interest groups articulate political demands in the society, seek support for these demands among other groups by advocacy and bargaining, and attempt to transform these demands into authoritative public policy by influencing the choice of political personnel, and the various processes of public policy-making and enforcement.[3]

Interest groups then are organizations designed to present such attitudes as are shared by the group. These attitudes are directed toward political realization, i.e., they have the potential of becoming political outputs, policies, or administrative decisions. Organized interest groups infuse policy demands into the political system and thereby take the first step toward obtaining political outputs in response to these demands.

We must distinguish interest groups from political parties. We could say simply that some organizations are called interest groups and others political parties, and that each set has distinctive organizational characteristics. However, the telling differentiation lies in their functioning, not in their names. Almond gives us a clear statement:

Political parties . . . are aggregative, i.e., seek to form the largest possible interest group coalitions by offering acceptable choices of political personnel and public policy. . . . [T]he party system stands between the interest group system and the authoritative policy-making agencies and screens them from the particularistic and disintegrative impact of special interests. The party system aggregates interests and transforms them into a relatively small number of alternative general policies.[4]

Relations between the party and interest systems, Almond tells us, permit legislatures to choose among general policies, and bureaucracies to administer these policies neutrally.

Thus, the main function of parties vis-à-vis interests is aggregation. In order to avoid confusion, let us distinguish aggregation from articulation. Articulation is the voicing or the raising of demands. The term is used here in this voicing, not in the joining, sense. An articulated demand is

---

[1] Gabriel A. Almond, "Introduction," *The Politics of the Developing Areas*, eds. G. A. Almond and J. S. Coleman (Princeton: Princeton University Press, 1960) , pp. 33-38.

[2] David B. Truman, *The Governmental Process* (New York: Alfred A. Knopf, Inc., 1951) , pp. 33-34.

[3] Gabriel A. Almond, "Interest Groups and the Political Process," *Comparative Politics: Notes and Readings*, eds. R. C. Macridis and B. E. Brown (Homewood, Ill.: The Dorsey Press, Inc., 1961), pp. 129-30.

[4] *Ibid.*, p. 130.

one that has been voiced. Aggregation, on the other hand, means the combining of articulated demands in such a way that they are related to the selection of governmental leaders and to the making of policy and administrative decisions. There is a significant distinction between these functions; yet, lest the reader make too facile the equation that organized interest groups equal articulation, and political parties equal aggregation, a few *caveats* are in order.

(1) In North America, major parties aggregate most of the demands of the major organized interest groups. The aggregation differs, however, to the extent to which the party leaders evoke differing expectations regarding policy and its administration. Third parties may not aggregate all major interests. For instance, the CCF/NDP would claim that it does not combine corporate economic interests with farm or labour interests in fashioning policy alternatives.

(2) Some major interest groups do some aggregating themselves. This is true of the Canadian Labour Congress, the Canadian Manufacturers' Association, the Canadian Chamber of Commerce, and the Canadian Federation of Agriculture. All of these groups combine some and reject some of the demands articulated by the organized groups in their field.

(3) Much important aggregation takes place within the civil service. Interest groups tend to have direct channels to the civil service, and parties are not usually involved in this kind of aggregation.

(4) In the case of the many instances of aggregation within the "political" structure of the government, e.g., Cabinet and legislative caucus, we do not know the extent to which the activation of party loyalties is involved. Cabinet and caucus are closely tied to party, but it does not follow that the accommodation of interests necessarily changes with a party change in the government.

Despite these caveats, the basic distinction between interest groups and parties should now be clear: interest groups articulate interests, while parties transform these interests into policy alternatives for transmission to the governmental structure. The parties' exact role in interest aggregation cannot always be definitely established, but parties do provide the leadership personnel of the governmental structure through which the demands of the interests can be put into effect.

Demands articulated by interest groups are among the major inputs received by the parties. Such demands as are transmitted through the party system to the governmental structure are combined there with other demands to form or influence authoritative decisions of a legislative or an administrative nature.

•

THE WORLD OF CANADIAN INTERESTS

A Taxonomy of Canadian Interest Groups

We are concerned here not with presenting a complete listing of Canadian interest groups, but with giving the reader a notion of the fullness

THE SHAPING OF POLITICAL PARTIES

of organized interest life in Canada, and a picture of the wide range of interests that organize. There is no generally agreed upon categorization. We have devised one that is explained in the following paragraphs.

Organized economic interests are customarily classified into agricultural, labour, and business interests. There is a plethora of these interests in Canada. Examples of organized agricultural groups are the Canadian Federation of Agriculture, the various farmers' unions, the various wheat pools, and the National Dairy Council of Canada. There are many organized labour groups but we will restrict ourselves to the two major trade union congresses: the Canadian Labour Congress and the Confederation of National Trade Unions. The major business groups are the Canadian Chamber of Commerce and the Canadian Manufacturers' Association. Among more specialized business groups, we find the Association of Canadian Advertisers, the various better business bureaus, the Brewers' Association of Canada, the Canadian Association of Real Estate Boards, the Canadian Bankers' Association, the Canadian Construction Association, and the Life Underwriters' Association of Canada.

On other categories of interests, there is less common agreement. The following nine categories of non-economic, or not primarily economic, organized interest groups are not exhaustive, but they are all distinctive. The first is that of professional groups, among which are the Canadian Association of University Teachers, the Canadian Bar Association, the Canadian Medical Association, the Canadian Nurses' Association, and the Canadian Teachers' Federation.

The second category covers the field of public administration and includes organizations of public servants at the various levels of government, among which are the Civil Service Federation of Canada, the Canadian Association of Chiefs of Police, and the Canadian Federation of Mayors and Municipalities.

The third category covers non-professional interests in the communications field. Among these, we find the Canadian Association of Broadcasters and the Canadian Daily Newspaper Publishers' Association.

The fourth category covers non-professional interests in the field of education. Among these are the Canadian Home and School and Parent-Teacher Federation, the Canadian Union of Students, and the Association of Universities and Colleges in Canada.

The fifth category is that of organized veterans' groups. These include the Army, Navy, and Air Force Veterans of Canada, the Canadian Naval Association, and the Royal Canadian Legion.

Our sixth category covers ethnic interests. Anglo-Canadian ethnocentrists may prefer to refer to some of these groups as patriotic groups. In this category we find the Empire Club of Canada, the English-Speaking Union of the Commonwealth, the Imperial Order Daughters of the Empire, the Loyal Orange Association, the Native Sons of Canada, the Ukrainian Canadian Organizations, and the Société St. Jean-Baptiste.

The seventh category comprises religious interest groups. Among these are the Canadian Council of Churches, the Catholic Women's League of

Canada, the Canadian Jewish Congress, the Knights of Columbus, and the Student Christian Movement of Canada.

The eighth category comprises organized women's groups among which we find the Canadian Federation of Business and Professional Women's Clubs, the Canadian Federation of University Women, the Canadian Women's Club, and the National Council of Women of Canada.

The ninth category is a complex one and includes social action and ideological groups. Among them are groups concerned with the protection of certain segments of the population or the restructuring of Canadian society. Among these groups are the Association for Civil Liberties, the Canadian Council of Christians and Jews, the Canadian Mental Health Association, the Canadian Peace Congress, the Canadian Society for the Abolition of the Death Penalty, the Canadian Women's Christian Temperance Union, Moral Re-Armament, the Royal Canadian Humane Association, the United Nations Association in Canada, and the Voice of Women. The Consumers Association of Canada, a women's group till 1961, now admits men and properly belongs in the social action category.

Characteristics of Organized Interest Groups in Canada

The aim of interest articulation is to affect governmental outputs. Any interest sytsem must, therefore, be oriented toward the maximization of access to the governmental structure and, therefore, be adapted to this structure. The result is that most of Canada's major interest groups have a federated organization.[5]

Such federated organization is logical in fields like business, industry, agriculture, and labour. These major economic interests are all regulated by the federal government and by the various provinces. Groups representing them, therefore, require access at both levels of government if they are to articulate their demands for concessions and protection adequately. This access normally requires an organizational base, with a bureaucracy, in Ottawa and in the provincial capitals. Some national headquarters, however, are located to suit the clientele and not the seat of government. For the Canadian Manufacturers' Association, it is in Toronto; for the Canadian Farmers' Union, in Saskatoon. The latter group does not even have a branch office in Ottawa.

The Canadian Chamber of Commerce is the national roof organization of about 850 local chambers in Canada's large and small commercial centres. It assures access to the federal government for Canada's major commercial interest group. Chambers of Commerce also have provincial organizations which provide access to the provincial governments. While the various levels of Chambers of Commerce are not linked hierarchically, the Canadian Chamber has provincial branches, each of which is closely coordinated with the respective provincial chamber. Local chambers have their own bureaucracies, and each has a good measure of autonomy. Membership in a local chamber is held by businesses, not by individuals. The major share of financing the Canadian Chamber, incidentally, is not borne by the individual chambers, but by the large corporations with nation-wide operations; these corporations pay direct national fees.

THE SHAPING OF POLITICAL PARTIES

The Canadian Manufacturers' Association also has a federated structure, but it places more emphasis on the national level of organization.
The Association, a rather loose confederation of its twenty-seven individual trade sections, is concerned primarily with access to the federal government. The Association has divisions, but not in every province. Manitoba and Saskatchewan are combined in one division, as are all four
Atlantic provinces. Membership is by industrial firms, with one-half of
the more than 6,000 members located in Ontario.

The Canadian Federation of Agriculture, formed during the depression years, is now the major nation-wide interest representative of Canadian farmers. It also has a federal principle of organization. There is a
small bureaucracy in Ottawa, charged with carrying the Federation's
demands to the Government of Canada. The principle of federated organization is not applied evenly in the CFA. Eight of the provinces have
one provincial federation, Quebec has three, and Newfoundland, none.

The organization of Canada's labour interest is complex.[6] Three-
fourths of the million and one-half organized workers belong to the
Canadian Labour Congress (CLC), and the vast majority of these are in
unions also affiliated with the American Federation of Labor and Congress of Industrial Organizations (AFL-CIO). Eight per cent belong to
the Confederation of National Trade Unions (CNTU), a congress comprising Catholic unions in Quebec; the remainder are unaffiliated. Both
CLC and CNTU maintain national headquarters and bureaucracies, the
former in Ottawa, the latter in Montreal. The CLC is organized according to the principle of federated organization and takes care of its access
to provincial governments through the provincial federations of labour,
which exist in all provinces except Prince Edward Island. In addition,
the CLC is organized into 109 district labour councils.

The federated organization of Canadian interest groups is least important when these groups represent interests clearly subject to national
regulation. This applies particularly to the Canadian Bankers' Association and to the Royal Canadian Legion.

•

THE POLITICAL RELEVANCE OF CANADIAN INTERESTS

At the outset, we stated that the main function of political parties is to
provide leadership and decisions for a society. There will be little quarrel
with the statement that providing leadership is the role of parties. Surely
everyone will agree that, as of 1965, Lester B. Pearson is Prime Minister
because he is the leader of the Liberal Party. John G. Diefenbaker is

---

[5] For much of the information regarding specific interest groups, we are indebted to
the following, all former students at the University of Calgary: Hans Brown, Brian
Coulter, Eileen Ellinson Kaul, Heinz Kaul, David Surplis, and Martin Westmacott.
Helen Jones Dawson furnished information beyond that contained in her publications.

[6] For more detailed information, see Canada, Department of Labour, *Labour Organization in Canada* (Ottawa, Canada: Queen's Printer and Controller of Stationery,
1966).

Leader of the Opposition because he is the leader of the Progressive Conservative Party, and the members of the Cabinet hold their posts because they have been selected by the leader of the Liberal Party. But would everyone agree that wheat sales, the trusteeship of the Seafarers' International Union (SIU), and the short-lived tax cut of 1965 are decisions of the Liberal Party? Perhaps—or could it not be argued that such decisions stem directly from organized interest groups: the wheat sales policy from the CFA, the SIU trusteeship from the CLC, and the tax cut from business groups in need of additional investments? Do parties provide leaders and leave it to organized interest groups to provide decisions? The correct answer is suggested by Harry Eckstein when he writes, with special application to the United Kingdom:

In democratic systems parties must perform simultaneously two functions which are, on the evidence, irreconcilable: to furnish effective decision-makers and to represent accurately opinions. The best way to reconcile these functions in practice is to supplement the parties with an alternative set of representative organizations which can affect decisions without affecting the position of the decision-makers. This is the pre-eminent function of pressure groups in effective democratic systems, as the competition for power is the pre-eminent function of the parties.[7]

Applying Eckstein's statement to Canada, we find that here also, parties furnish effective decision makers. Here also, the impact of interest groups on parties makes it possible to have day-to-day opinion affect policy decisions, while the same decision makers, that is, the Prime Minister and his Cabinet, remain in office. The answer to our question is that parties provide decisions as well as leaders, but that the former are influenced strongly by demands stemming from interest groups.

We do not want to evoke the impression that group access to the governmental structure in Canada is totally regulated by political parties. The Canadian system of government leads to much more channeling of policy through party then does the system of government in the United States. Such agencies as the civil service or a Royal Commission, however, are approached by interests without the offices of political parties. Channeling of interests to these agencies through parties might be considered a breach of Canadian political mores. Interest groups may, and often do, approach the Cabinet, federal or provincial, and members of the Federal Parliament or the provincial legislatures, without awareness of political party at all. However, the "aggregation" of the specific demand in question—the determination whether or not it will be made part of a policy—is often made by the governing party. Direct approaches of interests to parties will be discussed in the next section.

Direct Impact of Interest Groups on Civil Service, Boards, and Royal Commissions

"Lobbying" is usually viewed as the prototype of interest group activity. Historically, this notion is true in the United States, where the lack of

THE SHAPING OF POLITICAL PARTIES

party discipline permitted interest group representatives to do their most effective work in the lobbies of legislative halls. But the vast expansion of governmental activity during the past half-century shifted much interest group activity from work with and on legislators to work with and on bureaucrats, and the importance of the latter has come to be of great significance in Canada also. Certainly Harmon Zeigler's observation, made in the U.S., applies to Canada also:

Very often decisions which may be interpreted by a group as having life or death consequences are made in the relatively secretive atmosphere surrounding administrative agencies, far from the glare of public scrutiny which permeates the legislative process. Therefore, groups hoping to influence public policy often exhibit strong interest in the establishment [and, we would add, the behaviour] of administrative agencies responsible for policy in the areas of the groups' concern.[8]

Canada's principal interest groups maintain close liaison with that part of the Ottawa bureaucracy that affects them most directly. In the case of the CLC, this is the Department of Labour, in the case of the CFA, the Department of Agriculture, and in the case of the CMA, the Departments of Industry, Finance, Trade and Commerce, and Labour. The Consumers Association of Canada, whose interest spans many departments of government, at one point claimed relations of mutual trust and friendship with the civil service in six of these departments. Direct group access to the bureaucracy exists at the provincial level also. In Alberta, for instance, lower-level officials of the Alberta Wheat Pool maintain close contact with such lower-level provincial civil servants as seed inspectors. The Alberta Teachers' Association maintains a direct influence on the decisions of the Department of Education through representation on all of the Department's major committees. In his discussion of interest group activity on the Ottawa scene, Don McGillivray points to the "continuous two-way consultation" between group representatives and civil servants. He also refers to the importance to the group representative of knowing who is who in the bureaucracy:

If a decision is going to be made by five civil servants, the lobbyist's special knowledge can pick out the man who will dominate the meeting and any persuasive efforts can be focussed on him. It's no use lobbying people who won't stay lobbied.[9]

Occasionally, representatives of interest groups manage to have themselves appointed to government boards that have advisory or regulatory powers over their interest. For instance, the President of the Alberta Wheat Pool is a member of the Canadian Wheat Board, and the Alberta

---

[7] Harry Eckstein, *Pressure Group Politics* (London: Allen & Unwin, 1960), p. 163.

[8] Harmon Zeigler, *Interest Groups in American Society* (Englewood Cliffs, N.J.: Prentice-Hall, Inc., 1964), p. 278.

[9] Don McGillivray, columns on lobbyist activities in Ottawa, *The Calgary Herald* (April 3-8, 1964).

Division of the Canadian Manufacturers' Association has two representatives on the Alberta Productivity Council. McGillivray says about group representatives in Ottawa: "They nominate members for bodies like the Economic Council of Canada and dozens of advisory committees in the departments." This generalization is corroborated by scholarly studies. Malcolm Taylor points to the influence wielded by the Canadian Medical Association in the appointment of health officials. He also reports that (as of 1959) the Advisory Committee to the Department of National Health and Welfare is a standing committee of the Canadian Medical Association. The Canadian Federation of Agriculture, according to Helen Dawson's report, has been particularly influential in regard to appointments. In 1959, the CFA claimed to be represented on the following boards and committees: the Advisory Committee of the Agricultural Prices Stabilization Board, the National Employment Committee, the National Vocational Training Advisory Councils, the Board of Broadcast Governors, the Advisory Committee to the Canadian Wheat Board, and the National Council of 4-H Clubs. J.G. Taggart, who had formed close relations with the CFA while Saskatchewan Minister of Agriculture, probably owed his original federal appointment (to the wartime Meat Board) to nomination by the CFA; he later became Deputy Minister of Agriculture. In 1952, C. D. Howe, the Minister of Trade and Commerce, specifically asked the CFA to nominate four representatives for the Canadian delegation to the International Wheat Council.

Whenever Royal Commissions are appointed, interest groups may present briefs or attempt to exert influence by securing the appointment to the commission of a representative of the group. For instance, both the CMA and the Canadian Chamber of Commerce presented briefs to the Carter Royal Commission on Taxation, the CMA to the MacPherson Commission on Transportation, and the Canadian Chamber to the Dunton-Laurendeau Royal Commission on Bilingualism and Biculturalism. G. L. Harrold, the President of the Alberta Wheat Pool, was a member of the Porter Royal Commission on Banking and Finance. McGillivray writes that "the Hall Commission on Health Insurance was appointed in 1961 on the request of the Canadian Medical Association which also had a big role in its terms of reference and personnel." If this was so, reports of hearings in 1962 indicate considerable tension between commissioners and spokesmen of the CMA. At that time, the CMA became apprehensive that the Hall Commission might propose a compulsory scheme. It can now be said that the Canadian Medical Association, despite an initial influence on its terms and personnel, did not have much influence on the *recommendations* of the Hall Royal Commission.

The normal interest group access to the bureaucracy and to Royal Commissions, whether at the federal or the provincial level, is, as we have indicated earlier, of a non-partisan nature. The role of party as an agency interposed between the organized group and the governmental structure looms larger as we examine the impact of groups on the Cabinet, the ministers, and the Members of Parliament and the legislatures.

Impact of Interest Groups on Cabinet and Parliament

The most traditional and best known contact of organized interest groups with the governmental structure is the annual submission made by many groups to the federal Cabinet. It was this event which early leaders of the CCF had in mind when they advocated direct labour representation in the federal Parliament, so that Canada's trade unionists would not have to present themselves to the Cabinet "with hat in hand." Yet the formal presentation of submissions of all major nation-wide interest groups to the federal Cabinet has continued. These annual submissions cover all the subjects of likely or desirable outputs of possible concern to the group making the submission.

Dealings of provincial and local interest groups with the federal government may be direct or channeled through the nationwide organization of the group. Both modes of contact are found in the groups we present as examples: the Alberta Wheat Pool and the Calgary Chamber of Commerce. The Alberta Wheat Pool, a group stemming from the traditions of the cooperative movement, bases all of its dealings with the federal Cabinet on policy resolutions concerned with either agriculture or marketing. In the former case they are communicated to the Alberta Federation of Agriculture, with the hope that they will eventually get to the Cabinet in Ottawa *via* the CFA. In the latter case, resolutions go to the Canadian Co-operative Wheat Producers Limited (CCWP), the group made up of the wheat pools of the three prairie provinces. From the CCWP, resolutions are usually submitted to the federal government in person by the president. He will meet with the Prime Minister and the Ministers of Agriculture, Transport, and Trade and Commerce, and with ministers of such other departments as may be involved in the Pool demands.

The Calgary Chamber of Commerce forwards its resolutions of interest to the Government of Canada, insofar as they deal with nation-wide matters, to the Montreal office of the Chamber, where they are screened. Some are returned to be acted upon by the Calgary Chamber. Those adopted make their way to the annual meeting of the Canadian Chamber and if passed, are incorporated in the annual submission of the Canadian Chamber to the federal Cabinet. Should Calgary have a local problem under the jurisdiction of the federal government (for example, the proposed closing of the Canadian Pacific Airlines' servicing depot in Calgary), the Calgary Chamber deals directly with the Prime Minister, other ministers concerned, local MP's, and, when there is one, the federal Cabinet Minister from Alberta.

Contacts between organized interest groups and provincial governments are similar to those in Ottawa. The Alberta Federation of Labour, for instance, presents an annual brief to the Executive Council of the Province of Alberta prior to the opening of the Legislative Assembly. The Alberta Federation of Agriculture presents a lengthy and strongly worded annual brief to the provincial Cabinet. Since the early 1950's, the brief has normally been presented jointly with the Farmers' Union of

Alberta. The Alberta Wheat Pool presents to the provincial Cabinet such resolutions as call for the enactment of provincial policies. The Alberta Chamber of Commerce submits to the government in Edmonton an annual brief which has been worked on by the major chambers in the province, and which is presented by a group in which these major chambers are represented. Premier Manning is said to take a strong personal interest in these annual meetings with the Alberta Chamber. In matters of local concern to Calgary, the Calgary Chamber of Commerce has direct access to the provincial government; it dispatches a delegation to Edmonton to discuss the problem at hand.

Our examples have indicated that a group's contact with the executive government is not restricted to formal annual submissions to the entire Cabinet. At both the federal and provincial levels, individual ministers may be approached by interest groups, either formally or informally. The Canadian Manufacturers' Association submits numerous briefs to individual ministers. These briefs are usually submitted in writing and are followed by an oral discussion with the minister. The CMA acquired the benefit of "personal union" with the Pearson Government of 1963, as both C. M. Drury, the Minister of Industry, and Mitchell Sharp, then the Minister of Trade and Commerce, were CMA members. The Canadian Chamber of Commerce also makes submissions to individual federal ministers. In 1963, such submissions were made to the Ministers of Finance, National Revenue, and Trade and Commerce. It is, of course, difficult to ascertain just when ministers act because of organized group pressure. Occasionally, a communication to an interest group makes specific mention of ministerial action based on that group's initiative. The Consumers Association of Canada was told in 1952 that, as a result of their representations, the Government Specifications Board had been ordered by C. D. Howe to investigate the technical aspects of the standardization of garment sizes.[10] In the 1950's, J. G. Gardiner, the Minister of Agriculture, and other ministers claimed to be faithful listeners of (and to be effectively "lobbied" by) the Canadian Federation of Agriculture's broadcasting program *Farm Radio Forum*. In the field of health, relations between medical associations and ministers have been cemented by the frequent practice of having physicians serve as federal and provincial ministers. Malcolm Taylor's figures indicate that, in eight provinces, physicians have served as Ministers of Health one-half of the time since the First World War.[11]

Since the sparse literature gives us one account of a crucial turn in the relationship between an interest group and a Cabinet Minister, we report this account fully:

At the time of its organization [the Canadian Federation of Agriculture] had to contend with a general ignorance of its existence. This ignorance apparently extended to the federal Department of Agriculture and to its Minister, the Hon. J. G. Gardiner. The Federation realized that if Mr. Gardiner could be won over, the departmental officials would also be more approachable. After 1938, Mr. Gardiner . . . received [CFA] depu-

tations with coolness or hostility. Then in 1941 he accepted an invitation to speak to the Annual Meeting of the Ontario Federation of Agriculture in London, Ontario. This occasion has become known in the Federation as the "Battle of London." Mr. Gardiner was treated to an especially scathing address by Dr. Hannam [CFA president] with the vocal support of 2,000 extremely angry farmers from all over Canada who made no bones about the fact that they thought Dr. Hannam's speech was a very mild expression of their feelings. Dr. Hannam concluded his address by saying that farm people had lost confidence in Mr. Gardiner and that this confidence would not be restored until he assured them that he would fight vigorously for their interests before the Cabinet. Mr. Gardiner met their challenge. He defended departmental policies and defended his decisions. Meanwhile the farmers present became even more enraged and hurled further accusations at him. They refused to allow him to leave the meeting until they had extracted some concessions from him in the early hours of the next morning. Ever since then the Federation has been recognized by the federal Department of Agriculture and by the entire Cabinet. It can hardly be accidental that it was first requested to submit a brief to the Cabinet two weeks after the 'Battle of London.' The change in attitude was quick. The Federation was almost immediately requested to nominate representatives for the various war-time advisory committees which dealt with subjects of interest to the farmers. In 1943 Dr. Hannam was made chairman of the advisory committee on food and after the war he was frequently invited to be an adviser on the Candian delegation to the Food and Agricultural Organization of the United Nations. Perhaps the rapid change is best typified by Mr. Gardiner's 1947 statement: 'Never before in the history of Canadian agriculture has the voice of agriculture been more effectively and unitedly expressed than during the past six years.'[12]

Despite their journalistic nature, McGillivray's articles contain the only published generalizations about relations between a federal minister and such interest groups as he takes into his confidence. It is significant that his "rules of the game" do not make reference to any aggregative activity by political parties. He states the rules as follows:

On non-fiscal matters, interest groups are given hints of the government's intentions. Or they may be plainly told, or even handed a copy of a draft bill.

At this point, what Ottawa insiders call 'the rules of the game' come into play.

These unwritten rules prevent a group which has been taken into the

[10] Helen Jones Dawson, "The Consumers Association of Canada," *Canadian Public Administration*, VI (1963), 107.

[11] Malcolm G. Taylor, "The Role of the Medical Profession in the Formulation and Execution of Public Policy," *Canadian Public Administration*, III (1960), 242 n.

[12] Helen Jones Dawson, "The Canadian Federation of Agriculture," *Canadian Public Administration*, III (1960), 143-44.

minister's confidence from starting a public campaign against his bill before it even reaches the Commons.

They also prevent the group from agreeing privately then raising a public fuss when the minister makes his plan public.

The rules of the game are binding on ministers too. If a minister puts forward a plan a pressure group views as strictly second best, the group may still work with him to make it as bearable as possible.

But it would be a grave breach of lobbying etiquette for the minister to stand up and claim that the plan had been endorsed by the farmers, oilmen, union leaders, or whatever the group might be.

Breaking the rules brings a breakdown in consultation, sometimes recriminations on both sides.[13]

McGillivray's rules could be tested only by extensive empirical investigations. But conversations with some knowledgeable observers enable us to make a few observations about them.

There appears to be much disputing of McGillivray's assertion that copies of bills are handed to interest group representatives. However, the "hints" mentioned may well include broad outlines, and details on some technicalities. Of the specific rules mentioned, the one broken most frequently appears to be that designed to prevent a minister from mentioning in the Commons the interests endorsing a bill. The recriminations for breaking the rules are strong, and ministers as well as MP's have on occasion vented their displeasure on the floor of the House or in committee.

At the provincial level, groups have numerous dealings with individual provincial ministers. Here, possibly in view of the fact that there are fewer expert bureaucrats then we find in Ottawa, provincial ministers frequently take the initiative in contacting interest groups when policy changes are contemplated. For example, the Alberta Division of the CMA was asked to advise the Department of Municipal Affairs in Edmonton on municipal tax regulations. Also, the Alberta Chamber of Commerce and some local chambers, including the Calgary Chamber, were involved in the amending of the Alberta Labour Act. The Calgary Chamber was among the groups notified of the planned changes, and it presented its views at a meeting in Edmonton. Once the legislation was drafted, the provincial Ministers of Labour and Industry and Development, came to Calgary to discuss the draft with the Council of the Calgary Chamber of Commerce.

Canada's federal system occasionally provides provincial branches of interest groups with opportunities to use the governmental structure in an attempt to reach goals they cannot reach within their own interest group. For example, potato growers from various provinces have been unable to agree on potato grading. The potato growers of Prince Edward Island, thwarted in their national organization, have on occasion asked the P.E.I. representative in the federal Cabinet to persuade his colleagues to adopt nationally a policy which was solely a P.E.I. demand.

The individual legislator may remain one of the prime targets of interest group pressure in the United States, but caucus discipline in Canada largely precludes him from this enviable or unenviable position. However, U.S. patterns of group influence are impressed so strongly on Canadians that the general expectation seems to be that lobbying is effective. Almost every lobbyist, asked about his ways of securing access, feels bound, therefore, to volunteer the information that approaching individual MP's or MLA's has only limited utility. McGillivray gives a most telling description of the status and image of the interest group approach to the individual MP:

'What can a member of Parliament do for you?' asks one lobbyist. 'He can make a speech in caucus if he's on the government side, or in the House if he's in Opposition. But that's all.

'When I see members of Parliament being lobbied, it's a sure sign to me that the lobby lost its fight in the civil service and the cabinet.'[14]

McGillivray adds, however, that individual Members of Parliament may make themselves personal spokesmen for special interests for three reasons. The first is the individual member's standing in the House of Commons. "What they [MP's] do get is research help which can make them look good in the House of Commons. Many a well-timed question or information packed speech in the Commons owes much to the invisible lobbyist." (On this point, one of our informants claims that few questions are in fact planted.) The second reason is a special local interest in the MP's consituency. This applies to such things as Maritime fishing, Prairie wheat, and tobacco-growing and cheese-producing ridings. The final reason is a search for individual recognition by taking up a cause. Here McGillivray cites

. . . Conservative Reynold Rapp's fight for a better deal for rape-seed growers, or the battle of Liberal Ralph Cowan to keep CJBC Toronto from going French. Bagpiping Senator Tom Reid last year made himself into a one-man lobby and got the tariff taken off the chanters used for piping practice.

Individual Members of Parliament are occasionally targets of letter-writing campaigns organized by interest groups. The Consumers Association of Canada uses this approach fairly frequently, and allegedly with some success. Agricultural lobbyists do not deal much with private members because most members representing agricultural areas are towns'folk who do not have the technical knowledge to be lobbied effectively.

Interest groups may under certain circumstances address themselves to legislative committees. For instance, the Alberta Federation of Labour submitted a brief to a special committee of the Legislative Assembly charged with revising the Workmen's Compensation Act. Some interest groups, in Ottawa and in the provinces, manage to have themselves well represented on legislative committees. Most striking is the prominent

---

[13] McGillivray, *loc. cit.*
[14] McGillivray, *loc. cit.*

representation of the Royal Canadian Legion on the Committee on Veterans' Affairs in Ottawa.

The Aggregative Function of Parties

We have now given a limited survey of the areas of contact between organized interest groups and the elective portions of Canada's governmental structure. We can no longer elude the question posed at the beginning of this section: to what extent do political parties in Canada aggregate the demands raised by organized interest groups, demands which lead to policy decisions by the elective part of the governmental structure, i.e., Cabinet and Parliament? There seems at first to be an easy answer to this question: political parties do furnish the governmental leaders, and their policy decisions are therefore party decisions. After all, with the exceptional independent who proves the rule, every Canadian legislator and every Canadian minister holds his office by virtue of a partisan nomination and election, and in every normal situation does find himself subject to party discipline. It would be ludicrous to maintain that a Cabinet carefully balances the intrinsic merit of interests and accommodates them without regard to party. Therefore, Canadian parties aggregate interests, period.

But our answer may be a bit too facile. Are there really Liberal and Conservative ways of cutting taxes, Liberal and Conservative ways of keeping watch over a corrupt union, Liberal and Conservative ways of selling wheat? Or are there Liberal and CCF ways of widening the highway between Regina and Saskatoon, and Social Credit and NDP ways of preventing rock slides on the road between Hope and Princeton, B.C.? Could it be that the input to governmental decisions is a simple relationship between organized interest groups and the governmental structure? Does all significant aggregation take place within the bureaucracy, without regard to party?

Not only is the first answer—that every interest input is aggregated by parties—too facile, but so also is the second answer—that every interest input is directly carried to the governmental structure and aggregated by the bureaucracy. In the Canadian political system, party may perform an aggregative function with respect to (a) the formation and transmittal of inputs to the governmental structure, and (b) the formation of policy outputs by the governmental structure. To distinguish party and non-party involvement in (a) as well as in (b), we present this paradigm:

	party	*non-party*
(a) INPUT FORMATION	Appointment of Royal Commission on Bilingualism and Biculturalism	Negotiation of Wheat sales with Communist countries
(b) OUTPUT DECISION	Maple leaf flag	Proposed abolition of death penalty

Let us look at examples of both kinds of inputs. The "B and B" Commission was appointed by the Liberal Government in response to French-Canadian demands, against the will of the Conservative Opposition. Wheat sales to Communist countries were initiated by the Conservatives in response to a demand from farm interests for surplus disposal, and supported by the diplomatic "thaw" of the late fifties; their continuation by the Liberals is based not on a party decision, but on the continuing availability of Canadian supply and Communist demand. As an example of a party output, in response to a demand to give symbolic expression to Canadian national indentity, the Liberal Government implemented plans for a maple leaf flag, despite fierce Conservative opposition. The proposed abolition of the death penalty arose from demands by humanitarian interests; its implementation would have followed a positive outcome of the "free" vote (i.e., a vote free of party discipline) in Parliament.

Let us come back to assessing the role of party in the aggregation of policy inputs in Canada. The most valid generalizations appear to be the following: (1) *The articulators of demands tend to turn to the governmental structure itself, and not to parties.* There are notable exceptions, especially with trade unions, but even these conform to our first generalization more than meets the eye. (2) *The parties, and primarily the governing party, are in a position to aggregate interest demands, and also to refuse to accommodate such demands.* Let us turn to a discussion of our first generalization.

It would require the kind of empirical research bordering on military intelligence work to obtain a full picture of the extent to which interest groups seek access to parties on their way to the governmental structure. Most organized interests feel that to admit an approach to party is tantamount to "going into politics." It is obviously as impossible for an interest group to shun politics, as it is for a businessman to shun economics. What interest groups *do* fear by admitting approaches to party is the impression of attaching themselves to *one* party, and thereby closing routes of access to other parties. We must, therefore, expect standard answers of non-partisanship from interest group spokesmen, unless the group has openly attached itself to *one* party. Access of groups to both major parties (during the same period of time) or indeed to all parties could probably be determined only through participant-observation.

It will appear to the standard observer that the ordinary interest group is seeking access to the governmental structure directly, and not to one or more political parties. Some of the declarations of non-partisanship ring particularly true. The Wheat Pools, for instance, can point to the time when they got their fingers burned when the United Farmers' parties, through which they had operated, sustained permanent defeat. The Canadian Federation of Agriculture can claim permanence in its relations with the federal government by avoiding party channels. This non-partisanship in the CFA is enforced. Helen Dawson reports:

For instance, during the 1953 provincial elections in Ontario three of the federation's County secretaries resigned because they had been nominated for political office. It is perhaps even more revealing to note that one was nominated by the Conservative party, one by the Liberal party and one by the C.C.F.[15]

In the Consumers Association of Canada, officers are dissuaded from taking an active part in partisan politics during their term of office with the group, but Ellen Fairclough held office while she was a Conservative M.P. and Pauline Jewett resigned from the executive only after she was elected to Parliament in 1963.

Some of the avowed non-partisanship of groups seems to be limited. A case in point is the Chambers of Commerce, whose assertions of non-partisanship seem restricted to the two major parties. In late 1961, they launched "Operation Freedom," a pro-free enterprise, anti-socialist, anti-communist program with much fanfare. In 1962, the "operation" was abandoned, mainly because many local chapters did not identify with the venture and refused to participate. The abortive "operation" may be an indication that the chambers' non-partisanship might become inoperative should the NDP ever attain the status of the principal opposition party.

McGillivray lists three important successes of interest lobbying wrested from the Pearson Government of 1963: " (1) Walter Gordon's withdrawal of the 'foreign take-over' tax from the budget in June, 1963, (2) the modification, by the same Minister of Finance, of the sales tax on building materials, one week later, and (3) the cancellation of the shut-down of TCA's overhaul base in Winnipeg." The interests involved were (1) the stock exchanges, led in this role by Eric Kierans, (2) the trade association of the construction industry, (3) the province of Manitoba, led by Duff Roblin, its Conservative Premier. In the case of the 30 per cent "take-over" tax, Mr. Kierans took direct action. He delivered his attack on the tax to the presidents of all companies whose shares were listed with the Montreal exchange. This precipitated a market crash of sufficient magnitude to cause the Minister to withdraw the tax. The sales tax issue was less urgent; however, reports indicate that spokesmen of the various trade associations spared no effort to inform Mr. Gordon of their views.

The classic example of an interest group that managed to avoid open identification with one party while closely working through it (and in fact *against* the other major party) was that of the Canadian Manufacturers' Association in the early years of this century.[16] The CMA strongly favoured the tariff policies of the Conservatives, and strongly opposed those of the Liberals, yet it did not go so far as to cut its lines to the Liberals by openly supporting the Conservatives.

Open identification of some interest groups with parties has occurred in Canada, principally with the CCF/NDP, and with some of the parties connected with the Progressive and United Farmers' movement of the twenties. This open identification of interest (primarily trade unions) with party has taken the form of actual affiliation with direct financial support, and of political action support—electorally, educationally, and financially.

The next section of this chapter will deal with overt and covert exceptions to our first generalization, i.e., cases of access of interest groups to political parties. The second generalization, concerning the responsiveness of parties to organized interest groups, will have to stand as an hypothesis. We are persuaded that research into the accommodation of demands of organized interest groups will bear out the hypothesis. At the present stage of development of research on Canadian interest groups, attempts to make conclusive statements on this point would amount to dangerous guesswork.

●

THE ACCESS OF INTERESTS TO PARTIES

We will begin with interest groups that have regularized, and apparently rigidified, their access to political parties by formally affiliating with one of them. Following the indirect pattern of the British Labour Party, whereby a party establishes considerable reliable financial and voting strength through the direct affiliation of interest groups with large membership, the CCF attempted to encourage the affiliation of farm, cooperative, and labour groups. However, except for indefinite and temporary affiliation arrangements with the declining United Farmers of Alberta, the CCF did not succeed in obtaining the affiliation of farm and cooperative groups. We should not infer from the affiliation to the CCF in 1937 of District 26 of the United Mine Workers of America (the coal miners of Cape Breton, N.S.), that the party succeeded on the labour front either. Nonetheless, by 1952, forty-four local trade unions had affiliated with the CCF.[17] None of the trade unions, however, affiliated on a nation-wide basis. Trade union affiliation has increased since the formation of the NDP, but again on a local basis. Groups other than local trade unions have not affiliated. The importance of affiliation to interest articulation is thus bound to be limited and for two reasons: (1) no nation-wide interest is affiliated, and (2) all affiliation is with the NDP, which is neither the government nor the principal opposition party. Affiliation is, however, of considerable fiscal importance to the NDP.

Considerably more important than affiliation as a channel of regularizing access of interest group to party is political action support. Here again, we are dealing with the trade union interest on one side, and the CCF/NDP on the other. It was the former Canadian Congress of Labour (CCL) that devised the notion of political action support. At its annual convention in 1943, the CCL decided to endorse the CCF as "the political arm of labour in Canada." The CCF was at that time the

---

[15] Dawson, "The Canadian Federation of Agriculture," 137-38 n.

[16] S. D. Clark, *The Canadian Manufacturers' Association* (Toronto: The University of Toronto Press, 1939).

[17] Frederick C. Engelmann, "Membership Participation in Policy-Making in the C.C.F.," *The Canadian Journal of Economics and Political Science*, XXII (1956), 170.

principal opposition party in the Ontario legislature; moreover, its standing in national public opinion polls was then on a par with that of the two major parties. Following the CCL's declaration in 1944, the labour congress formed the Political Action Committee. The Committee's primary function was

to carry out the decisions of the convention, involving a program of education among affiliated locals to act as a liaison between the Congress and the national office of the CCF, and between member unions of the Congress and the provincial CCF offices.[18]

The Committee consisted of important trade union personages, originally including leading figures of the Steel Workers, the Transport Workers, the Amalgamated Clothing Workers, the Mine, Mill and Smelter Workers, the Packinghouse Workers, the Auto Workers, and the Rubber Workers. The 1948 National Convention of the CCF was addressed by A. R. Mosher, President, and Pat Conroy, Secretary-Treasurer, of the CCL. The very poor showing of the CCF, in the federal election of 1949, in Ontario ridings with a heavy concentration of industrial workers, and again in the Ontario election of 1951, led to the decentralization of the CCL's political action organization.

The Trades and Labor Congress of Canada (TLC), the senior trade union congress, had developed in the tradition of the American Federation of Labor. This tradition was to support labour's friends, to defeat labour's enemies, and not to pledge support to a particular political party. When TLC and CCL merged in 1956 to form the Canadian Labour Congress (CLC), the question of political action was left open, and it soon became obvious that the supporters of the CCF were gaining the upper hand. At its convention in 1958, the CLC passed the following resolution:

The time has come for a fundamental realignment of political forces in Canada. There is the need for a broadly based people's political movement, which embraces the CCF, the Labour movement, farm organizations, professional people and other liberally minded persons interested in basic social reform and reconstruction through our parliamentary system of government. Such a broadly based political instrument should provide that Labour and other people's organizations may, together with the CCF, participate directly in the establishment of such a movement, its organizational structure and basic philosophy and program, as well as in its financing and choice of candidates for public office.[19]

The National Convention of the CCF adopted the CLC's invitation to launch a new party, and the CLC-CCF Joint National Committee, later the National Committee for the New Party, was formed. Most of the leading CLC figures, including the President, Claude Jodoin, were members. The Committee's work led to the formation, in 1961, of the New Democratic Party.

Trade union support was placed on a firmer basis when the NDP was formed. Yet this change of 1958 to 1961 did not turn out to be fundamental. The CLC continued to be Canada's leading trade union-congress and not a part of a political party. It was not even as thoroughly committed to the NDP as the British Trade Union Congress is to the British Labour Party. The NDP remained well behind the two principal political parties in strength and had to be satisfied with no more than a substantial minority of the votes of Canadian industrial workers. The pattern of the forties and fifties has not changed greatly. However, the NDP now has the formal backing of the entire CLC, not just the formal backing of the former CCL unions which the CCF enjoyed. But in political reality the basic nature of the pre-1958 political action relationship remains about the same.

The effect of the political action pattern, whether in its earlier or present form, on the access of the trade union interest to Canada's political structure would have to be assessed through a detailed empirical study. One limit emerges clearly: the party through which the CLC has channeled its access remains a third party, forming neither the government nor the official opposition. A thorough investigation would very likely show that the labour interest is adequately taken care of through open channels to the upper echelon of the civil service in the Department of Labour and to the Minister of Labour himself. But the formal commitment of much of the labour elite to the NDP probably hampers direct access to the major parties, though the parties themselves are interested in communication with the trade union leadership. In late 1965, organized Labour obtained a Cabinet representative. The seat did not go to the CLC, but to the CNTU, whose President, Jean Marchand, became Minister of Manpower.

The situation vis-à-vis the parties of the Canadian Manufacturers' Association, in the early decades of this century, was a sensitive one. Around 1900, the orientation of the CMA was clearly non-partisan. S. D. Clark quotes the following statements by CMA spokesmen, all dating from 1903:

My politics today . . . are my business. We do not care a fig for party, . . . [W]e go to the Minister of Customs because he is a Minister of Customs, not because he is a Reformer or Conservative. The intention of the Association . . . is, that being non-political, believing that we should have influence with whatever Government may be in power, that it would be . . . extraordinary if the business interests . . . should have no influence with the Government in power. . . . [T]hey are our representatives, whether they are of our political stripe or many of our political stripes or not. The feeling is to so arouse the interests . . . that each manufacturer

[18] Frederick C. Engelmann, "The Cooperative Commonwealth Federation of Canada: A Study of Membership Participation in Party Policy-Making" (Unpublished Ph.D. Dissertation, Department of Political Science, Yale University, 1954), p. 141.
[19] Stanley Knowles, *The New Party* (Toronto: McClelland and Stewart Limited, 1961), p. 127.

. . . will personally approach the representative of the constituency, be that representative Reform or Conservative. . . .[20]

In the election campaign of 1904, the CMA recommended that members "support those candidates, irrespective of party, who announce themselves publicly in favour of an immediate tariff revision." Dissatisfaction with the tariff revision of 1907 brought an abortive effort to align the CMA with the party of protection. Many of the CMA leaders had been Liberals, but during the Reciprocity crisis many prominent Liberals in the CMA broke from the party. After 1921, the CMA's opposition to tariff reduction was so strong that the temptation was great to give open support to the Conservative Oppositon. It was resisted, however, out of fear that an open political commitment would force agricultural interests into an even closer alliance with the Liberal Government. In the periods discussed by Clark, it is clear that the CMA leaned toward the Conservatives whenever the tariff was a partisan issue. It is equally clear that the CMA preferred to keep open channels to both parties. They did not want their programmatic agreement with the Conservatives to jeopardize their access to the Liberals.

Hugh Thorburn presents a concrete example of an organized interest seeking access through one political party. He recounts the partially successful effort of the Retail Merchants Association (RMA) to obtain resale price maintenance from the Diefenbaker Government.[21] Since the Liberal governments, in office for twenty-two years, had opposed combines in general, and the Conservatives had championed resale price maintenance in 1951, there was good reason for the RMA to turn to the Conservatives. It approached Messrs. Diefenbaker and Fulton prior to the 1957 election. Over-lobbying by the RMA and vacillation by the Government marred the success of the campaign.

It is a fact that many interests deal simultaneously with the two major parties. Estimates of splitting of campaign contributions by corporations as well as by organized interest groups are legion; they are usually quoted as 60 per cent for the Government, 40 per cent for the Opposition. More significantly, interest groups often have policy dealings with more than one party. The CFA, after submitting its annual brief to the federal Cabinet in February, spends part of February and March submitting it not only to the regional caucuses of the federal House of Commons, but also to the federal caucuses of all the political parties. The Consumers Association of Canada sometimes forwards its resolutions to both the governing party and the opposition parties.[22] On one occasion, Mrs. Fairclough, when in opposition, flaunted on the floor of the House of Commons private information she had received from the Consumers Association—a small counterpoise indeed to the information available to the Government through the civil service.

There is virtually no evidence to suggest that Canadian interest groups, like their British and U.S. counterparts, seek to nominate "captive" candidates who will do their bidding once they have been nominated and elected. The CFA not only does not attempt to influence

nominations; it even removes from association office those who have succeeded in obtaining nominations. This does not, however, stop the CFA
from suggesting to its members that they vote for the candidate who is the
best friend of agriculture, nor does it stop the CFA from making use of its
friends in the high echelons of party organization. The late Senator
Lambert, once the chief organizer of the Liberal Party, had a background
in the Progressive movement which predisposed him in favour of agricultural groups; in his party activities, he was said to have been very helpful
to the CFA. The organizational relationship of the NDP and the labour
movement is cemented by numerous "personal unions" in the hierarchies
of labour and the party.

Unless the access of an interest group is entirely non-partisan or clearly
all-partisan, the group's mode of behaviour will depend on the position
of the party. Thorburn's example of the RMA shows one fruitful approach: elect the Opposition and then influence the newly elected Government. A group's behaviour toward a third party is important in two
ways. Labour, Canada's most numerous economic interest, continues, in
the formal sense at least, to seek access through a third party. And in
some of the provinces, third parties have formed and do form provincial
governments; in such situations, interest groups do of course deal with
them prominently.

●

SUMMARY

In reporting and assessing the channels of access used by organized
interest groups in Canada, we found that political parties may or may
not be involved in carrying interest demands to the governmental structure. The civil service, most regulatory boards, and Royal Commissions,
are approached by interest groups without the interposition of party. In
conveying interest demands to the central parts of the governmental
structure, the Cabinet and the Parliament, political parties may perform
the function of aggregating—i.e., bringing together, combining, sorting
out—these demands. When parties perform this function, they do so not
only in the formation and transmittal of such demands, but also in
turning them into policy outputs.

We found a tendency among organized interest groups to transmit
their demands directly to the governmental structure, and not to parties.
By not "going into politics," a misleading phrase used by groups when
they deny working through parties, interests give expression to their fear
of being identified with *one* party, and of facing isolation by the others.
Atypical is the formal, if not always real, behaviour of those trade unions

---

[20] Clark, *The Canadian Manufacturers' Association*, pp. 15-18, 23, 91.
[21] Hugh G. Thorburn, "Pressure Groups in Canadian Politics: Recent Revisions of
the Anti-Combines Legislation," *The Canadian Journal of Economics and Political
Science*, XXX (1964), 160-62.
[22] Dawson, "The Consumers Association of Canada," 108.

who have made common cause with the NDP through affiliation, or through giving regular support to that party by means of political action and education. A pattern used occasionally by groups is to elect the opposition party and then to influence the newly elected Government.

We have attempted to give an accurate picture of the role of party in interest aggregation in Canada. Paucity of material was not the only handicap. We found that both actors in, and observers of, Canadian political life hesitate to face up to the realities of interest-party relations and tend to maintain that these are illegitimate, or non-existent.

6

The System of Government

•

The governmental structure affects the total political system, including parties, by placing certain demands on the political forces of the society. In Canada the party system and individual parties are affected by demands arising from three aspects of the system of government: the parliamentary system, the electoral system, and the federal system.

•

DEMANDS OF THE PARLIAMENTARY SYSTEM

The parliamentary system, by its very nature, makes pervasive demands on political parties. These arise largely from the nature of the Cabinet, whose central leadership position depends on the support of a parliamentary majority. Parties are called upon to both bring about and keep together such majorities: the former by nominating candidates throughout the country under a common party label, and the latter by maintaining voting discipline within the party caucus.[1]

The Provision of Government through Party

In contributing the governmental leader and keeping him and his colleagues in office, parties interact with the system of government. Modern political analysts emphasize the dominant role of governmental leaders in their political parties.[2] In discussions of Canadian politics and

---

[1] Readers desiring information on Canada's governmental structure are referred to Robert MacGregor Dawson, *The Government of Canada*, 3rd ed. (Toronto: The University of Toronto Press, 1957). See also Dawson, *The Government of Canada*, 4th ed. rev. by N. Ward (Toronto: University of Toronto Press, 1963).

[2] See, among others, R. T. McKenzie, *British Political Parties*, 2nd ed., (New York: Frederick A. Praeger, Publisher, 1963), Chs. 2, 3, 6, 7; Avery Leiserson, *Parties and Politics* (New York: Alfred A. Knopf, Inc., 1958), Ch. 8, Sec. 47; Alfred de Grazia, *Political Behavior*, new rev. ed., (New York: Collier Books, 1962), pp. 225-28.

government, this emphasis has been pervasive. Hugh McD. Clokie concluded at a time when Canada had seventy-five years' experience with Confederation:

> . . . the major Canadian parties have been groupings of politically minded individuals in different sections of the Dominion who agree on one thing—acceptance of the leadership of a particular politician. The chief basis of union within each party has been allegiance to the leader of the party. It is the leader who chooses the chief issues upon which his party is to campaign. . . . It is the leader's prerogative to give direction to the parliamentary activities of the party. . . . The leader's first duty to his party is to create and preserve some semblance of unity among the diverse elements which constitute the party and its adherents. . . . Once a leader is selected he becomes both the organ of party opinion and policy and the director of party organization.[3]

The focal position of the Prime Minister in Canada's political life, emphasized here, has become a commonplace of Canadian political history. It shows up strongly in the biographies of, and other writings on, John A. Macdonald, Mackenzie King, and John Diefenbaker. It is the need to provide government under a parliamentary system that has resulted in this development.

Canadian parties developed out of the need to provide government. This was so in the days of John A. Macdonald, when the main task of the Conservative Party (often called Liberal-Conservative until 1878) was to supply enough members of the House of Commons to enable him to govern, and to put into effect his National Policy. Support of the Government was the chief element structuring political life. It was facilitated by open voting (the secret ballot was not instituted until 1874), and by deferred elections in the West, the part of the country depending on the federal government for its very existence. Civil servants and government contractors felt the need to transform their dependence on the Government into political support. The common term for Macdonald's supporters was, significantly, "ministerialists." Some candidates had themselves elected as independents, "loose fish," as Macdonald called them, so that they could defer pledging their support to the government once its return to office was assured. In later decades, both programmatic and organizational factors rivaled the provision of government as demands on the party system, but it seems evident that Laurier, King, St. Laurent, and Diefenbaker (in 1958) consolidated their electoral support because they were, at various times, the only ones likely to be able to provide stable and effective government.

Ever since the identity of Canadian parties has been clearly established, there has been strict party discipline in the governing party's parliamentary caucus. The workings of the parliamentary system strongly require that the caucus lend continuous support to the Government; any deliberate abstention from voting for the Government is a highly news worthy event.[4] A striking instance of members of the governing party

THE SHAPING OF POLITICAL PARTIES

actually voting against the Government on the floor of the House was the vote of 34 Liberals against the King Government's motion of confidence on conscription on December 7, 1944. Mr. Cowan's vote against the Pearson Government on the Flag Resolution of 1964 is not really a valid example, as the vote on the resolution was billed officially as a free vote.[5]

The governing party must arrive at an agreement on specific policies before these reach the floor, as these are presented to the House under the aegis of the Cabinet. Normally, mere sponsorship by the Cabinet assures such agreement. If there is known disagreement, a private meeting of the party's parliamentary caucus is convened. The leader settles on a course of action after, in the words of Mackenzie King, the Cabinet has ascertained ". . . through its following what the views and opinions of the public as represented by their various constituencies may be."[6]

Possibly the most striking way in which Canada's parliamentary system gives support to the governing party is through the prerogative power to dissolve the House of Commons. Dissolution, by giving the leader of the governing party the power to call an election, permits him to decide when the parties will compete for votes. With a maximum five-year term for Parliament,[7] the Prime Minister has considerable discretion in calling an election, and the governing party a substantial advantage in the process of popular consultation. That Prime Ministers seek to avail themselves of such advantages is indicated by the fact that the only peacetime Parliament in this century which was permitted to last its full term was the one elected in 1930. This was the Parliament sustaining the Conservative Cabinet of R. B. Bennett, at a time when by-elections and provincial elections showed a strong trend away from the Conservative Party. All peacetime elections in this century were called at times deemed propitious by the Prime Minister, except those of 1926 and 1963, which were brought on by the defeat of the Government in the House of Commons. This is not the place to argue the constitutionality of the refusal of Lord Byng, the Governor-General, to grant Mackenzie King's request to dissolve the Commons in 1926. Politically, however, the fact remains that when Arthur Meighen, like King, his opponent, the leader of a minority government, was subsequently granted a dissolution, he was defeated at the polls. Thus, the party thwarted by the representative of the Crown won

---

[3] H. McD. Clokie, *Canadian Government and Politics* (Toronto: Longmans, Green and Company, 1944), pp. 90, 94. Reprinted by permission of the publishers, Longmans Canada Limited.

[4] See Peter C. Newman, *Renegade in Power: The Diefenbaker Years* (Toronto: McClelland and Stewart Limited, 1963), p. 374.

[5] In respect to parliamentary voting discipline, Canadian parties have, in recent years, been similar to those in the United Kingdom. There, the famous Conservative oppositions to Chamberlain's conduct of the war and to Eden's conduct of the Suez venture, brought forth no more than abstentions. An exception, in 1947, was the vote of 72 Labour MP's against the original version of the Attlee Government's conscription bill. McKenzie, *British Political Parties*, p. 451.

[6] Quoted in Dawson, *The Government of Canada*, 3rd ed., p. 245. See also 4th ed., p. 224.

[7] Exceptions to the maximum term are provided for in The British North America (No. 2) Act, 1949.

the election. It seems unlikely, therefore, that any Cabinet, even a minority Cabinet, will in future meet with vice-regal interference in trying to reap the fruit of victory offered by the dissolution function.[8]

Another strong support given the governing party by the parliamentary system is the Cabinet's power to direct the civil service. This direction is political only and does not affect the administration of policy. Ministers do, however, monopolize the access to bureaucratic information. The governing party thus has exclusive use of unpublished information available to the bureaucracy. Such information can be used for partisan advantage in parliamentary debate, in election campaigns, in speeches by ministers, and in public-relations releases,[9] all of which gives the governing party a distinct advantage in political competition.

The demands of the parliamentary system normally have a profound influence on the power structure of the governing party. The power position of a member within his party improves through election. This strengthening effect can be seen in all parties, but only the governing party has within it Ministers of the Crown, and the holding of ministerial office constitutes a particularly strong basis of support within the power structure of the party. Most ministers are in a position to do some favours, however legitimate, and their organizational and campaign work tends to make them widely known in party circles. Individually and collectively, they commit the party to day-to-day policy positions, giving them a privileged place in the party's prime function of aggregating demands.

The effect of the parliamentary system on political parties can also be seen at the provincial level. A number of provincial premiers have been impressive party leaders: Oliver Mowat of Ontario, L. A. Taschereau and Maurice Duplessis of Quebec, and in recent years, T. C. Douglas of Saskatchewan and E. C. Manning of Alberta who, at present, holds the tenure record among governmental leaders in the British Commonwealth. Periods of office for one or the other party have been long in some provinces, and many provincial oppositions, particularly those in Alberta, have been extremely weak. The provision of government is as strong a demand on some provincial party systems as it was on the federal party system in the early years of Confederation.

As it does at the federal level, the parliamentary system also enforces legislative discipline on provincial parties. Provincial caucuses have integrative roles similar to that of the caucuses in Ottawa, though at the provincial level there tends to be considerably less initial disagreement on policy issues within each party.

The support given the governing party by the prerogative of dissoluton is as strong in the provinces as in Ottawa. All provinces have five-year limits on their legislatures, but since the Second World War, only the Manitoba legislature of 1953-58 was permitted to expire naturally, to the detriment of the incumbent Government. The almost universal use to which early dissolution is put in the provinces has probably helped provincial governments to assure their re-election, and re-election has certainly been frequent.

118

In the provinces, as in Ottawa, governing parties have available a monopoly of bureaucratic information and governmental public relations. While these are advantages for any governing party, they loom large particularly when a party is firmly entrenched in office for a long period of time. In Alberta particularly, it is difficult to make a meaningful distinction between the Social Credit Goverment and the provincial bureaucracy. When the bureacracy is little more than a patronage enterprise, as it was under Duplessis' Union Nationale Government, it is one of the mainstays of the governing party.[10] Governmental public relations of a government long in office may become indistinguishable from party public relations.

At the provincial level, the elected member of a governing party has a position of importance similar to his federal counterpart. If the elected member is a Minister of the Crown, this influence is particularly great. Provincial ministers have usually managed to shape policy even in third parties committed to some measure of lay participation in policy making, such as the CCF of Saskatchewan and the early Social Credit Party of Alberta.

The Provision of Opposition

The provision of opposition as well as the provision of government shapes Canadian parties. The effect varies, depending on whether the party is the official opposition, normally the party second in strength, or a "third" (normally a minor) party. In Ottawa, the role of official opposition has been played alternately by the Liberal and Conservative parties, despite the fact that, in the election of 1921, the Progressive Party, and not the Conservative Party, attained the second largest number of seats in the House of Commons.

The demands of the parliamentary system affect the attitude and tactics of the principal opposition party. Frustrated in efforts to replace the Government before an election is called, the principal opposition party is confined to the business of opposing. Between elections, this opposition is carried on principally within the House of Commons.

The parliamentary system virtually forces parties to carry on opposition on a continuous basis. Parliamentary opposition extends to practically all matters in which the Government initiates new policy, and to many aspects of its administration of established policy. The latter is

---

[8] The reader should note that we emphasize the role of dissolution as a weapon of the governing party, and not as a tool of the leader in maintaining party discipline. The latter, once an important part of the lore of cabinet government, has been questioned recently, in the case of Canada, by Donald V. Smiley, "The Two-Party System and One Party Dominance in the Liberal Democratic State", *The Canadian Journal of Economics and Political Science*, XXIV (1958), 318-9.

[9] For the latter, see T. Joseph Scanlon, "Promoting the Government of Canada: a Study of the Information, Explanation, and Promotional Activities of the Federal Government Departments" (Unpublished M.A. Thesis, Department of Political Studies, Queen's University, 1964).

[10] Herbert F. Quinn, *The Union Nationale* (Toronto: The University of Toronto Press, 1963), Ch. 7.

continually the subject of parliamentary questions. As parliamentary convention demands answers to these questions, the opposition party is in a position not only to air matters, but also to engage the governing party in a dialogue. Such a dialogue is even more effective when a department's budget estimates are debated in the House. The adversary nature of parliamentary procedure affords few opportunities for bargaining between Opposition and Government. Bargaining may go on, however, when policies are worked on by parliamentary committees.

The Leader of the Opposition, as a salaried official, is clearly charged with providing opposition in the House of Commons. Some holders of this office, in the past half-century notably Arthur Meighen and John Diefenbaker, have been able to structure the interparty dialogue through their supreme debating skills. Yet even a Prime Minister who is no match for his adversary does not relinquish office. Only Meighen's minority government of 1926 can be said to have been toppled through the skill of the Leader of the Opposition. In this case, Mackenzie King's exploitation, in debate, of the fact that Meighen's Cabinet consisted of ministers who had not taken an oath of office moved a sufficient number of Progressives in the House to bring it down.[11]

Normally then, the parliamentary activities of the Opposition are essentially electoral in character. No matter how superior may be their arguments, opposition members do not expect to persuade their parliamentary adversaries, the disciplined members of the government caucus. Their speeches are designed rather to appeal to the more volatile part of the electorate, in an effort to improve the party's vote at the next election. Even here, the electoral fortunes of Meighen, and of Diefenbaker after 1963, appear to indicate that the electoral impact of a superb parliamentary leader is at most a slight one.

The continual electoral stance of the Opposition does, however, affect the position of its leader within his party. Under normal circumstances, he is viewed as the alternate Prime Minister. This contributes to the influence he has with his parliamentary colleagues, and with his party's organizational structure. John Diefenbaker's position as undisputed leader of the parliamentary caucus is the principal reason for his retention of the leadership of the Conservative Party through years of strong intraparty opposition.

The Leader of the Opposition does not have an equivalent to the Prime Minister's dissolution power, but even a passive role vis-à-vis the next election confers power. The Opposition's continual electoral posture in Parliament gives power not only to the party leader, but also to his principal parliamentary advisers and, to a lesser extent, to all members of the Commons representing the party.

In recent years, both major parties have had the opportunity of being the principal opposition party facing a minority government. While a governing party with a minority in the Commons is weakened, the obverse position does not give additional strength to the Opposition. Power beneficiaries, if any, are the third parties holding the balance of the seats.

120

In the provinces, the function of the principal opposition party is similar to that of the Opposition in Ottawa. Here also, the business of the Opposition is to oppose, and efforts are directed not to the persuasion of the Government but to the electorate. Provincial opposition parties are greatly affected by the demands the system of government makes on the party most likely to replace the Government. Over periods of time, and in some provinces, the difference in strength between Government and Opposition may be so great that the role of the official opposition does not differ greatly from that of a minor party.

Third parties are affected strongly by the system of government, principally in regard to their electoral fortunes, which are adversely affected by the electoral system, as we shall show in the next section. The parliamentary system itself has one important impact on third parties. Members of a third party elected to the House of Commons tend to assume a preferred power position within their party. In the case of the NDP, the MP's salary and perquisites are a definite help to a party that has been, traditionally, short of funds.

When neither of the major parties has a majority in the House of Commons, the power position of third parties is magnified. The Government can stay in office only with the support of one or more of these third parties. In 1921, Mackenzie King governed with the support of the Progressives, whose 65 members made them the second strongest party in the House. In the ensuing years, King used his position as Prime Minister in order to manipulate the inexperienced Progressives. Their strength would have declined in any case, but by 1925 King had almost smothered them by his embrace. The effect on third parties of the minority government situations after 1962 cannot as yet be assessed.

Other Demands of the Parliamentary System

The constitution of the Senate also reflects the way in which the parliamentary system affects parties. The Senate was originally intended to be a protector of provincial rights. However, it was created as a body whose entire membership was appointed for life by the Government in Ottawa. Thus this governmental structure has been a support to the governing party. This support is limited only by its minor governmental significance. Virtually all of the appointees have been partisans of the appointing Prime Minister, and therefore a party coming into office after a long period in opposition has on occasion faced a hostile Senate. Time and tide tends to reduce the imbalance, though the Liberal majority accumulated between 1935 and 1957 managed to outlast the ensuing six

---

[11] Because ministers at that time vacated their seats when appointed, Meighen, in order not to risk their seats, had them appointed as acting ministers. For accounts of the episode see Roger Graham, *Arthur Meighen*, II (Toronto: Clarke, Irwin & Company Limited, 1963), pp. 430-45; Bruce Hutchison, *The Incredible Canadian* (Toronto: Longmans, Green and Company, 1952), pp. 125-38; H. Blair Neatby, *William Lyon Mackenzie King: The Lonely Heights* (Toronto: University of Toronto Press, 1963), pp. 154-56; Eugene A. Forsey, *The Royal Power of Dissolution of Parliament in the British Commonwealth* (Toronto: Oxford University Press, 1943).

years of Conservative rule. Appointments to the Senate are supportive of the organizational structure of the governing party, as they tend to be patronage appointments. Mr. Diefenbaker has been aided in his dominance of the Conservative caucus by the presence of Senators appointed by him.

Patronage extends also to the position of Lieutenant-Governor, judgeships, some diplomatic positions, and occasionally to deputy ministers. Governing parties in the provinces have considerably more opportunities to use patronage in bureaucratic appointments, the granting of franchises, and the letting of contracts.

•

DEMANDS OF THE ELECTORAL SYSTEM

Political scientists have long been concerned with the influence of electoral systems on political parties and party systems.[12] In the case of Canada, all legislative seats, federal and provincial, are subject to plurality election, that is, the candidate who obtains more votes than any other candidate wins. The plurality principle has always been in effect in elections to the House of Commons. Single-member districts are used throughout, with the exception of two double-member districts (Kings, P.E.I., and Halifax).[13] Provincially, at various times and places, some schemes of multi-member districts with alternate votes have been in effect. Now, there are all multi-member districts in New Brunswick and Prince Edward Island, some in British Columbia, Nova Scotia, and Newfoundland, and all single-members districts in Quebec, Ontario, Manitoba, and Alberta.

The electoral system affects party fortunes in that the party with the largest vote tends to obtain an inordinate number of seats, thus favouring it over the second party. The first two parties, in turn, are at an even greater advantage over third parties in respect to vote getting. In the case of the latter, relatively many more votes are required to gain a seat. An important remaining question is whether it is first or second position in a constituency, or first or second position in the Parliament as a whole, which gives these parties an electoral advantage over third parties. Colin Leys[14] assumes that "polarization occurs in favour *not* of the two parties which are in the lead locally, but *in favour of the two parties which have the largest number of seats in Parliament, regardless of their local strength.*" This means that the advantage in representation tends to go to the two parties with the largest nation-wide vote. But Leys adds that parties are *"inherently* local in character—e.g., nationalist or agrarian movements," will tend *not* to suffer under-representation, even when they do not rank first or second nationally. This exception would account for the representation in the House of Commons of Social Credit, the Créditistes, and for the western seats of the old CCF.

The electoral system of Canada affects not only the party system as a whole, but it also makes demands on individual parties. The single-member-district system tends to impose a strategy on political parties. The first aspect of this strategy is the drawing of the constituency map. In the United States, this map-drawing has been one of the most celebrated political games ever since the first districts not dictated entirely by tradition were drawn in the late 18th Century. From the very first, the leading party in the various states shaped the legislative districts to its own advantage, and the "gerrymander" was born. In Canada, both for the House of Commons and the provincial legislatures, the drawing of constituencies was until 1964, the business of the governing party. Rural romanticism and just plain political lag have brought more definite advantages to rural areas than to the governing party as such, but the latter has always been suspect. The federal statute of 1964 transfered the business of redrawing the boundaries of constituencies for the House of Commons (under the aegis of Parliament, to be sure) to ten provincial commissions, the common member of which is the Representation Commission of Canada. Of the three remaining members of each commission, two were appointed by the Speaker of the House, and one by the provincial Chief Justice (a federal appointee). The Speaker's appointees, in each case, were one represenave of higher education in the province, and the provincial Chief Electoral Officer. Much preparatory work was done by the Representation Commissioner. This work was based, as purely as was humanly possible, on a simple count of voters, which was then plotted on the provincial map without reference to past election returns. For each constituency, a tolerance of 25 per cent above and below the provincial average was instituted, a provision which will help urban-based parties. Beyond this, partisanship will have only a narrow range of capability in redistribution. The scheme just mentioned is in effect only for the federal House of Commons, though the 1965 election was still based on the old ridings. At present, provincial constituencies continue to be drawn by, and largely in the interest of, the provincial governing party. The most extreme case of maldistribution exists in Alberta, where the federal example has led to demands for non-partisan redistribution by all three opposition parties, who with 45 per cent of the vote, obtained a total of 3 out of 63 seats in 1963.[15] In that year, the two major urban centres in Alberta had almost one-half of the provincial population, but only 18 of its 63 seats.

Drawing the electoral map, until 1964 at least, tended to favour the governing party. The second impact on parties of the electoral system,

---

[12] See John Stuart Mill, *Utilitarianism, Liberty and Representative Government* (London: J. M. Dent & Sons Ltd., 1964), Ch. 7; F. A. Hermens, *Democracy or Anarchy* (Notre Dame, Ind.: University of Notre Dame Press, 1941); Maurice Duverger, *Political Parties*, trs. Barbara and Robert North (New York: John Wiley & Sons, Inc., 1954), pp. 207-55.

[13] Because of redistribution, all seats will be filled by single-member-district election after 1966.

[14] Colin Leys, "Models, Theories, and the Theory of Political Parties," *Comparative Politics: a Reader*, eds. Harry Eckstein and David E. Apter (New York: The Free Press of Glencoe, 1963), pp. 305-15.

[15] Some of the provinces have now appointed non-partisan redistribution commissions.

the devising of an electoral strategy based on the shape of the districts, tends to affect all parties equally. The demands of the electoral system call for the maximization of pluralities in constituencies. A party's vote expectation in a particular constituency will do much to determine its campaign there. If the likelihood of obtaining a plurality in a constituency is nil, its organizational effort is reduced to a minimum.

One more impact of the electoral system, involving the election law, should be considered. Federal candidates must deposit $200 when they file their candidacy, and this deposit is forfeited when the candidate fails to poll one-half as many votes as the winner. The deposit rule does not seriously affect major parties, but any third party must arrange its candidacies with the financial consequences in mind. However, the possible loss of deposit has not been a serious deterrent to minor party and independent candidacies; there have been more such candidates than in the United States, where there is no deposit requirement.

The electoral system does have a slight impact on party leadership in that leaders must get themselves elected from single-member constituencies. Thus, all those who want to become governmental leaders must be "electable." There is no residence requirement for candidates for the House of Commons, but most candidates live in or near their constituency. A suitable candidate for a Cabinet position, or some other position of parliamentary leadership, must find a constituency in which he can win. Those who cannot win are effectively excluded from such leadership positons. General McNaughton, who twice failed to obtain a seat, is the classic example of the man tapped for a position of political leadership by Mackenzie King but vetoed by the workings of the electoral system. The party leader himself, however, need not be disabled when he loses his seat. After electoral defeats, seats were "found" twice for Mackenzie King and, in 1962, for T.C. Douglas.

By-elections have only a slight impact on parties. They cause parties to compete, and thus show their strength, at times and in places accidentally arrived at. The accident of time is somewhat modified, as the Prime Minister may within limits select the date of the by-election.

Our discussion in this section has centred on the federal scene. Provinces show a similar picture because of their similar electoral systems. The electoral calendar, determined by dissolution, is different in each of Canada's eleven jurisdictions. A government with a comfortable majority may permit a parliament to last about four years; but even if earlier dissolutions did not occur, each province would, on the average, experience an election (federal or provincial) every two years. This means that elections affect Canadian parties almost continually.

•

DEMANDS OF THE FEDERAL SYSTEM

Canadian Federalism

The Canadian polity is a federal system. It clearly fulfills the three conditions of William Riker's definition of federalism: " (1) two levels of

THE SHAPING OF POLITICAL PARTIES

government rule the same land and people, (2) each level has at least one area of action in which it is autonomous, and (3) there is some guarantee . . . of the autonomy of each government in its own sphere."[16] To explain how these conditions are met, let us cite the following examples: (1) Inhabitants of Winnipeg are governed by the Government of Canada and by the Government of Manitoba. (2) The Government of Canada is autonomous in regard to the minting of coins used in Winnipeg, while the Government of Manitoba is autonomous in regard to the establishment of provincial hospitals in Winnipeg. (3) Canada's autonomy stated in (2) is guaranteed by Article 91, Section 14, of the British North America Act, while Manitoba's autonomy stated in (2) is guaranteed by Article 92, Section 7, of the British North America Act.

Canadian federalism has six aspects that are of significance as we assess its effect on parties. These are (a) constitutional, (b) fiscal, (c) political, (d) regional, (e) ethnic, and (f) programmatic.

The Constitutional and Fiscal Aspects of Federalism in Operation: Their Effect upon the Party System

The division of powers between Canada and the provinces, as presented in the British North America Act, is not self-regulating. Until 1949, lines of demarcation were determined by the Judicial Committee of the Privy Council. Since 1875, these have also been laid down, and still are, by the Supreme Court of Canada. (From 1875 to 1949, the Supreme Court of Canada interpreted the BNA Act, but the losing party could appeal to the Judicial Committee of the Privy Council.) Judicial interpretation has had a profound effect on the constitutional-legal structure of Canada. Its effect on Canadian parties has been slight, with one exception: the power of the Attorney-General, of Canada or a province, to elicit a judicial ruling from the courts, can be of help to the governing party. It did enable the Liberal Government of Mackenzie King to obtain judicial rulings on the so-called "New Deal" legislation of the previous Conservative Government under R.B. Bennett. The rulings invalidated most of these statutes, thereby removing them from the scene without attaching to the Liberals the stigma of having repealed them.

Two aspects of the governmental structure that were established to maintain the federal bargain, the office of Lieutenant-Governor and the Senate, have had varying effects on the party system. A third part of the structure, the Cabinet, has turned out to be a more important nexus of federalism and party.

The office of Lieutenant-Governor has had little impact on party in this century. The Lieutenant-Governor has a dual position: the representation of Her Majesty in the province, and the representation of the Governor-General-in-Council. Of this duality (which made the Earl of Dufferin refer to the Lieutenant-Governor as a circus rider, riding two horses at the same time), only the second, the federal, element has

---

[16] William H. Riker, *Federalism: Origin, Operation, Significance* (Boston: Little, Brown and Company (Inc.), 1964), p. 11.

affected party at all. From the very first, governments in Ottawa had themselves represented in the provinces by their partisans. With only a few initial exceptions in the West, the practice has been to appoint residents of the province. Not only has the position often gone to political opponents of the provincial government of the day, but sometimes it has gone to a political leader who had been defeated at the polls by such a government. The political capabilities of the Lieutenant-Governor, and therefore opportunities to affect party, are twofold: he may dismiss ministers, and he may reserve provincial legislation and subject it to disallowance in Ottawa. The former has not been used for two generations. There have been two instances of reservation since 1930: the reservation of major pieces of Social Credit legislation in Alberta in 1937, and the reservation of a Saskatchewan CCF mineral rights bill in 1961. The former was a celebrated incident: it involved the reservation of several bills by Lieutenant-Governor Bowen, and their subsequent disallowance. As there is evidence that Bowen acted in response to Mr. Hugill, the legalistically-minded provincial Attorney-General, and not to the federal government, his action constitutes an impact on party policy by an agent of the Crown acting at his own discretion.[17] The action affected the policies, and quite possibly the fortunes, of William Aberhart's Social Credit Government. Lieutenant-Governor Bastedo's reservation in 1961, which might have affected Saskatchewan's CCF Government, was not prompted by the Conservative Government in Ottawa, and was quickly disavowed by it.[18] Any future exercise of discretionary powers by the Lieutenant-Governor, and certainly future impacts of the office on the party system, are unlikely.

The Senate was constituted carefully to represent regions, provinces, and in Quebec, even specific districts. However, the central appointment of Senators has kept the Senate from having any centrifugal impact at all. The partisan composition of provincial Senate delegations has depended not on public opinion in the province, but on the partisanship of present and past federal Cabinets. It has differed, about as often as not, from the partisan composition of provincial delegations in the House of Commons, and even more so of provincial legislatures. There has never been a CCF/NDP or a Social Credit Senator, and these parties have governed three of the Western provinces for an aggregate of more than two generations. The Senate certainly does not enable provincial governments in such provinces to influence the governing party in Ottawa. The impact of the Senate on party has been the reverse of the intended one: it has been centripetal. Often, Senators from the provinces are agents of the governing party in Ottawa: they may handle its finances in their home province, or conduct its campaigns. In such cases, their function is to attempt to bring the provincial electorate in line with the nationally favoured party.

The party system has indeed been affected, and has had demands made on it, by provincial interests in an area of central importance: the composition of the national Cabinet. Provinces are not the only interests represented in the Cabinet but their representation is the most reliable and the most striking. In R.M. Dawson's judgment "the Cabinet has, in fact, taken over the allotted role of the Senate as the protector of the rights of the provinces. . . ."[19] To permit the Cabinet to function in this way, its composition has been affected by the federal system to the point of having all provinces represented, though Prince Edward Island may have to be satisfied with a parliamentary assistant.

Provincial representatives are not always easy to find when, as has occurred several times since the rise of third parties after World War I, the major party forming the government has not been able to gain adequate, or any, parliamentary representation from one or more provinces. Writing in 1947, Dawson notes the problems presented by the practice of having regional representation in the Cabinet:

The strength of this practice, which has during the past thirty years hardened into a rigid convention of the constitution, was well illustrated in 1921 when Mr. Mackenzie King formed his first Cabinet. The Province of Alberta had by a singular oversight neglected to return even one Liberal to Parliament, and none of the twelve United Farmers of Alberta would betray his party for a portfolio or help Mr. King and advance the provincial interest by resigning in favour of a Liberal. The new Prime Minister, however, was not easily discouraged, and after some inquiry and negotiation found a solution: he appointed to the Cabinet Charles Stewart, a Liberal ex-Premier of Alberta, and then opened up a seat for him in the Province of Quebec. In 1935, Alberta again caused some worry, for the province returned one Liberal, one Conservative, and fifteen Social Crediters; but after some hesitation, extending over three years, the sole Liberal was made member of the Cabinet without portfolio.[20]

The Liberals experienced a similar dearth of choice in 1963, when only one Liberal was elected in Alberta. But there was no hesitation in appointing him Minister of Agriculture, since he was not only the lone Alberta representative, but one of only three to be elected from the prairie provinces.

These appointments indicate that federal requirements greatly limit the Prime Minister's choice of is colleagues. The federal bargain is indeed enforced at the most crucial site of central policy making, the Cabinet: all provinces have a say in the body that represents the highest counsels of both governing party and country.

The fiscal aspects of Canadian federalism have been highly problematic from the beginning of Confederation. For the first seventy years, the

[17] John T. Saywell, *The Office of the Lieutenant-Governor* (Toronto: University of Toronto Press, 1957) , pp. 215-18.

[18] J. R. Mallory, "The Lieutenant-Governor's Discretionary Powers: The Reservation of Bill 56," *The Canadian Journal of Economics and Political Science,* XXVII (1961) , 518-22.

[19] Dawson, *The Government of Canada,* 3rd ed., pp. 211-12. See also 4th ed., p. 194.

[20] *Ibid.,* 3rd ed., p. 212; 4th ed., p. 194.

problem was exacerbated by four factors: (a) the superior taxing powers of the federal government, (b) the vast increases in expenditures in policy fields delegated to the provinces, e.g. education and highways, (c) the virtual preemption of the income tax by the federal government since its inception during the First World War, and (d) the inequality of the tax resources available to the various provinces. Throughout this period, provincial demands for subsidies and grants-in-aid increased. This brought about, in 1937, the appointment of the Rowell-Sirois Royal Commission on Dominion-Provincial Relations. Its Report, issued in 1940, looked toward a system whereby income taxes would be preempted by the federal government, but numerous other taxes would be left to the provinces, of which the poorer ones were also to receive adjustment grants. Implementation had to await the end of the war, but since 1946 "rent" and then "sharing" arrangements have given provinces payments for the tax fields the Government of Canada preempts. Is is these arrangements which have channeled provincial demands during the past two decades. From time to time, provincial premiers and treasurers meet with the Prime Minister and the Minister of Finance, and the Government is bombarded by provincial fiscal demands. The influence of these demands on the party system has been negligible. Provincial governments controlled by the party in control in Ottawa have been no gentler in their demands than governments controlled by the opposition party or by third parties. Recently, federal Cabinets of both parties have been under similar pressures from the provinces. Thus, the most significant provincial demands have been raised by the provinces as demanding interests, without regard to partisan considerations.

Political, Regional, Ethnic, and Progammatic Aspects of Federalism

The simple facts that Canada has ten provincial governments, and that political parties in Canada have provincial organizations in all or some of the provinces, have an effect on the party system. There are certain "political" demands, and these may be categorized as (a) organizational demands, and (b) leadership demands.

Federalism has profoundly influenced party organization in Canada. The organization of the Liberal, Conservative, NDP, and Social Credit parties is so structured as to make the provincial organization the most significant unit. It is fair to say that the national organization is the superstructure, and constituency organizations the substructure. (We are speaking here, of course, of the parties' electoral or membership organizations, not of their governmental leaders.) The significance of this emphasis on the province as organizational unit varies from party to party. In both the Liberal and Conservative parties, the legislative leaders, if any (in 1965, the Conservatives had one member in the legislature of Saskatchewan, and none in that of Alberta), tend to be dominant, leaving the membership, or electoral, organization in a subordinate position. In the CCF/NDP, however, the membership organization itself is a significant demand-raising group. This can be seen in its resolutions, passed by a provincial convention. When such a resolution deals with a subject within the jurisdiction of the federal government, it is normally passed on to the national convention, from where it may or may not be forwarded to the NDP caucus in the House of Commons. In the CCF/NDP, the organization as well as governmental leaders may speak on behalf of provincial interests.

The most important political demands, particularly in the major parties, arise from the provincial party leaders. Regardless of his policy agreement or disagreement with his national party leader, the provincial leader, when Premier, competes with him for funds, particularly when the national leader is also the Prime Minister. Riker defines the position of the Premier in these terms (which apply of course also to the Conservative Party) : "Even within the Liberal party, provincial prime ministers look to Liberal leaders in Ottawa, not for leadership, but for bargaining concessions of exactly the same sort that might be gained by Social Credit or Union Nationale provincial ministers. And there is something to bargain about."[21] Some provincial leaders, whether in office or not, are of course serious contenders for the national leadership of their party, especially when the tenure of the national leader is in question, and they can be expected to bring forth their demands reinforced by their claims to national leadership. But these claims also carry with them the obligation to be reasonable in demands made on the national leader. For this reason, the more serious instances of tension with Ottawa in recent decades have been on the part of premiers who did not contend openly for the national leadership, such as Hepburn of Ontario, Robarts of Ontario, and Thatcher of Saskatchewan. On balance then, the mere existence of provincial premiers as demanders places a strain on the governing party —a strain that is mitigated only when a provincial premier has the ambition to become the national leader of the governing party.

"Political" demands from the provinces tend to increase, on balance, when the province is controlled by a party which does not govern Canada. This notion is cited frequently as one of the chief reasons for the perseverance of the minor parties. The argument goes like this: any party other than the one in control in Ottawa will "get more" for the province. We have no evidence at this point that third parties or the federal opposition party gain votes provincially because individual voters cast a ballot "against" the federal government. All we can be sure of is the overt campaigning behaviour of provincial parties. We do know that Social Credit governments in Alberta and British Columbia, the CCF Government in Saskatchewan, and the Union Nationale Government in Quebec, did at times oppose the Government in Ottawa in successful provincial campaigns. We also know that provincial leaders of major parties occasionally indicate in campaigns that they will behave in the fashion described by Riker. This applies, in the sixties, to the Liberals in Quebec and in Saskatchewan.

---

[21]Riker, *Federalism*, p. 118.

The demands mentioned so far are essentially jurisdictional; they arise because the legal-constitutional framework of Canada consists of ten provinces with distinct governments and party organizations. However, some of the pressures from provincial governments or parties have been regional. These have been exerted by the province—a legal, political entity —on behalf of the region—a socio-economic entity.

There are numerous examples of such provincial demands which can be classified as primarily regional. There were the activities of the United Farmers' governments in the 1920's in Alberta and Manitoba, and those of the coalition governments of Manitoba, insofar as these governments exerted pressure on behalf of the agricultural prairie population as a whole. In pressing for its terms in a Columbia River treaty, the Bennett Government in British Columbia may have acted fully as much on behalf of Pacific Canada as for the province. The strains placed on the Liberal Party by the Smallwood regime in Newfoundland (the only government Newfoundland has had since it entered Confederation) are also essentially of a regional, if not, in view of Newfoundland's previous status, of a "national" nature.

Quebec is both a province and a region. Yet demands emanating from Quebec have been paramountly of an ethnic, or, in the French-Canadian sense of the term, of a "national" nature. These demands have been significant throughout the past century. Since Laurier succeeded in attracting the loyalty of many French-speaking Canadians to the Liberal Party, demands have been directed to the Liberal Party as well as to the Government of Canada. Probably the main achievement of Mackenzie King's statecraft was the accommodation of French-Canadian demands, thereby bridging some of the cleavages produced by the national coalition of 1917. On the provincial level, French-Canadian demands, particularly under Maurice Duplessis' Union Nationale Government, were raised on behalf of the relatively small groups in control of the economy and of the polity. The nature of the provincial-"national" demands made by the Liberal Lesage Government were of a very different nature. In regard to the Government of Canada, they were economic ("opting out" of federal policies, sharp increases of taxing autonomy, control of offshore mineral rights) and secular-cultural (among these was the demand for the control of Eskimos); in regard to the Liberal Party, they led to the establishment of provincial autonomy within the party's federal structure.

Recently, demands on the political system have taken a novel direction. The federal pension program (the Canada Pension Plan) brought on, once its terms were revealed, competing plans from the governments of Ontario and Quebec. Features of the latter were later incorporated in the federal scheme. Provincial demands are crystallizing around the proposed national health scheme, possibly resulting once again in some form of cooperative federal policy making. Provincial demands are thus likely to continue to shape the national programs. It remains to be seen whether or not their nature and the response to them will have partisan overtones.

SUMMARY

We have found that Canadian parties are influenced strongly by Canada's system of government. All the major aspects of this system are influential: the parliamentary (or cabinet) system, whose principles determine the shape of the governmental structures, federal and provincial; the single-member-district system used in federal and provincial elections; and the federal system, according to whose principles the Canadian polity is organized.

The parliamentary system assigns definite functions to political parties and makes them the chief actors within the governmental sphere. In all parties, it encourages and virtually forces cohesion within the parliamentary group; this cohesion in turn tends to bring about consistency in the entire behaviour of the party. The parliamentary system also requires that parties select a parliamentary leader, and the system assists this person in becoming the actual as well as nominal leader of the entire party. In any party, those elected to Parliament become important members of their party organization.

The influence of the parliamentary system is felt most keenly in the party that is called upon to form the Government. Its leader becomes the Prime Minister of Canada, a factor which strongly reinforces his party leadership. The system of government permits the party to transform its decisions into public policy, through legislation and through the direction of the civil service. The system also gives the governing party a strategic advantage over competing parties by giving its leader the function of dissolving Parliament and thus deciding the timing of an election. When the governing party fails to obtain a majority and has to form a minority government or a governing coalition, its power position tends to be weakened.

The parliamentary system affects the non-governing parties in similar ways. However, it does place these parties in a passive role in at least two ways: they are forced to respond to, rather than to initiate, proposed or effected policy decisions, and they must, under normal circumstances, adapt passively to the election timetable decided by the Government.

Canada's electoral system tends to favour the strongest over the second strongest party and both of these over all other parties. The single-member-district system affects the parties' general electoral strategy in at least two ways: the election deposit tends to discourage small splinter parties from competing, and virtually all party leaders must clear the hurdle of election in a constituency. Any advantage governing parties may have derived from past distribution of constituencies may be removed, at the federal level, as a result of the redistribution legislation introduced in 1964.

Canadian parties are affected by the constitutional division of power between Canada and the provinces and, decreasingly, by the power of the Lieutenant-Governor. Federalism has a strong influence on Cabinet selection and, through it, on federal party leadership. The loose determination of fiscal powers by Canada's constitution has enhanced the strength of the governing parties in the provinces.

Canadian federalism has a profound influence on the organization of political parties. It also provides avenues to federal party leadership, or in turn, to positions from which federal party leaders can be challenged effectively, or bargained with successfully. The impact of federalism on the parties is reinforced by the following two facts: (1) Quebec acts not only as a province but also as the source of French-Canadian demands. (2) Three of the provinces, Quebec, Ontario, and British Columbia, coincide with socio-economic regions. Their ethnic and regional demands are brought not only to the national government by the provincial governments, but also to the various national parties by their provincial sections.

7

The Consequences of External Influences

•

In the five preceding chapters, we have presented some of the conditions affecting Canadian political parties. However, if we are to account adequately for the shaping of Canadian parties, we must attempt to answer the following questions: (1) How do these conditions—social structure, organized interest groups, elites, and the system of government—affect party structures, and what kinds of party structures result? (2) How do these conditions (i.e., the inputs into the Canadian party system) affect policies, programs, and ideologies, (i.e., its outputs)? In answering these questions, we will be summarizing much of the material of Section II.

•

CONSEQUENCES FOR PARTY ORGANIZATION

Social Structure and Party Structure

We have described Canada's population as one that is ethnically and religiously heterogeneous, has a geographically differentiated growth rate, is urbanizing and industrializing, has many recent immigrants who are neither British nor French, and loses many of its best trained people to the United States. We indicated also that elitist positions are held in an inordinate proportion by those of British extraction. There is much objective evidence (though much less individual perception) of class-like status divisions in Canadian society.[1]

---

[1] S. Peter Regenstreif, "Group Perceptions and the Vote: Some Avenues of Opinion Formation in the 1962 Campaign" in *Papers on the 1962 Election*, ed. John Meisel (Toronto: University of Toronto Press, 1964), p. 239 n.

How does a society with this kind of population and social structure affect the organizational structure of political parties? Alford found in *Party and Society*[2] that there is less class voting in Canada than in Britain, Australia, or the United States. In fact, there is no discernible class voting at all. His findings support our own conclusion that the regional-ethnic and regional-economic cleavages in Canadian voting behaviour (and especially in Canadian party formation) are the most significant. In his 1962 election study he concludes that there may be literally no stable social bases for Canadian parties, ". . . except on a very *local* basis."[3] We have specifically pointed to the lack of a major labour party in Canada, and to the lack of stable support from workers for one party, such as the Democratic Party in the U.S. has been enjoying during the past generation. The social base of Canadian parties hence is not a primary reflection of social class differences. Instead, each party's base is characteristically diversified, sustaining what on balance are pragmatic, electoral-success-oriented parties.

This lack of connection between social class structure and party support has encouraged what Maurice Duverger calls a cadre structure of political parties, and defines as:

. . . the grouping of notabilities for the preparation of elections, conducting campaigns and maintaining contact with the candidates. Influential persons, in the first place, whose name, prestige, or connections can provide a backing for the candidate and secure him votes; experts, in the second place, who know how to handle the electors and how to organize a campaign; last of all financiers, who can bring the sinews of war [sic]. . . . Adherence to it . . . is restricted to a few.[4]

By adherence, Duverger means formal individual party membership. He describes cadre parties as being "decentralized and weakly knit."[5] These parties stem from a period of limited franchise, when mass enrolment was pointless.

Canada's major parties both in theory and practice, and some of the minor parties in practice, fit the model of the cadre party. Conservatives and Liberals have individual members, but the aggregate of membership fees does not constitute a substantial portion of the parties' income as it does in what Duverger calls mass parties. A regular or fairly regular party supporter may do no more than cast his vote for the party candidate. He can afford to "let George do it," as there are numerous Georges around, and some "angels" to pay them. Most of the party work is done by paid or volunteer workers. They prepare the voters' lists, canvass, help in campaigning, and get people to the polls. At the headquarters level, where the work is organizational, propagandistic, financial, and research, the structure is quite bureaucratized, and occasionally professionalized. This type of party structure, which involves professionals, hired non-professionals, and only occasional help from rank-and-file citizens, seems to fit Canada's consumer-oriented, mass-society politics, just as it had been suitable for Canadian politics in the days of the restricted suffrage. It leaves the average individual free to go about his business, with minimum partisan involvement.

There are two elements in Canada's social structure which have not adapted easily to the prevailing cadre-party structure: the first are certain groups of prairie farmers, and the second, pockets of immigrants, some from the United Kingdom and some from Eastern Europe. Their impact on party structure has come about through the interplay of ethnic and ideological factors, but it is easier to define them by means of the ideological components: the former are the Prairie Populists, the latter Social Democrats. Both have organized for political action, and both have espoused, at least in principle, a mass-party structure. This structure, according to Duverger, has two functions: (1) the political education of the individual, and (2) the financing of the party through individual membership fees. To perform these functions, "the recruiting of members is a fundamental activity."[6]

Among many prairie farmers, Lipset tells us, "politics is organized to be a daily concern and responsibility of the common citizen."[7] This organization of politics has affected the structure of three parties: the Progressive Party and related United Farmers' parties, the Social Credit Party, and the Cooperative Commonwealth Federation. The United Farmers, especially in Alberta and Saskatchewan, maintained a broadly based membership movement throughout the twenties and early thirties. Social Credit was organized as a mass party, albeit a highly centralized one, during its first decade. In the structure of the CCF, the influence of prairie populism must be understood in conjunction with that of social democracy.

When the CCF was founded, among its components were the prairie populist United Farmers of Canada (Saskatchewan Section) as well as the Socialist Party of Canada (British Columbia) and a few eastern social democratic coteries, including former members of the Polish Jewish *Bund*. The Socialist groups, whether British or continental European, were organized along the lines of the British Socialist societies or of Marxist parties. In either case, the mass-structure principle applied. The members paid dues, which normally were the group's only sustenance, and ideological discussion and education was a central and continuing activity. The Populist strain, and the various Socialist ones, combined to shape CCF organization along mass-party lines. The CCF continued, and

---

[2] Robert R. Alford, *Party and Society* (Chicago: Rand McNally & Company, 1963), Ch. 9.

[3] Robert R. Alford, "The Social Bases of Political Cleavage in 1962" in *Papers on the 1962 Election*, ed. John Meisel, p. 232.

[4] Maurice Duverger, *Political Parties*, trs. Barbara and Robert North (New York: John Wiley & Sons, Inc., 1954), p. 64.

[5] *Ibid.*, p. 67.

[6] *Ibid.*, p. 63.

[7] S. M. Lipset, *Agrarian Socialism: the Cooperative Commonwealth Federation in Saskatchewan* (Berkeley and Los Angeles: University of California Press, 1950), p. 218.

the NDP continues, to have a mass-party structure in form, but mass-party reality has suffered for at least three reasons: (1) the subjection of agricultural life to consumer-oriented mass communication, leading to less direct participation in farm politics, (2) the de-ideologization of the CCF itself, and (3) the slow shift from an individual membership base to trade union affiliation.[8]

One Canadian party, the Communist Party, has maintained its mass-party structure. Its structure, following the Leninist tradition, is indeed of the cell type. The party's small membership keeps it from being a significant addition to the typology of Canadian parties.

French-Canadian parties have tended to be volatile. The only major all-Canadian party with a complete structure in Quebec is the Liberal Party. The Quebec Liberals of the "Quiet Revolution" have now separated from the old-fashioned, patronage-oriented federal Liberal structure in Quebec. Within the latter, a struggle between the "Old Guard" and the federal elements of the Lesage party—prominent among whom are men like Jean Marchand, Maurice Sauvé, Gérard Pelletier, and Pierre-Elliott Trudeau—was not resolved when the Quebec Liberals lost provincial office in 1966.

Interest Groups and Party Structure

In Chapter 5, we pointed out that interest groups may regularize their access to political parties through actual affiliation or through pledging electoral support to a party. This latter relationship is called "political action support," and was established between the Canadian Congress of Labour and the CCF. Such regularized access has definite implications for the structure of the party concerned, particularly if there is actual affiliation.

AFFILIATION   A political party which consists entirely of affiliated interest group components is, according to Duverger, an indirect party.[9] Duverger tailored this classification to the British Labour Party prior to 1918, the year in which the party admitted individual members in addition to trade unions, corporations, and socialist societies. No Canadian party answers to his description of an indirect party. There is, however, the existence of group affiliation with the CCF/NDP. This provision for group affiliation has had a significant impact on the structure, first of the CCF, and now of the NDP.

The CCF showed considerable concern, beginning in 1942, lest its internal policy-making machinery, especially its delegate conventions, be dominated by affiliated trade unions. The party did not want to repeat the experience of the British Labour Party, whose annual conferences are dominated by the bloc votes of the major affiliated unions. All of the formulae laid down for the representation of affiliated groups at national and provincial conventions of the CCF had one feature in common: affiliated members (i.e., members of groups that affiliated, not individual members of the party) were entitled to a ratio of delegates considerably

136   THE SHAPING OF POLITICAL PARTIES

below that provided for individual members. Most CCF constitutions also required convention delegates from affiliated groups to be either CCF supporters or at least not members of any other political party. The latter provision was designed primarily to prevent the infiltration into CCF conventions by members of the Communist or Labour Progressive Party.[10] A similar provision is now in force for delegates to the federal convention of the NDP. Large groups affiliated with the NDP are entitled to a federal convention representation only somewhat in excess of one-tenth of that of constituency associations of comparable size.[11]

Since the CCF/NDP remains the only Canadian party showing what Duverger would call "indirect" features, group affiliation is not a factor in the structure of other parties.

SIGNIFICANCE OF GROUP SUPPORT   The influence of group support on party structure is related to the group's strategy and tactics. Where organized groups, as prime articulators of demands, turn to the party for access, they may attempt to influence the party structure. The impact on party structure by articulators of demands whose effort is oriented directly to the governmental structure, is more subtle if it is felt at all.

During the decade when the Canadian Congress of Labour gave political action support to the CCF, most of the CCL's impact on CCF structure was informal. Several consultation committees were set up, and informal contacts took place most of the time. During this period there were never more than two members of the CCF National Executive who owed their designation primarily to their prominence within the labour movement.[12]

The structure of the two major parties is designed primarily, both in theory and practice, to elect the maximum number of legislative members. In these parties, the impact of interest group on party structure is essentially fourfold: (1) pressure, the propagation of policies bringing rewards to the group, (2) protection, the prevention of policies bringing deprivations to the group, (3) financing, the providing of channels to permit the flow of funds from the group to the party, and (4) electoral activity, the mobilizaton of group voters on behalf of the party. Pressure and protection affect the shape of party structure only in the relatively rare instances in which there is discussion of policy by lay party members. In these instances, interest group representatives attempt to secure representation within the party structure. Financing, of course, comes into play

[8] Leo Zakuta, *A Protest Movement Becalmed: a Study of Change in the CCF* (Toronto: University of Toronto Press, 1964), see also Frederick C. Engelmann, "Membership Participation in Policy-Making in the C.C.F.," *The Canadian Journal of Economics and Political Science*, XXII (1956), 161-73.

[9] Duverger, *Political Parties*, pp. 5-17.

[10] Engelmann, "Membership Participation in Policy-Making in the CCF.," p. 170.

[11] Stanley Knowles, *The New Party* (Toronto: McClelland and Stewart Limited, 1961), App. I., p. 11.

[12] Frederick C. Engelmann, "The Cooperative Commonwealth Federation of Canada: a Study of Membership Participation in Party Policy-Making" (Unpublished Ph.D. Dissertation, Department of Political Science, Yale University, 1954), Chs. 4,5.

whenever a group gives financial support to one or both of the major parties. A group may plant a representative somewhere in the party structure or, more frequently, individuals will obtain positions of some importance because they obtain group funds for the use of the party. Where the groups involved are major corporations, the party men who obtain funds from them are known pejoratively as "bagmen." Electoral activity is important in the case of groups with a committed membership. Cases in point would be representatives of ethnic groups trying to deliver their group vote to one or the other of the major parties. Such representatives may obtain a prominent place within the party structure.

Elites and Party Structure

Elites may have an impact on party structure in several possible ways, though the ones we list are suggestive only and by no means exhaustive. At the totalitarian extreme, we find Hitler's *Fuehrerprinzip*: the *Fuehrer* is the elite in every respect, and especially in the decision-making agency of the polity, the party. Close to this extreme is the Leninist concept: here the party is the vanguard of the proletariat, and is directed by a few individuals who have thoroughly mastered the principles of Marxism-Leninism. Well along the spectrum toward the pluralistic side is the democratic socialist concept. Ideally, the socialist party is directed by a democratically controlled intellectual elite. Most akin to the Canadian situation is the role of the elite of the Fabian Society within the British Labour Party. At the pluralistic extreme the various societal elites have no particular political mission. Nonetheless, members of some of the elites will be found willing to give their counsel to the various political parties. Here, we have Weber's *Honoratioren* or Duverger's *notables*.[13] They will not aspire to governmental leadership, and often not even to key party office.

The latter concept, that of elite members as notables, comes closest to the prevailing mode in Canada's major political parties. The role of the notables is not outlined as distinctly as, say, in the Radical Socialist Party of France, where notables help direct the party's electoral effort. But in Canada, members of the non-political elite have been called upon to hold office, direct strategy, and give counsel. For example, officeholders have included M. W. McCutcheon and Eric Kierans of the corporate elite, Louis St. Laurent of the legal elite, and W. L. Mackenzie King, Lester B. Pearson, and J. W. Pickersgill of the bureaucratic elite.

Advice on electoral tactics and on policy formation have come from the communications and intellectual elites, particularly in recent years, in response to the growing professionalization of politics. The role of communications elites within parties will increase as parties spend more of their energies and resources in utilizing the mass media. This in turn will likely have an impact on the role of the party leader, in that greater premium will be placed on his popular appeal, putting him in a position resembling that of a U.S. presidential candidate. There are distinct limits on this movement, however, as the 1963 election demonstrated, when the

THE SHAPING OF POLITICAL PARTIES

stronger party was able to defeat (however inconclusively) the more electable leader.

Utilization of the intellectual elite has never been consistent, but recently concerted attempts to involve intellectuals in party politics have been made by the major parties. Both in order to improve the party's image and the calibre of its policy content, the two parties have arranged "thinkers' conferences": the Liberals, the Kingston Conference of 1960 and the Conservatives, the Fredericton Conference of 1964. Intellectuals have also contributed to elected officeholders. The most successful former academician in Canadian politics has been Mackenzie King. Academic-political types found in the Parliament elected in 1963 included Pauline Jewett, Jean-Luc Pépin, Maurice Lamontagne, and Heath Macquarrie.

The Fabian-type concept of elite impact on party structure was of at least initial importance in the CCF, and elements persist in the NDP. The League for Social Reconstruction (LSR), a Fabian-like group of Canadian intellectuals, performed a service in the CCF similar to that of Plato's or Rousseau's legislator: the LSR helped launch the party without becoming part of its organizational structure. However, one LSR member, F. R. Scott, the celebrated Canadian jurist, later served as national (organizational) chairman of the party. Michael Oliver, a political scientist, served as the first federal president of the NDP. In the early years of the CCF, part of the organizational structure, the CCF clubs (of particular importance in B.C.) took the autonomous place held by the Socialist societies within the British Labour Party.

The integration of the friendly trade union elite into the structure of the CCF became a problem as soon as the CCL committed itself to political action support. In the forties and fifties, a few prominent labour bureaucrats served on the CCF National Executive; but all of these were enrolled in the party as individual, dues-paying members. John Porter reports that, as of the late fifties, not only did nearly all of the leaders of unions formerly with the CCL declare themselves to be CCF supporters, but also nearly one-half of the leaders of unions formerly with the TLC.[14] In view of the meagre electoral support of the party in French Canada, it is remarkable that three-fourths of the leaders of unions affiliated with the *Confédération des Syndicates Nationaux* said that the CCF corresponded better to their ideas than any other party.[15]

Within the Social Credit structure, the Douglasite elite was very strong in the early days of Aberhart. In resisting their more radical Social Credit notions, Aberhart also weakened their position within the Social Credit League. Since the abolition of the Social Credit Board the impact of ideological Social Credit on the party has been weak.

---

[13] Max Weber, "Politics as a Vocation," *From Max Weber*, trs. and eds. H. H. Gerth and C. Wright Mills (New York: Oxford University Press, 1958), pp. 77-128; Duverger, *Political Parties*, Book I, Ch. 3.

[14] John Porter, *The Vertical Mosaic: an Analysis of Social Class and Power in Canada* (Toronto: University of Toronto Press, 1965), pp. 350-51.

[15] *Ibid.*, pp. 363-64.

The System of Government and Party Structure

In Chapter 6 we discussed the impact of the Canadian system of government on parties and the party system. In this section, we will concentrate on the impact of the governmental system on the nature of party structure in Canada. How do the chief functions of Canadian parties—the provision of leadership and decisions—and particularly the structure within which governmental outputs are generated, affect the structure of these parties themselves? We propose to demonstrate the specific effects on party structure of these crucial aspects of the Canadian system of government: the electoral system, the federal system, and the parliamentary system.

THE ELECTORAL SYSTEM   The general election is the arena in which political parties stage the crucial competition for the provision of leadership. The electoral decision, federal as well as provincial, provides the most clear-cut output of the party system, the answer to the question: Who governs? To compete for the successful answer to this question, parties must adapt their structure to the electoral system. The electoral system, according to which the institution of elections in Canada is structured, is, with the exceptions noted in Chapter 6, the single-member-district system. Under this system, the electoral map of Canada (or of a province) is divided into as many constituencies as there are seats, and the candidate who leads the poll in a constituency is elected. The object of the electoral effort of the party is to assure the election of a majority of members, and this object is achieved by the attaining of at least pluralities of the vote in the majority of constituencies.

The rules of the electoral game affect the structure of all parties throughout the nation. The standard local organization of a party is not determined so much by the intensity of local interest, or the magnitude of the local following, as it is by the way in which the electoral map is drawn up. Effect and cause alike of the major-party status of the Liberal and Conservative parties is that they have maintained, through most of the years since Confederation, federal constituency associations throughout Canada. The failure of the Conservative Party to maintain functioning constituency associations in much of Quebec is, at present, a major factor in rendering unequal competitive conditions between the two major parties.

There is a public electoral jurisdiction below the constituency—the poll. This is the area comprising the population voting in one polling place. Any party contesting a constituency is represented, on election day, at every polling place. The average number of voters residing in a poll is about 200, and the average number of polls in a federal constituency is also about 200. (The actual number tends to vary with the size of the constituency.) Parties need not be represented at the polling place on election day by permanent poll organizations, nor do such normally exist. Most Canadian constituency party organizations are thus not structured as minutely as are electoral districts in the United States, where the traditions of patronage and the larger size of districts have continued widespread precinct (i.e., poll) organization, especially in urban areas. In Canada there has been more significant poll organization in rural areas. This condition was found for the major parties in Ontario by the research assistants of R. MacGregor Dawson.[16] In the heyday of the Saskatchewan CCF, the party had viable permanent organizations in many polls of rural provincial constituencies. While these poll organizations consisted of dues-paying party members, such poll organization as is found in the major parties consists normally of people who have been assigned to the task of keeping in touch with friendly voters, and of getting them to vote on election day. Brian Land describes in some detail the poll organizations of the major parties during a crucial constituency campaign.[17]

The aspect of party structure most directly affected by the electoral system is the constituency association. Its importance is brought out in Dawson's description, applicable directly but not solely to the riding associations of the major parties in Ontario:

Its nominating convention is by far the party's most vital representative body: it has the major responsibility for securing the election of its nominees; its vigilance is in large measure essential to secure activity in the polling subdivision, especially in such formal matters as revision of voters' lists; it serves directly or through local bodies as a dispenser of patronage; it transmits opinions, suggestions, and complaints from the party members to the elected representative in Parliament or in the Legislative Assembly.[18]

We are concerned here primarily with the first three functions listed by Dawson—nomination, election, and enumeration—which we will discuss briefly in reverse order.

While public enumeration of voters in Canada does not evoke as much party activity as does personal voting registration in the United States, the constituency associations assist in the preparation and revision of voters' lists. The parties that placed first and second in the last federal election compile the voters' list in that particular constituency. This is an example of a public function vested in the party at the constituency level.

In the age of mass communication, the strategic aspects of election campaigns are waged far above the constituency level, but the tactical importance of the campaign in the constituency continues unabated. It is here that the individual candidate stands for election, and it is here that the voters must, in the last analysis, be persuaded to go to the polls; it is here then, that the individual scores are achieved, the sum total of which

[16] Robert MacGregor Dawson, *The Government of Canada*, 3rd ed. (Toronto: University of Toronto Press, 1957), pp. 518.

[17] Brian Land, *Eglinton: the Election Study of a Federal Constituency* (Toronto: Peter Martin Associates, 1965), pp. 64-69, 74-78.

[18] Dawson, *The Government of Canada*, 3rd ed., p. 520. See also 4th ed., p. 480.

determines electoral victory. These facts of electoral life impel all parties to maintain at least some organization in all constituencies from which they seek legislative seats.

Possibly the most crucial demand made by the single-member-district electoral system on a party's constituency association is the nomination of the candidate. It is here that the party structure at the constituency level must be ready to play its essential role in the provision of leadership. The voters in a general election have a choice only from among candidates whom the constituency parties have put forward. (Independents, candidates without party nomination, have been extremely rare in recent elections.) In cases where the party has any strength at all in the particular constituency, a delegate convention is normally held to nominate the candidate. Even sitting members normally require renomination by such a convention. Exceptions are sufficiently notorious as to merit the special mention given to instances in which the Taschereau regime in Quebec and subsequent Liberal organizations up to 1960, refused to hold nominating conventions and simply assumed the renomination of sitting members.[19]

These functions of the constituency association may take only several weeks out of the year, but they do require that a party cadre be maintained on a permanent basis. In the major parties, where these electoral functions are paramount among local party functions, such cadres essentially form what we might call the local party. Only in parties with a mission, where there is call for an actual or potential mass membership, like the CCF/NDP and to some extent Social Credit, is there a necessity for a more elaborate constituency party structure.

THE FEDERAL SYSTEM   The structure of Canadian parties is profoundly affected by Canada's federal system. The result is that, like parties in other federal systems, parties in Canada must maintain a multiple structure, with a component for each jurisdiction in which they compete. This makes for one federal and ten provincial structures in the Liberal and Conservative parties. The NDP maintains a federal structure and provincial structures everywhere except in New Brunswick, Prince Edward Island, and Newfoundland. Social Credit has a federal structure and provincial structures everywhere except in Nova Scotia, Prince Edward Island, and Newfoundland.

Because there are invariably more provincial than federal constituencies, parties are forced to maintain two sets of constituency associations. The discrepancy between the two sets of constituency associations is smallest in Ontario, and there, a number of federal and provincial constituencies were identical, at least prior to the redistribution of 1965-66.

It would not be farfetched to assert that a principle of cooperative federalism obtains in Canadian party structure. It is certain that there is no subordination of provincial to federal (or rather national) party structure. The high degree of autonomy of the provinces is reflected in the high degree of autonomy of the provincial party structure. This autonomy was enjoyed even during the brief periods in which the Canadian constitutional system appeared to tilt toward federal supremacy.

The autonomy of the various provincial party structures is not only a function of the nature of Canadian federalism; it is also a function of the distinctive nature of the eleven governments of Canada. The national party structure is designed to help provide leaders and decisions in Ottawa; the provincial party structures help to perform these functions in the various provincial governments.

As a result, we find in all parties (except the Communist Party, the weakness of which makes the exception unimportant) provincial structures that differ from province to province, that are constituted autonomously, and that are not in a hierarchic relationship to the national party structure. The National Liberal Federation, the National Progressive Conservative Association, the national organization of the Social Credit Party, and even the national organization of the more compulsively structured NDP, are agencies that coordinate rather than integrate parties on a nation-wide scale. This holds true even at the time of a federal election campaign. Like the federations of the United States and Australia, the Canadian federation is served by party structures that are highly peripheralized.

The relative strength of a party in a province affects the relative power position of the provincial structure within the party's organization. Because Social Credit is more important in Alberta than nationally, its provincial structure far outweighs its national structure in significance. In Quebec, during the Duplessis regime, the federal Liberal party structure became much more important than the provincial structure. With the "Quiet Revolution" and the accession of Lesage, the importance of the provincial Liberals increased. Lacking sympathy with the personnel, aims, and methods of the federal Liberals in Quebec, they obtained complete structural separation from them. This separation in turn reflected the view, held by most provincial Liberals in Quebec, that Quebec is to enjoy a particular status within Confederation.

THE PARLIAMENTARY SYSTEM Party structure is affected by the fact that the Conservative and Liberal parties developed initially in order to facilitate the workings of the developing system of responsible government. Much of their initial development took place in the early parliaments and cabinets; it was, as Ranney and Kendall call it, intra-governmental.[20] A widening suffrage required a more complex organization. As long as the Liberal Party was primarily a grouping of parliamentarians, as it was under Mackenzie and Blake, it was hard put to compete with Macdonald's Conservatives. Only the development of a strong electoral—according to Ranney and Kendall, extra-governmental—organization under Laurier facilitated competition with the Conservatives. They in turn had to improve their own electoral organization in competing with the Liberals.

---

[19] *Ibid.*, 3rd ed., p. 522 n.

[20] Austin Ranney and Willmoore Kendall, *Democracy and the American Party System* (New York: Harcourt, Brace and Company, Inc., 1956), Ch. 5.

The origins of the Progressives, the CCF/NDP, and Social Credit, were quite different from those of the two "old" parties. They faced an existing, mature two-party system, operating a system of parliamentary government. Their origins were extra-governmental. They created an electoral party structure to enable them to establish themselves within the governmental structure, an objective they could achieve only by displacing, through election, some of the Liberals and Conservatives who were then preempting the parliamentary seats. Once they elected members to Parliaments, they also acquired an intra-governmental party structure.

It would be foolish to claim that a clear division of function exists between a party's intra- and extra-governmental structures. Yet there is enough difference in functions to warrant a brief explanation of the two aspects of party structure.

The intra-governmental aspects of party structure in a parliamentary democracy are those involving elected legislative personnel: the legislative caucuses of the various parties, the Cabinet, and, wherever it exists, the opposition's shadow cabinet. The extra-governmental aspects of party structure include constituency, provincial, and national associations, committees, conventions, and headquarters. Both aspects deal with the provision of leadership and decisions. However, the intra-governmental structure is primarily concerned with decisions. It is here that the party engages in day-to-day consideration of policy matters, either as the Government, the principal opposition, or as a minor party. Questions of leadership do not come up directly; however, the behaviour of individuals as members of the caucus may affect their eventual selection as leaders. The extra-governmental structure, on the other hand, is primarily concerned with leadership. Nominations for legislative seats, attempts to elect those nominated, and the selection of the party leader (by a leadership convention) all take place here. Matters relating to policy decisions do come up from time to time in the committee and convention structure (especially in the CCF/NDP), and more regularly in the research work done at party headquarters.

The impact of the parliamentary system tends to give a dominant position to the intra-governmental parts of the party structure. The party leader, though more directly part of the intra-governmental structure, is in charge of both aspects of the structure. This is most clearly the case in the Conservative Party.[21] In times of actual stress, the intra-governmental position of the leader puts him at a great advantage. This was illustrated dramatically when John Diefenbaker, in early 1965, maintained his position as leader of the Conservative Party. He did so by means of his leadership of the caucus, and in the face of opposition from the top echelon of the extra-governmental structure.

Extra-governmental elements are, as we might expect, strongest when a tradition of lay participation in politics is combined with lack of experience in government. The strength of such elements was shown in the early days of the CCF Government in Saskatchewan, and, to a lesser extent,

THE SHAPING OF POLITICAL PARTIES

in the Social Credit Government in Alberta. Thirty years' experience in government has now resulted in firm intra-governmental control within the Alberta Social Credit Party. We can generalize that any experience in government, and even in the position of the principal opposition, aids the power position of the intra-governmental party structure.

The Resulting Party Structure

The system of government has a greater influence on the actual structure of Canadian parties than any other factor. On the national level of organization, federalism is of paramount importance; to a notable degree, the national organizations of all three truly nation-wide parties—Liberal, Conservative, and New Democratic—are federations. The National Liberal Federation is the only one that recognizes this in its name, however; the national organization of the Conservatives is called National Progressive Conservative Association. In each of these parties, the national party structure includes a meeting or convention, a council, an executive, table officers, and a central party bureaucracy.[22]

The meeting, called "General Annual Meeting" by the Conservatives, "Convention" by the Liberals, and "Federal Convention" by the NDP, is as a rule held annually by the Conservatives, biennially by the Liberals, and at regular biennial intervals by the NDP. In the two major parties, the basis of representation at the national meeting is similar. The meeting of both parties includes all Senators, Members of Commons, and defeated candidates for the House. It also includes equal representation from each federal constituency association—six in the case of the Liberals, two in the case of the Conservatives. Both parties seat (accord convention seats with voting power) representatives-at-large from the provinces—the Conservatives more than the Liberals—including representative women and young people. The Conservatives seat all of their provincial legislators; in the case of the Liberals, provincial legislators and defeated candidates select one-fourth from their midst. Conservatives, but not Liberals, seat all members of their national council, called the Executive Officers. The basis of representation of Liberal meetings applies also to national leadership conventions of the Liberal Party.

In the make-up of the NDP federal convention, two additional factors are considered: the importance of individual dues-paying members, and the fact of group affiliation. Because of the former, federal constituencies are represented, not proportionately according to party members, but along a sliding scale. Affiliated organizations are entitled to representation in their own right, on a scale of about one-tenth of the representation of individual members. The NDP national convention includes all national council members; beyond this, there is no special provision for

---

[21] John Meisel, *The Canadian General Election of 1957* (Toronto: University of Toronto Press, 1962), p. 73.

[22] Most of the data in this section are derived from the national (federal) constitutions of the respective parties.

provincial representation. Of NDP legislators, only elected federal members are seated in their own right, not defeated candidates nor provincial legislators.

In all three parties, the national councils have special functions related to intraparty federal-provincial relations. Therefore, the federal principle of representation is pronouncedly applied in all these bodies, with equal-number representatives of the provinces making up the bulk of the members. The National Council of the Liberal Party meets approximately every second year and is made up of eleven representatives from each province (among them the provincial leader, women, and youths), ten representatives of the federal caucus, and about thirty others, including the leader and the table officers (such officials as president, vice-president (s), secretary, treasurer). The council of the Conservatives, called the Executive Officers of the National Association, meets twice yearly, with the low quorum of twenty. In this body, each province has eight representatives, among them the provincial leader, a woman, a youth, and a student; the caucus has about thirty representatives: two members (if necessary, defeated candidates) from each province, one from each territory, and one Senator from each province which has one. There are about thirty other members, again including the leader and the table officers. In the Federal Council of the NDP, each province has five representatives, including the provincial leader. There are two representatives of the federal caucus, and about thirty others, including the federal officers.

Each national party organization has an executive committee, which can be convened easily. The membership totals about twenty, except in the Conservative Party, where it is smaller. Only the Liberals have all provinces represented in this body.

The number of national table officers varies. The Liberals have only four: president, two vice-presidents, and secretary-treasurer. The Conservatives do not list theirs specifically, but they include president, three vice-presidents, secretary, treasurer, the Leader, and the National Director. The listed table officers of the NDP are, in addition to the leader, president and associate president, five vice-presidents, treasurer, secretary and associate secretary.

Each party retains a small professional staff and some office help at its national (or, in case of the NDP, federal) headquarters in Ottawa. These Ottawa offices are headed by the National Organizer in the Liberal Party, by the National Director in the Conservative Party, and by the Federal Secretary in the NDP. Their activities are conducted under the over-all direction of the table officers in the case of the Liberals and the NDP, and of the National Leader in the case of the Conservatives.

At the provincial level, party organization coordinates both federal and provincial campaigns, and services the party's contingent in the provincial legislature. This crucial level of the party structure, therefore, is also influenced by the system of government; in this case, by its electoral and parliamentary aspects.

THE SHAPING OF POLITICAL PARTIES

Provincial party structure is influenced by the party's notion of membership. The NDP has members because it follows the originally socialist tradition of involving the maximum number of individuals in a day-to-day identification with the movement, and because memberships are an important source of finances. The number of members is important in establishing the amount of influence constituency associations are to have in the provincial party. In the provincial Liberal and Conservative parties, the object is simply to conduct a campaign in all constituencies, and to have all constituencies represented in the party's councils. Therefore, constituencies are represented equally and the device of delegate members is used. Provincial associations, which means principally their annual meetings, are made up of what is normally an equal number of delegate members from every constituency. There are other, ordinary members in these parties who are entitled to attend meetings and, while they are not entitled to vote, they are on occasion in a position to influence the proceedings. They may be sources of financial support, or of volunteer labour. However, there is nothing about the Liberal and Conservative parties, as presently constituted, that provides a regularized base of influence for these private members.

The provincial structures of the major parties have annual meetings of delegate members, executive committees, and table officers. They may also have wider executive councils. NDP provincial structures, on the other hand, have annual provincial conventions, with the dues-paying members normally represented proportionally and provincial councils representing the constituencies, executives, and table officers. The three parties maintain small bureaucracies in their respective provincial offices. These offices tend to be more elaborate in provinces in which the respective parties have strong representation in the legislature.

Below the provincial level, there may be, as with the Ontario Conservatives, district associations, but normally there is no intervening level between province and constituency. Provincial constituency associations, in all parties and provinces, show the most signs of life during election time, when they are charged with nominating the candidate and with campaign functions.[23] In periods between elections, constituency associations do little or nothing, and many have difficulty getting people together for the frequently mandatory annual constituency association meeting. In the early years of the CCF, and primarily in its Saskatchewan section, some vital party life took place in the constituency associations, but by now intensive local activity within the NDP has become extremely rare.

We have been very general and schematic in our description of actual party structure. There are of course regional, provincial, urban-rural, and local differences in a country as vast as Canada, but a detailed discussion of these goes beyond the scope of this volume.

---

[23] These aspects will be discussed in Chapter 8.

CONSEQUENCES FOR POLICIES, PROGRAMS, IDEOLOGIES

Social Structure and Party Pragmatism

The pragmatism of Canadian politics has been affirmed by most of the observers and analysts of Canada's political system. Two of the leading analysts, R. M. Dawson and J. A. Corry, use different approaches to affirm this pragmatism: Dawson employs the traditional institutional approach,[24] centring on the institution of the Cabinet, while Corry's approach borders on the behavioural in his consideration of Canadian interests and opinions.[25] Yet this pragmatism needs a bit of bolstering up, especially as a recent monumental study of Canadian society[26] (a) questions its existence and (b) denies, at any rate, its desirability.

This book cannot come to grips with (b). It is not our task to tell the Canadian people what to want. This does not mean that we do not care whether Canada is a democracy or a dictatorship, whether or not Canadians enjoy civil rights and liberties, whether or not the rule of law reigns in the land, and whether or not the political system takes care of the needs of Canadian society. But it is incumbent on us to come to grips with (a), whether or not Canadian politics is in fact pragmatic politics. In a way, this entire volume presents evidence to affirm the question. We do not view Canadian politics as a second-string game that is being played while the real decisions affecting the society are being made behind closed doors in corporate boardrooms. We conclude rather that the economic elite is *one* of the shaping forces of Canadian politics, and that the real decisions are made within the governmental structure. We feel also that it is beyond proof that something other than pragmatic politics—e.g., a system in which a progressive party would oppose a conservative one—would give Canada more dynamic politics, mobilizing better the creative energies of Canadian society and therefore, presumably, doing more to meet Canada's needs.[27]

It should be obvious by now that we do not feel that Canada's political system distorts her social structure. We expect that outputs issuing from the governmental structure will tend to satisfy articulated demands and, hopefully, real needs of our society, provided there is sufficient consensus to bridge the gulf between British and French Canada. But we will address ourselves to these questions in Chapter 11.

What then is the impact of Canada's social structure on party policies, programs, and ideology? Let us take policies and programs first. Canada is a new, diversified, geographically far extended, and highly mobile nation. Unlike the United States, which is similar though less diversified, Canada did not emerge out of a deliberate wrenching away from colonial status nor did it start on the road to nationhood with a set of guiding principles. Despite these differences with its southern neighbour, Canadian governmental outputs resembled those of the U.S. Matching the latter's laissez faire government, Canadian society appeared to be largely satisfied with minimal governmental outputs in the half-century following Confederation. Until the Great Depression, these minimal outputs continued to satisfy most of the industrial elements of the social structure, including most of the non-owners. Even during the Depression, welfare demands were articulated less strongly than in most industrialized nations. The war put Canda back to work, and the ensuing prosperity has kept her at work ever since. The non-prosperous Atlantic provinces have kept themselves in equilibrium, in part, by losing some of the most demanding elements of the population through migration. Whether primarily because of prosperity, or because of the vast population changes (especially through immigration), the industrial sections of post-war Canada have to a large degree been satisfied by minimum welfare outputs, such as family allowances and a pension policy which only recently went beyond the embryonic stage.

Much of the social system, then, has demanded little in the way of policy or program. To what demands there have been from the industrial sector, the policy responses of the major parties have been similar. In the early sixties, both stood for a moderate extension of welfare, the Progressive Conservatives taking the first initiative in health, the Liberals in pensions; both have paid lip service to the need for more and better education (the federal system hardly permits them to do more), and both have stood for further economic development.

Some demands have strained the capacities of the major parties to the breaking point. These have been of a regional-ethnic nature and have related both to domestic and foreign policy. The Manitoba School crisis of the 1890's and the conscription crisis of 1917 are the leading examples. But in recent decades the conciliatory policies of the Liberal leadership have avoided extreme strains along regional-ethnic lines. Major examples are the handling of the conscription issue during the Second World War, the appointment of the Royal Commission on Bilingualism and Biculturalism, and the accommodation of various demands arising from the "Quiet Revolution" in Quebec.

Other demands of a pressing nature have come from western agriculture. As we pointed out in Chapter 3, the development of minor parties in the West—United Farmers, Progressives, Social Credit, and CCF—came about through dissatisfaction with the traditional parties, which were held to be dominated by eastern urban and financial interests. If these minor parties have something in common, it has been a concern for forming policies and programs that would be especially attuned to the problems of western agriculture. It is significant that the Conservative Party under the leadership of John Diefenbaker, and particularly when Alvin Hamilton was Minister of Agriculture, also followed policies stemming from the traditions of western populism.

The North American political tradition on the whole has been one of

---

[24] Dawson, *The Government of Canada*, 3rd and 4th eds.

[25] J. A. Corry and J. E. Hodgetts, *Democratic Government and Politics*, 3rd ed. (Toronto: University of Toronto Press, 1959).

[26] Porter, *The Vertical Mosaic*, especially Ch. 12.

[27] *Ibid.* p. 377.

little ideology; in Canada where, unlike in the U.S., there have been significant minor parties to drain off ideology from the major ones, these major parties have been less ideological than their counterparts to the south. It could be maintained that the major parties have stood for democracy and for competitive enterprise. However, they have expressly emphasized only the latter and this only when they were opposed by the real or imagined socialist ideology of the CCF/NDP.

The Canadian attempt to identify socialism with an organized political party has certainly been stronger than in the U.S. When the CCF was founded, urban socialists from British Columbia, Alberta, and Manitoba, agrarian socialists from Saskatchewan and Alberta, and some socialist ideologists from eastern centres combined to give the party a socialist program. The party maintained this program for twenty-three years, and even now segments of the party, especially on the Pacific Coast, do not mind being called socialist. Yet it would be gross exaggeration, if not falsification, to call the present NDP a socialist ideological force. The de-ideologization of a party that was never prominently ideological is closely related to its social composition. There never were many socialists among workers supporting the CCF—much of this is due to the influence o business unionism in the U.S., even in the former C.I.O. unions. Regarding farmers in the CCF, agrarian socialism weakened as farms became more part of a consumer-oriented society, and as farmers became more prosperous. The leaven of ideological socialists was not strong enough to maintain ideology as a major force in the NDP, with the possible exception of the British Columbia section. If there is ideology in the party in the mid-sixties, it is a mixture of a welfarism not much stronger than that advocated by labour elements in the major parties, and of a neutralism (far from universal), consisting primarily of skepticism toward U.S. foreign policy.

Our discussion of social structure and ideology can end here: there is not enough ideology in present-day Social Credit and not enough social structure in the Communist Party. Ideology in French-Canadian Liberalism is too closely connected with ethnicity to permit generalizations.

Implications of Group Support

POLICIES AND PROGRAMS   The consequences of group support for party policies and programs depend primarily on two factors, (a) the nature of the demands of the group supporting the party, and (b) the nature of the party's focus of appeal. With respect to focus of appeal, parties range from those oriented toward principle (whether based on organized interest groups, issues, ideology, or any combination of these) to those oriented primarily toward electoral success. The critical questions concerning demands are whether the group voices these directly or indirectly, and whether the demands are overt or covert. When the demand is voiced directly, it also voiced overtly; the voiced and the real demand are one and the same. For instance, a trade union congress demanding a higher minimum wage really wants a higher minimum wage. When the demand is voiced indirectly, the demand voiced may not be the real one. For instance, an organized interest group of manufacturers using some new process may be interested in a franchise. In private dealings with office-holders or candidates of a party, they will voice their real demand, i.e., the franchise. Publicly, however, they will state their demand not in terms of a franchise, which they have reason to believe is unpopular, but rather in terms of the desirability of fostering industries venturing in new directions. Here then, the covert, not the overt demand, is the real one.

From the foregoing it appears that the raising of direct demands by a group is related to the expected popularity of such demands. It is related also to the internal structure of the group. Where we find a large number of people involved directly in the activity of the group, we can expect the group to come forward with direct demands. A trade union, because it has a large dues-paying membership, and many members involved in such activities as strike ballots and the election of officers, is likely to be such a group. Some unions show a very intensive involvement of members.[28] Many of the farmers' groups in the twenties and thirties had highly intensive involvement of members which resulted in the voicing of many direct, overt policy demands. On the other hand, the specialized trade association that brings forth indirect demands does not have a large, directly involved membership. Somewhere between the type of group just mentioned and groups with a large, involved membership are the Canadian Chamber of Commerce with its large, though not necessarily much involved, membership, and the Canadian Medical Association, with a relatively small, but rather highly involved, membership. We would expect such groups to raise demands that are less direct than those raised by large-membership trade unions (or by some of the farm groups of an earlier generation), but more direct than those of a specialized trade association seeking favoured treatment.

When a group raising direct, overt demands deals with a party oriented toward principle, the demands will find a formal place in the party's program. An example here would be a trade union's stand for an increase in the minimum wage placed in the program of the NDP. Here, the relationship would probably lead to the following course of action: the program item would be worked out formally by a trade union (or a trade union congress), and then be adopted formally by the party's convention (or, between annual or biennial conventions, by its council or executive). On either side, group as well as party, the shaping of the particular program item would involve elites responsible to a relatively large and involved membership, and this responsibility would tend to make the elites communicate to the members, and also to the public at large, the nature of the program item, and possibly also the means that were employed in its adoption.

At the other extreme, we have program formation when a group with

---

[28] S. M. Lipset, M. Trow, and J. S. Coleman, *Union Democracy* (Glencoe, Ill.: The Free Press, 1956).

indirect demands interacts with a party oriented primarily toward electoral success. Here we take for an example the relationship between private health insurers and the governing Conservative Party in Ontario, in the period prior to the unveiling of a compulsory medicare scheme by the Pearson Government. Surely, the Robarts Government knew that those benefiting from compulsory health insurance have more votes than the stockholders and discretionary employees of the private insurance companies. Yet, in adopting a position preferring voluntary coverage under a provincial health scheme, the Robarts Government took into consideration not only the covert, direct pressures from a small group, possible financial enticements by the group, and its own predisposition to favour private over public enterprise. But the private insurers also brought to bear overt, indirect pressures the tenor of which was the maintenance of freedom of choice by the patient, and the maintenance of the private relationship between patient and physician. Pressures from the private insurers were no doubt accompanied by messages from other business interests in the province, indicating apprehension lest one member of the business community be sacrificed to a public policy. The electoral orientation of the Ontario Conservatives permitted the Government to fashion its stand on health insurance without submitting a formal proposal to a policy-making body of the party meeting in public. Because of the interest in compulsory health insurance shown by the federal government, it is unlikely that the Robarts Government will have to face the voters on the basis of having put into operation a private health insurance scheme. Should it have had to do so, it would have justified the voluntary scheme not by the admission that it had accommodated the direct demand of protecting private profit-making insurers, but probably by a claim that it was preserving freedom of choice regarding health insurance on the part of the general public.

The relationship between groups that raise direct demands and electoral-success-oriented parties has been observed on many occasions in the United States, where both parties are oriented toward electoral success, and where they fashion their platforms every four years. A group, especially where its leaders are held responsible to the members, makes a formal representation to the party body charged with drawing up the election platform. The electoral-success-oriented party is free to determine the degree of attention it will give to its platform planks during the ensuing electoral campaign, or indeed during its future performance. The group-party relationship is similar to the one that prevailed in past decades between Canadian trade union congresses and governing parties, when the annual presentation of demands by the congress to the Cabinet—"hat in hand," as militant unionists mockingly called it—was the principal contact between the labour congresses and the governing party.

Principle-oriented parties have few dealings with groups that raise indirect demands. The CCF/NDP has derided such groups as "special interests," who find accommodation of their covert demands by the major parties, but not (or so at least they claim) by themselves.

THE SHAPING OF POLITICAL PARTIES

Much too little is known about the contact with electoral-success-oriented parties by the major groups, such as the Canadian Chamber of Commerce, the Canadian Manufacturers' Association, and the Canadian Medical Association, who fall in the middle range of our demand dimension. We may assume, however, that such contacts are, if not continuous, then at least frequent, and that their impact on party policy is important. In information made public or divulged privately, such groups frequently refer to their contacts with Cabinet Ministers, but rarely with non-governmental party agencies.

IDEOLOGY In Canada a party's group support has little influence on ideology. The major parties are generally committed to constitutional democracy and to the free enterprise system. (The latter commitment, while not universal, has never been openly attacked by spokesmen of either party.) They do not accommodate anti-democratic groups, and such collectivist pressures as come from labour and welfare groups (and now and then from business groups requiring special protection) are watched by the relevant party bodies with an eye to at least preventing the demolition of an essentially competitive economic system.

Since the late fifties, the major parties have had to face the quasi-ideological problem of the ethnic nature of Canadian society. But even here no permanent cleavage appears to be developing. The Liberals have been more receptive to French-Canadian demands for the recognition of biculturalism, while the Conservatives have been more susceptible to pressures from Anglo-Canadian interests. This susceptibility was apparent during the flag debate of 1964.

Such ideological stands as are still taken by the NDP and Social Credit are due largely to tradition. In the past, groups like the League for Social Reconstruction and the Socialist Party of British Columbia (technically a party itself) have done their part in trying to keep the CCF socialist. On the Social Credit side, the Social Credit League was the vessel of Major Douglas' ideology until the early days of the Manning Government in Alberta. Today, the ideological influence of Social Credit groups is largely restricted to provinces in which the party is unimportant.

The political involvement of Canadian intellectuals is of relatively recent origin. In addition, it is, as John Porter points out, more an involvement with the administrative bureaucracy than with political parties.[29] Even the recent activities of intellectuals with the major parties has been organizational and programmatic rather than ideological. There is a trend toward the employment of intellectuals in the formulation of campaign strategy and of party strategy in general. It is too early to tell whether the major parties' "thinkers' conferences" will lead to an increased leaning on intellectuals in the formulation of policies. Ideological contributions of intellectuals to any party have been slim, certainly since the League for Social Reconstruction helped the young CCF

---

[29] Porter, *The Vertical Mosaic*, pp. 503-4.

draft the Regina Manifesto of 1933. Those who make programmatic contributions to parties today may fail to contribute ideologically for the simple reason that to them a non-pragmatic view of Canadian politics does not make sense.

The Mass Media

In French Canada, the press has given some ideological as well as programmatic leadership. The English-Canadian press has done less, with the possible exception of the *Globe and Mail* and such personages as George Brown of the *Globe* and J. W. Dafoe of the *Free Press*. Editorially, the major papers, whether singly or chain-owned, have at times shifted support from one major party to the other, without having any great influence on party policy anywhere. The press is useful occasionally in turning on alleged maladministration; in the early 1960's, it did so in the case of Hal Banks, the alleged labour racketeer, and Lucien Rivard, the convicted dope smuggler.

Outside of the press, media are not of great importance policywise; most are American-owned or influenced. Possible exceptions are the Canadian-owned periodicals, with *Maclean's* seeing itself as a journal with the mission of integrating the Canadian nation. The CBC is, of course, government-operated; understandably, it is under attack whenever it is even so much as alleged to interfere in "politics." It is noteworthy that, in minor matters, the CBC's now defunct public affairs program "This Hour Has Seven Days" had occasionally played the role of an ombudsman, seeking to protect individuals from acts of maladministration. These episodes, however, were not meant to have partisan significance.

The System of Government

THE PARLIAMENTARY SYSTEM   In his classic treatment of parliamentary democracy, Sir Ernest Barker presents it as a discussion process *par excellence*.[30] Some parliamentary democracies have bred more fruitful discussion that others, and even the Mother of Parliaments had difficulty keeping discussion within bounds during the Irish Question. But the parliaments of Canada, and especially the Parliament in Ottawa, have by and large served to channel and moderate the discourse between the parties. This channeling of discussion, the permitting of alternate, equal debate under what has at best been an impartial Speaker, but hardly ever an avowedly partisan one—Mr. Speaker Beaudoin's partisan behaviour in 1956 was a notable exception—may well be the most significant impact of the parliamentary system on party policies and programs. Ideally at least, the process assures that policy decisions are reached only after some debate, and that an invariably victorious Government will present only such policies as can stand up to oral controversy.

This applies to all parties with parliamentary representation. But the various positions occupied by parties in the parliamentary system—Government, Opposition, and minor parties—each have unique influences on a party's policies and programs.

Under a parliamentary system, many of the policy proposals in the electoral program of the victorious party will be turned into public policy. If a party has any chance at all of winning an election, it fashions its electoral program not only with a view to winning votes, but also with a view to the realizability of the proposed policies. Coming up with realizable policies, or promising continuation of existing policies (by the Government), or "better" administration, or a different style in the implementation of existing policies (by the Opposition), have all been more significant in Canadian electoral history than the clash of opposing issues. The election of 1911 was an exception, when the Opposition was known to be diametrically opposed to the Government on the major issues of reciprocity with the United States, and the support of the Imperial navy. A more normal campaign in regard to issues was 1957. In his analysis of that election, John Meisel lists eight issues: fiscal policy, agriculture, trade, development, social welfare, dominion-provincial relations, foreign policy, and Parliament.[31] Only the latter was a sharp issue, stemming from the Liberals' riding roughshod over the Opposition concerning the Defence Production Act of 1955, and especially in the pipeline debate of 1956. Even here, the issue was sharp only on the Opposition side, with the Government trying to ignore it. None of the other issues seemed clear-cut even at the time. In retrospect, the Conservative attacks on St. Laurent's censure of British and French action in the Suez crisis, and on the centralizing tendencies of the St. Laurent Government, seem particularly artificial. That agriculture was an issue between the parties could be noticed only when the portfolio was taken over by Alvin Hamilton, in late 1960.

In general, a party seriously aspiring to form the federal government will either restrict itself to policy issues that are capable of realization by its ministers and the civil service, or it will at least restrict itself to such policies once it forms the government. As far as the winning party goes, and this appears true for all recent elections, the main reason for its winning was not that it had one or more winning issues, but that its leaders appeared to the marginal voters to be more likely to give competent government to Canada. This certainly helps to account for the Liberal victory in 1963, the heavy Liberal gains in 1962, the Conservative sweep in 1958, the Conservative victory in 1957, and the Liberal victories in the five preceding elections.

Once in the Government, the policies of either party are limited by the realities of government, as these are perceived by the bureaucracy. An alleged nexus between the civil service in Ottawa and the Liberal Party was frequently used by Conservatives as an alibi for the relatively low

---

[30] Ernest Barker, *Reflections on Government* (London: Oxford University Press, 1942), pp. 36-72.

[31] Meisel, *The Canadian General Election of 1957*, pp. 45-61.

legislative output issuing from their vast parliamentary majority of 1958-62.

The Opposition has much of the area of its policy stands, and sometimes even their nature, determined by the Government. As opposition in Ottawa has always been of an office-seeking kind, and never an opposition of principle, the main job of the Opposition between elections has been simply to oppose—to oppose policies or, more often, details of policies brought down as legislation, and to oppose the administration of established policy. In recent years, unduly strong opposition to legislation brought in by the Government has even been tarred with the brush of obstruction. This occurred in regard to the Conservatives' opposition to C. D. Howe's pipeline bill, and especially to Mr. Diefenbaker's stand against the Maple Leaf flag. It appears as though Canada shares with other parliamentary democracies a recent feeling that opposition for the sake of opposition should be de-emphasized. We are not aware of a single major instance in recent years in which the Opposition (Liberal or Conservative) developed, between elections, an entirely new policy stand and introduced it as a bill or resolution in Parliament.

If minor parties in Ottawa have been freer in the selection of policy stands than the Opposition, this may be due more to the nature of these parties than to their less "responsible" position within the parliamentary system. No third party has ever entered a general election with the serious expectation of winning, or even of achieving second place (though the Progressives actually did so in 1921). Third parties, therefore, have not been under an injunction to propose realizable policies in their election programs. Even so, the parliamentary system has had a moderating influence on the programs of all serious competitors in Canadian general elections. The CCF was committed to a socialist manifesto from 1933 to 1956. Yet, its election program for 1949 contained a provision for the nationalization of chartered banks only on the insistence of the 1948 National Convention,[32] while the 1953 program did not mention any outright socialist measure. Similarly, recent Social Credit programs have not contained any of Major Douglas' ideology.

Thus, the pragmatic pull of the parliamentary system—along with the North American environment—has influenced the program and policy stands not only of the two major, electoral-oriented parties, but also of such minor parties as have been able to obtain seats. The system has contributed to discourage these parties from asserting such ideological principles as they may have.

That this pragmatic effect of the parliamentary system is not due simply to the dominance of two pragmatic parties in Ottawa can be ascertained by a brief look at the provinces. Here, Social Credit has governed two provinces (Alberta and British Columbia) for a total of over forty years, the CCF has governed Saskatchewan for twenty years, and the Union Nationale reached its twentieth year of governing Quebec in 1967. Social Credit and the CCF entered politics with an ideological commitment. It would be foolhardy to ascribe the pragmatic behaviour of the governments of these parties to the parliamentary system alone. However, in the first decade of Social Credit rule in Alberta, and throughout the CCF rule in Saskatchewan, the membership organization of the parties propagated far-reaching applications of ideology to policy, while the governments by the same party almost invariably took a pragmatic position in discussing policy within the party structure, and in their governmental behaviour. The CCF Government's medicare position in 1962 is hardly an exception, as the interest-group opposition to the policy was at least as ideologically based as the policy itself.

THE FEDERAL SYSTEM Traditionally, the Cabinet, the focus of policy making, has had representation from all or most of the provinces. The chief purpose of this arrangement is to give the provinces a voice in the policies and program of the governing party. Electoral programs of both major parties have traditionally been fashioned by bodies with representatives from the various provinces, again safeguarding provincial interests. The front bench of the Opposition, where the day-to-day Opposition policy is made, also has wide provincial representation. Yet the provinces have not always felt that they have had all the impact they wanted on policy, in either government or opposition party.

Several general elections were fought by one major party in the interest of a stronger provincial voice in national affairs. In salient instances, the party raising the issue won the election and replaced the Government. This occurred in 1896, when one of the main issues was the insufficient accommodation of the interests of Ontario as viewed by its Liberal Government. 1921 brought to the fore regional and provinical interests of the Western prairies. The party least mindful of these interests, the Conservative Party, finished a poor third. The 1957 campaign was waged and won by the Conservatives, with the issues including more accommodation of provincial demands; the election possibly had a long-range effect on policies through the gradual acceleration of these demands. In 1963, when the Liberals campaigned in part for a stronger position in Confederation for Quebec, they returned to office once again. Their victory led to a significant accommodation of Quebec policy demands by Ottawa. Many of these accommodations were arrived at in the now fashionable quasi-diplomatic dealings between the federal government and the provinces, but there has also been some legislation, such as the renaming of TCA to Air Canada and the adoption of the Maple Leaf flag, and there have been administrative directives, such as the introduction of more bilingualism into the civil service. It is interesting to note that, as of 1966, the Conservative Opposition is not espousing any policies demanded by the provinces, despite the fact that the party has governed Ontario for more than two decades. On the contrary, the Conservatives are assuming a national stance in opposition to the alleged over-accommodation of the provinces by the Liberal Government.

Third-party provincial governments, particularly the Social Credit

---

[32] Engelmann, "Membership Participation in Policy-Making in the C.C.F.," 167.

governments of Alberta and British Columbia, have done little to have their case presented nationally by the small band of Social Credit MP's. They have instead taken the much more effective route of presenting their demands directly to the federal government in federal-provincial relations, thereby influencing some of the policies of the governing party.

•

SUMMARY

In this chapter, we have oriented information about the factors shaping Canadian parties along two lines: how these factors affect party organization, and how they affect party policies, programs, and ideologies.

The social structure of Canada is reflected in a cadre structure of political parties. This structure, according to Duverger, emphasizes influentials, experts, and financiers, rather than a dues-paying mass membership. The latter is found historically only among western farm and immigrant-influenced labour groups, and currently (to a limited degree) in the NDP. Group support has a very slight impact on party structure, with the NDP again forming an exception. Non-party elites have had their impact on party structure primarily as influentials, with the professionalization of politics drawing an increasing number from the mass media, and the professionalization of government from the intelligentsia.

Canada's system of government has affected party organization profoundly. The electoral system, with its demands that polls be manned, that candidates be nominated, and that constituencies be won, has done much to give shape to the lower echelons of party organization. Canadian federalism has given a federal organizational structure, with far-reaching provincial autonomy, to all parties. The workings of the parliamentary system have tended to give a paramount place in the structure of the party to the parliamentary leader and his ministerial colleagues. Extra-governmental elements are strongest in parties with a tradition of lay participation, at least until such parties acquire governmental experience.

We have found overwhelming evidence of pragmatism in the policies and programs of the major parties, and we contend that this pragmatism is a reflection of Canada's social structure. The aspect of Canadian society least conducive to such pragmatism has been the ethnic cleavage between British and French Canada. The impact of group support on party programs is most clearly visible when a group makes direct, overt demands on a party of principle. The impact of groups on parties oriented primarily toward electoral success tends to take less visible and less rigid forms. Intellectual elites have as yet had little impact on party programs (with the exception of the influence of the League for Social Reconstruction on the CCF program of 1933), but these influences may be on the rise. Economic elites have been concerned mainly with the preservation of a climate friendly to competitive enterprise.

Canada's parliamentary system has exercised a pragmatic pull on the programs of all parties. Elections fought along sharply cutting issues are rare. The federal system has influenced party programs in recent years primarily because the habitat of most of the French-Canadian population is also the province of Quebec.

If the influence of all the shaping factors on ideology has been of a rather slight significance, this fact is in turn due to the slight significance of ideology in Canadian political life altogether.

Section III

THE EFFECTS OF POLITICAL PARTIES

8

Provision of Leadership and Decisions: The Electoral Process

•

Two of the most central functions of any political system are the provision of leadership and the making of decisions. Political parties play a major role in carrying out these functions, certainly in the Canadian political system. Let us look at how they do this and, in our examination, address ourselves to two questions: (1) Who decides? (2) How are decisions made?

There are two stages in the analysis of the role played by parties in carrying out the two central functions: the election stage and the inter-election stage. This chapter will be devoted to the electoral stage or the electoral process and will deal with the various activities connected with elections: the informal recruitment and the formal nomination of candidates, the formation of electoral platforms, and the actual election campaign.

•

RECRUITMENT AND NOMINATION OF CANDIDATES

In every system of representative government, there is a way of limiting the number of candidates for electoral office. If there is a free candidacy for all those qualified by law, there is at least a procedural narrowing down to those whose names appear on the printed ballot. Other candidates are relegated to the near-hopeless position of "write-in" candidates. Generally the limiting is done by insisting that candidates undergo certain formal legal procedures. However, the formal legal nomination is normally preceded by a political nomination. This process of actual political nomination and the recruiting process before it, are done, in all competitive political systems we know, by political parties.

The function of the party in nominating is to assure that, for each available seat or office, one and only one candidate is put forth toward whose election the party will eventually attempt to mobilize its maximal voting support. The ways of nominating vary with each formal legal structure of government, but the essence remains the same;[1] it is the structured narrowing of the number of possible candidates with a view to electing them under a particular party label.[2]

When we speak of the nominating function of parties, what do we mean by "parties"? Nominations are made within and by each constituency. This geographic pattern of nomination obtains in all political systems with single-member-district legislatures. But the meaning of "party" in regard to nominations depends on the degree of centralization of the party system. In the United Kingdom, there is usually open consultation between central office and constituency, and there is a rarely used central veto on candidates. Austin Ranney, however, shows that in practice most decisions are in fact local.[3] In the United States, the pattern is one of complete local autonomy. In fact, the prevailing system is that of the direct primary, in which the local party members (and the primary may not even be restricted to these) elect the candidate, occasionally with severe consequences for party cohesion. The Canadian norm in nominating is closer to the British, though there is never a formal list of approved names. Formally, the choice is always purely local; actually, we find either local autonomy or veiled central control, though such control as there may be is often provincial. There may be veiled national control when he provincial party is weak. Regenstreif reports instances where Liberal Cabinet Ministers influenced vacant nominations in several parts of the country.[4]

It is exceptional for national party headquarters, or the party leader personally, openly to take a hand in nominations. Such an exceptional situation obtains when the party leader finds himself defeated. Should his party win the election, it is of course imperative that an apparently safe seat be found for him, as indeed it was found for the victorious, but personally defeated, Mackenzie King in 1925 and in 1945. A seat may also be found for the defeated leader of a defeated party; this happened in 1962, when Erhard Regier of the NDP resigned his seat in Burnaby-Coquitlam so that his leader, T.C. Douglas, defeated in Regina, could

---

[1] For an explanation and illustration of the principle underlying nominations by parties see Austin Ranney and Willmoore Kendall, *Democracy and the American Party System* (New York: Harcourt, Brace and Company, Inc., 1956), pp. 265-66.

[2] Joseph A. Schlesinger considers nominations to be the prime function of political parties. See his "Political Party Organization," *Handbook of Organizations*, ed. James G. March (Chicago: Rand McNally & Company, 1965), pp. 764-801.

[3] Austin Ranney, *Pathways to Parliament* (Madison: University of Wisconsin Press, 1965).

[4] S. Peter Regenstreif, "The Liberal Party of Canada: a Political Analysis" (Unpublished Ph.D. Dissertation, Cornell University, 1963), pp. 158-66.

sit in the House of Commons. Occasionally, a Prime Minister may use the influence of the national party to obtain a nomination for someone he wants in his Cabinet. King was instrumental in obtaining two (unsuccessful) nominations for General A.G.L. McNaughton.

In competitive situations, when a vacancy exists, the rule is that the nomination is decided by the constituency on local grounds. But in assessing local control over nominations, it must be realized that not all nominations are sought after. Even one of the major parties may be in a truly hopeless competitive situation in several constituencies. Minor parties are in this position in a majority of constituencies, but they still often nominate in most of them. In such circumstances, many of the candidates literally have to be found. When central encouragement is needed in a situation of this kind, it is the provincial and not the national organization of the party that takes on the task of finding someone to stand as a candidate. Provincial influence over hopeful nominations, however, has to be used with the utmost subtlety. Occasionally, prominent figures who do not hold seats become interested in a parliamentary nomination. They must then interest a vacant constituency in nominating them. Several such prominent figures sought nominations in 1965: Robert Winters, Jean Marchand, Gérard Pelletier, and Pierre-Elliott Trudeau on the Liberal side, and George Hees, Dalton Camp, and Davie Fulton on the side of the Conservatives. Mr. Fulton was given the nomination in the riding he had held prior to his earlier retirement from national politics (Kamloops, B.C.) ; several of the others had to put up a struggle to obtain a nomination.

The legal requirements for the nomination of candidates for the House of Commons are simple. Nomination papers may be filed by any ten qualified voters, and a deposit of $200 must be made. This is refundable if the candidate wins, or obtains at least one-half of the vote of the winner.

Most nominations filed in this manner have been arrived at through the instrumentality of one of Canada's political parties. In all parties, nomination procedures are laid down locally or at the provincial level. A clause in the federal constitution of the NDP permitting the Federal Council to intervene in federal nominations is, in practice, as vestigal as are the provisions in various party constitutions giving provincial bodies the power to veto candidates nominated locally. Meisel, for example, was not aware of any such veto in the federal election of 1957.[5]

Various methods are used in the nomination of candidates. At one extreme we find the automatic renomination of sitting members. This mode was employed by both the Liberal and Conservative parties in Quebec under the Taschereau regime and subsequently. Dawson mentions an instance in which Taschereau refused a request of a federal constituency to hold a nominating convention designed to unseat the incumbent MP.[6] Another method of nominating is reported by George Perlin:

The method of selecting Liberal candidates for both federal and provincial elections is revealing of the nature of the Newfoundland Liberal

THE EFFECTS OF POLITICAL PARTIES

*party. Although a general nominating convention was held in 1949, can-
didates since then have been appointed by the party. In fact this has
meant that the selection of candidates has been entirely the prerogative
of Mr. Smallwood. There is nothing covert about the use of this process
for the names of candidates always are announced either in personal
statements by the Premier or in statements issued by his office.*[7]

At the other extreme, we find the "open convention." Howard Scarrow
describes its operation in the case of the federal nomination in a riding
in urban Ontario, in 1962:

> *. . . anyone who lives in the riding and who is a 'Liberal supporter' can
> attend the convention and cast a ballot. Proof of the former can be found
> in the city directory; proof of the latter is possible only in the negative
> sense that scrutineers placed by the competing candidates can spot per-
> sons who have been conspicuously identified with another party.*[8]

Scarrow claims that this system, once instituted in a particular consti-
uency, is likely to be retained because ". . . any change in favour of a
more structured procedure is likely to be regarded with suspicion."[9]

There are indeed more structured procedures. Among Liberals and
Conservatives, the decision as to what kind of procedure to employ may
be within the discretion of the constituency association, acting through
the annual meeting or the executive. Delegate conventions appear to be
the most conventional mode of organizing nominations. They have the
advantage, from the party's point of view, of involving many if not all
polls of the constituency, and of assuring some party regularity on the
part of the nominators. An open convention, on the other hand, is open
to "packing" by adherents of a particular aspirant, and to the involvement of neutrals or even opponents. A thoroughly organized constituency
like the Conservative federal constituency association of Carleton (Ontario) has a carefully structured delegate convention. This constituency,
with (in 1963) a Conservative vote of 31,168, had 4,700 enrolled party
members in 1957.[10] In order to make a federal nomination in 1957, the
constituency association employed a nominating convention of five delegates for each of the 215 polling subdivisions, a total of 1,075. Surprisingly all 1,075 were selected and attended, giving to this one federal
constituency a body of the size, and evidently of the political seriousness,
of a major party national convention in the United States. Equal seriousness, both in regard to structure and performance, prevails in case of
nominations in many federal and provincial constituency associations of

[5] John Meisel, *The Canadian General Election of 1957* (Toronto: University of Toronto Press, 1962), p. 121.

[6] Robert MacGregor Dawson, *The Government of Canada*, 3rd ed. (Toronto: University of Toronto Press, 1957), p. 522 n.

[7] George Perlin, "St. John's West" in *Papers on the 1962 Election*, ed. John Meisel
(Toronto: University of Toronto Press, 1964), p. 7 n.

[8] Howard A. Scarrow, "Three Dimensions of a Local Political Party" in *Papers on
the 1962 Election*, ed. John Meisel, p. 54.

[9] *Ibid.*

[10] Meisel, *The Canadian General Election of 1957*, p. 122.

the CCF/NDP. Whenever there are sufficient dues-paying members, particularly in Saskatchewan, nominating conventions are carefully structured and representative of every poll in the constituency.

Other cases in the Meisel election studies shed additional light on nominating procedures. The volume on the 1957 election indicates that sitting Liberals in Quebec were given renomination as automatically as in the days of Taschereau. However, this procedure led to discontent and to the local nomination of a number of Independent Liberals to oppose incumbents who were disliked in their constituencies. In Drummond-Arthabasca, the locally selected insurgent actually defeated the sitting member in the general election.[11] Meisel also reports two provincial-local problems among Ontario Conservatives.[12] One provincially proposed, and already announced, federal candidate was turned down by his constituency association. In a Toronto riding, a mining executive, who was proposed by the Provincial Office and who was to receive only token opposition, failed even to be placed in nomination at the local meeting. The token candidate withdrew dutifully, and the nomination went to a third man who had never been a serious candidate.

Nominating conventions give party luminaries an opportunity to appear in public before the official campaign starts. Almost invariably, there is a major address: by a Cabinet Minister, a parliamentary assistant, a Senator, or an MP. Cabinet Ministers especially are drawn into this pre-campaign campaigning. Prior to the 1962 election, one Conservative minister was scheduled to address seven nominating conventions in a period of fifteen days.[13] A number of them visit conventions outside their province, possibly to emphasize the national character of the party. We cannot determine whether or not the involvement of a prominent party figure influences a convention which is to nominate a new candidate. Prominent visitors no doubt aid an incumbent whose renomination is contested, but he would generally have things going for him anyway.

In the federal election of 1963, the parties came close to preempting nominations. Of the slightly more than 1,000 candidates for the 265 seats there were, in addition to the few Communist candidates, and an even smaller number under the labels Nationaliste and Socialist Labour, only twenty-one who were not nominees of one of the four principal contenders: eight Independents, six Independent Liberals, five Independent Conservatives, one Independent Social Credit, and one Independent Labour. The election deposit probably helped to bring about this situation, but it was a tribute to the force of the four (five in 1965) major contending parties that they were able to account for over 95 per cent of the 1963 federal nominations. No candidate who had not been nominated by one of the four parties—Liberal, Conservative, Social Credit, New Democratic—amassed a significant number of votes. In 1965, however, two Independent candidates were elected—a reappearance of a phenomenon of earlier years.

But the output of the parties in the nomination of candidates should be measured not only by the fact that there are now so very few other

166

candidates. Equally significant is the fact that the parties, despite the decentralized nominations, remain in control of the candidates once they are selected. Epstein rightly states that

[I]t is noteworthy that this control of candidate selection by the party organization is exercised in Canada despite the absence of the other organizational features of British and European extra-parliamentary parties, but that nevertheless it seems effective in selecting candidates who, when elected, are loyal to the national party cause as defined by their parliamentary leadership and caucus.[14]

Nominations of candidates are so much the act of the party that the party can usually count on its nominees once it elects them. The recent break-up of the Quebec wing of Social Credit, preceded by only one similar event—the break-up of the Progressives after 1921—is, like the earlier case, an instance of an unstable parliamentary caucus, and does not vitiate the application of our conclusion to the major parties and, for that matter, to the NDP. That party held on to seven of the eight CCF caucus members when it reconstituted itself in 1961.

The nomination of candidates, then, is an effective output of Canadian parties. Party leaders—the Prime Minister, Cabinet Ministers, the Leader of the Opposition, Opposition front benchers, leaders of other parties—emerge during the inter-election stage, and not at the nominating stage. However, their selection is almost invariably limited to those who have been elected to Parliament in the first place, and these qualify for election by partisan nomination.

•

FORMATION AND PRESENTATION OF PARTY PLATFORMS

It would be tempting to say that the provision of policy decisions is as effective an output as the nomination of candidates. Early analyses of parliamentary government, especially in the United Kingdom, did in fact say so. The following sequence would be specified: (1) Parties prepare and present platforms. (2) In voting for a candidate, the voter also casts a ballot for the platform of the candidate's party. (3) The winning platform (i.e., the platform of the party able to form the government) then becomes the governing party's "election mandate." (4) Implementation of the policies contained in the "mandate" is then scheduled in the Speech from the Throne and usually takes place before Parliament is dissolved.

This picture is no longer held unreservedly even by observers of the

---

[11] *Ibid.*, p. 124.

[12] *Ibid.*, p. 122.

[13] This is based on information supplied by the National Office of the Progressive Conservative Party.

[14] Leon D. Epstein, "A Comparative Study of Canadian Parties," *The American Political Science Review*, LVIII (March 1964), 55.

British parliamentary system, and observers of other systems have been more skeptical. One poignant example should help prepare the reader's skeptical attitude: no amount of searching in the winning Conservative platform of 1930 will unearth even a trace of R.B. Bennett's "New Deal," which was enacted later by his Government.

We contend that the formation and presentation of platforms is a party output qualitatively different, and much more tentative, than the nomination of candidates. However, party platforms as party outputs should not be downgraded too far. In every election, each party that competes on anywhere near a national basis does come forward with a platform; and an effort is made to acquaint the voting public with the contents of such a platform. Throughout the political history of Canada, at least some elements of the winning party's platform have been among the policies enacted during its term in office.

Election platforms may contain at least three different aspects, which often appear in uneasy combination. First there are declarations of principle, which may be quite old when they are used. The Liberals, for instance, made wide use, in the 1957 campaign, of a statement of principles adopted at their national convention of 1948.[15] Second, there are resolutions passed by the party's last national convention, or by its last annual meeting. These may come into play through omission as much as through commission. When the Conservatives faced the voters in 1957, their last national convention was only a few months behind them, and its expressions of opinion were quite timely. However, the party had been placed under the progressive leadership of Mr. Diefenbaker, while some of the resolutions adopted had been the handiwork of the "old guard." Some of the convention resolutions were therefore suppressed during the campaign, particularly one that was ambiguous about the requirement of a means test for old age pensioners.[16] The third and final aspect is the manifesto of the leader. Such a manifesto tends to be of foremost importance, for two reasons: (a) it derives from the man who will have primary responsibility for the party's performance in Government or Opposition, and (b) it has the quality of timeliness.

The foregoing indicates that, while nominations are overwhelmingly the work of the electoral organization (and, what is more, of its local components), platform making reflects the tension between the intra- and extra-governmental aspects of party structure. Generally, in the major parties at least, the balance of power rests with the governmental leaders. Dawson's generalization applies certainly to Liberals and Conservatives:

'Our platform is our leader, and our leader is our platform' is sometimes openly avowed, and it is a maxim that is almost always accepted in practice. It follows, therefore, that the leader is the master of the platform, and tends to accept it as a general indication of the way in which the party would like him to move when and if he finds it desirable to do so.[17]

Dawson himself refers to voluminous evidence in support of his generalization.[18] Mackenzie King time and again proclaimed his mastery of the Liberal platform of 1919. He claimed that all the party had done when it met in national convention and adopted the platform was to provide him with "chart and compass." Once in office, he was to use this "chart and compass" but otherwise steer the ship of state himself. This notion guided him during his twenty-nine years of party leadership; when the 1948 National Convention was held upon his resignation, he took great care that the views of the Cabinet would prevail in the drawing of the platform.[19] King's many Conservative opponents, especially Meighen, Bennett, and Bracken, were guided by similar notions regarding platforms. As we mentioned above, Mr. Diefenbaker veered off the compass in 1957 and he kept covert part of his chart. However, the predominance of the leader should not be overdrawn. For a balanced view, we may be guided by the conclusions Leiserson arrives at, despite his specific reference to party ideology rather than platforms:

This separation of the electoral and intragovernmental party organization does not mean that the formulation and reformulation of party ideology is an exclusive province of either. On the contrary, in countries like Great Britain where the parliamentary party controls party propaganda policy, leaders of the electoral party are carefully consulted in its formulation; in the United States, where the electoral party organization through the national convention draws up the party platform, legislative party leaders usually play a prominent role on the drafting committee.[20]

It is of course the remark on Britain that is particularly applicable to the interaction between intra- and extra-governmental party structure in the preparation of party platforms in Canada.

In the constituency associations of the Liberal and Conservative parties, there is much more concern with organizational matters than with policy. While two decades have elapsed since Dawson commented on policy resolutions passed by annual meetings of Liberal and Conservative constitutency associations, his remark regarding their frequency still holds: "Occasionally the meeting, quite daring, may place on record its opinion on a special measure or policy but this is uncommon."[21] There may be considerable platform-designing activity at provincial leadership conventions, but these deal with provincial platforms. On the national level of the extra-governmental party structure, for both major parties, policy resolutions are drafted at two kinds of meetings, the annual

---

[15] Meisel, *The Canadian General Election of 1957*, p. 39.

[16] *Ibid.* p. 170.

[17] Dawson, *The Government of Canada*, 3rd ed., p. 506. See also 4th ed., p. 472.

[18] *Ibid.*, 3rd ed., pp. 226, 577-81. For a full discussion of King's notion of "chart and compass" see *Constitutional Issues in Canada, 1900-1931*, ed. R. M. Dawson (Oxford University Press; London: Humphrey Milford, 1933), pp. 397-405.

[19] Regenstreif, The Liberal Party of Canada . . . ," pp. 204-7.

[20] Avery Leiserson, *Parties and Politics* (New York: Alfred A. Knopf, Inc., 1958), p. 275.

[21] Dawson, *The Government of Canada*, 3rd ed., p. 521. See also 4th ed., pp. 481-82.

meeting of the Liberal Federation or the Progressive Conservative Association and the national convention. The annual meeting has primarily organizational purposes. It does, however, pass policy resolutions which assume some importance when a general election is impending. With the national convention the drafting of the program may be a major activity. At the Conservative national conventions of 1942 and 1956, for instance, the platform was hammered together from resolutions passed by lower party echelons.[22] Unlike policy resolutions of the annual meeting which are, at most, a gentle admonition to the party's governmental leaders, platforms passed by national conventions must be reckoned with by these leaders.

In the CCF/NDP, the extra-governmental structure is taken more seriously in platform formation. The atmosphere surrounding the activity is that of intraparty democracy, which stems from the CCF's populist forebears. Some of this lay policymaking will be discussed in the next chapter; here we are concerned with it only as it relates to the party platform. With its set biennial national conventions, the CCF/NDP is tied to a time schedule more rigid than that of the major parties, and less adaptable to the electoral timetable (which, in any case, has so far been beyond the control of the party's leaders). There is, therefore, need for some tactical flexibility at election time, even if a convention succeeds in putting together a complete platform. M.J. Coldwell, then the party's national leader, pointed out this need to the 1948 National Convention, after it had boldly passed a First Term Program for a CCF Government of the future:

We must try to visualize the task which would confront a CCF government on its accession to power. We should avoid making promises which we might find it difficult to fulfil. What we adopt should be regarded as a minimum we intend to carry out, as time and circumstances permit.

That, and the manner of fulfilment, must be left to the judgement of the Parliamentary group whose activities will be assessed by the Canadian electorate to whom in the final analysis under our democratic and parliamentary system they will always be responsible.[23]

Here too the exigencies of time and the system of government demand an election manifesto which will, to some extent, bear the imprint of the party's governmental leadership.

Recent studies afford some insight into platform formation of the major parties in the late fifties.[24] An analysis of the Conservative platform of 1956 indicates that it was more "progressive" than the party's platform in 1948, but much less revolutionary a departure from earlier party stands than was the nomination of Mr. Diefenbaker. The platform was the work of a large representative resolutions committee, which worked over many proposals, some of grass-roots origin. This platform was widely ignored by Mr. Diefenbaker in his victorious 1957 campaign. His actual election program was determined largely by personal advisers, often in complete disregard of earlier party decisions. In sharp contrast,

THE EFFECTS OF POLITICAL PARTIES

the fashioning of the Liberal platform was a continuous interaction between the Cabinet and the civil service, an agency which, far from extra-governmental, was extra-partisan. Prior to the 1958 election, the tables were turned and the Liberals, now out of office, used the national convention, called to select a successor to Mr. St. Laurent, to form its platform in a committee which digested 360 policy resolutions.[25]

In comparing platforms and nominations as party outputs, we conclude: the nominated candidate who is elected stays elected, while the platform of a winning party though adopted may not stay adopted. However, if it is employed during the campaign by the party's governmental leadership, it does have some effect on the electorate.

•

CAMPAIGNS

An election is not the only process bringing into play popular consultation, but it is its most visible and telling aspect. The election brings into focus the bridging function of parties, and it performs better in providing leadership than in providing decisions. Not all the provision of leadership takes place at the moment of election, however. There are, during inter-election periods, occasional Cabinet shuffles and movements to and from the Opposition front bench, and even the rare change of a party leader. But it is at election time that the society at large is asked whom it wants to direct the political system, and it is the political parties that organize and structure the asking of this question.

In Canada, parties have waged election campaigns from the beginning of responsible government. Campaigns were part of the scene before Confederation, and long before manhood suffrage became nearly universal. The first seven years of Confederation lacked not only a federal control of the franchise, but also minimum federal electoral standards: there was no secret ballot, and no requirement to hold the election at the same time throughout Canada. The Act of 1874 established minimum standards of regularity, and from 1885 to 1898, Canada had a federally determined franchise with low property qualifications. In order to permit diversity within the federal system, the Laurier Government re-established provincial determination of the franchise, and the federal government did not re-enter the picture until 1917. That year brought a major setback in Canada's movement toward universal suffrage. This was Arthur Meighen's bill which was designed to enfranchise all those, and

---

[22] *Ibid.*, p. 550.

[23] Frederick C. Engelmann, "Membership Participation in Policy-Making in the C.C.F.," *The Canadian Journal of Economics and Political Science*, XXII (1956), 173.

[24] Meisel, *The Canadian General Election of 1957*, pp. 22-25, 37-44; Meisel, "The Formulation of Liberal and Conservative Programmes in the 1957 Canadian Election," *The Canadian Journal of Economics and Political Science*, XXVI (1960), 567.

[25] Norman Ward, "The Liberals in Convention", in *Party Politics in Canada*, 2nd ed., ed. Hugh G. Thorburn (Toronto: Prentice-Hall of Canada, Ltd., 1967), pp. 96-103.

only those, who were likely to vote for conscription and the vigorous prosecution of the War. No paraphrase could improve on Norman Ward's statement of what he calls "the most remarkable franchise act ever passed in Canada, and very possibly in the democratic world:"

The wartime franchise of 1917 could hardly fail to return a majority in Parliament for the party which enacted it. Women were enfranchised, for example, but only those women who had, or had had, husbands, sons, brothers, or fathers in the Canadian or British armed forces. Men were enfranchised who might be disqualified by provincial property or income qualification but who had sons or grandsons in the services. The franchise was granted, under the Military Voters Act, to virtually all members of the Canadian armed forces, whether or not they were ordinarily resident in Canada, were minors, or Indians. On the other hand, the following categories were disfranchised: conscientious objectors and those who applied for certificates as such; Mennonites and Doukhobors, and not only all naturalized British subjects born in an enemy country and naturalized after March 31, 1902, but all who even spoke an enemy language habitually and were naturalized after that date.

On the positive side, the newly enfranchised soldiers and their sisters and their cousins and their aunts were expected to vote for the Government; on the negative side, the disfranchised group (most particularly the naturalized aliens) were those who would, on their record between 1900 and 1911, be likely to vote Liberal.[26]

In the broad sweep of Canadian franchise development, the statute of 1917 stands out as a short-lived aberration. Since 1920, virtually all Canadians twenty-one years or older, and British subjects resident in Canada for one year, have been eligible to vote.

Canada's electorate then is broadly inclusive and constitutes most of the adult population. In the campaign period preceding a general election, normally less than two months, political parties come close to having a monopoly in dealing with the voters. It is the parties that wage the campaign, from national headquarters, through the leaders, and in the constituencies. The parties are essentially alone in doing so. Except for financial aid, known and unknown, Canada's interest world sits on the sidelines. The major exceptions are the political action and education efforts by organized labour on behalf of the CCF/NDP. Radio and television are used, but by the parties. The only notable exception to the party monopoly in campaigning is the press, whose role as an input we discussed in Chapter 4, and whose role in campaigns, as we will indicate later, defies easy generalization. Election campaigns, the clearest manifestations of political competition in democracies, are fought nearly everywhere, and certainly in Canada, almost exclusively by political parties, and thus form a striking and significant output of those parties.

How do Canadian parties go about providing this crucial output? To describe this, we will answer the following questions: (1) What does party headquarters do during a campaign? (2) What do the leaders do?

(3) What goes on in the constituencies? (4) Who works for the parties? (5) What kind of money is spent? (6) What does the press do?

Significant national headquarters work is done by all parties that nominate candidates on a nation-wide scale. In the case of the Social Credit Party, however, the very nature of its support forces concentration on the areas where there is some chance of success, and this occasions a primarily provincial organization of federal campaigns. In 1965, in fact, the party elected members only in the provinces in which it formed the government. In the CCF/NDP, in contrast, the federal campaign is strong in most provinces, in all urban population centres from Vancouver to Montreal, and in Halifax.

The federal structure of Canada affects the direction of the national campaign, certainly in parties that are important on both national and provincial levels. Yet Meisel gives this convincing account of national primacy in the campaigns of both major parties:

Notwithstanding the great importance of the party organizations within the provinces, the main actors in a federal election are the national leaders and their chief lieutenants—members of the cabinet or of the shadow cabinet. The ministers are, it is true, spokesmen in the cabinet for the provincial interests, but they are not delegates of the provinces in a federal assembly. Those ministers who become the spokesmen for their provinces in the cabinet are responsible to the cabinet *for the state of the party's organization in their province; in no sense are they responsible to the provincial organization for the activities of the cabinet. It is consequently the task of the ministers to see that the decisions about the national campaign—the strategy and tactics as determined by the national leadership—are carried out in the provinces and regions for which they bear particular responsibility.*[27]

Headquarters in both major and minor parties issue campaign literature, manage the campaign trips of the leader and other national figures, arrange for broadcasting, employ one or more public relations firms, collect their own public opinion data or contract for the use of existing ones, issue news releases, and generally coordinate campaign activities. Strategy and tactics are determined by the leader and his chief advisers, both within the intra-governmental and the electoral party structure.

The agenda of the initial campaign meeting at the national headquarters of a major party, in one of the campaigns of the early sixties, probably sums up the typical concerns of a national headquarters.[28] The national items up for discussion were the campaign themes and the leader's campaign itinerary. All other items on the agenda dealt with federal-provincial liaison during the prospective campaign. These included candidates, the schedule of nominating conventions, speakers, and publicity.

---

[26] Norman Ward, *The Canadian House of Commons: Representation* (Toronto: University of Toronto Press, 1950), pp. 226.

[27] Meisel, *The Canadian General Election of 1957*, pp. 64-65.

[28] Descriptive data on campaigns are based on information supplied by the national offices of the Liberal and Progressive Conservative parties.

The latter covered a multitude of topics: television, radio, the daily, weekly, and ethnic press, magazines, pamphlets, posters, and "gimmicks."

The party leader must carry a major burden in the campaign. He must act both as director of the campaign and, more importantly, as chief bearer of the party's image. This function is becoming increasingly like that of a presidential candidate in the United States, and it is shared by the national leaders of all parties. The leader is expected to appear in the party's major campaign telecasts; he is also expected to appear live in all provinces and in all major population centres. These appearances, and the travel connected with it, constitute a grueling task. They are physically and intellectually taxing, the latter especially because the leader affects his party's image through everything he says. They also contribute to making his position within the party paramount.

The nature of the leader's campaign activity can best be demonstrated by giving some details of a specific campaign. The information we present is from the federal campaign of 1963.

As Leader of the Opposition, Mr. Pearson opened his campaign for the April 8 election on February 22, five days earlier than Mr. Diefenbaker. The first five days were spent in Quebec. Travel was by train, and the schedule of meetings was interrupted by two television appearances. The next three days brought a swing through the Maritimes, by air, rail, and car. Again, there were two television appearances on the program. A few days in Ottawa and Toronto were followed by the first western swing of the tour, four days in Saskatchewan and Manitoba; travel was by air. During the next week, Mr. Pearson traveled through Quebec and Ontario by air and car, with one TV appearance. There followed a week's flying visit to all four Atlantic provinces, during which two television programs were scheduled. Another two days of campaigning in Ontario were followed by the second flight west. This time, Mr. Pearson spent one week in the West and visited all four provinces. April 4 was spent in his constituency of Algoma East in Northern Ontario, and the campaign culminated in a rally in Toronto's Maple Leaf Gardens on April 5.

The campaign of Mr. Diefenbaker, the Prime Minister, began on February 27. The first big event was the nominating convention in Prince Albert, Saskatchewan, to which he took a "whistle-stopping" train trip of three days. He returned east by train and plane, with a telecast on the way. After four days of campaigning in Ontario, Mr. Diefenbaker toured the Atlantic provinces by air and rail and video-taped a TV address. Two days of "whistle-stopping" in Ontario were followed by a flight west; more than a week was spent in Saskatchewan, Alberta, and British Columbia. The final week of campaigning took the Prime Minister to Ontario and Quebec, and he spent election day in Prince Albert.

On their seven and six weeks' tours, respectively, the leaders were accompanied by a permanent staff. In the case of Mr. Diefenbaker, this staff numbered about ten people. In addition, both leaders were followed by press correspondents. The leaders' time was taken up not only with major and minor meetings, TV appearances, and campaign staff conferences, but also with frequent meetings with the press entourage. The strain on the leaders, one of whom is also responsible for the government of the country, is considerable. But the campaign tours appear to be here to stay. During their encounters, and there have now been four, Mr. Diefenbaker likes to taunt Mr. Pearson by saying that *he* does not fly over the people's heads in an airplane, but that he meets them from the train platform. Exaggerated though these statements are, Mr. Diefenbaker has a good claim to being Canada's champion campaigner. His campaigning activities accounted for the narrow Conservative victory in 1957, the monumental extent of that party's landslide in 1958, and most probably for the staving off of defeat in 1962 and for the prevention of a Liberal majority in the election of 1963. How much he contributed to the unexpectedly good Conservative showing in 1965 remains a matter for conjecture.

It is not only the party leaders who engage in centrally managed campaign swings through the country. The governing party always has a number of ministers who are effective platform speakers, and who are, therefore, in demand in a number of constituencies. We have already referred to their appearance at nominating conventions; their trips through various parts of the country also extend into the later stages of the campaign. The principal opposition party also uses at least a few national campaigners. Even in as personal an opposition campaign as that of Mr. Diefenbaker in 1965, Alvin Hamilton was a frequent speaker.

National campaigns have become increasingly important, especially because of developments in transportation and communication, but votes continue to be cast for constituency candidates. For this reason, much of the essential campaign work continues to be done there. In Chapter 10, we will deal in some detail with the relative importance of party and candidate in voter decision; but even if it is apparent that party voting is more significant than candidate voting, the candidate's individual effort during the campaign is of great importance. If the candidate is an important challenger of an important incumbent, as Mitchell Sharp was of Donald Fleming in Eglinton (Toronto) in 1962,[29] or Dalton Camp of Mitchell Sharp in the same riding in 1965, the constituency campaign assumes national significance. An incumbent is in a good position to advertise all the things he claims to have done for the constituency. Open meetings, and the way candidates perform in them when under fire, continue to be important. Also, observers continue to emphasize that candidates help their own cause by meeting as many voters as they can: at tea or coffee parties or, better still, through personal house-to-house canvassing. In a recent campaign, one of the major parties made the following suggestion for distribution of the candidate's time: personal

---

[29] The 1962 campaign in Eglinton is described in Denis Smith, "The Campaign in Eglinton" in *Papers on the 1962 Election*, ed. John Meisel, pp. 68-90, and Brian Land, *Eglinton: the Election Study of a Federal Constituency* (Toronto: Peter Martin Associates, 1965).

calls 65 per cent; small meetings 25 per cent; large meetings and receptions 4 per cent; press, radio, TV 5 per cent; administration (including managers' meetings and speech preparation) 1 per cent.[30] In actual practice, time distribution varies with the nature of the constituency. Certainly TV should be more important in rural areas; the urban candidate would invariably be seen by large numbers who live in different constituencies and therefore cannot vote for him. The same party urges its candidates to be available for work, at least on the telephone, by 7:30 a.m. Practitioners on all sides have confirmed for us the relevance of this particular party's emphasis on direct contact between candidate and voter. Its circular emphasizes: "Most voters have never met a federal candidate in all their lives. The first candidate to fill this gap makes a tremendous and lasting impression."

Each candidate is assisted by a campaign manager. This manager must be in constant touch with the candidate, he must be continually aware of the progress of the various aspects of the campaign, and he must make sure that all campaign workers are doing their assigned tasks. The official agent is responsible for campaign finances within the constituency. We do not know how representative is the following suggestion, made by one of the major parties in the sixties, for a constituency campaign budget: general organization (including wages, gratuities, and expenses) 40 per cent or less, public relations and advertising 40 per cent or more, election day expenses 20 per cent. The latter, including cars, babysitters, poll workers, and lunches, are of course crucial in bringing about a favourable turnout. The activation effort on election day remains an entirely local function. No amount of people at national headquarters can assure that the party will actually deliver its maximum vote at the polls.

We owe to Howard Scarrow the first attempt to demonstrate what kind of people do the actual work for the party in the constituency.[31] In an urban riding in Ontario (in 1962) he found that poll captains, the group he studied, showed the following characteristics in the Liberal and Conservative parties: they were impermanent, paid, and most were women. The second and third characteristics were not shared by NDP workers; these were mostly male, and they were unpaid, though some of them were union employees. Scarrow found that virtually all of the NDP poll captains came from households, the head of which was a manual labourer; more significantly, the majority of the Liberal and Conservative poll captains showed the same characteristic. Second among major-party poll captains ranked "white-collar, sales, managerial," and third "retired, and widow." Only 2 per cent of the major parties' poll captains were either businessmen or professionals, while professionals made up 5 per cent of the NDP poll captains. Scarrow presents the following conclusion:

The preponderance of manual workers can be explained by the highly industrialized nature of the community, the conscious attempt by parties to have workers 'fit' the neighbourhood and, probably also, by the remuneration associated with the job. Whatever the explanation, however, the consequence is that election campaigns serve to inject a high

176   THE EFFECTS OF POLITICAL PARTIES

degree of personal involvement into a stratum of the community which otherwise has been shown to be low on the scale of political participation.

"Elections are not won by prayers," Israel Tarte is reported to have said.[32] Observers of Canadian parties and elections have long whispered about the financing of parties and campaigns; fortunately, political scientists have recently begun to shed some light on the matter. Expenditures of parties are covered in John Meisel's study of the 1957 election.[33] Constituency expenditures reported for that election range from $385 for one rural Conservative in Saskatchewan to $58,000 for one urban Liberal in Quebec. Meisel estimates the average expenditure for an effective campaign at $10,000 for a rural riding, and at about $20,000 for an urban one. Nationally, Meisel reports that the Conservatives spent $1.7 million in 1957, and he suspects the Liberals of having spent about twice as much. He estimates that the CCF spent only about $200,000, but the nexus with organized labour must be taken into consideration when comparing its finances with those of the major parties. There is, incidentally, no legal ceiling on campaign expenditures, and no legal requirement to disclose either source or amount of contributions.

E. E. Harrill's study,[34] which is based in part on conversations with "bagmen," collectors of party funds (occasionally, he reports, men working for the same firm act as "bagmen" for competing parties), helps to shed some light on the opaque area of party income. Most Liberal and Conservative party funds come from corporations, businessmen, and trade associations. The main reason given for contributions to parties were found to be, in the order listed, preservation of free enterprise, preservation of the two-party system, preservation of a climate of opinion that is favourable to business, civic duty, and habit. The creation of a favourable climate for specific demands and the actual obtaining of specific favours received some mention, but the assessment of a subordinate place to them is probably realistic.

A post-election poll taken early in 1966 gives us the first survey data on Canadian party and electoral finance—data relating both to behaviour and attitude.[35] Five per cent of those polled indicated that they or their families had been canvassed for funds by a political party. Four-fifths of those canvassed actually contributed. One-fifth of those polled were aware

---

[30] Information supplied by the national office of one of the major parties.

[31] Scarrow, "Three Dimensions of a Local Political Party" in *Papers on the 1962 Election*, ed. John Meisel, pp. 57-63.

[32] Quoted in Dawson, *The Government of Canada*, 3rd ed., p. 565. See also 4th ed., p. 519.

[33] Meisel, *The Canadian General Election of 1957*, pp. 116-19, 172-73, 216.

[34] E. E. Harrill, "Money in Canadian Politics" in *Party Politics in Canada*, ed. H. G. Thorburn, pp. 60-9.

[35] "Canadian Attitudes to Election Expenses 1965-6; a Report on Part of a National Survey." Presented to the Committee on Election Expenses by John Meisel, May 1966. The National Survey was directed by John Meisel and designed by Philip Converse, Maurice Pinard, Peter Regenstreif, Mildred Schwartz, and the survey director. Advice on questions regarding election expenses was also given by the Committee's research director, K. Z. Paltiel.

that parties did canvass for funds, and a similar number (not necessarily the same people) would have given had they been approached. Considerably more respondents would have been willing to give some of their time to the party or candidate of their choice. A slight majority of those polled opposed corporate and union giving to parties; attitudes toward giving by the two types of organizations were surprisingly similar. While a large majority favoured the publication of election costs by parties, the publications of donors or amounts given were rejected by small margins. Only one-third wanted to allow tax deductions on contributions to parties, but 30 per cent favoured total, and 38 per cent partial, government subsidization of campaign costs.

A general election costs close to $15 million in the mid-sixties. Surely, only the sensationalist would consider this sum high. The difficulty is that there is no obvious source for this relatively small sum, though we know since the 1966 survey that about two million voters would make at least token contributions if approached. The surprisingly friendly attitude toward public support of campaigns marks this particular avenue as potentially fruitful. If means and a formula could be found for drawing the money from the public purse, no taxpayer would feel the difference. But as long as there is no agreement on public financing, the money will have to be found where it is. Since the CCF became the NDP, that party has firmer financial support from unions and no longer suffers too great a disadvantage.

If parties occasionally derive money from nefarious sources they do so because some major-party collectors feel that they cannot afford to shun money from any source. This understandable, though not necessarily forgivable, lack of discrimination on the part of collectors for the major parties has given Canada two major political scandals: the Pacific Scandal of the 1870's and the Beauharnois affair of the 1930's. The first brought swift retribution to Macdonald and his Government. The second had no discernible effect, because the Liberals, who were primarily implicated, had just lost to the Conservatives. By the time the next election came, the depression had brought on the disintegration of the Bennett Goverment and had all but removed the scandals from the consciousness of the voters. The scandals of the mid-sixties, and primarily the one linking the narcotics smuggler Rivard with some of the Liberal "old guard" in Quebec, indicate that some "bagmen" are still willing to accept money from unsavoury sources. Mr. Diefenbaker's pursuit of the Rivard theme in 1965 no doubt contributed to Mr. Pearson's unexpected failure to obtain a parliamentary majority. This connection may in future help to discourage "bagmen" who lack discrimination, but then again it may not. There is always the possibility that the fear of scandal will confirm parties and their collectors in their determination to keep a shroud of mystery over contributions, a condition most conducive to future scandals.

Despite the scandals mentioned, our tentative conclusion is that contributions to the major federal parties, allegedly given at 60 per cent to the Government and 40 per cent to the Opposition, affect public policy primarily in a general way, in maintaining an atmosphere favourable to private property and a more or less competitive economy. A number of provincial governing parties have used and do use patronage to exact contributions. Possibly the starkest—certainly the most discussed—was that of Maurice Duplessis' Union Nationale Government in Quebec, which awarded and withheld jobs, roads, public buildings, and franchises on the basis of contributions.[36]

Finally, here are a few words about the role of the press in campaigns. While most Canadian dailies favour one or the other of the major parties in their editorial columns, none is directly connected with either party. But the daily newspapers report on the campaign, and editorialize about it. They are the one major extra-party force operative in an election campaign.

A content analysis of eight Ontario dailies during the 1962 campaign justifies our designation of the press as "extra-party."[37] While seven of the eight dailies were preponderantly partisan in their editorials, only two were devoid of an editorial favouring the other major party, and four each carried some editorials favourable to the NDP and to Social Credit. A careful tabulation of the position of news in the papers indicates that all papers, including the strongly Liberal Toronto *Star*, gave more prominent coverage to the Conservatives as the party in office. The NDP and Social Credit fared worse than the major parties in regard to news coverage throughout, but not very badly. With the possible exception of one paper, the NDP received more prominent coverage than Social Credit.

The press is likely to continue to be active in campaigns, and its activity will in all probability favour the major parties, but both of them about equally. Meanwhile, the bulk of the working press does not hesitate to show its prejudices. In 1963, most columnists and major reporters took the side of the Pearson team against Diefenbaker; in 1965, the general tone was one of disappointment with the election call. If the working press did not influence uncommitted voters in either of these elections, it at least had many of them on its side to begin with.

Our discussion of the press in this chapter concerns the press only as it affects the parties' output function, the election result. We are in no position to assess the magnitude of this influence, but we suspect it is slight. We do know, however, that the press, in covering and constantly

---

[36] Herbert F. Quinn, *The Union Nationale: a Study in Quebec Nationalism* (Toronto: University of Toronto Press, 1963), Ch. 7. While this volume went to press, the Committee on Election Expenses submitted its report. It recommended (1) legal responsibility of political parties for campaign funds; (2) certain subsidies to all candidates and parties; (3) tax concessions for contributors; (4) shortening of campaigns and limits on expenditures; (5) disclosure of finances by parties and candidates; (6) public auditing and publishing of financial reports; and (7) improvement of political communication by the media. *Report of the Committee on Election Expenses, 1966* (Ottawa: Queen's Printer, 1966), p. 37.

[37] T. H. Qualter and K. A. MacKirdy, "The Press of Ontario and the Election" in *Papers on the 1962 Election*, ed. John Meisel, pp. 145-68.

assessing the current campaign, serves as a constantly active force on the electorate. It is the only medium which often produces partisan information not generated by the parties themselves.

Our distinction, in this section, between the campaign effort at national headquarters and that in the constituencies is useful, but not preemptive. Despite our agreement with Meisel on the primacy of the national effort, we want to point out that some important activity is also carried on at the provincial level. The major parties have a distinctive provincial campaign organization in all provinces, and the NDP and Social Credit in the provinces in which they expect a considerable vote. Such provincial organization handles some of the campaign finances, and exercises important direction and control of campaigning through the communications media, especially radio and television.

•

SUMMARY

In the process of popular consultation in Canada, political parties are centrally involved in the providing of leadership and decisions. In regard to leadership, parties select the candidates from among whom the voters are asked to choose. While such partisan nominations of candidates are important in any competitive political system, in Canada they are all but preemptive. Nominations are made within constituencies and, formally at least, they are entirely under local control. Actually, there may be a give-and-take between constituency and province, or contituency and national party. In any case, the result is a thoroughgoing party solidarity in legislative behaviour. The methods of nominating vary, and are controlled locally or by the provincial party. Throughout Canada, nominating conventions are used, and the bulk of these are held after the dissolution of Parliament is announced.

The role of parties in submitting policy alternatives for electoral decision is exercised less fully and significantly. In Canada, a direct line between the electoral platform of the winning party and the Speech from the Throne of the next Government exists in political mythology only. Policy proposals submitted by parties to the electorate may take the form of guiding principles, platforms, or leader's manifestos. The standard view taken by the government of the platform accompanying its election is exemplified by Mackenzie King's metaphor of the chart and the compass. In all parties, the extra-governmental part of the structure is in some way involved in the drawing up of election programs. This involvement is more important in parties that have a participatory dues-paying membership.

Campaigns are the structured sequences of events in which parties put their nominees and platforms to the popular test. Canadian suffrage, never highly restrictive, has been nearly universal since 1920. Campaigns are therefore directed to a large electorate. All campaign activity is directed and financed by the competing parties; the only significant exception is the activity of the non-party press. The salient features in a national campaign take place on two levels, the national and the local. National headquarters is the nerve centre of the campaign: it arranges the leader's tour and concerns itself with nation-wide campaign publicity. As the actual election takes place in the constituency, it is there that the candidates wage their campaign; activity on polling day is of course restricted to the constituency. Between national headquarters and constituency organization, provincial headquarters performs some financial and public relations tasks.

Highly publicized scandals have brought the entire complex of party finances into disrepute. As long as the financing of campaigns remains covert—and many managers claim that it must remain so—the image of party finance is not likely to change. It is obvious, meanwhile, that campaigns cost money. Normally there is no simple relationship between campaign contributions and policy favours to donors; but there has been enough smoke to make worthwhile attempts to locate the fire.

Radio and television are partly under public ownership, and entirely under public control. All activity using these media, with the exception of news reporting, is within the control of parties. This is not true of the press. Here, parties have control over advertisements only. Otherwise, the press operates according to the editorial policy of the newspapers, and the orientations of its reporters and commentators. Press campaigning activity then, though it may be highly partisan, is farthest removed from direct party control.

9

Provision of Leadership and Decisions: The Operation of the System of Government

•

In this chapter we will look at the Canadian party system and examine its effect on the Government of the country, primarily during the inter-election stage. Our subject is the effect of parties on determining who governs Canada and what policies are enacted. We will approach this topic by examining five aspects of the political system. First we will look at the party that provides the government. Secondly we will look at the parties in opposition. Our attention will be focused on the principle opposition party but parties in minor opposition roles will also be discussed. Our third concern will be the relationship between that part of the party which operates the electoral activity and that which operates the system of government: in other words the relationship of the party's extra- and intra-parliamentary organizations. The fourth aspect will be the selection of national leaders. Some may wonder why we include this process in the inter-election stage, as it may be confused with its famed counterpart, the national convention in the United States, which is definitely part of the electoral process. In the past half-century, Canadian parties have also adopted the national convention. However, the national convention in Canada, in the major parties at least, occurs during the inter-election stage, when there is a vacancy due to death or resignation. The last aspect to be examined will be the effect of Canadian parties on federalism. This will involve a discussion of the effect of national parties on provincial politics, the effect of provincial parties on national politics, and the effect of parties on federal-provincial relations.

PARTIES AS GOVERNMENT

Canada is, most of the time, in the inter-election stage. This is so despite the recent frequency of elections. In a number of countries (for example, the United States, Switzerland, and France), parties show in this stage much less output than at election time. In Canada, however, the nature of the parties together with the system of government, results in significant party outputs between elections as well. This is most noticeable in the case of the governing party.

In Chapter 6, we dealt with the impact of the system of government on the party system. Now let us consider the reverse impact. How does the governing party affect the Government, during the inter-election stage? What impact does the party have on the system of government, as the party goes about its crucial work of providing Canada with leadership and decisions? We will assume that the governing party has majority control, and we will account for minority-government and coalition conditions separately.

Since Confederation the Canadian party system has been successful in providing Canada with a Prime Minister. Throughout this period the leader designated by the majority or the plurality party was promptly designated by the Governor-General to head the Government. The party output of providing a Prime Minister has been a highly stable one. The instability of the Conservative Party from 1891 to 1896 was exceptional. It had three leaders in the few years between Macdonald and Tupper. The two Meighen governments, the brevity of which was caused by two electoral defeats, were also exceptions. Up to 1963, eight Prime Ministers governed Canada for a total period of eighty-nine years. This is an average of more than eleven years each. This leaves no doubt that Canadian parties have provided the Government with stable and durable leadership.

The Prime Minister's position as party leader facilitates the full exercise of his powers of government; that is, he is able to lead his Cabinet colleagues and the members of his parliamentary caucus because his party has selected him as its leader. His constitutional position is reinforced by his party position as he appoints, dismisses, promotes, demotes, and shuffles his Cabinet colleagues. Pressure of executive business has brought about, in recent years, the separation of the positions of Prime Minister and Leader of the House of Commons. But even when the Prime Minister does not personally lead his party in the Commons, his party position makes him his House Leader's leader.

Along with his Cabinet colleagues, who may or may not be party leaders in their own right, the Prime Minister gives day-to-day expression of party policy. The party has two output channels for this day-to-day policy. Traditionally, both are confidential. The first is the Cabinet meeting itself. The second is the meeting of the party caucus. In the case of the governing party, the caucus is bound to be large; it is as representative of the country as the seats captured by the governing party. It is in caucus that the more clearly legislative aspects of party policy are fashioned in reportedly free, because secret, debate. In the caucus, the governing party can also pronounce itself occasionally on matters of administration.

There are, in addition to government policy, other outputs of the governing party. One is the control of administration. The civil service does the actual implementing of policy, but both direction and responsibility rest with the minister concerned. As selectee and representative of his party, and as a member of its highest councils, he exercises this direction along lines determined by his party.

The governing party affects Government personnel through the practice of patronage. Patronage in Canada has been whittled down by civil service reform, and recruitment to the highest positions within the civil service takes place within the service and essentially in a non-partisan manner. The move of Tom Kent, from top-level political adviser to Lester B. Pearson, to Deputy Minister is an unusual phenomenon. But numerous minor positions and, at the other extreme, prominent positions —including many judgeships and some ambassadorships—are filled on the basis of partisan advice; such advice may come from a minister, or from a Member of Parliament of the governing party, or even from one of its defeated candidates. Then there is the most distinctly Canadian patronage appointment, a Senatorship. Here, the governing party not only pensions off one of its governmental or organizational activists, however meritorious he may be, but it also gives him the capability of doing the party's bidding within the policy-making structure. However, Senatorial interference with the will of the Commons, traditionally restricted to periods in which the opposition party controlled the Senate, has become extremely rare. It was only during the Diefenbaker years that the heavily Liberal Senate showed two signs of life. Firstly, it refused to pass—claiming that it was a bill of attainder—the Commons bill terminating the appointment of James Coyne as Governor of the Bank of Canada. Secondly, it refused to pass, though not for reasons of party, a tariff bill on the grounds that the bill would have given to the Minister of National Revenue discretionary powers that could not be appealed to the Tariff Board. But the partisan circumstances of those years were such that this spate of activity on the part of the Senate may not be repeated. In the province of Quebec—the only province with a bicameral legislature—interference of the Union Nationale-controlled Legislative Council with policies of the Liberal Legislative Assembly led to an effort on the part of the Lesage Government to curb the powers of that second chamber.

Because of the rules of the game in parliamentary government, the party output, not only in regard to decisions but also to leadership, depends on discipline within the caucus of the governing party. This legislative cohesion is present with such regularity, that the few instances in which there have been slight breaks in it have become historic occasions. Lack of cohesion among the Conservatives in the Manitoba school crisis fell in the formative years of full party solidarity. Of the other instances, all but one arose from the English-French cleavage. During the Second World War, the conscription issue led to a break in Liberal cohesion which, however, had no major consequences for the fortunes of the party. Strong consensus-building efforts by King, Lapointe, St. Laurent, and other party leaders healed the rift. The instance not related to the English-French cleavage was the nuclear warheads crisis of 1963. Lack of cohesion among the Conservatives precipitated the fall of the Diefenbaker Government, although it did not cause it; it was a minority government, and it toppled in part because of the withdrawal of passive support by the third parties. It was this last crisis that led Epstein to write:

The continued Conservative party support for Diefenbaker, despite at least substantial disagreement with his policy and his handling of the defence dispute, represents the strongest possible evidence, from a single case, of the establishment of parliamentary party cohesion in Canada.[1]

Canada's divisions—regional-ethnic, regional-economic, and federal-provincial—and the nearly constant bargaining arising from these divisions, quite often make it profitable for the governing party to be temporarily inactive. By *not* acting, the party may be averting a sectional break-up, and inactivity may thus be the most effective output of the governing party. Mackenzie King, by placing consensus building over governmental activity, was the master of this style of inactivity. It is too early to evaluate the occasional inactivity in terms of output of later Canadian Governments.

How does lack of orthodox majority status affect the effectiveness of the governing party? The Canadian experience tells us little about coalitions. The Union Government of 1917 arose from the English-French conscription issue, with the imperial wing of the Liberals joining the Conservative Government. An electorate gerrymandered in a martial direction blessed this union in what was Canada's ugliest election ever. The armistice removed the cause of the coalition but the senior partner, the Conservative Party, tried to maintain it. This coalition left such a bitter taste that it militated gravely against the Conservatives in the election of 1921. Coalitions appear to have ceased to be a viable mode of government formation in Canada on the federal level. They have, on occasion, been successful in the provinces, primarily in Manitoba and British Columbia.

Minority governments have been numerous in Canada. In King's minority government of 1921, the Liberal Party was allowed to govern effectively, but his minority government of 1925, and Meighen's Conservative minority government of the next year, foundered. Observation of three recent minority governments (Diefenbaker 1957, Diefenbaker 1962, Pearson 1963) leads us to the following tentative conclusion: minority governments are effective governments when the parties expect the Government to win an election, were it to dissolve the House. The significant legislative output of the Pearson Government of 1963-65 is a case in point, though this very government did not in fact "win" the election once it

---

[1] Leon D. Epstein, "A Comparative Study of Canadian Parties," *The American Political Science Review*, LVIII (March 1964), 54.

was called. Minority governments are ineffective in terms of the governing party when the major opposition party and the minor parties, as in the case of the Diefenbaker Government of 1962-63, feel that it would lose such an election. The dissension in the Conservative Party was only a minor factor in the paralysis of the Diefenbaker Government of 1962-63. The close election in 1962, following their devastating defeat in 1958, had made the Liberals "taste blood." Their opposition tactics were designed to bring about an early election, with an almost certain promise of victory.

Much of what we have said applies to the provinces. By and large, they have had highly effective party government, with the governing party providing leadership and decisions. Many provincial premiers have been effective chiefs of government because they have been strong party leaders. Duplessis, Douglas, Manning, Bennett, Lesage, Smallwood, Robichaud, Robarts, Stanfield, and Roblin are significant current or recent examples. In recent decades, there has been more patronage provincially than in Ottawa. Therefore, party changes in provincial governments have had more thoroughgoing effects on the civil service than have similar changes in Ottawa. Even when there have been what might be called ideological changes in provincial government, only some civil servants have been replaced. Our discussion in Chapter 4 of the Saskatchewan civil service after the provincial elections of 1944 and 1964 illustrates this. In the provincial legislatures, party cohesion has been nearly as thorough as in the House of Commons in Ottawa.

•

PARTIES AS OPPOSITION

While one party provides the government, the other parties provide opposition. The function of opposition is built into parliamentary government, and a case could be made for the proposition that, if there were no opposition, the system of government would invent one. In the years after Confederation, the main site of opposition was the House of Commons. In the 1890's, with the development of party organization in the country, opposition came to approach the British conditions of the time. Canadian opposition strategy came to be what Robert Dahl calls office-seeking opposition. Neither of the major contending parties has wanted to change the structure of the society or the government. Rather, the principal opposition party has been trying, between elections as well as during elections, to replace the governing party. This office-seeking opposition has continued to be the Canadian pattern right up to the present time.

Since Confederation, the Liberal and Conservative parties have between them monopolized government and the principal opposition. They have maintained this monopoly despite the fact that the Progressives came out second strongest in seats (though not in votes) in 1921. The two major parties have never differed on matters regarding the basic structure of Canadian society, and they have maintained a competition for the votes of all major strata of society, with occasional lapses in the relationship between the Conservatives and French Canada. Such demographic imbalances as exist and have existed between them will be discussed in Chapter 11. Throughout the past century, there has not been a definite ideological difference between Conservatives and Liberals, no matter how significant the temporary differences in style have been. Between elections, the Opposition has concentrated on the criticism of Government policies and their administration. Here, the Opposition's message to society has been not so much that they would do things differently but that they would do them better.

The opposition we have just described was essentially all the opposition there was during the first half-century of Confederation. Regional-economic and regional-ethnic cleavages during the second half-century have made the opposition picture more kaleidoscopic. In addition to the outputs of government and principal, office-seeking opposition, the Canadian party system since the First World War has given rise to an additional form of opposition. While the parties, and primarily the Liberal Party, have been able, at least until 1962, to accommodate the regional-ethnic cleavage, the regional-economic cleavage has given rise to an opposition with at least some designs for changing the socio-economic structure of Canada. Only the Communist Party has provided a sustained ideological opposition. With temporary exceptions, socialist and populist opposition has concentrated on a redistribution of rewards: at times to regions, at times to economic groups, at times to both.

In assessing briefly the effect of party on opposition in Canada, we will concentrate first on the function of principal opposition. Here, the principal opposition party gives rise to the Leader of the Opposition. His original selection is like that of the Prime Minister, and the two offices are often held alternately by the same person. Since 1942, all Leaders of the Opposition have been selected initially by their party's national convention. Just as the Prime Minister selects his Cabinet colleagues, so the Leader of the Opposition determines the make-up of the Opposition front bench, with a number of MP's, whether previous ministers or not, assigned the task of criticizing the administration of specific departments of government.

All MP's of the principal opposition party form the Oppositon caucus. Like the Government caucus, it meets regularly, and its proceedings are equally confidential. There also tends to be the same free discussion that meets the psychological pre-condition for the ensuing party cohesion. This cohesion is as nearly complete as it is in the governing party. The only major breakdown in opposition cohesion was the ethnic split over conscription in the Liberal Party during the First World War. Mr. Pearson, an electorally trounced leader with little experience in politics, maintained a cohesive Opposition from 1958 to 1963, and Mr. Diefenbaker, though repudiated in many respects by many in his party, has maintained an Opposition displaying almost entirely cohesive behaviour from 1963 until the present.

The actual outputs of the Opposition during the inter-election period take various forms. In Parliament there are amendments to bills and resolutions, most of which are introduced with the expectation of immediate failure, but with the hope of contributing to eventual success in a later election. There are parliamentary questions, some designed to prevent maladministration, others to embarrass the minister questioned. There are full-dress debates, beginning with the Debate on the Address, in which the Opposition may indicate its general approach to questions facing the society. Then there is the exposé; a noted recent example is the revelation, in 1964, by Erik Nielsen, Conservative MP from the Yukon, that parliamentary assistants of the Pearson Government were involved in an effort to prevent the extradition to the United States of Lucien Rivard, now a convicted narcotics smuggler. This revelation led to a commission of inquiry, under Mr. Justice Dorion, whose findings made possible the apparently successful exploitation of the scandal by the Conservatives in the 1965 campaign.

In addition to the parliamentary opposition activities, some of the opposition work is done outside of Parliament. Though sporadic, the research and propagandistic activity carried on at the headquarters of the principal opposition party, or by ancillary organizations, is occasionally of importance. Effective opposition work was done, for instance, during the latter years of the Diefenbaker Government by the National Liberal Federation.

In view of the volatility of some of the third parties, it is difficult to generalize about third-party opposition. Parliamentary leaders of third parties with twelve seats or more are now recognized by a special increment to their parliamentary salaries. Third-party leaders serve as the chief spokesmen of their parties, and they have considerable impact on opposition strategy and tactics. The members of their respective parties in the House of Commons form caucuses; in the case of the CCF/NDP these have an elaborate committee structure, and most of the few members are assigned duties pertaining to specific areas of government.

Recent absences of parliamentary majorities for governing parties have increased the power of third parties. However, experience to date has shown that this power is exercised only when third parties are ready to provoke a dissolution. They were prepared to do so at the time of the nuclear weapons crisis of 1963. The ensuing election cost each of the third parties a few seats, but a change from one minority government to another left them in their balance-of-power position. The same result issued from the election of 1965, which had been called by the Pearson minority government without opposition provocation. Once again, third parties are extremely unlikely to bring on a dissolution. Despite the surge of NDP strength—the most remarkable result of the election of 1965—Canadian political scientists continue to be of more than one mind concerning the future of third parties. It seems clear, however, that third parties in a minority position attempt to persuade the Government to enact some of their policies. The "persuader" in such a case is the chance that enactment of the policies will give the Government a majority the next time.

•

ARTICULATION OF INTRA- AND EXTRA-PARLIAMENTARY PARTY ORGANIZATION

Party structure itself has some influence on the way in which leadership and decisions are provided. An assessment of this influence must take into consideration the manner in which parties connect their intra- and extra-governmental structures. Such an examination tells us something about the source of party policy and the flow of policy within the party. In Canada, however, the policy-making role of the extra-governmental party structure is, generally speaking, slight.

In seeking to account for the relationship between the intra- and extra-governmental aspects of party structures, we refer to our approach to the categorization of parties. This approach was introduced in Chapter 1 in terms of origin, support, organization, appeal, and relation to government.

In a party that originated within the government, we would expect the parliamentary leadership to dominate, with the electoral and other extra-governmental organization subservient to it. The latter would be expected to nominate, to promulgate (though hardly to originate) the platform, to campaign and, between elections, to be seen, but not heard. Parties with extra-governmental origins, on the other hand, tend to have their extra-governmental organization participate in the inter-election, day-to-day provision of leadership and decisions.

While we would not expect to find social base significantly correlated to intra- and extra-governmental party relations, we would assume that a restricted base would encourage a more prominent position within the party for the extra-governmental structure.

Cadre parties we would expect to correlate with intra-governmental structure dominance. The connection between mass parties and significant extra-governmental party elements is patent; here, the mass membership contributes greatly to the attention given not only to the extra-governmental structure itself, but also to its activities, including participation in policy making.

Focus of appeal is relevant to intra-party relations in that, in a party with an appeal directed at electoral success, much business is likely to be transacted between parliamentary leaders and interest groups. In a party of principle, militant members are likely to use their extra-governmental position to influence the party.

Any governmental experience is likely to strengthen a party's intra-governmental elements. Lack of governmental experience, on the other hand, tends to leave the extra-governmental party structure in its initial position of strength, whatever such strength may be.

From the foregoing, we would expect the Liberal and Conservative parties, both federally and provincially, to show intra-governmental dominance in policy making, whether in Government or in Opposition. We would expect the Communists to show extra-governmental dominance (there is at present no Communist legislator on whom to test the power relationship) ; certainly Fred Rose, the party's sole MP, using his position as MP to spy[2] at the behest of the party organization in 1964, is an extreme case in point. We would expect the third parties to have at least extra-governmental participation at the inter-election stage, but strong intra-governmental influence wherever the party has governmental experience.

The evidence tends to bear out our expectations. Aside from the platform-creating activities that ideally precede the election stage—national conventions and the onset of an election campaign coincide infrequently—there are instances when the annual meetings of the federal Liberal or Conservative parties concern themselves with policy resolutions. Such resolutions are also presented to many of the provincial annual meetings of the two major parties. But the discussion, and even the passage, of such policy resolutions are not considered matters of great moment in either party. If anything, they are considered more important when the party is in opposition. Much of R. M. Dawson's discussion of parties in *The Government of Canada* is a tirade against the involvement of the extra-governmental party structure in policy making, but his pungent remarks about the annual meetings of the two major parties in 1947 probably present the true feeling then existing within them:

> . . . there are unmistakable signs that both Liberal and Conservative parliamentary authorities are becoming increasingly perturbed about the capers of this latest offspring [the annual meeting] which promises to become for each a family trouble-maker. In 1947 the resolutions of the Liberal Federation were buried for three weeks before being given to the public, an interval which was presumably devoted to their revision and possible emasculation by the parliamentary members. . . . The Progressive-Conservative Association in 1947 passed resolutions which did not seem to be particularly startling . . . but they apparently caused consternation in Ottawa. For although the party had all the scope in these matters which comes from being in opposition, the resolutions were advanced with the astonishing proviso that there was no intention of committing the whole party membership to the Association's proposals. The meeting, it was added, was not a policy-making convention, because its sessions were too short to permit of adequate research, consultation, and consideration. . . . [T]he statement almost certainly indicates a growing uneasiness on the part of the parliamentary group at the prospect of having its hands forced by a rival party body.[3]

There is little evidence, almost two decades later, that the fears of the two parties' parliamentary groups were well founded.

In the CCF, extra-parliamentary influence on policy making has *not* been inversely proportional to governmental experience, because the

190   THE EFFECTS OF POLITICAL PARTIES

tradition of lay policy making is strongest in precisely the province the CCF has governed, Saskatchewan. It was concluded about the Saskatchewan experience a decade ago, that:

There have been no major clashes between the Douglas Government and the lay organization. Some of the minor clashes have resulted in the caucus' disregarding conventions' decisions, but conventions have prevailed over the Government by insisting successfully on such matters as the enactment of the 44-hour week and the granting to married women of the right to work for the government. In other disputes, such as the controversy over private exploitation of Saskatchewan's oil resources, the Government won, but not without prolonged sullenness on the part of conventions.

Saskatchewan parliamentary leaders have asserted themselves most successfully where they have been able to make themselves part of the organizational machinery of the party. Premier Douglas and his colleagues combine the gaining of influence and goodwill by meeting annually with the provincial council, at the beginning of each legislative session. Equally significant parliamentary influence is brought to bear on the movement when the members of the Cabinet appear individually before the various panels of the provincial convention. It is here that some resolutions that run counter to the government's policy are nipped in the bud.[4]

National conventions of the CCF have throughout the years passed many policy resolutions. An analysis of both origin and disposition of 721 of the 742 resolutions that came before the CCF National Conventions of 1946, 1948, 1950, and 1952 is found in Table 9-1. Here, four categories of origin and three categories of disposition appear. The national leadership bodies listed are the Resolutions Committee of the National Convention, the National Council, and the National Executive. The provincial leadership bodies are provincial councils and executives. Local bodies are constituency associations and clubs. A positive disposition is adoption, with or without amendment, adoption by the National Council after reference to that body, or a statement that the resolution parallels existing CCF policy. Negative disposition includes rejection, tabling, withdrawal, a statement of conflict with CCF policy, or rejection by the National Council after reference. All other modes of disposition (e.g., a statement, in the proceedings, without accompanying explanation that the resolution is covered by CCF policy; or reference to the National Council without any record of action there) are labeled as "neutral."

Table 9-1 indicates that resolutions from leadership bodies fared much

---

[2] He was convicted of conspiracy to violate the Official Secrets Act.

[3] Robert MacGregor Dawson, *The Government of Canada*, 3rd ed. (Toronto: University of Toronto Press, 1957), pp. 544-45. See also 4th ed., pp. 501-2.

[4] Frederick C. Engelmann, "Membership Participation in Policy-Making in the C.C.F.," *The Canadian Journal of Economics and Political Science*, XXII (1956), 171-72.

TABLE 9-1

ORIGIN AND DISPOSITION OF RESOLUTIONS AT CCF
NATIONAL CONVENTIONS, 1946-1952

Origin	Disposition of Resolutions			Number of Resolutions
	Positive	Neutral	Negative	
	%	%	%	
National leadership	90	9	1	69
Provincial leadership	50	43	7	105
Provincial convention	29	56	15	157
Local body	24	55	21	390
All Resolutions	35	49	16	721

Source: Adapted from F. C. Engelmann "The CCF of Canada: A Study of Membership Participation in Party Policy-Making" (Unpublished Ph.D. Dissertation, Yale University, 1954).

better than resolutions from meetings (including provincial conventions). The friendliest treatment was accorded resolutions from national leadership bodies. Most of the leadership bodies, and especially the national ones, were made up overwhelmingly of individuals whose views were in sympathy with those of the federal parliamentary caucus. The caucus, therefore, was not saddled with many resolutions with which it was not in sympathy.

•

SELECTION OF NATIONAL PARTY LEADERS

The tenure of a Canadian party leader extends to his death, retirement, or resignation. These events coincide only rarely with the calling of an election, and the selection of a national party leader is therefore usually an inter-election function, as in the United Kingdom, and not an electoral function, as in the United States. The selection of a national party leader is a party output of the greatest importance. If the party is or becomes first in Parliament, the leader it designates becomes Prime Minister; if it is or becomes second, its leader becomes Leader of the Opposition. No representative of the Crown in Ottawa has failed to place in office the man selected by his party.

Like many other Canadian ways of doing things, the present mode of national leadership selection of the two major parties is a British-American hybrid. While the current Canadian mode is the national convention, such a convention is not, as in the United States, composed entirely of constituency and provincial delegates. In the Canadian convention, the parliamentary caucus plays a considerable, though not necessarily a decisive, role. The convention mode evolved slowly. Selection by a parliamentary caucus was the accepted way until the Liberals called a national convention in 1893. This convention retained Laurier, the party's caucus-selected leader, in his party office. R. L. Borden's selection as Conservative leader in 1901, the first instance after the Liberal Convention of 1893, was a traditional caucus nomination. But the connection of the national convention idea with leadership selection in the United States eventually had its impact on Canada. When the Liberals had to select a leader to follow Laurier, they did so in national convention. This resulted in the selection of William Lyon Mackenzie King in 1919. The Conservatives responded in 1920 with a curious procedure, out of which emerged the selection of Arthur Meighen. The Conservatives were in office at the time, and Borden insisted on a procedure which would not presume to take from the Governor-General the power to select the Prime Minister. Borden therefore asked Conservative MP's and Senators to submit names to him in writing. No tally was ever released, but Meighen appears to have "won" by a comfortable margin. In 1927, the Conservatives were in Opposition, and therefore the party felt free to choose its leader openly. It has been alleged that the good luck of the Liberals after their two national conventions, and the Conservative fiasco after the procedure leading to Meighen's selection, were instrumental in settling the party on the national convention device. The first Conservative national convention of 1927 selected Richard B. Bennett as leader. Since then, the national convention has become the accepted mode, the only exception being the short-lived caucus selections of Hanson and Meighen (the latter's second selection) as Conservative leaders.

It would be tempting to state that the major parties of Canada gave up the British way for the American. But we have already stated that the Canadian national convention is not really the equivalent of the American. And the curious modes employed in the selection of Mr. Macmillan and the Earl of Home as leaders of the British Conservative Party have spoiled generalizations about British leadership selection by the parliamentary parties.

The major parties of Canada have now held nine national conventions, eight of which (three Liberal and five Conservative) resulted in the selection of a national party leader. We believe that the stage is past at which, according to the inveterate opponent of the national convention, R. M. Dawson, "neither Liberals nor Conservatives have accepted wholeheartedly and with genuine conviction the system of choosing a national leader by the convention system."[5] We are assuming that national conventions are here to stay on the Canadian scene. Their make-up is complicated. Members of Parliament, Senators, and occasionally members of the provincial legislatures, are members *ex officio*. There are many delegates at large; these represent various interests, including youth, from the

---

[5] Dawson, *The Government of Canada*, 3rd ed., p. 547. See also 4th ed., p. 504.

various provinces. And then there is a full complement of delegates, from federal constituencies, normally three from each, with an equal number of alternates. The total number of voting delegates is between one and two thousand, and a majority vote is needed to select the leader. The most important divergence from the national conventions in the United States is that voting in Canada is secret and individual, not open and by state delegation. The conduct of a Canadian national convention is more restrained than that prevailing in the U.S. But the convention is more than a simple morale builder. Local elitists, from coast to coast, share in selecting the leader. This binding together of party activists, even at such rare intervals, in the performance of a crucial function adds significantly to party cohesion and facilitates the task of party leadership.

What has been the output of past national conventions? Whom and on what grounds have they chosen? In the case of Liberal national conventions, the selection of leaders who had not climbed up the political ladder has been noted.[6] Fielding in 1919, Power in 1948, and Martin in 1958, far exceeded their successful opponents in parliamentary experience. As King, St. Laurent, and Pearson all owed their Cabinet appointment from "outside" to the previous leader, we feel justified in saying that the selection, in the last two cases at least, came close to appointment by the predecessor. We know of no particular reason to assume that in any of the three cases a caucus would have chosen differently; in fact, the choices of St. Laurent and Pearson were foregone conclusions.[7]

Conservative convention nominations do not lend themselves easily to generalizations. R. B. Bennett, the wealthy corporation lawyer from Calgary, was the strongest candidate going into the Winnipeg Convention of 1927. The nominee of the Ottawa Convention of 1938, R. J. Manion, had all the "availability" of a typical U.S. presidential candidate: he was a Roman Catholic of Irish ancestry, was married to a French Canadian, yet had broken with the Liberals in 1917 over the conscription issue. In 1942, the Winnipeg Convention ratified Arthur Meighen's revolutionary notion of drafting John Bracken, the academic Liberal-Progressive Premier of Manitoba, who insisted on re-fashioning the party into the Progressive Conservative Party. In 1948, the balance swung back to "Conservative": George Drew, Premier of Ontario—the Tory incarnate and, as was to show soon, unacceptable to most floating voters—received an unprecedented first-ballot nomination at the Ottawa Convention. The balance swung back to "Progressive" in 1956, with the first-ballot selection of the also-ran of 1942 and 1948, John G. Diefenbaker.

Dawson's statement that "a Maritimer or Westerner has the best chance of success"[8] surely applies only to the Conservatives. In this century, four of its national leaders (Meighen, Bennett, Bracken, and Diefenbaker) have been from the West, three (Tupper, Borden, and Hanson) from the Maritimes, and only two (Manion and Drew) from Ontario. Dawson's statement is totally inapplicable to the Liberals. Their national

THE EFFECTS OF POLITICAL PARTIES

leaders in this century have been either Catholic French Canadians from Quebec (Laurier and St. Laurent) or Protestant British Canadians from Ontario (King and Pearson). Ward's speculation as to whether a Roman Catholic from Ontario is ineligible for the Liberal leadership[9] is interesting, but the sample (Paul Martin) is small.

Of the third parties, Social Credit seems to have adopted the major parties' mode of leadership selection. Robert N. Thompson was selected national leader by the party's national convention in 1961.

The selection process is essentially different in the CCF/NDP. Here, the national leader is formally elected by the biennial convention. But there is no necessary connection between the regular convention dates and the need to select a leader. Therefore, with one exception, the acts of the national conventions have been politically meaningless acclamations of the leader. The exception was the founding convention of the New Democratic Party in 1961, when T.C. Douglas, who was then re-entering federal politics after two decades on the Saskatchewan scene—mostly as Premier—defeated Hazen Argue, who had been selected by the CCF parliamentary caucus. With this exception the CCF (possibly the NDP will again do so in the future) has followed the paradoxically conservative mode of doing the selecting of its national leader through election by the parliamentary caucus. J. S. Woodsworth, M. J. Coldwell, and Hazen Argue were all selected in this manner. In the subsequent convention elections of Woodsworth and Coldwell, there was never a contest. However, the biennial national convention has at least the opportunity to retire the leader legitimately.

Whatever the method of selection—and Prime Ministers and Leaders of the Opposition in the foreseeable future will probably be selected by specially convened national conventions—the output has generally been effective. Periods of instability have been confined to the Conservative Party, and to the brief periods 1891-1896 and 1938-1942. The terms of the major party leaders have been long indeed, and their leadership (with the exception of the last years of Laurier and, possibly, of St. Laurent) was effective. John A. Macdonald was deprived of a possible endurance record by both the date of Confederation and his death. Laurier and King were national leaders for three decades, Borden and Coldwell for two. If anything, leadership has been too stable. The experience of the Conservatives after 1962 shows that it may be impossible even to raise the question of replacing the leader in a loyal fashion. At a time in which many opinions are voiced that both major parties, and possibly all parties in Canada, might benefit from a change of leaders, the lack of a regular

[6] Norman Ward, "The Liberals in Convention" in *Party Politics in Canada*, 2nd ed., ed. Hugh G. Thorburn (Toronto: Prentice-Hall of Canada, Ltd., 1967), pp. 96-103.

[7] S. Peter Regenstreif, *The Liberal Party of Canada: a Political Analysis* (Unpublished Ph.D. Dissertation, Cornell University, 1963), p. 408.

[8] Dawson, *The Government of Canada*, 3rd ed., p. 553. See also 4th ed., p. 509.

[9] Ward, "The Liberals in Convention" in *Party Politics in Canada*, 2nd ed., ed. H. G. Thorburn, p. 101.

procedure for changing leaders, even at considerable intervals, is dysfunctional.[10]

Provincial parties also selected their leaders in legislative caucus at first. They may still have to do so should a vacancy occur suddenly; but the permanent selection of what is often a permanent leader is now safely lodged in conventions held for that purpose. These conventions are representative primarily of provincial constituencies. Some of the delegates represent the provincial party organization. Seats are also given to legislative members and defeated candidates at the provincial and federal levels. The latter may be real or attempted carriers of national party influence in provincial conventions of the governing party in Ottawa.

Both major parties selected their Ontario leaders in provincial convention in the early 1960's.[11] Both nominations were hotly contested, each by seven active candidates. Both conventions needed six ballots to nominate. The rules of both parties require a majority vote for nomination, and the dropping of the candidate with the lowest vote after each ballot. In neither case had there been an obvious front-runner prior to the convention.

Unlike the Conservatives, who had met in October 1961 to select the next Premier of Ontario, the Liberals met in September 1964 to select the leader of a rather weak Opposition. Nonetheless, there were seven candidates, three of them strong contenders. Andrew Thompson and Robert F. Nixon, both MPP's, divided between them the support of the bulk of the party regulars. The pre-convention campaign was made interesting through the candidacy of Charles Templeton, the defeated candidate in the provincial by-election in Riverdale. A former evangelist, cartoonist, and journalist, Templeton received most of his support from outside the regular party circles. Only his spell-binding oratory and his announced intention to change the party into a mass party, with many members from all walks of life, made him a serious challenger. However, the regulars won. Thompson defeated Templeton on the sixth ballot. His energetic campaign, with impressions of youth and vigour, put him ahead of Nixon. A mixture of these qualities, and his party regularity, made him defeat Templeton, who was also subjected to a measure of personal attack. Thompson's connection with federal leaders, especially Walter Gordon, was held against him by some, but without success. The convention was well reported and occasioned considerable interest, despite the highly dubious nature of the prize it offered.

That prize had been real and immediate when the Ontario Conservatives met in 1961 to select the successor to Premier Frost, who had announced his retirement from active politics. The party had been in office for eighteen years under two premiers, and it held a commanding lead in votes and seats, as indeed it continues to do. Premier Frost had not attempted to name his successor, nor had the caucus expressed any preference. Of the seven contenders, there were four principal ones, all Cabinet Ministers: James Allan, Provincial Treasurer (67 years old), Kelso Roberts, Attorney-General (62 years old), John Robarts, Minister of Ed-

THE EFFECTS OF POLITICAL PARTIES

ucation (44 years old), and Robert Macaulay, Minister of Energy Resources (40 years old). Allan and Robarts came from Western Ontario, Roberts and Macaulay from Toronto.

There was a lengthy pre-convention campaign, with the candidates travelling through the province. Macaulay's campaign lasted three months, Roberts' and Robarts', two months, while Allan did not enter the race until four weeks before the convention. Macaulay had the most elaborate campaign organization; the Robarts campaign, in contrast, was directed by himself in conjunction with a close political associate, Ernest Jackson.

Roberts was the strong and active outsider. He had lost the leadership contest in 1949, and he was going to gain it this time and rejuvenate the organization. Macaulay was the vigorous idea man. Allan was the caretaker who felt called upon to offer his services as there was no obvious candidate. Robarts was the methodical plodder whose simply organized campaign was carefully planned and timed.

Roberts was slightly ahead on the first ballot. From then on, Robarts pulled ahead. His "soft sell" approach, his general acceptability, and his shunning of controversy made him emerge more and more as the consensus-building candidate, and gave him the nomination on the seventh ballot.

•

THE EFFECT OF PARTIES ON FEDERALISM

By and large, the same political parties operate in Ottawa and in the provincial capitals. Only one major party in a province, the Union Nationale, has no direct counterpart in Ottawa, and even it is historically, and to some extent electorally, the Quebec adaptation of the Conservative Party. With parties reaching across federal lines we would expect them to have some impact on Canadian federalism. Theoretically, the

---

[10] Political "de-recruitment" has not been studied systematically, though such a study is suggested in an unpublished paper by Lester G. Seligman ("Political Leadership: Status Loss and Downward Mobility," prepared for delivery at the 1966 Annual Meeting of the American Political Science Association, Statler-Hilton Hotel, New York City, September 6-10; copyright, 1966, The American Political Science Association). Of special significance in the mid-sixties is Lester B. Pearson's reply to Peter Regenstreif on how a Liberal leader might be deposed: "There is no institutional way . . . I suggest you study the Conservative Party and see how it's done . . . we haven't had to dispose of leaders. We've had very few leaders. As you know, I'm the fourth. . . . The Leader deposes himself. I don't know what other arrangements there could be." (Regenstreif, *The Liberal Party of Canada*, p. 294.) Presently, the Liberals have resolved to have a secret ballot biennially, in national convention, on the desirability of a leadership convention, and the Conservatives may be planning something similar. It is too early to say whether we are confronted with a new attitude toward leader retirement or merely with an attempt to accommodate dissatisfaction with present leaders.

[11] Information on the Liberals was supplied by an official of the Ontario Liberal Federation; information on the Conservatives is derived from David E. Allin, *The Making of a Leader 1961* (Unpublished B.A. (hons.) Thesis, Queen's University, 1962). Any interpretation is that of the authors.

Canadian party system could centralize Canada, fragment Canadian federalism further, or have little effect on federalism. As we will see, the impact varies. We will discuss the influence of national parties on provincial governments, the influence of provincial parties on the federal government, and the influence of parties on federal-provincial relations. In the first two sets of influences, our concern will be with both principal party functions, the provision of leadership and decisions.

In assessing the influence of national parties on provincial governments, it would be reasonable to begin with the assumption that the greatest influence is wielded by the governing party in Ottawa, since it has the capability of making and implementing policy decisions, many of which have a direct impact on provincial governments. The second assumption would be that the influence is greater where the nationally governing party also governs the province. The contacts discussed here cover a vast field, and our approach will have to be highly selective. Both assumptions are reasonable in actual practice, though they represent tendencies only. In the case of the second assumption there are indeed striking divergences.

The influence of federal parties on provincial government personnel is slight in any event. No federal party attempts to nominate its provincial counterpart's candidates for office. There also is little national party influence on provincial elections. National parties may "send in" prominent figures to campaign for the provincial ticket, on provincial request. The extent to which this is done is not affected by the strength of the party in Ottawa. The one strong provincial effort made by a national party was made by a governing party: it was the (temporarily) successful effort of Mackenzie King's federal Liberals to elect the Quebec Liberals and to defeat Duplessis' Union Nationale Government in 1939. The need for this unprecedented effort was manifest: to preserve national unity by replacing a government with which there could be no wartime dialogue by one with which the King Government could communicate. The leading Quebeckers in the Cabinet, Lapointe, Power, and Cardin, were mobilized, and the hazardous gamble paid off.

The example just cited is exceptional; it is also of only small theoretical significance. Normally, massive federal intervention in provincial elections is not likely to affect the outcome. Federal governing parties "win" some provincial elections and lose others. We have placed the word win in quotation marks, because the provincial counterpart's victory does not necessarily help the national party. Mitchell Hepburn's Liberals were a bane to Mackenzie King; John Robarts' Conservatives were not exactly a boon to John Diefenbaker; an assessment of the effect of the Lesage Liberals on the federal party is premature. Important, but *not* as a federal influence, is the selection as provincial leaders of such MP's as Lesage, Douglas, and Thatcher.

Regarding policy decisions, the governing party in Ottawa is the only one likely to attempt to influence provincial governments. Outside of the area of federal-provincial relations, federal parties cannot be said to have any particular policies which they attempt to foist on provincial governments. King's attempt to gain cooperation from Quebec during the war was made, as we just indicated, by changing the provincial government. An earlier instance, which appeared to be the epitome of federal party interference in provincial policy, was really an attempt to change leadership. The episode is that of King's notorious "five-cent" speech. King had been wont to aid provincial Liberals in policy matters. At the onset of the depression, King stated callously that he would refuse to help Conservative governments in the provinces for, as he called them, "these alleged unemployment purposes." In a tone which apparently backfired in the ensuing election of 1930, King said to the Commons: ". . . I would not give a single cent to any Tory government. . . . May I repeat what I have said? With respect to giving moneys out of the federal treasury to any Tory government . . . I would not give them a five-cent piece."[12] Not only the acceptance of welfare responsibility but also the present-day stature of the provincial governments make this speech sound utterly archaic.

But King stated fifteen years later that he had in fact meant to persuade all provinces to elect Liberal governments. This, as he put it, would be "a guarantee of provincial co-operation."[13] In the light of election returns over the years, there is no strong evidence that voters accept such a view of federal-provincial cooperation through national party influence on provincial governments.

Provinces represented in the Commons by one or more members of the governing party are almost invariably represented in the Cabinet. In provinces that have a single minister in the Cabinet, this minister in turn tends to assume functions on behalf of the federal party. But he is much more likely to concern himself with federal patronage, and possibly with the organizational affairs of his provincial party (especially should it be weak), than to affect personnel or policies of the provincial government.

In looking at the reverse influence, that of provincial parties on the federal government, we find that it is on balance of greater magnitude. The influence is greater on leadership than on decisions. The provision of federal governmental leadership is influenced by provincial parties through recruitment and campaigning.

Provincial party influence on recruitment extends from parliamentary candidates up to the national leadership. We have, in the preceding chapter, assigned the principal weight in the nomination of parliamentary candidates to the local constituency. Without the benefit of the results of intensive investigations, it is difficult to state how much of this local influence is in fact the influence of local provincial rather than local federal party organization. We know that several provincial party organizations, major and minor, make it their business to help supply candidates in constituencies in which the party is unlikely to make a good race. We do not know how many of the party notables who participate in the

[12] Dawson, *The Government of Canada*, 3rd ed., p. 573. See also 4th ed., p. 526.
[13] *Ibid.*

selection of federal candidates are active primarily in the provincial rather than the federal party organization.

Provincial party influence in the selection of the national party leader is no less difficult to assess. John R. Williams gives us exact figures on delegates for the Conservative National Convention of 1948,[14] but the interpretation of these figures for the purpose at hand presents difficulties. Out of a total of 1,313, 18 per cent were *ex officio* delegates, 24 per cent delegates at large, and 58 per cent riding delegates. It appears that the majority of the *ex officio* delegates were in the categories "members of Provincial legislative assemblies and the Quebec legislative council who supported the federal Progressive Conservative party" and "all Provincial Progressive Conservative leaders," and therefore represented provincial rather than federal party organization. The same may be assumed of the preponderance of the delegates at large (one *for* rather than from each federal constituency), who were to be selected by provincial associations *"not by districts, but province-wide* to represent the leading activities, educational, press, labor, agriculture, professions, business and so forth . . . ."[15] The riding delegates are as difficult to assign to the federal or provincial parties as were the notables.

The classification of delegates in the Report of the 1948 National Liberal Convention[16] labels only 20 per cent of the 1,302 delegates as provincial, while 24 per cent must be considered "national" (national officers, MP's and Senators, federal candidates); 56 per cent were riding delegates. This classification should be considered along with Norman Ward's judgment, made on the occasion of the Liberals' 1958 National Convention, that "as in 1948, but not as in 1893 and 1919, federal leaders clearly overshadowed their provincial counterparts at the convention."[17] Ward's reference to the Liberals in 1919 strengthens our conviction that, on balance, provincial influence at national conventions does exist. It is smaller than is state influence at the much more widely and deeply discussed national conventions in the United States, because voting in Canadian conventions is by secret and individual ballot, and not open by provincial delegation.[18]

The influence of provincial parties in the selection of national leaders can be assessed by looking at both the selectors and selected. Here, national politics has a commanding lead over political politics. Of the eight national leaders selected by national conventions between 1919 and 1958, only two, Bracken and Drew, had earned their spurs in provincial politics. However, even if a provincial career is not the safest avenue to national leadership, it definitely *is* an avenue. In 1966, the provincial premiers of Nova Scotia, Quebec, Ontario, and Manitoba, one-half of the major party contingent of premiers, were all being mentioned as possible national party leaders. We demonstrated in Table 4-2 that provincial office experience is a not unimportant stepping stone to federal Cabinet posts. On the other hand, for many, and by no means the least of Canada's political leaders, a provincial office career is sufficient in itself.[19]

The system of government keeps narrow the range of provincial party influence on positive policy decisions of the federal government. If Canada's Senate were representative of provincial governments, like Germany's *Bundesrat*, it could be the site of provincial party influences on national policy. As it is, such influences are brought to bear, when at all, in the secrecy of the governing party's caucus. Provincial party pressures on policy may show up within the extra-parliamentary structure of the party, but here again they are limited to the scant policy concerns of these structures. Provincial pressures are most visible in the party in which the policy-making structure itself is most visible: the CCF/NDP. In that party it is not the federal government that is influenced, but only the federal parliamentary caucus.

A rather stark instance of attempted influencing of federal policy by provincial parties was Mitchell Hepburn's quixotic effort in January 1940. The Liberal Premier of Ontario, in what he assumed would be a challenge to Mackenzie King, his party's leader and Prime Minister, introduced in the Ontario legislature a motion regretting that the King Government had "made so little effort to prosecute Canada's duty in the war in the vigorous manner the people of Canada desire to see."[20] Liberals and Conservatives in Queen's Park voted for the resolution; nationally, all it did was to help King call an election on the propitious theme of needing national unity for the prosecution of the war.

While the positive influencing of federal policy by provincial parties has been greatly limited, provincial governing parties have had a long record of serving as *de facto* opposition to the federal government. This they have done regardless of party. The Liberals of British Columbia under Pattullo, the Liberals of Ontario under Hepburn, and the Liberals of Quebec under Lesage did, just as the Liberals of Saskatchewan under Thatcher do, oppose Liberal governments in Ottawa on various issues. There are many instances of provincial party opposition to federal governments of different parties. Here we list the opposition of the Ontario Liberals under Mowat to the federal Conservatives under Macdonald, of the Quebec Union Nationale under Duplessis to the federal Liberals under King and St. Laurent, and of the Alberta and British Columbia

[14] John R. Williams, *The Conservative Party of Canada: 1920-1949* (Durham, North Carolina: Duke University Press, 1956), p. 89.

[15] *Ibid.*, pp. 87-88 (emphasis either Williams' or the party's).

[16] *Report of the Proceedings of the National Liberal Convention, Ottawa, 1948* (Ottawa: National Liberal Federation of Canada, n.d.), p. 25.

[17] Ward, "The Liberals in Convention" in *Party Politics in Canada*, 2nd ed., ed. H. G. Thorburn, pp. 96-103.

[18] Regenstreif asserts that all Liberal national conventions were controlled by the parliamentary party (*The Liberal Party of Canada*, p. 408).

[19] This point is made in an unpublished paper by Joseph A. Schlesinger ("Political Careers and Party Leadership," prepared for delivery at the 1966 Annual Meeting of the American Political Science Association, Statler-Hilton Hotel, New York City, September 6-10; copyright, The American Political Science Association, p. 11n).

[20] Bruce Hutchison, *The Incredible Canadian* (Toronto: Longmans, Green and Company, 1952), p. 270.

Social Crediters under Manning and Bennett to the federal Conservatives and Liberals under Diefenbaker and Pearson. This opposition role of provincial governing parties is important, and appears to be endemic to most federal systems. However, the often repeated claim that provincial governments have replaced federal parties as agencies of opposition to the Government of Canada is exaggerated.

In assessing the influence of party on federal-provincial relations, one might assume that party is one of the chief determinants of the atmosphere of federal-provincial relations. The assumption here would be that a Conservative Government in Ottawa would be on good terms with the Conservative governments in the provinces, and a Liberal Government with its Liberal provincial counterparts. The stormy history of federal-provincial relations in the postwar era has shown little to substantiate this assumption. Certainly, there is nothing like a Commons-like party division at federal-provincial conferences. If Premier Bennett of British Columbia is one of the chief demanders at these, he is so as spokesman of a heavily demanding province, showing more similarity to his Liberal colleagues, Lesage of Quebec and Smallwood of Newfoundland, than to his Social Credit colleague, Manning of Alberta.

Concluding this rather inconclusive section, we would say that the most important party output affecting Canadian federalism is the provincial party influence on political recruitment and campaigning in national politics. In this way, provincial parties take a significant hand in providing leadership for Canada's national parties.

●

SUMMARY

Canadian political parties have been successful in giving Canada "party government." They have done so by providing the Prime Minister and his Cabinet, by supplying a disciplined parliamentary group of the governing party, and by furnishing policies that become effective in the form of statutes and directives to the civil service. Party government in Canada has been sufficiently strong to permit parties to govern effectively without parliamentary majorities, and to make unnecessary the formation of coalition governments.

Since Confederation, Liberals and Conservatives have alternated in the roles of Government and Opposition. The pragmatic orientation of these parties, and the fact that both of them have, with only one important exception, drawn support from all of Canada, have combined to make the Opposition one that is designed primarily to replace the governing party. Only the third parties of the past half-century have had designs for changes in the structure of Canadian society. Opposition activity, especially by the major parties, centres on the creation of a favourable electoral image through a capable performance on the parliamentary scene. The most the Opposition tries to achieve substantially is some redistribution of rewards.

In assessing the importance of extra-parliamentary party organization, we found it to vary with a number of factors. Extra-governmental influence is greater with parties that originated outside of Parliament. It is greater also in parties with mass membership, a narrow social base, and a narrow focus of appeal. In any case, it tends to diminish as the party acquires governmental experience. Of the important parties in Canada, we found the CCF/NDP with the most significant extra-parliamentary influence.

While Canadian parties now select their national leaders in conventions called for this purpose, these conventions are not, as in the United States, tied to the electoral process. The leadership in Canadian parties tends to be "permanent," and conventions are called when a vacancy exists. Parliamentary members and candidates have considerable influence at these conventions. In the CCF/NDP, which holds regular conventions, the initial selection of a leader is made by the caucus, and the leader is up for confirmation at the regular convention time. Whatever the actual selection process employed, national leadership in Canadian parties has been highly stable. The main difficulty has been irremovability rather than instability of leadership.

The impact of parties on Canada's federal system has been complex. With a few exceptions, federal parties have had little influence on provincial government leaders and policies. Provincial parties, however, have had greater influence on the federal government. A number of provincial politicians have been recruited for federal leadership positions, and provincial organizations of a party have some, though not decisive, influence in its national convention. More and more, the governing parties in the provinces play a role of opposition to the federal government. In federal-provincial negotiations, the nature of the conflict between the two levels of government, and not the partisan make-up of the provincial government, is the chief determinant of the relations between Ottawa and the provinces.

10

The Shaping of Public Opinion

•

HOW DO PARTIES AFFECT VOTERS' OPINIONS?

In the last two chapters we have considered outputs from the party system in terms of the impact of parties on the political sphere, defining political in the conventional sense. In this and the following chapter, we shall move on to the broader social milieu. Our concern is with the effects, on society in general, which stem from the existence and operation of political parties.

At first glance, the connection between public opinion and political parties may appear tenuous. How is it possible for political parties, organizations concerned with attaining and exercising governmental power, to have a bearing on the way in which public opinion is formed and expressed? Before considering the evidence pertaining to such party effects in Canada, we will preface our discussion with an account of the characteristics, of parties in general and their operation in Canada specifically, which lead us to anticipate that parties will be among the important shapers of public opinion.

We have been referring to public opinion here as though it were completely undifferentiated. Rather, there are many publics, each with its own opinions on different issues, each displaying varying degrees of knowledge about issues and commitment to its views, and with varying degrees of likelihood that each can be mobilized to act in support of its opinions. For the most part, we will only be concerned with one aspect of this distinction: the existence of many publics. In terms of our interests, the focus will be on the opinions of each party's supporters.

The likelihood that a party's supporters will be affected by that support, so that the party is characterized by a high level of internal consensus, is related to at least three characteristics of parties: type of organization, social base, and focus of appeal. Our argument is that mass parties are more likely than cadre parties to influence the opinions of their supporters and hence to display more internal consensus, by virtue of the fact that they involve the wholehearted commitment and active participation of a relatively large part of their membership. Those parties which count among their supporters representatives of only a few of the principal social groups, such as one region, religion, or social class, have a greater likelihood of shaping their supporters' opinions because of this preexisting homogeneity, than do those parties which seek to draw support from all regions, religions, or social classes. When a party's primary focus of appeal is one of principle, it can be expected that its supporters will be more alike in their opinions than would be the case with a party oriented to electoral success, since the former party is openly seeking support with respect to its stand on some issues, policies, etc. In summary then, the three dimensions along which we have ordered parties—organization, social base, and appeal—can be viewed as interacting. The party type with the greatest internal consensus is the mass party of principle with a restricted base. At the other extreme is the broad-based, cadre party of electoral success, with the remaining party types falling in between, in the order suggested in Figure 10-1. We assign greatest priority in the achievement of internal consensus to the force of unifying principles. Next in importance is a narrow social base, while the membership structure is, comparatively, of least importance in shaping opinions.

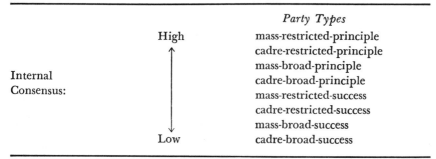

FIGURE 10-1

THE RELATION BETWEEN PARTY TYPES AND OPINIONS OF SUPPORTERS

		Party Types
	High	mass-restricted-principle
	↑	cadre-restricted-principle
Internal		mass-broad-principle
Consensus:		cadre-broad-principle
		mass-restricted-success
	↓	cadre-restricted-success
		mass-broad-success
	Low	cadre-broad-success

The typology described in the above paragraphs should be applicable to existing parties, no matter what the political setting. Other relevant aspects of parties stem more specifically from their location within a parliamentary system of government. Thus, one party serves as government and the other or others as opposition. The party as government must formulate policies and the opposition, in criticizing these, must also present alternatives. In so doing, all parties have a strong concern with issues, which the perceptive voter can at least discern from their parliamentary records. This association between parties and issues is further strengthened through election campaigns which, the concern with party images and the cult of personality notwithstanding, are often largely conducted on the basis of party stands on issues. Finally, the demand for internal party discipline, requiring that Members of Parliament follow the party line on all major issues brought to a vote, reinforces the consistency of each party's position with respect to issues. In actuality, the parliamentary system does not operate with such consistency or regularity, and parties can often find ways to gloss over policy stands when this interferes with their appeal for the largest number of votes. But theoretically at least, the operation of parties within a parliamentary system accentuates the connection between parties and their orientation to issues. The voter has for his guidance in formulating opinions the example of the party which he supports. Less frequently, his existing opinions may attract him to a party compatible with his views.

Every party system constitutes a frame imposed upon opinion, forming it as well as deforming it. The party system existing in a country is generally considered to be the result of the structure of its public opinion. But the converse is equally true: the structure of public opinion is to a large extent a consequence of the party system. . . . [1]

•

AREAS OF PARTY INFLUENCE

We have emphasized the various aspects of party systems which make it likely that parties will affect the opinions of their supporters, and we have spoken of this as opinions on issues. However, it is not only voters' views of issues which may be affected. Even more vulnerable to the influences of party attachments are perceptions of the parties themselves, perceptions of leaders, and choice of candidates.,

Opinions on Issues

INTERNAL CONSENSUS   The influence of parties on the opinions of their supporters with respect to issues can be discerned in two ways. The first is to look at the extent of consensus which exists among party supporters; the second is to compare the relative distinctiveness of each party's climate of opinion. Both procedures could be applied to a large number of political issues, extending over some period of time. We will not attempt such a comprehensive coverage of this topic but will instead rely on an existing study which dealt with the question of party influence on issues pertaining to public perceptions of Canada's identity. Data for this study were obtained from a number of surveys conducted by the Canadian Institute of Public Opinion, spanning in this part of the analysis, the years from 1951 to 1962. The examination of opinions proceeded from the assumption that different social groups frequently hold to different viewpoints, according to the way in which they see their interests affected. For example, workers may be opposed to immigration be-

THE EFFECTS OF POLITICAL PARTIES

cause they are fearful of increased competition in a limited job market, while farmers may be in favour of immigration because they welcome additional domestic markets for their products. But what happens when farmers and workers support the same political party? Does the party exist as a body of opposed supporters, held together by traditional loyalties, misperceptions, and favours? Or, and this may be in addition to the preceding rather than a distinct alternative, does the shared experience of support for the same party contribute to some modification of outlook, leading members of different social groups to be more like each other than their counterparts in other parties? For the study in question, it was found that the extent of consensus within parties varied according to the party, the characteristics of voters, and the issues considered. Issues were classified into three main categories: external, internal, and symbolic. External issues are those concerning independence and foreign commitments. Specific questions pertaining to independence are those concerned with relations with Britain, the United States, and the Commonwealth, while questions pertaining to foreign commitments are those concerned with the nature of Canada's involvement in international agencies and disputes. Internal issues are those stemming from the existence of diverse social interests and the role which government should play in the social and economic life of the country. Issues of symbolic representation arise where there is a lack of such potentially unifying symbols as flags, anthems, and national leaders. Specific questions used in the study concerned attitudes to such symbols.

As Tables 10-1 and 10-2 show, both with respect to issues and characteristics of supporters, the greatest degree of internal consensus was found in the CCF/NDP.[2] While the tables also indicate that Social Credit is internally consistent as well, conclusions must be tempered by the knowledge that data on this party's supporters were often incomplete. Much more definitive are data on the two older parties and these clearly show that internal consensus is at a relatively low level for the Conservatives and an even lower level for the Liberals.

These findings can largely be accounted for by what we have already said about the nature of parties. For example, the Conservative and Liberal parties can be characterized as broad-based cadre parties of electoral success. The data confirm our expectation that such parties are relatively unsuccessful in imposing a consistent point of view on their varied supporters. However, some differences do exist between the two parties, and the Conservatives seem somewhat more consistent in their opinions than do the Liberals. While data in support of this interpretation are not presented here, an examination of trends in opinions revealed that at least some of the greater internal consensus found for

---

[1] Maurice Duverger, *Political Parties*, rev. ed. (London: Methuen, 1954), p. 372.

[2] The examination of within-party differences (and also those among parties) was done through a statistical test termed the Index of Group Homogeneity (IGH). Internal differences in a party or other group are considered to be low when the IGH is low.

TABLE 10-1

RATING ON INTRAPARTY CONSENSUS BY PROBLEM AREA FOR EACH PARTY

	Conservative	Liberal	CCF/NDP	Social Credit
Problem Area:	%	%	%	%
Independence	68	51	80	70
Foreign Commitments	62	48	62	74
Internal Cleavages	56	57	77	74
Government Activities	52	44	60	69
Political Symbols	56	62	81	75
Total	59	53	75	72

Note: This table is adapted from Mildred A. Schwartz, "Canadian National Identity as Seen Through Public Opinion Polls: 1941-63" (Unpublished Ph.D. Dissertation. Columbia University, 1965). The higher the score, the greater the consensus. The problem areas refer to categories into which the survey questions were classified. It means, for example, that for Conservatives, on questions of independence, party viewpoints were relatively uniform regardless of the region, religion, occupation, etc., of party supporters in 68 per cent of the cases tested.

TABLE 10-2

THE INTERPLAY BETWEEN PARTY PREFERENCE AND OTHER CHARACTERISTICS
IN AFFECTING OPINIONS ON NATIONAL ISSUES

	(Rating of Intraparty Consensus)			
	Conservative	Liberal	CCF/NDP	Social Credit
Party Compared To:	%	%	%	%
Union household	84	84	83	90
Type of community	83	81	79	85
Martial status	80	70	86	70
Age	70	76	63	73
Sex	69	46	85	78
Occupation	58	53	67	70
Education	62	38	70	81
Birthplace	60	40	87	62
Official language	37	33	79	57
Region	23	20	61	56
Religion	13	26	63	35

Note: This table is derived from data presented in Schwartz, op. cit. The higher the score, the greater the consensus within the party. Consensus within parties is measured, regardless of the content of national issues, in contrast to each of the characteristics listed in the left-hand column. This means, for example, that for Conservatives, in 83 per cent of the cases tested, party viewpoints are relatively uniform whether supporters live in urban or rural communities.

THE EFFECTS OF POLITICAL PARTIES

Conservatives could be attributed to that party's longer opposition role. During the many years in which they remained out of office,

... support was more likely to come from those strongly committed to the Conservative party and influenced by the party climate of opinion. Although the accession to power of the Conservatives in 1957 and 1958 went along with a new concern with membership participation,[3] it was not accompanied by increased internal consensus. Presumably, increased responsiveness to the wishes of the rank and file would need to continue for a longer period before it would be manifested in a greater degree of intraparty consensus. For parties of this type, however, an opposition role often provides greatest opportunity for consolidation of differing viewpoints. This appeared to be true as well for Liberals when they lost favour with the voters.[4]

On questions pertaining to independence, foreign commitments, and government activities, the Conservatives showed a greater degree of internal consensus. In fostering these opinions, the Conservatives were aided by a long tradition of steadfastly standing by Britain, Empire, and Commonwealth. This perspective has frequently alienated French-speaking Canadians. Yet at the same time it has resulted in a greater ethnic homogeneity for the party, making it less difficult to reconcile differences among supporters which would otherwise stem from differing ethnic loyalties. It may appear surprising then that the Conservatives were less successful than the Liberals in imposing a unified outlook on questions of symbolic representation. Differences between the two parties are not great. There is, however, a time lag among the more traditionalist, British-oriented supporters and leaders of the Conservatives, which keeps them from responding to a growing nationalism that finds its expression in symbolic issues.

The CCF/NDP best approximates the mass party of principle with a restricted base. According to our expectations, such parties should manifest a high degree of internal consensus and Tables 10-1 and 10-2 confirm this. Homogeneity of outlook is achieved by encouraging considerable participation in policy making on the part of the membership. It is further aided by an ideological orientation notably more explicit and consistent than that of the two older parties. This ideology—in favour of extensive governmental participation in such areas as public ownership and social welfare, sympathetic to control by the central government, and suspicious of military commitments—alienates many, but to those favouring the party, its ideology is frequently a source of attraction and a guideline in responding to specific issues. Finally, this appeal to principles serves to preclude support from what turns out to be the majority of

---

[3] John Meisel, "The Formulation of Liberal and Conservative Programmes in the 1957 Canadian General Election," *Canadian Journal of Economics and Political Science*, XXVI (November, 1960), 565-74; J. M. Beck, "Quebec and the Canadian Elections of 1958," *Parliamentary Affairs*, XII (1958-59), 92-93.

[4] Mildred A. Schwartz, *Public Opinion and Canadian Identity* (Berkeley: University of California Press, 1967), p. 196.

Canadians. For example, the rejection of socialism which was explicitly preached by the Catholic Church up to the 1940's and carried over in practice until 1960, and the CCF/NDP's emphasis on centralism, have resulted in meagre support from French Canada. Beginning as a party of agrarian protest in the west, it has had difficulty moving into the cities and central and eastern Canada. With its strong social class appeal, it has had scant support from the middle class, except for its intellectual leadership. The formation of the NDP out of the CCF was designed to offset this restricted base, but the gains of the new party have been countered by the losses of the old. Thus, while the NDP has had some success in urban, industrialized areas and with workers, it has declined in appeal in Saskatchewan and with farmers generally. Internal consensus thus was achieved at the price of widespread electoral appeal.

Consensus within the CCF/NDP is of course relative, and never becomes complete. For example, compared to the degree of consensus revealed on other issues, opinions on foreign commitments and government activities are more varied. In both cases this is indicative of the tensions which exist within the party among western farmers, organized labour in central Canada, and middle class intellectuals. The latter have been most pronounced in their anti-Americanism, opposed to the acquisition of nuclear weapons, and reluctant to continue existing commitments to North American Air Defense (NORAD) or to the North Atlantic Treaty Organization (NATO). Westerners, including some labour supporters in British Columbia, have found these positions attractive, but this has been much less the case in Ontario. It may seem especially surprising, in the light of the CCF/NDP's espousal of socialist principles, that issues of government activities result in the lowest measure of consensus rather than the highest. But here again the same tensions among supporting groups are operating. An analysis of the relation between party preference, other characteristics of voters, and issues, revealed that CCF/NDP supporters were most often divided on social class lines in their evaluation of the government activities desired. Social class cleavages in this area were greater than for any other party. Beyond reporting these findings, it is difficult to interpret them, since the questions which proved most troublesome to the establishment of consensus were not repeated frequently enough to ascertain whether they indicated a clear-cut pattern and whether they were affected by the formation of the NDP, with its changed membership base.[5]

We are hesitant in saying much about Social Credit for several reasons. The public opinion data upon which this discussion is based did not produce a sample of Social Credit supporters adequate for intensive analysis. In addition, the data used was all collected prior to the June 1964 break in the party, which led dissident Members of Parliament from Quebec to form Le Ralliement des Créditistes, under the leadership of Réal Caouette. This development then could not be taken into account in the analysis of public opinions polls. The only portent of serious strains in the party, as this was reflected in the views of support-

THE EFFECTS OF POLITICAL PARTIES

ers, appears in Table 10-2, where we see the relatively low levels of consensus across regional and ethnic lines. At the outset of its establishment in Canada, Social Credit could have been characterized as a mass party of principle with a restricted base. It was a social movement, not just a political party, demanding intense commitment to its leadership and principles. But unlike the CCF, where study and debate were considered essential ingredients for meaningful social action, Social Credit principles were soon treated as beyond the understanding of most supporters. They were asked simply to put their faith in Aberhart, who would see that Social Credit policies were instituted as soon as possible. It was inevitable that the study groups which had formed the original nuclei for the spread of Social Credit in Alberta soon lost their primary function and became adjuncts of the party machinery. Not only has the party become more cadre than mass in membership structure, but its focus of appeal has altered as well. Its principles, especially concerning monetary reform, have been played down in the interests of electoral success. If its supporters then displayed considerable homogenity of outlook (assuming this was not solely the result of sampling variability when using small samples), this was probably due mainly to its base of support being restricted to the western provinces; this too must be qualified in the face of the upsurge of support for Social Credit in Quebec.

DIFFERENCES AMONG PARTIES Up to this point we have considered the extent of similarities among different kinds of supporters within the same party. Here we will deal with the uniqueness of each party's climate of opinion with respect to the same issues and based on the same data. The question we are raising here is not how successful a party is in submerging the particularistic interests of supporters and creating instead a party perspective on issues, but rather with how the collective opinions of supporters serve to differentiate the parties. It would be possible, and this occurs in some instances, for differences both within and between parties to be minor. This is the case, for example, on some social welfare issues, where an overwhelming majority of the supporters of all parties currently favour family allowances.[6]

We can in these instances speak of a general consensus. More frequently there is considerable division in opinions, according to the perspectives provided by party support or other social groups. At issue is whether or not it is possible to characterize parties by the distinctiveness of their supporters' opinions so that each party displays its own climate of opinion. From the available data it appears that there is considerable similarity between the views of Conservatives and Liberals and that the CCF/NDP is most unique in outlook. (There is probably also similarity between the two older parties and Social Credit; but as we have indicated, data are sparse, and do not reflect most recent events.) There is

---

[5] *Ibid.*, pp. 175-78.

[6] A Gallup Poll release of March 12, 1955 indicated that 90 per cent of the population favoured family allowances.

also some variation according to the issues considered and the time period under review. A summary of these differences is shown in Table 10-3. While it is self-explanatory in its general outlines, it does not reveal more specific differences, and it is these on which we will comment. On external issues, it was the Conservatives and CCF/NDP who were farthest apart in opinions; this was due mainly to views of the Commonwealth and, to a lesser extent, on international economic relations. Of all party supporters, Conservatives were most favourable to the continuation of ties with the Commonwealth while the CCF/NDP were more frequently advocates of an independent course for Canada. In economic matters, the CCF/NDP were inclined to favour ties with Britain, as were the Conservatives, but the former were much more suspicious of those with the United States and of foreign investment in Canada. The source of Conservative differences with the Social Credit was also related to the Commonwealth, but it reflected the extent of Social Credit support for union with the United States. Liberals and CCF/NDP lined up on different sides on economic issues relating to Canadian independence. The anti-Americanism of some CCF/NDP supporters led them to oppose overly close trade ties with the United States and foreign investment in Canada, and to favour trade ties with Britain. The majority of Liberal supporters expressed contrary views.

Again elaborating on Table 10-3, we find that the major difference on internal issues was between CCF/NDP supporters and those of the Liberal and Conservative parties. The greatest degree of differentiation occurred in response to such ideological questions as the desirability of government control over business and industry and governmental guarantee of steady work. Although the passing years have brought fairly widespread approval for social welfare measures from all parties, these issues still produce some differences between the CCF/NDP and others, as that party espouses an even broader application of such measures.

Symbolic issues have been one problem area dividing Conservatives and Liberals, as the former cling to British and old forms of symbolic representation for Canada and the latter pursue a more highly nationalistic approach. But these differences have been declining in recent years, as the Conservatives too look with more favour on Canadian symbols (the controversy over the introduction of the new flag notwithstanding). The opposition between Conservatives and CCF/NDP is not so clear-cut, but appears to be declining, not because of the Conservatives' growing nationalism, but through a number of instances when CCF/NDP supporters favoured British symbols. This could be considered surprising in the light of the CCF/NDP's less than wholehearted support for the Commonwealth. But favourability to ties with Britain may reflect both a way of countering American influence and involvements and the British origins of many CCF supporters.

Distinctive climates of opinion appear to emerge from the particular character of the supporters and the specific nature of the party's principles. For the CCF/NDP, for example, the consistency of views toward

TABLE 10-3

DIFFERENCES IN VIEWPOINTS BETWEEN PARTY SUPPORTERS,
ACCORDING TO PROBLEM AREA

| | Problem Area | | |
	External	Internal	Symbolic
Least different*	Liberal and Social Credit	Conservative and Liberal	Conservative and Social Credit
	Conservative and Liberal	Conservative and Social Credit	Liberal and CCF
	CCF and Social Credit	CCF and Social Credit	Liberal and Social Credit
		Liberal and Social Credit	CCF and Social Credit
	Liberal and CCF		
	Conservative and Social Credit	Liberal and CCF	Conservative and Liberal
Most different	Conservative and CCF	Conservative and CCF	Conservative and CCF

*Pairs of parties are arranged in order, from least to most different. The line divides differences in the views of supporters of less or greater than 10 per cent.

Note: Adapted from Mildred A. Schwartz, "Canadian National Identity as Seen Through Public Opinion Polls: 1941-1963" (Unpublished Ph.D. Dissertation, Faculty of Political Science, Columbia University, 1965.)

public ownership and social welfare derives partially from the ideology it advocates and partially from the farmers and workers it attracts. As far as that party's stands on international involvements are concerned, whether these are economic or political, it is not likely that the bulk of its supporters would normally be terribly concerned. Since leadership on such issues is provided by the middle class intellectuals in the party, when rank-and-file supporters do express an opinion, it is likely to be in the direction given by the leadership. This is so because all supporters of this party are more sensitized to policy orientations than is generally the case for the two older parties. For the latter parties, policies and actions undoubtedly play some part in producing the kinds of opinions found, even if these were not as sharply differentiated. Moreover, the kinds of supporters which they attract also affect their climates of opinion. The great proportions of those of British origin found in the Conservative Party contribute to that party's pro-British orientation. Conversely, the great proportions of Liberal supporters who are of French or other European origins encourage the Liberal Party's more nationalistic viewpoints.

Thus, while we began by positing that political parties would influence the opinions of their supporters, we obviously need to take into account the fact that their supporters will also have some effect on the kinds of policies and programs the parties present.

Perception of Parties

Support for a party is frequently accompanied by a general conception or image of that party, somewhat separate from particular issues. This may be partly the result of party positions on issues, but after the issues themselves have disappeared their impact can continue as part of the image which the party conveys.[7] It may also derive from more diffuse policy orientations, from appeals to special groups in the population, or even from historical accidents. But whatever the reasons, supporters are often able to ascribe characteristic features to their favoured party. Each party's supporters selects its own choice as the party best for hard times, for keeping the country prosperous, and under which the respondent and his family would be better off.[8]

The above findings are hardly surprising. It may be less self-evident, however, that party images have some existence independent of the perceptions of their own supporters. That is, in conformity with the intent of modern advertising techniques adapted to political campaigning, voters do hold relatively diffuse conceptions of political parties—whether they vote for a party or not—which are separate from their views of party stands on specific issues, or even from their knowledge of these. From the data we commented on above, it was possible, allowing for the tendency to see one's own party in favourable terms, to still discern fairly distinct party images. Of the two major parties, the Liberal was more frequently associated with prosperity, with doing a better job during hard times, and as being best for oneself and one's family.[9] The long years of Liberal reign and the association of the Conservative Party with the depression of the 1930's have apparently left their mark on the way many Canadians see the two parties, to some extent independently of how they vote. These findings further demonstrate the influence of parties on the opinions, not only of supporters but also of other voters.

Perception of Leaders

The political leader in Canadian politics has a particularly important position because of the demands placed on the machinery of government to provide leadership in a highly fragmented society. As a result, it has been argued that the leader personally plays a preeminent role in this system. "In Canada more than anywhere else it is possible to define a party as being a body of supporters following a given leader. Parliamentary elections are primarily occasions on which the electors choose between party leaders and prospective prime ministers."[10]

The alignment between voters' perceptions of party leaders and their partisan choice is shown in data from two surveys in Table 10-4. These data reveal a high correlation between a favourable evaluation of a party

TABLE 10-4

CHOICE AS BEST

PRIME MINISTER FOR CANADA

REGARDLESS OF OWN POLITICAL FEELINGS

	Conservative Supporters		Liberal Supporters	
	1960	1965	1960	1965
	%	%	%	%
Diefenbaker	77	64	12	4
Pearson	7	9	63	84
Both the same	10	14	14	8
Undecided	6	13	11	4

Sources: The 1960 data are from a Canadian Institute of Public Opinion survey conducted in July 1960 and specially tabulated for this book. The 1965 data are contained in a C.I.P.O. release dated January 20, 1965.

leader and support for his party. In addition, other surveys show that, while the great majority of a party's supporters approve of the way their leader is doing his job, some small proportion either disapprove or are undecided, while a moderate share (usually about 25 per cent) of the opposition party's supporters agree with the majority in their favourable evaluation of the nation's leader.[11] We can hardly use these data as a refutation of the dominating position of party leaders. But they do cause us to reflect on the independent effects of party. If we look back at Table 10-4 we can see how, when a party is out of office, its supporters become more doubtful of their leader than they do of their party. Party appears then both to contribute to favourable conceptions of party leaders and to retain loyalties which unsuccessful leaders (i.e., those who lose elections) are not able to keep.

While not directly relevant to the subject we are discussing here, some word should be said about the consequences of having party leadership perceived somewhat independently of partisan loyalties. In essence, these findings highlight the integrative potential of the party leader. The public opinion data reveal how party opponents as well as supporters acknowledge the fitness of party leaders to assume their leadership role. In

---

[7] Angus Campbell, Philip E. Converse, Warren E. Miller, Donald E. Stokes, *The American Voter* (New York: John Wiley & Sons, 1960) p. 60.

[8] Reference here is to Canadian Institute of Public Opinion surveys conducted in December 1957, July 1960, July 1961, and March 1962, from which ten relevant questions were obtained.

[9] Schwartz, *Public Opinion and Canadian Identity*, p. 207.

[10] H. McD Clokie, *Canadian Government and Politics* (Toronto: Longmans, Green, & Co., 1944), p. 91.

[11] While we have not reported on these data in detail, they have been obtained from unpublished tabulations made by one of the authors on Canadian Institute of Public Opinion surveys. Similar findings with respect to provincial party leaders appeared in an Ontario study, as yet unpublished, by Peter Regenstreif conducted under the auspices of the Toronto *Daily Star*.

all democratic states where there exist more than one party, this ability of the party leader to appeal to those outside his party has important consequences for the stability of the political system. In the United States, not a presidential election goes by without some individuals threatening to leave the country if Candidate X is elected. What is more noteworthy, however, is not that a few individuals actually do leave[12] but that almost all Americans remain and, what is more, do not plot the overthrow of the President beyond the peacable means available through the electoral process. Customarily, public opinion polls find that, after presidential elections, some proportion of the electorate who voted for the opposition party come to alter their views of the President despite his party affiliation, and to recognize his leadership ability.[13] Data on the favourable views of the national leader which are shared among governing and opposition party supporters are also available for other countries.[14] They contribute to an interpretation of one of the factors associated with the stability of political systems—political leaders who not only inspire loyalty and respect from their party and its supporters, but who are also able to convince some portion of the opposition that they possess abilities which fit them for leadership. These opponents, however grudgingly, ensure that the party leader becomes, on the assumption of office, truly a national leader.

Choice of Candidates

At each election the voter is presented with a ballot on which are listed the candidates running for office, with no identification of their party affiliation. To the confusion of those who immigrate to Canada as adults and who are not informed of the workings of the Canadian political system, only those voters resident in his constituency have an opportunity to vote for the party leader. Superficially, at least, these formal characteristics of the electoral process would seem to encourage a strong candidate orientation, at the expense of party loyalty or leaders' appeal. However, in terms of how voters assess influences on their decisions, it is party which outweighs the drawing power of the local candidate. In 1944 and again in 1962, the Canadian Institute of Public Opinion asked voters, "In an election, which influences your vote the most, the policies of a political party as a whole, or the kind of candidate the party has in your own riding?" In 1944, 53 per cent mentioned party and 36 per cent candidate; in 1962, it was 44 per cent for party and 39 per cent for candidate.[15] This particular question was not adapted to the subtleties of electoral decision making, but it indicates the relatively greater influence of party.

The above data also suggest a possible decline in party influence over the years. If this is the case, have all voters responded similarly, or are some more affected by the attractiveness of their local candidates? Some clues can be found in the victory of the Conservatives, especially in 1958. 1958 marks the Conservatives' sweeping victory, which brought with it into the Conservative fold a host of new voters, previously uncommitted ones, or those who had formerly voted for other parties. Observation

THE EFFECTS OF POLITICAL PARTIES

leads us to believe that a large part of these recent Conservative supporters voted the way they did because of their disillusionment with the
Liberals, their responsiveness to the promise of change, or their attraction
to John Diefenbaker, rather than because of any large-scale commitment
to the principles and policies of the Conservative Party. As a result, these
same voters were not as much under the influence of their party as they
might otherwise have been. In support of this we note that in the 1962
survey reported, it was Conservative supporters who were least likely to
answer that party was influential in deciding their electoral choice. Table
10-5 permits us to infer that the possible trend to the abatement of party

TABLE 10-5

RELATIVE INFLUENCE OF PARTY AND CANDIDATE
IN AFFECTING VOTING DECISION, 1962

Most influence	Conservatives	Liberals	Other
	%	%	%
Party	39	53	59
Candidate	44	36	30
Other	10	3	4
Undecided	7	8	7

Source: Canadian Institute of Public Opinion release April 4, 1962.

influence from 1944 to 1962 did not occur for supporters of other parties,
particularly the more ideologically-oriented CCF and Social Credit, cited
in the table under "other."

We conclude from these items that party influences the outlook of
supporters in national elections, but that this influence becomes attenu-
ated when a major political change occurs without providing either the
mechanisms or the time for new supporters to become socialized into the
new outlook of their party.

The Regenstreif study, conducted in Ontario prior to the 1963 provincial election, also collected data permitting an evaluation of the influences of candidates on voters' choices. While the relevant questions did
not specifically ask for respondents' behaviour in provincial elections,
since the focus of the interview was on this subject, we can presume that
those replying likely had such elections in mind. Voters were first asked,

---

[12] The only sizable exodus followed the Revolutionary War, but then the response
was to a new form of government rather than to the person of the president himself.

[13] For some examples see Elmo Roper, *You and Your Leaders* (New York: Morrow,
1957).

[14] See for example, Juan J. Linz, "The Cleavage Structure of West German Politics,"
a paper presented at the 5th World Congress of the International Sociological Association, Washington, D.C., 1962.

[15] In both years, the remainder either mentioned other influences or were undecided.
Canadian Institute of Public Opinion release, April 4, 1962.

"On the whole, which of the following is most important to you when you vote: the party itself, the party's leader or the local candidates in the constituency?" The largest proportion, 36 per cent, answered that party was most important, while 11 per cent selected the party leader, and another 5 per cent answered that the party and party leader were equally significant. Local considerations were relatively less important, with 26 per cent replying that the local candidate was most critical in affecting their decisions. Even more clear-cut are the results of the following question:

Suppose there was an election in which the party you happened to favour was running a candidate you did not like or did not agree with. Which of the following statements comes closest to what you think you would do?

I probably would vote for the candidate anyway	*51%*
I would consider another party's candidate	*30*
I probably would not vote for anyone in the election	*11*
Don't know	*9*
N = 988	

Source: Unpublished study of the 1963 Ontario provincial election, conducted by S. Peter Regenstreif for the Toronto *Daily Star*.

While it is possible that the wording of the question used in the above had some effect on the distribution of answers, this question in combination with the others lends support to the view that party has greater drawing power than do local candidates in determining the specific choices of voters. There is, of course, great variation in the way in which this influence operates, since some candidates have stronger personal appeal than others, and elections differ in the extent to which they are contests based on issues, the personalities of the leaders, or the strength of traditional partisan loyalties. But within these qualifications, it is possible to conclude that, in general, party is a prime consideration in affecting the likelihood that candidates will receive the support of voters.

•
LIMITS ON PARTY INFLUENCE ON OPINIONS

In each of the four areas considered—issues, party images, leaders, and candidates—it was possible to demonstrate that each of the four political parties displayed a unique perspective insofar as this was discernible through the views of supporters. From this it was inferred that parties influenced public opinion by affecting the opinions of at least their own supporters. But with each item of information presented, it was also possible to see that, with the possible exception of the CCF/NDP, the influence of party was far from overwhelming. Limitations on the effectiveness with which parties can establish a climate of opinion derive from at least three possible sources. These are voters' misperceptions of the current political situation, the deliberate efforts of parties to play down differences, and the significance of other cleavages, whose boundaries do not coincide with those of parties.

Voters' Misperceptions

While we have not specifically sought evidence of the misperceptions voters may have of the stands which their parties take on specific issues, we can rest assured that such misperceptions are not unusual. These may arise as a result of a low level of education, which leads to lack of interest or understanding of political issues. Limited exposure to the information communicated by the mass media, often a correlate of low educational attainment, also contributes to distorted evaluations of party stands. The nature of the issues themselves may cause confusion, insofar as these require technical or specialized knowledge or lend themselves to distortion through their emotional overtones. Finally, irregular support for a party or weak partisanship diminishes the likelihood of following the party line as a guide in the formation of opinion.[16] Even for those who almost always vote for the same party, however, there may still be considerable distortion in the way the party's programs are seen. As our typology of parties indicated, a broad-based, cadre party of electoral success would not be expected to display high consensus among its supporters because of the way in which supporters are attracted, involved in the party, and recruited from diverse social origins. One of the consequences of all these factors associated with the possibility of misperception is revealed in Table 10-3, where we showed that the views of major party supporters were frequently very similar, despite differences in their parties' programs and policies.

Attempts to Minimize Differences

Differences in the ways in which parties approach political issues arise in the conduct of Parliament, during party conventions, and through policy-making decisions at the leadership level. No party is a monolithic structure, and considerable diversity exists among regions and other subgroupings both at the provincial and national levels. In addition, the longer the party's history, the greater the likelihood that policy stands taken at one point in time will be abandoned or even reversed at another period. Hence the decisions made by any one group of policy makers or at any one time are vulnerable to the opposition of other elements in the same party. This is especially the case when the positions taken are perceived as alienating important segments of the electorate. For example, during the controversy over the adoption of a new flag, Mr. Diefenbaker, as leader of the Conservatives, voiced strong opposition to the abandonment of the Red Ensign, or at least, to the exclusion of the Union Jack on some part of a new flag. Many influential Conservatives, concerned by the impact of such a policy on French-speaking voters, as well as on the

---

[16] For an elaboration of these and related points based on empirical evidence from the United States, see Bernard R. Berelson, Paul F. Lazarsfeld, William N. McPhee, *Voting* (Chicago: University of Chicago Press, 1954) ; Lewis A. Froman, Jr. and James K. Skipper, Jr., "Factors Related to Misperceiving Party Stands on Issues," *Public Opinion Quarterly*, XXVI (Summer, 1962) , 265-72.

growing nationalist spirit in the country as a whole, were led to repudiate this position. Under less emotionally tense circumstances, similar tendencies also emerge. A party may begin by opposing a policy initiated by its rivals. However, when this policy appears to provoke wide public appeal, the initial opponents may adopt it as their own and attempt to outdo those who originated it. While everything we have said about parties thus far would lead us to anticipate that such policy switches would most often occur among parties of electoral success, even more ideologically oriented parties are not immune to the need for playing down policy differences in order to attract more voters. For example, during the 1962 election, some leaders of the NDP proposed that Canada withdraw from NORAD, and under some circumstances, from NATO. Not all NDP leaders were united in their approval of these plans and this reservation was felt by many candidates. In the Toronto area, where candidates sought support from European immigrants often militantly anti-Communist, NDP policies on international military commitments were tactfully ignored by the campaigners wherever possible.[17] Yet in general, it is correct to assume that parties of electoral success (the Conservatives and Liberals) will be more prone to move in similar directions. Insofar as the opinions of their supporters reflect this movement, a relatively low level of differentiation between the two parties appears in Table 10-3.

Another potential for minimizing party differences arises whenever candidates represent a coalition of parties, or when the Government is formed through a coalition. By their very nature, coalitions de-emphasize the uniqueness of individual parties in order to achieve electoral success and governmental stability. In so doing, they necessarily play down individual differences and emphasize instead common interests and goals. In the course of Canadian history there have been several instances of coalitions—the Union Government of 1917, the coalition governments in Manitoba and British Columbia in the 1940's, the informal alliance of the Conservative and Union Nationale parties in Quebec, and numerous candidates who have run as the representatives of more than one party, either openly or tacitly. Unfortunately, we do not have available survey data to show how such coalitions affected partisan loyalties and outlooks. We would expect that partisanship was lessened in British Columbia and Manitoba. The coalition of 1917 was, however, a special case, brought about by the wartime issues. The re-emergence of traditional party alignments in 1919 showed how transitory had been the effect of the Union Government. We can hardly use it then as an instance of the lessening of party differences.

In total, the pressures of campaigning for elections and attracting the widest possible body of support are among the factors leading parties, at times, to downgrade the distinctiveness of their programs and policies and hence to diminish the potency of their opinion-shaping role. This may also be true when they emphasize such non-issue concerns as the character of the leader or of individual candidates.

220

The Significant Cleavages

Empirical evidence on the opinions of party supporters indicates that, compared to support for parties, opinions of voters are much more strongly affected by ties of region and origin. This is true for all parties, except the minor ones or at least the CCF/NDP. In the case of the CCF/NDP, party was able to exert a major influence partly because of the absence of widespread support from all regions and origin groups. These public opinion data accord with our summary analysis of Canadian society in Chapter 2, where we showed, from demographic and economic trends, how the cleavage structure emerged and has been perpetuated. Regional loyalties, reinforced by ethnic and economic considerations, have resulted in distinct divisions within the country, and these in turn have shaped the viewpoints of Canadians. To the extent that these are the basic loyalties of many Canadians, political parties have been limited in their impact on supporters. On the national level, this has been especially the case of the major parties, since the lines of party and other social cleavages do not coincide. The full implications of these relations between parties and other cleavages will be explored in the following chapter.

•

SUMMARY

To some extent then, political parties are able to influence the opinions of their supporters, at least on significant national issues. The scope of this influence is related to the nature of the particular party. This influence extends not only to opinions on issues, but also to the way in which the parties themselves are perceived. Partisanship was shown to have an effect on the way in which party leaders are evaluated, although in this case we also demonstrated that voters' views of leaders are somewhat independent of support for a party. Finally, there was evidence that, disregarding local conditions, in national elections, it was the party which had most effect on the voters' selection of candidates.

The degree to which parties are able to exert influence on the views of the public are limited in at least three ways. Probably the most significant are the limitations which derive from the strength of alternative loyalties and interests. In the case of Canada, parties have run a second place to the more pressing claims of regionally-based ethnic and economic cleavages. Some of the lack of party influence is due to the misperceptions of voters, who are, for various reasons, unable to detect the full extent of differences or similarities between parties. Finally, since the impact of a party on the opinions of its supporters is strongly conditioned by the uniqueness of that party, we could expect that party influence would be low where parties deliberately attempt to play down inter-party differences.

---

[17] Mildred A. Schwartz, "Political Behaviour and Ethnic Origin" in *Papers on the 1962 Election*, ed. John Meisel (Toronto: University of Toronto Press, 1964), p. 265.

11

The Impact of Parties on Societal Consensus and Conflict

•

THE ROLE OF PARTIES

In their influence on the social milieu generally, parties play two apparently contradictory roles: they foster consensus and provide a focus for conflict.

The conflict-inducing aspects of parties are quite self-evident, since the essence of party politics is competition. Each party has support from only parts of the electorate, and in acquiring and maintaining this support, it inevitably makes claim to special concessions and access to scarce resources. As a consequence it comes in conflict with other parties representing other interests. Parties deal with issues, creating new ones and directing old ones into partisan channels. They continually emphasize the unique contributions they can make to solving problems as compared to the blundering outcomes of the actions of opposing parties. The issues they raise are then a source of conflict. Controversies can rage over many different issues, and those affected by these issues can publicly express many shades of opinion. However, parties have an important function in organizing such controversies, often by simplifying the issues involved and directing them into partisan channels. In this fashion parties mobilize an otherwise passive electorate into opposing factions.

Disturbed by the possible fragmentation of society, leading as a natural course from the conflicts generated by the activities of political parties, commentators on the political scene have looked for countervailing tendencies or mechanisms. They have found these to lie in the existence of some measure of consensus cross-cutting lines of conflict. For example,

Lord Balfour wrote that parliamentary government "pre-supposes a people so fundamentally at one that they can safely afford to bicker."[1] What Balfour and later writers have had in mind is essentially a consensus on the "rules of the game"—those beliefs and values about how the political system should operate, which make up a part of each nation's political culture.[2]

The part played by political parties in the fostering of consensus has been most fully elaborated by Austin Ranney and Willmoore Kendall. They consider "nurturing consensus" to be one of the major functions of the American party system.[3] The party system makes this kind of contribution because each of the major parties in the United States draws support from all social strata, although not to an equal extent. Yet all or most social groups are viewed by the parties as at least potential supporters and hence appeals are directed to them and promises are made (and frequently kept), to satisfy the specific needs of different elements of the population. But what satisfies one group, displeases another. As a result, each party frequently contains within its platforms and programs conflicting ideas and ideologies. At the same time, by deliberately giving scope to opposing interests and ideals within each of the major parties, the opportunity for mobilizing an ideologically consistent political movement on any large scale tends to be undercut and "the likelihood of ideological strife triggering our civil-war potential"[4] is played down. Ranney and Kendall also feel that consensus is promoted by the personal touch which parties and their leaders give to the otherwise impersonal laws and structures making up the government, thereby providing a more human quality to capture the loyalties of citizens. The search of the major parties for support from many different groups and the consequent need to satisfy at least some of these means that the parties help keep a pluralistic society going; this is indicated in the United States by the absence of new revolutionary minor parties and the weakness of existing ones.

The consensual aspect of party politics has also been a favoured theme of Canadian commentators. They have apparently been influenced by

---

[1] Quoted in John T. McLeod, "Party Structure and Party Reform" in *The Prospect of Change*, ed. Abraham Rotstein (Toronto: McGraw- Hill Co., of Canada Ltd., 1965), p. 4.

[2] This is an area where a great deal has been written. Our references have been selected to give some indication of the nature of the views expressed and the range of theoretical interests represented. As a sample see, Herbert J. Spiro, *Government by Constitution* (New York: Random House, 1959); Talcott Parsons, " 'Voting' and the Equilibrium of the Political System," in *The American Voter*, eds. Eugene Burdick and Arthur J. Brodbeck (New York: Free Press, 1959), pp. 80-120; Bernard R. Berelson, Paul F. Lazarsfeld, William N. McPhee, *Voting* (Chicago: University of Chicago Press, 1954), pp. 305-23; Robert MacIver, *The Web of Government* (New York: Macmillan Co. Ltd., 1947); Gabriel A. Almond, "Introduction: A Functional Approach to Comparative Politics" in *The Politics of the Developing Areas*, eds. G. A. Almond and J. S. Coleman (Princeton: Princeton University Press, 1959), pp. 3-64.

[3] Austin Ranney and Willmoore Kendall, *Democracy and the American Party System* (New York: Harcourt, Brace & Co., 1956), pp. 504-513.

[4] Ranney & Kendall, *Democracy and the American Party System*, p. 509.

Pendleton Herring's concept of brokerage politics, where parties are seen to function primarily as conciliating intermediaries between opposing interests.[5] In the case of Canada, this view of parties has evolved rather easily out of the experience of the pressing need for national unity. For example, we find Corry first viewing the functions of political parties in this light and then making the easy transition to Canadian parties.

Party politicians are not, and cannot be, crusaders, men of single-minded passionate purpose, who drive straight to the realization of their ideals. They are not even generally the inventors of the ideas they expound. In the aptest phrase yet applied to them, they are brokers of ideas. They are middlemen who select from all the ideas pressing for recognition as public policy those they think can be shaped to have the widest appeal and, through their party organization, they try to sell a carefully sifted and edited selection of these ideas (their programme) to enough members of the electorate to produce a majority in the legislature. . . .

Perhaps the simplest illustration of the necessity for such accommodation is to be found in Canadian politics. The people of the Province of Quebec, overwhelmingly French-speaking and Roman Catholic, make up about one-quarter of the population of Canada. Therefore, it is only rarely that a political party can win power without getting substantial support in Quebec. But Quebec opinion on what the national Parliament should be instructed to do for the common good shows marked divergences from the lines of policy for which majorities can be found in the rest of Canada. Accordingly, political parties must modify their programmes to find a compromise that will produce a nation-wide majority. This compromise will be something that neither Quebec nor the rest of the country would plump for if each were going its own way.[6]

This is a position also taken by other prominent Canadian political scientists, among them Brady, Clokie, and Dawson.[7]

Our own perspective is that the relation between the consensus- and conflict-inducing roles of parties is an empirical problem, requiring detailed examination of the workings of parties in their respective sociopolitical milieus. For example, exponents of the consensual nature of American party politics, at least as this applies to such fundamental issues as the nature of American democracy, need to qualify their generalizations about the widespread acceptance of democratic values if they take seriously the results of surveys reported by Herbert McClosky. In his study he found such consensus to exist among only the more politically sophisticated party activists, and even there it was limited.[8] For Canada then, we shall attempt to assess, in as objective a fashion as possible, the relative contribution made by parties to encouraging either consensus or conflict, having neither a commitment to the conservative orientation of the consensus theorists nor to the radical orientation of the conflict theorists. We will view these party outputs in terms of those four aspects of Canadian society according to which we organized much of our previous discussion on inputs to the party system: social class, religion, ethnicity, and region.

•

SOCIAL CLASS

In almost all industrialized societies in the Western World, a primary focus of cleavage has been along social class lines and this cleavage has found expression and has frequently been augmented through the activities of class-based political parties. Canada is a notable exception to this generalization. In meeting the potential conflict inherent in the existence of different social classes, the major Canadian political parties have made their contribution mainly by searching for consensus across class lines. For the most part, the search has been marked with success. Evidence for the consensus-inducing role of parties is revealed by the lack of polarization of voters along class lines, in either their voting behaviour or their political opinions.[9]

Many of the reasons for this lack of a partisan base for class conflict in Canada have already been discussed in the context of the social structural factors underlying the formation and operation of political parties. Some of these factors merit discussion here as well, as we consider the impact of parties on society.

To some extent, the conditions of life in Canada, as in the United States, have permitted what might otherwise be class hostility to be channelled off in other directions. Among the conditions that have been suggested are the absence of a feudal past (despite a transplanted seignorial system in New France), an underpopulated country rich in resources with great room for expansion, an extensive frontier that could absorb both the malcontents and those whose opportunities were limited in more settled regions, large scale immigration which reinforced cleavages along ethnic rather than class lines, and an unequal growth rate for regions which focused conflict on regional rather than nationally-based cleavages.[10] Other contributing factors are a slow rate of industrialization,

---

[5] E. Pendleton Herring, *The Politics of Democracy* (New York: Norton, 1940). The concept was first employed in A. Lawrence Lowell, *Public Opinion and Popular Government*, rev. ed. (New York: Longmans, Green Ltd., 1914).

[6] J. A. Corry and J. E. Hodgetts, *Democratic Government and Politics*, 3rd ed., rev. (Toronto: University of Toronto Press, 1959), pp. 221-22.

[7] Alexander Brady, *Democracy in the Dominions*, 3rd ed. (Toronto: University of Toronto Press, 1958), p. 102; H. McD. Clokie, *Canadian Government and Politics* (Toronto: Longmans, Green Ltd., 1944), p. 80; R. MacGregor Dawson, *The Government of Canada*, 3rd ed. (Toronto: University of Toronto Press, 1957), p. 508.

[8] Herbert McClosky, "Consensus and Ideology in American Politics," *American Political Science Review*, LVIII (June 1964), 361-82.

[9] Robert R. Alford, *Party and Society* (Chicago: Rand McNally, 1963); Mildred A. Schwartz, *Public Opinion and Canadian Identity* (Berkeley: University of California Press, 1967).

[10] This is adapted from Lipset's discussion of the reasons which have been given for the lack of a strong socialist movement in the United States. S. M. Lipset, *Agrarian Socialism* (Berkeley and Los Angeles: University of California Press, 1950), p. 2.

accompanied by a slow growth of labour unions, and relative to these factors, prior recognition of the rights of workers through the provision of public education and the right to vote.[11] None of these factors are intended to suggest that there have not been and will not continue to be gross inequalities in the social and economic rewards enjoyed by Canadians. But what we reiterate is that the existence of inequality does not necessarily lead to overt hostility which can be mobilized by specific political parties. Such class hostility as does exist has not led to widespread demands for a major overhaul of the society. To varying degrees, the two major parties have been responsive to demands for social welfare. On issues such as public education or government ownership, they have usually avoided quarrels of an ideological nature and have thus sidestepped class issues *per se*.

The class conflict which does exist in Canada has, for the most part, been conducted in arenas outside those of national party politics. Overt conflict has been expressed at the provincial level, by minor parties, and by rural interests. Obviously, given the Canadian situation, these three are interrelated, but we will look at each arena of conflict separately.

Partly because of jurisdictional grounds, class issues have been relatively confined to provincial politics. The framers of the British North America Act allotted to provincial governments powers which hardly seemed considerable at the time of Confederation, but which increased with growing industrialization to encompass much of the legislation covering the conduct of business within the confines of each province. We have already discussed how this has had implications for unevenness in the wage structure and weakness in the trade union movement. In addition, it has normally been provincial governments who have intervened in major strikes, such as that of the asbestos workers in Murdochville, the automobile workers in Windsor, and the woodworkers in Newfoundland. The party forming the government in these instances was Union Nationale in Quebec and Liberal in Ontario and Newfoundland. Even the CCF Government in Saskatchewan was not immune to labour conflicts, if we view the doctors' strike in that province as a conflict between government and labour. The main exception to the involvement of provincial governments occurred during the Winnipeg General Strike of 1919, when the federal Conservative Government, alarmed by fears of insurrection, moved directly to quell the strike. The federal government also deals with problems of labour unrest in such government-regulated, nation-wide industries as railways and airlines.

In the political arena, it has been mainly the minor parties which have provided the foci for class interests. We recall that these same parties have been predominantly local rather than national in scope and effectiveness. Since Confederation many representatives of labour have appeared, but mainly they have been short-lived and of fleeting impact.[12] Prior to the formation of the CCF, there were numerous labour parties at the provincial level, some of which joined into two larger federations, the Independent Labour Party and the Canadian Labour Party. Of the

THE EFFECTS OF POLITICAL PARTIES

smaller groups with some ideological cohesion, of main historical interest is the Socialist Party of British Columbia. It was founded in 1904 and possessed remarkable durability and vitality, yet it never had more than a few thousand members. This was apparently the first socialist party in Canada, though not the last. The minor party with greatest impact as a class party has been the CCF. But its history in this regard is an important lesson in understanding the role of class issues in Canadian politics. In 1933, the Regina Convention of the CCF began with an ideological attack on Canadian society and a dedication to its complete restructuring. Delegates promised, just as soon as they would achieve power, to do away completely with all forms of capitalist society. In the 1956 Winnipeg Convention, attended by some of the same people who had been present at the birth of the CCF, this ideological promise was disregarded and no mention was made of the evils of capitalism. This is not to say that the NDP now, like the CCF before it, does not continue to attract many voters because it is perceived as the spokesman of the working class against the interests of business. In fact, in attracting such class-conscious support, the CCF/NDP has probably served to channel off class hostility that might otherwise have been expressed in fiercer conflict between the major parties. Yet the position taken by the 1956 convention is instructive in that it represents the assessment of seasoned political leaders and party theoreticians, that an emphasis on class issues gives a party only limited mileage in the Canadian political milieu.

One of the peculiarities of class conflict in Canada, shared to some extent with the United States, has been its manifestation as agrarian protest.

The history of American political class consciousness has been primarily a story of agrarian upheavals. From Shay's Rebellion through the Jeffersonian and Jacksonian movements in the United States and the "Clear Grits" in Canada, American farmers have been in the forefront of the battle against the control of society by business. The agrarian revolt became significant as part of the world-wide movements for economic collectivism after the Civil War, when western wheat-belt farmers had to resort to various collectivist schemes to alleviate the coercions of a growing monopoly capitalism.[13]

The precursors of a more elaborated conflict of interests between East and West and urban and rural dwellers were in existence in pre-Confederation days. Historically, the tension between free trade or low tariff versus high tariff advocates had its roots in the search for profitable

---

[11] For an elaboration of the significance of these and related factors, see the provocative essay in Reinhard Bendix, *Nation-Building and Citizenship* (New York: John Wiley & Sons, 1964), pp. 55-101.

[13] See the comments by Howard Scarrow on the difficulty of distinguishing between genuine labour parties and candidates who independently listed themselves as representing labour. Howard Scarrow, *Canada Votes* (New Orleans: Hauser, 1962), pp. 9-10.

[13] Lipset, *Agrarian Socialism*, p. 3.

markets for primary, agricultural products rather than for manufactured goods. Manufacturers said they required tariff protection in order for industry in Canada to emerge and flourish in the face of competition from more densely populated and highly industrialized nations. Farmers, and also fishermen, loggers, and fur trappers, wanted to be able to sell as great a quantity of their products as possible, especially in larger markets than those provided by the Canadian population. At the same time they wanted to be able to buy the manufactured products they required at the lowest possible prices. The political focus for these economic views were the Clear Grits of Upper Canada. Especially during the decade preceding Confederation, these doctrines were vigorously presented by George Brown and the Toronto *Globe*. Then, as the West became settled and large-scale farming was instituted at the turn of the century, the sense of exploitation by Eastern business interests grew. Not only did the Easterners control the sale of manufactured products, but the difficulties of financing so uncertain an enterprise as farming were apparently aggravated by the fact that banking too was in the hands of unsympathetic Easterners. Populist movements to revamp the economy and give farmers a greater share of the rewards, along with greater control over their financial destinies, had then their greatest appeal among one-crop farmers in Western Canada. These farmers were peculiarly vulnerable, because of geography and concentration on one crop, to natural disasters, international market fluctuations, and dependence on outside financial assistance.[14] That these difficulties and interests were not confined to Western farmers is attested to by the strength of the United Farmers of Ontario around 1920. Agrarian protest in the rest of the country was given political expression by the United Farmers' parties and the Progressive Party. But once these parties achieved some impact on the political scene and were able to make the major parties and Eastern business acknowledge their legitimate claims to share more equitably in the resources of Canada, the movements passed from the scene. The CCF, aided in its popular appeal by the disasters of the 1930's, later picked up where the Progressives left off. And, in the case of that party, as the farmer has become less radical and the need for new and additional electoral support has become pressing, the shift has been increasingly to urban, working class interests, especially with the formation of the NDP.

Our argument has been then that conditions, both political and other, have led Canadian parties to foster consensus on social class issues. The major parties have been aided in this role by the diversion of class hostility into provincial politics, the activities of minor parties, and the focus on rural interests.

•

RELIGION

Throughout Canada's history as a nation, the political relevance of religion has always existed. Leadership provided by political parties has frequently reflected religious tensions and sometimes exacerbated them, but has rarely served to foster a spirit of ecumenism. The reasons why this should be so are not immediately self-evident. British rule over the former French possessions began with an auspicious air of tolerance that was unusual for the time. Catholics in Canada were from the outset permitted freedoms that were still forbidden to their co-religionists in England.[15] Again, unlike the English situation, there was to be no established church in Canada. The existence of a conquered people, who were set apart by their language, religion, and way of life, and whose indigenous leadership was now pretty well confined to that provided by the Catholic Church, meant that those concerned with protecting French identity were almost irresistibly drawn into politics. And who was there to serve as the spokesman of French interests but the Catholic Church? In the meantime, settlement from both England and the thirteen colonies, by those accustomed to Anglican privileges, led such settlers to political involvement in order to perpetuate their advantages, especially in the face of concessions granted to Catholics. The ancestor of the Conservative Party answered the purposes of both groups, aided in this apparently contradictory role by the separation of Upper and Lower Canada. Not all Protestants were Anglicans, and there were objections to the political ascendancy of the Anglicans, spiritually and temporally. Land set aside from Crown land grants for the support of Protestant clergy and the disposition of these so-called clergy reserves became the subject of bitter controversy, which added to the grievances of non-Anglicans participating in the Rebellion of Upper Canada in 1837. The antecedent of the modern Liberal Party hence had, as one of its bases, opposition to both the Anglican and Catholic Churches.

In the present century, one significant change has been the realignment of Catholic voters, who now support the Liberal Party in the majority of cases. This transformation was mainly the result of the leadership of Sir Wilfrid Laurier. Support for the Liberals from the Catholic Church hierarchy was not so rapid to develop, and there is evidence[16] that even in recent times there have been more feelings of affinity with the Conservatives. Be that as it may, Laurier's leadership marks a turning point in the nature of Catholics' partisan loyalties. But Laurier was not unaided by his opponents, both then and now. At times, actions which served to turn Catholics away from the Conservative Party were those which affected them at least as much because of their French origin. Such was the case, for example, with the Manitoba school question, the treatment of Riel, and the conscription crises of the two World Wars. But

---

[14] *Ibid.*; W. L. Morton, *The Progressive Party in Canada* (Toronto: University of Toronto Press, 1950); C. B. Macpherson, *Democracy in Alberta* (Toronto: University of Toronto Press, 1953).

[15] For a legal history of religious liberty in Canada, see D. A. Schmeiser, *Civil Liberties in Canada* (London: Oxford University Press, 1964), pp. 54-117.

[16] John Meisel, "Religious Affiliation and Electoral Behaviour: A Case Study," *Canadian Journal of Economics and Political Science*, XXII (November, 1956), 481-96.

Catholicism, regardless of national origin, was at issue in other instances. One such example must now appear strange to Canadians, who associate the Ku Klux Klan with outrages against Negroes in the southern United States. But strange or not, the Ku Klux Klan was active in Canada during the 1920's. Its program was violently anti-Catholic and it gave support to the provincial Conservatives in Saskatchewan. While this support seems to have been uninvited, it was not actively repudiated, and it lived on to taunt Mr. Diefenbaker. While Mr. Diefenbaker was a candidate in Saskatchewan at the time of the Klan's activities, he disavowed himself from its extremist sentiments. Yet some opponents tried to tie him in with Klan support, particularly during the 1957 election campaign.

The sources of Catholic estrangement from the Conservative Party are many and these few examples give only some possible sources for this. The effects, however, are clear. Both in terms of voting behaviour and political opinions, Catholics are and continue to remain distinguishable from Protestants.[17] While the findings are partly the result of the coincidence of Catholic religion and French origin, so that conceivably our findings are due to French opposition to the Conservatives, this is not solely the case. In a study of the 1962 general election, Alford found that, province by province, Catholics were more likely to support the Liberal Party and less likely to support the Conservatives than were Protestants. Frequently in fact, a majority of Catholic voters in each province supported the Liberals.[18] The Conservatives, in turn, have helped perpetuate these patterns by an apparent reluctance to learn from the past and to find ways of attracting Catholic support.

It is hardly fair to blame the Conservatives for a deliberate policy of alienating Catholics when this end result has often been the outcome of adventitious historical factors. In other words, it is only rarely that they have either actively or tacitly engaged in deliberately anti-Catholic policies, as in their tie-in with the Ku Klux Klan and the more vociferously anti-Catholic pronouncements of the Orange Order. But such active antagonism to particular religious groups has not been foreign to Canadian politics. The anti-Semitism of French-Canadian nationalist parties such as Bloc Populaire, the repressive policies of the Union Nationale Government against Jehovah's Witnesses, restrictions on Amish and Hutterite settlements by the Social Credit Government of Alberta, and the conflicts between the Social Credit Government in British Columbia and the Doukhobours, bespeak an intolerance of religious minorities. While nowhere so overt in the major parties—there is some unpublished evidence which suggests that, federally at least, minority religions vote Liberal most frequently—both of the older parties reveal a lack of representation in their leadership echelons from among the smaller, less "prestigious" religious groups.

If we could imagine Karl Marx reading the foregoing passages on religion, we might predict his reactions. Aside from some scathing criticism of the moral bankruptcy of bourgeois parties, which align themselves on religious rather than social class lines, he would bemoan the "false

THE EFFECTS OF POLITICAL PARTIES

consciousness" of the workers, which permits them to be distracted from following their class interests. Forgetting for the moment the emotion-laden language, freely adapted from Marx, in which these imaginary criticisms are couched, they still have considerable relevance. Why, in a modern, industrialized nation, should religious cleavages have such primacy in party politics? To some extent we know the answers, lying as they do in the historical conditions of Canada's development and in the long-range stability of political patterns. At the same time, there may be some portents that religion will be of declining importance in political attitudes and behaviour and in the subsequent actions of parties. (We say subsequent here since this is not an area where parties are likely to take the initiative until they are certain it is safe to do so.) Membership in churches is high, but attendance is declining, suggesting that the social rather than the theological content of religion has become important. And while memberships in different groups will always be divisive, it is a different kind of divisiveness than that based on beliefs and values. In Quebec, the pervasiveness of the Catholic Church shows signs of weakening. Greater participation of the laity, loosening Church control over education, evidence of self-criticism, and even the emergence of an anti-clericalism dormant since the decline of Le Parti Rouge, suggest a weakening of Church influence over all facets of life. This is now an era of ecumenism and if different religions can begin a dialogue, then we might anticipate that political parties will be influenced by this as well. Finally, we would suggest that practical politics will be an ever increasing consideration in contributing to the decline of religious-based political cleavages. Take the example of Toronto. Toronto was the centre of Conservative strength, of the Protestant establishment, and the Loyal Orange Order. After World War II the city became transformed and now the single largest denomination is Catholic. Picture then the annual Orange parade on July 12th, intended to commemorate William III's victory for Protestantism. In recent years the streets leading to City Hall have been lined with Catholic bystanders, many who could not yet speak English but who could still enjoy the band, the drum majorettes, and King Billy on his white horse. The final ludicrous touch came when the marchers were received on the steps of City Hall by a Jewish mayor—altogether then, a far cry from the days when Orangemen were ready to use force against Catholics in the interests of the Conservatives.

•

ETHNICITY

Was Lord Durham really surprised when he reported, several decades before Confederation, on finding "two races warring in the bosom of a

---

[17] *Ibid.*; Alford, *Party and Society*; Schwartz, *Public Opinion and Canadian Identity.*
[18] Robert R. Alford, "The Social Bases of Political Cleavage" in *Papers on the 1962 Election,* ed. John Meisel (Toronto: University of Toronto Press, 1964), p. 215.

single state"? After the British victories, which came at a period of growing discontent in the thirteen colonies, the British authorities had made important concessions to the French settlers (after the Acadian repressions), much to the objection of English settlers both coming into Canada and remaining in the colonies. These concessions were important later for retaining the loyalty, or at least passivity, of the French during the Revolutionary War. Our point is that there have always been those who have believed that the French were a conquered people and should be treated accordingly,[19] kept in a submissive position, made to give up their cultural identity, and eventually made to become English. It may come as something of a shock to American readers, for example, to discover that French-speaking Canadians have sometimes been told by their English-speaking compatriots to "speak white." Yet at no time in the history of Canada have the divisions between English and French been more salient than they are at present. So acute have become the tensions, or at least so aware has become the Government, that a Royal Commission on Bilingualism and Biculturalism was appointed in 1963, empowered "to inquire into and report upon the existing state of bilingualism and biculturalism in Canada and to recommend what steps should be taken to develop the Canadian Confederation on the basis of an equal partnership between the two founding races. . . ."[20] Why such pressing dissatisfaction should have emerged now, after generations of apparent satisfaction with the arrangements of 1867, is not easy to answer. Perhaps it is, that as Quebec has become more industrialized, urbanized, and prosperous, its more educated members have become painfully conscious of how they have lagged behind the rest of Canada, particularly in comparison to Ontario, in social and economic welfare. At the same time, increased education and prosperity have been accompanied by increased self-pride and a new awareness of the value of sustaining a French-Canadian identity.[21] Whatever the reasons, and they are undoubtedly complex ones, it is enough for us at this point to be reminded of the existence of *le fait français* in relation to the role of political parties.

In our preceding discussion we noted examples of how parties had faced important problems related to religion in content or implications. Many of the examples we cited frequently had even greater implications for ethnic tensions. Specifically, those times when the Conservative Party has, by its positions, reflected or increased tensions between Catholics and Protestants, it has also done so between French and English. Riel, the Boer War, the conscription crises, and the flag issue have all been instances in which Conservative policies have served to divide the population primarily along ethnic lines.

Attempts at consensus building include the representation of ethnic interests within parties, culminating in the institution of the "lieutenant." While the skillful use of a French language deputy was first employed by John A. Macdonald, it has been the Liberal Party which has used this device most successfully since then.

The minor parties have frequently served as a focus for conflict. In the case of the CCF/NDP, this has probably been largely unintentional. Its identification as a socialist party has aroused some religious scruples among French Catholics, while its centralist policies have repelled others. Especially since the formation of the NDP, there have been special efforts made to attract French voters, but thus far without much success, at least outside of Montreal. More deliberately provocative are those Quebec-based parties whose main rationale is narrowly nationalistic in nature, and thus sets them apart from the rest of Canada.

In terms of population composition, Canada is a multi-ethnic, rather than a bi-ethnic, society. At present, those of non-British, non-French origin constitute almost as large a share of the population as do those of French origin. The political impact of a growing population realignment is not yet clear. But there is little doubt that the existence of other European origins has the potential for new conflict. While the terms of reference of the Royal Commission on Bilingualism and Biculturalism began by stressing the equality between the "two founding races," that same introductory sentence continued with the injunction that the Commissioners take "into account the contribution made by other ethnic groups to the cultural enrichment of Canada and the measures that should be taken to safeguard that contribution."[22] Unlike the French minority, however, those of other European origins are diverse in background and social interests and, except in the most general terms, cannot be treated as any kind of united group.

To the political parties, as other origins have increased in numbers, they have also increased in significance as voters. And as such, they are important for the parties to deal with. There is, however, a qualitatively different manner of dealing with these ethnic groups than with the French. To varying degrees the political parties present policies and programs to members of what the "B and B" Commission call "the founding races," or what John Porter terms "the charter groups,"[23] which acknowledge the legitimacy of their claims to the leadership of Canadian society. But as far as other ethnic groups are concerned, they are primarily of interest to political parties as voters and not as co-partners in the nation. This does not mean that other ethnic groups are ignored, nor that they are given second-class status. But nonetheless, there is an important difference in the way parties approach these ethnic groups.

There is unfortunately not much data available on the activities of parties in relation to non-British, non-French origin groups. A survey of activities in the Toronto area during the 1962 federal election indicated

---

[19] French-Canadian nationalists are also inclined to see themselves as a conquered people, but the implications they draw from this are quite different from what we are discussing in the text.

[20] Canada, P. C. 1963-1106.

[21] See the brief discussion in Canada, *A Preliminary Report of the Royal Commission on Bilingualism and Biculturalism*, Ottawa: Queen's Printer, 1965, pp. 109-10.

[22] Canada, P. C. 1963-1106.

[23] John Porter, *The Vertical Mosaic* (Toronto: University of Toronto Press, 1965), p. 60.

that the Conservatives, Liberals, and NDP all made special efforts to contact ethnic voters.[24] Both the Conservative and Liberal parties had specially designated officials for liaison with these groups. The NDP did not have any organizational relationships with ethnic groups, but did have some satisfactory contacts through trade unions. Of the three parties, the Conservative was assessed as having made "the most thoroughgoing efforts to maintain close relations with ethnic voters. These include[d] such things as providing speakers for organizations, supplying press releases for the ethnic press, and serving as a clearing house for reports and recommendations from ethnic representatives. To keep in tune with developments, the ethnic press was carefully scanned, some research was undertaken, and ethnic leaders and party supporters were eagerly sought after for opinions and advice."[25] At the riding level, ethnic representatives were frequently on hand to give their support at the nomination of candidates, as were pretty girls in national costume. Voters' lists were examined and subdivided according to the presumed origin of voters and the voters were then contacted by canvassers of the same origin. Campaign literature was also often available in languages other than English.

At times, the courtship of leaders of ethnic organizations and the ethnic press can be pursued too assiduously. "For the rank-and-file voter, being courted by a party specifically as a member of an ethnic group can lead to feelings of suspicion as to how he is viewed as a Canadian and he may resent the implication that he is under the political control of his ethnic community leaders."[26] Be that as it may, ethnic group members, especially if they are immigrants, often face many problems with which party candidates can help. If aid can be given in bringing relatives to Canada or, less directly, in passing new social welfare legislation beneficial to all lower income groups, candidates and parties can thereby contribute to forging bonds of partisan loyalty.

On balance, the Conservatives, Liberals, and CCF/NDP, while not always successful, at least have directed their efforts to building consensus across ethnic lines, where the lines of ethnicity have not included the French. In the case of the Conservatives, the leadership of John Diefenbaker was important in making the transition from a Protestant, Anglo-Saxon party to one which more truly represented the multiplicity of ethnic origin groups presently living in Canada.

•

REGION

In combination with ethnic and economic factors, regional divisions make up the most critical cleavages in Canadian society. Efforts directed toward the establishment of a consensus across regional lines include those accommodative policies designed to deal with specifically regional problems and to overcome regionally-based inequalities. The Atlantic Development Board, the Canadian Wheat Board, and the Maritime

Marshland Rehabilitation Act are examples of the instruments used by both major parties, when they form the national government, to deal with the special regional-economic problems. Less directly instrumental in compensating for unequal economic development, but an important avenue for making known special regional grievances and assuring regions that they are a major concern of the federal government, is the custom of ensuring that regional spokesmen are present in the federal government. The Senate had originally been intended to safeguard provincial interests, but as it became clear that a body appointed for life by the central government was not well suited for this purpose, other agencies had to be found. Some protection was provided by the judiciary, in the decisions pronounced by the Supreme Court and the judicial committee of the Privy Council. More satisfying, both symbolically and in practice, has been the custom of appointing regional representatives to the Cabinet. As discussed in Chapter 6, each province, if at all possible, is represented by at least one Cabinet Minister, and the larger ones by several. In addition, it is traditional that the Minister of Fisheries come from the Maritimes, or less usually, from British Columbia and the Minister of Agriculture from the West. In 1965, only one Liberal was returned from the three prairie provinces, a situation which necessitated giving the Ministry of Agriculture to John J. Greene, representing the Ontario riding of Renfrew South.

Having been out of office since the election of 1896, the Conservatives had the task of forming a government under Borden in 1911. Heath MacQuarrie has given us a colourful description of the political debts paid and the tightrope balancing between divergent interests practiced in the formation of Borden's first Cabinet.[27] One Conservative had been elected from Saskatchewan and one from Alberta, but only the member from Calgary, R. B. Bennett, was deemed worthy of filling the role of provincial representative. In an effort to encourage national unity and regain Conservative support in French Canada, Borden brought together a strange fellowship. His Cabinet included French-speaking members of Bourassa's Nationalist movement, imperialists strongly in favour of ties with Britain, staunch Catholics and staunch Orangemen. Perhaps if there had been no war and no conscription crisis, Borden's efforts would have been successful. But unhappily these events did occur, and after the election of 1917, the new Union Government could call on no elected members from French Canada to take their place in the Cabinet.

While not quite as decimated, the Conservatives were in similar straits when they formed the government in 1957 and had to choose ministers from only eight members elected in Quebec. Unlike the earlier situation

---

[24] Mildred A. Schwartz, "Political Behaviour and Ethnic Origin" in *Papers on the 1962 Election*, ed. John Meisel, pp. 253-71.

[25] *Ibid.*, p. 267.

[26] *Ibid.*, p. 268.

[27] H. N. MacQuarrie, "The Formation of Borden's First Cabinet," *Canadian Journal of Economics and Political Science*, XXIII (February 1957), 90-104.

of the Liberals, that experienced by both major parties in 1917, the late 1950's, and the 1960's represents another order of phenomena: a poor showing regionally was not the result of losing out to a third party but the effect of an imbalance between the two major parties in their regional appeal. Whatever the conditions contributing to the breakdown of the principle of regional representation in the Cabinet, the end results are the same. One of the major parties may display an apparent indifference to local problems and a reluctance to engage in a tough electoral struggle because a province does not represent many seats. The espousal of local interests may be left to minor parties, which are consequently reinforced in their role as conflict leaders. A major party may become so closely identified with a region and its interests that it appears reluctant to expend the energy necessary to diversify its appeal. In the end, however, the major parties as much as the minor ones lose their claim to be the representatives of national interests. Failing to gain broad support, they can make little justifiable assertion of an ability to contribute to a genuine consensus on issues and political goals across regional lines.

•

PARTIES AND THE DEVELOPMENT OF A NATIONAL CONSCIOUSNESS

To summarize our account of the interplay between consensus and conflict in the roles played by Canadian parties, we can conclude with no simple, one-way relationship. We have noted instances of parties acting both to foster consensus and to further conflict. Under what circumstances these occur and in relation to which parties is not easy to generalize. But some indistinct patterns do emerge. For example, in respect to issues of social class, the major parties come out on the side of consensus. They have been aided in their efforts by a host of factors associated with the social structure of Canada. In addition, the class conflict which has occurred has been outside of national major party politics. It has been expressed at the provincial level, by minor parties, and by rural interests.

Unlike social class issues, those of religion have been highly relevant to the major parties as well as the minor. History has repeated itself often enough in Canada to have kept Catholics away from the Conservatives and in the Liberal fold. Other religious groups are dispersed among the parties, although there is some suggestion that minorities have been attracted disproportionately to the Liberal Party and to third parties. In concluding our discussion of religion, while we were faced with continuing evidence of the significance of religion in aligning voters, we also looked for hopeful signs of a decline in its political relevance.

Like religion, ethnic origin is a salient factor bearing on the effects of political parties on the society. Most overt conflict has centred on the place of the French-speaking in Canadian society, and as a consequence of such conflict, the majority of French Canadians in this century have given their loyalty to the Liberal Party, diverted only by the more pressing claims of parties indigenous to French Canada. Parties, however, play more of a consensus-inducing role with respect to voters of neither French nor British origin.

Region appears to be one important social division in which the major parties direct their attention to fostering consensus. This is done through the presentation of special policies designed to ameliorate conditions peculiar to one or more areas and devices for representing regional interests. But not infrequently a major party with the potential for forming the national government, fails to draw adequate support from a province because of competition from a third party or from the other major party. Whenever this occurs, even when a party achieves enough national support to form the government, it is seriously curtailed, both symbolically and practically, in providing leadership supportive of national unity.

Section IV

CONCLUSIONS

12

Canadian Parties:
Classification and Interpretation

•

One hundred years of Confederation have done little to change the clearly visible aspects of the Canadian party system. In the 1870's, the effective choice of the Canadian voter was between a government of the Conservative or the Liberal Party; in the 1960's, his effective choice remains the same. These parties grew out of the early experiences with responsible government in pre-Confederation Canada; the original components of their social bases can be found in the social matrix of that era.

But the fact that the same parties face each other after a century does not tell the whole story. The relevant part of the story on the Canadian party system involves the entire interaction of society and party since the parties came into existence. Canadian society began with French and English Canada and the Maritimes; it then developed the West, took in myriads of immigrants, and became industrialized, without ever equalizing or homogenizing people, resources, or rewards.

In the course of these developments in Canadian society during the past century, several new parties have been formed. We have shown in the early chapters that neither social class nor ethnicity nor religion were prime factors in the formation of national parties in Canada, though ethnicity and social class have been significant in regional party formation. The recently formed NDP, however, may be developing into a party which is differentiated along social class lines on a national scale. Durable new parties have come about when the ethnic or the economic factor has been linked with regional differentiation. The partial alienation of

French Canada and the agricultural West from the polity has led to new parties that are still with us.

This formation of new parties in the second half-century of Confederation has had two important effects. The first has been to give some differentiation and volatility to party life in French Canada without, however, leading to the development of a party which pits most of French Canada against the rest. The second has been the linking within the CCF of forces of Western agrarian protest with elements of organized labour. Now that the CCF has become the NDP, a party in which labour strongly outweighs Western agriculture, it is becoming increasingly based on social class. However, it is far from being in a position to pit the manual against the non-manual occupation groups.

While the changes in Canadian society since Confederation have given rise to new parties, the major parties have adapted to these changes and have gone a long way toward accommodating them. As a result, while the rise of third parties has affected the competitive conditions among parties in Ottawa and in the provinces, the primacy of the Liberals and the Conservatives in national politics remains.

●

THE DIMENSIONS OF CANADIAN PARTIES

In the first chapter, we introduced five dimensions along which political parties may be characterized: circumstances of party origin, breadth of party support, party organization and leadership, focus of appeal, and relation to government. Much about these dimensions has been implied in our discussion throughout the book. Now, in concluding, we are ready to discuss the application of these dimensions to Canada, and to use them to classify Canadian parties.

Circumstances of Party Origin

While it is possible to tie the origins of both the Liberal-Conservatives and what was to become the Liberals to particular social groupings, both Conservatives and Liberals attained a clear organizational status, and organizational permanence within Parliament. Canada is therefore one of the few countries whose major parties can be said to have parliamentary origins. The origins of all subsequent parties, transient or lasting, locally confined or nation-wide, have been extra-governmental. All of these parties were formed to give representation to one (or more) particular interest, ideology, or distinct population grouping.

Breadth of Party Support

Originally, the precursors of the Conservatives and the Liberals came from different social groupings. It was Tories versus Clear Grits in Canada West, and Bleus (and the Montreal business community) versus

Rouges in Canada East. But competition for office in the new Confederation made both parties broaden their bases. Two-party competition was taken to the new West, and the competitive position of the Liberals was improved when Laurier made his peace with the Roman Catholic Church. Numerous ethnic issues tended to polarize French-Canadian support around the Liberal Party; but after this polarization reached its maximum proportion in the conscription issue of the First World War, the Liberals managed to re-extend their base to English Canada. During the past generation, on the other hand, the Conservatives have come dangerously close to losing their national support base in French Canada. No third party has been able to establish a broad base of support in national politics.

As we classify Canadian parties along the support base dimension, we must differentiate between national and provincial parties. Nationally, as we have just indicated, only Liberals and Conservatives have a broad base of support, crossing regional, ethnic, religious, and social class lines. A point of serious reservation here is the extension of the Conservative support base into French Canada, and a less serious one the extension of the national Liberal support base into the Prairies.

In provincial politics, both Liberals and Conservatives have maintained broad support bases even in provinces where their support, such as that of both parties in Alberta, is very meagre. An exception, however, is Quebec, where the provincial Conservatives find expression through the broadly-based Union Nationale. Two decades of governing Saskatchewan turned the CCF into a broadly-based party, and the wide appeal of the Manning regime has given Alberta Social Credit a broad support base. Social Credit in British Columbia has had a broad base from its inception.

Most prominent among parties with a restricted base in the national NDP. During its history, the CCF/NDP shifted its base from wheat farmers, socialist workers, and intellectuals to a widening segment of Canada's trade unionists; but the party's base remains essentially restricted, regionally, ethnically, and with respect to social class. The support base of the national Social Credit Party, while difficult to describe, is restricted essentially to those who support provincial Social Credit governments, to French-Canadian Social Crediters and Créditistes, and to the few who still support Social Credit ideology with a missionary zeal. The NDP and Social Credit are also narrowly based in provinces they have not governed. The base of French-Canadian separatism appears to be restricted even within the French-Canadian community. The social base of Canadian Communists is restricted, as were the social bases of such successful farmers' parties as the national Progressive Party and the United Farmers of Alberta, Manitoba, Ontario, and New Brunswick.

The principal effect of social base on the Canadian party system has been the failure of any third party to establish a broad support base on the federal scene. As for the Conservative Party, its otherwise unrestricted support base has been narrowed principally by lack of support in French

242

Canada. While religion has tended to divide Liberals and Conservatives, both parties are in fact supported by numerous Catholics and Protestants. Both parties have bridged social class differences, both have some sizeable support among non-British and non-French Canadians, and both compete at least in the Maritimes, in Ontario, and on the Pacific Coast. No party competes effectively for every vote in any polity; but the breadth of the area in which Canada's major parties compete for votes is indeed remarkable.

Party Organization and Leadership

Canada had representative institutions and responsible government prior to the introduction of universal suffrage. It is not surprising, therefore, that the Conservative and Liberal parties developed as agencies more for the election of legislators than for the representation of certain popular groups. For this electoral purpose, the cadre-type organization, developed earlier in the United Kingdom, was functional. Cadre-type organization prevailed until disaffected groups—prairie farmers and some industrial labourers—sought representation outside the traditional parties. These groups challenged the Liberals and Conservatives on various grounds, an important one being those parties' mode of organization. The "boys in the back room" who allegedly arranged the financing of, and otherwise engineered, the election of legislators, and who were said to control the "old" parties, were to be replaced by masses of individuals who prized the democratic control of their party as highly as they did the democratic control of the country. The parties launched by the disaffected groups were organized, then, on the principle of mass control. The earlier organizations especially—Progressives and United Farmers—added, to more conventional European mass-membership characteristics, the radical North American feature of the recall of leaders and legislators by the collective membership.

The Liberal and Conservative parties have remained cadre parties on national and provincial levels. There are a few constituency associations in which there are many individual members, appearing not only as election workers but also as quasi-stockholders engaged in the nomination of candidates. But none of these associations has the populist notion of possessing the right to direct the destinies of the party. The national Social Credit Party and most of its provincial counterparts are also organized along cadre lines, as is the Union Nationale.

Canada's most important mass party is the CCF/NDP. While its dues-paying membership in the country has never reached 100,000, the term "mass" is based on the party's organizational principles. Throughout the party's history, the legitimate controlling power of the party's direct and indirect dues-paying members has been asserted, and has at least formal support in many intricate provisions of the party's constitutions. The mass principle has withstood twenty years of government status in Saskatchewan, buttressed by the populist tradition of the province, and a quarter century of major opposition status in British Columbia, supported by that province's socialist tradition. It is too early to say how it will maintain itself in the face of the recent, largely trade-union derived, voting support in federal politics, primarily in the urban centres of Ontario.

Social Credit in Alberta has become a cadre party during three decades of electoral success. There remain, however, elements in the party to whom early populist notions about the party remain important; these people, however, seem to be dying out. The mass principle of organization did prevail among the various United Farmers parties and in the Socialist Party of British Columbia, and it does prevail in the Communist Party.

It is quite possible that cadre-type organization, with its attending flexibility, has contributed to the longevity of the Conservative and Liberal parties. It may have helped to prolong the terms of the parties' leaders (with the exception of the blatantly unsuccessful Conservative ones), but the mass principle has done virtually nothing to encourage the rotation of CCF/NDP leaders, either in Ottawa or the provinces in which the party is important. Canada has so far followed the example of the United States, where the cadre parties have maintained their primacy, and not that of the United Kingdom, where a mass party has replaced one of the leading cadre parties; but surely organizational principle is only one of several factors responsible for this phenomenon. More clearly, the continued dominance of cadre parties has encouraged the pragmatism of Canadian political life.

Focus of Appeal

There are at least four reasons why electoral success, rather than fixed principles, has been the focus of so much of Canadian party politics. First, the colonies that united into the Dominion had the highly pragmatic task of building a nation. Second, this task needed to be accomplished by a small population with few fixed interests, and this population was continually replenished by newcomers. Third, the great neighbour to the south had already done much to build a nation along pragmatic lines with non-ideological parties. Fourth, the system of government was imported from the United Kingdom, where it had already interacted with rather pragmatic, electoral-success-oriented parties.

Canadian party politics based on principle, on the other hand, was not introduced to any important extent until the turn of the century. It began with the French-Canadian nationalism of Bourassa and socialism in British Columbia. These were followed by labour socialism elsewhere, and by populism on the Prairies. Although significant parties of principle were founded with the CCF and Social Credit, no segment of the population—neither western agriculture, nor industrial labour, nor French Canada—has given majority support to principle-oriented party politics, and certainly not for any length of time.

Both Liberals and Conservatives, nationally and provincially, have been and are oriented toward electoral success. In saying this, we are mindful of the Tory tradition with its elitism and inegalitarianism,[1] stemming from the United Empire Loyalists and sustained, sporadically as to both time and place, by the Conservative Party. A Tory leader like Arthur Meighen was surely unusual as a major party leader in Canada; pragmatists like John A. Macdonald and John Diefenbaker, although different were more typical leaders, as were their opposite numbers Laurier and King. The Tory style, sometimes combined with an imperial ideology, is the property of some Conservatives. Elitism and inegalitarianism are, however, not appealing at the hustings, not even as styles, and thus hardly affect the party's electoral stance at all. Imperial ideology as a principle finds sporadic use in Conservative electoral appeal. In Quebec, the provincial "Conservatives," the Union Nationale, have throughout been oriented toward electoral success.

Social Credit began as a party of principle. It lured Alberta populists from the UFA's cooperative notions to an utopian economic scheme which was preached with religious fervour. Social Credit as an ideology has not been repudiated officially by the party, and the ideological aspects are important among the few supporters the party musters in the eastern part of the Prairies, in Ontario, and in the Maritimes. The Quebec party, and the related Créditistes, use elements of Social Credit ideology in their federal electoral efforts in that province. The electoral effort of the national party in the mid-sixties has been a mixture of electoral-success orientation and one in the general direction of free enterprise. In the two provinces with Social Credit governments, however, the party is clearly oriented toward electoral success. In British Columbia, it has been this way ever since the party was catapulted into provincial office. In Alberta, Ernest Manning's leadership transformed the party from one of fading principle to one that could claim credit for the province's prosperity which began with the oil boom of 1947.

Among Canada's parties of principle, we find the Communists and the separatist parties of French Canada. The CCF/NDP has never ceased to be a party of principle, but its most poignant principle, socialism, has not been emphasized since the Winnipeg Declaration of 1956. However, the party continues to be a bit more than "Liberals in a hurry," especially to its opponents, who campaign against the NDP as though its purpose continued to be a major restructuring of Canadian society.

The effect of the electoral-success orientation of Canada's major parties has been to cast Canadian party politics in a pragmatic mould. Major exceptions were brought on by the disaffection of prairie farmers, by the Great Depression, and by French-Canadian nationalism. This last issue is still unresolved and may well put an unprecedented strain on the political system.

Pragmatic politics has not meant unresponsive politics. Both Liberal

---

[1] For an excellent discussion of Toryism in Canada, see G. Horowitz. "Conservatism, Liberalism, and Socialism in Canada: an Interpretation," *The Canadian Journal of Economics and Politicial Science*, XXXII (1966), 143-71.

and Conservative governments have accommodated demands of farmers and workers, and Liberals have gone far toward meeting French-Canadians demands. No one has championed effectively the cause of various segments of the underprivileged, but even chronic poverty may be about to be attacked by government. If liberal capitalism, whatever its contemporary meaning, has not been challenged successfully, it is because attempts to do so have not been strong enough; the same applies to the control of much of Canada's economy by the United States. Should these issues become much more salient, the very pragmatism of the parties will likely cause them to take up these issues, just as some modifications of the free enterprise system have already been undertaken by governing parties. We cannot predict that the major parties—much less the major parties as we know them today—will make all the adjustments that may be demanded.

Relation to Government

Of countries with competitive systems of long duration, Canada is the only one that has been governed by only two parties. The fact that two parties have governed Canada for long periods of time, and the others not at all, has significantly differentiated Liberals and Conservatives from all other parties. Only Conservatives and Liberals have had the kind of experience a party gains by governing, directing the civil service, or for that matter, occupying the official opposition benches. The distinction between them and third parties is mitigated only by the fact that third parties have governed provinces.

The Liberal Party has governmental experience in all eleven jurisdictions—Canada and the ten provinces. The Conservatives have not governed Newfoundland since Confederation, and have never governed Alberta. The governmental experience of the CCF is restricted to Saskatchewan, and that of Social Credit to Alberta and British Columbia. The Union Nationale has governmental experience in Quebec, the United Farmers' parties in Alberta and Ontario. Manitoba has been governed by several coalitions, involving at various times, along with the major parties, United Farmers, Progressives, and even the CCF and Social Credit.

Additional provincial parties have had experience as the official opposition. This includes the Conservatives of Alberta and Newfoundland, and the CCF/NDP of British Columbia, Manitoba, Ontario, and Nova Scotia.

On the national scene, the monopoly of governmental experience, shared by the Liberals and Conservatives, has probably had a self-reinforcing effect. It is futile but interesting to speculate on what might have happened to party competition in Canada had the Progressives, in 1921, assumed the official opposition role which was rightfully theirs. On the provincial scene, Social Credit in Alberta and British Columbia, the Saskatchewan CCF, and the Quebec Union Nationale, probably owe some of their staying power to their rapid accession to office. Social Credit may well have remained on the national scene primarily because of its striking electoral success in the two most western provinces. This success has since given the party a continuous hold on the governments of both provinces.

•

THE CLASSIFICATION OF CANADIAN PARTIES AND ITS IMPLICATIONS

As in Chapter 1, we here again follow our discussion of the dimensions of party characteristics with an integrative classification of parties—this time, those of Canada. Once again there is no need to include party origin in our classification, since intra-parliamentary origin is subsumed by the categories of broad base, cadre organization, electoral-success focus of appeal, and governmental experience.

Chart 12-1 indicates that Canadian parties cluster primarily into two types: broad-based, cadre parties of electoral success with governmental experience, and mass parties of principle with restricted bases and no governmental experience. The remainder of our discussion will be directed to an examination, necessarily speculative, of the implications of this pattern of party types in Canada.

The most successful parties in Canada, in terms of popular appeal and the exercise of power, both nationally and provincially, have been broad-based, cadre parties of electoral success. These include Social Credit in British Columbia and in its later stage in Alberta, Union Nationale in Quebec, and primarily, the Liberal and Conservative parties. Given Canada's inheritance of British political traditions, the nature of the governmental system, and the cleavage structure of Canadian society, it is no accident that such parties have dominated the political scene. But what have these parties contributed to Canadian society? How effectively have they provided leadership and decisions? To attempt to answer these questions we must resort to a partial dissection of party types and look separately at focus of appeal and party organization, and to a lesser extent, at base of support.

One thing which is so striking about parties that focus on electoral success is the absence of an appeal based on major policy issues. To critics of such parties, it is amazing that they have been able to convince voters to distinguish between them. Tommy Douglas, leader of the NDP, has frequently described the Conservatives and Liberals as Tweedledee and Tweedledum. In other circumstances in the United States, but again responding to the apparent absence of principle, the unsuccessful Republican presidential candidate, Barry Goldwater, emphasized that he was finally offering the voters a choice and not an echo. Can a broad-based cadre party find success governing a society by focusing on principle? The experiences of other countries are not very helpful. In the Western democracies, we could find no major parties of this type. But let us not forget that the Conservative Party under Macdonald did in fact make an appeal of principle—the National Policy.[2] Despite his style of brokerage

---

[2] Frank Underhill, "Foreword" in *Nationalism in Canada* ed. Peter Russell (Toronto: McGraw-Hill of Canada, 1966), p. xviii; Craig Brown, "The Nationalism of the National Policy" in *Nationalism in Canada*, pp. 155-62.

CHART 12-1

A CLASSIFICATION OF CANADIAN PARTIES

	Cadre		Mass	
	Government	Non-Government	Government	Non-Government
Broad — *Success*	Liberals (federal, provincial) Conservatives (federal, provincial excluding Alta. & Nfld.) Union Nationale Social Credit (Alta. & B.C.)	Conservatives (Alta. & Nfld.) Reconstructionist		
Broad — *Principle*			CCF (Sask.) early Social Credit (Alta.)	
Restricted — *Success*		Social Credit (federal, provincial excluding Alta. & B.C.)	UFA UFO	
Restricted — *Principle*		Bloc Populaire	UFM	CCF/NDP (federal, provincial excluding Sask.) UFNB Progressives Communists Socialists Rassemblement pour l'indépendence nationale

politics, he went after long-range goals and solutions rather than short-run patching. He looked for the bold, active, positive reconciliation of interests that was needed in the early years of the Dominion. A recent version of an appeal of principle, Diefenbaker's "northern vision" of 1957 and 1958, with its challenge to conquer new frontiers, was transitory and weak by comparison, but its effect on wide segments of the electorate must be noted.

While the major parties have occasionally tended to be like parties of principle, orientation to principle has more often been characteristic of minor parties. In Chart 12-1, we list the Saskatchewan CCF and the early years of Alberta Social Credit as examples of broad-based parties of principle with governmental experience. It is instructive that such parties have emerged at the provincial level, where unifying principles have been easier to promote in the face of widespread common problems, largely of an economic nature. But as Social Credit in Alberta exemplifies, an orientation to principle becomes much less attractive to the bulk of voters and much less feasible as a focus for party organization when the social structure of the province becomes increasingly complex.

The most enduring party of principle in Canada has been the CCF/NDP, in Saskatchewan as the governing party for two decades and in British Columbia as the official opposition since 1941. The party has a mass form of organization; in Saskatchewan, it also has a broad support base. The Saskatchewan CCF has thus a combination of characteristics unusual in Western democracies, but found in anti-colonial parties in emerging nations as well as in the major Communist and Fascist parties in developed countries. In Canada, mass parties of principle usually have a restricted base. The United Farmers managed to form governments in rural provinces, though in Ontario their base was too slender to maintain them in office beyond one term. Most of the Canadian mass parties, of course, have not had any governmental experience.

What then has been the relative effectiveness of parties of electoral success and parties of principle in Canada? The latter have rarely been in a position to provide governmental leaders, the former nearly always have. And the Saskatchewan CCF is the only party whose principles have been blurred—or broadened—but little by prolonged governmental leadership. But whether in office or not, parties of principle have always sought to affect decisions. They have done this as quasi-interest groups, as third parties holding the balance of power in the legislature, and as governing parties. While we do not necessarily feel that politics becomes meaningful only when parties of principle vie for power, their presence may add spirit to an occasionally stale interest brokerage.

But our dwelling on parties of principle should not deflect from the fact of dominance of success-oriented parties in Canada. Electoral success, and therefore governmental leadership, has usually gone to one or the other of the parties that have sought it above any specific principle. Forming the Government or the Opposition most times in most places, they have also done most to determine policy. They have given us passively effective leaders like Mackenzie King, but also imaginative ones like Macdonald, Laurier, and the "early" Diefenbaker. Their policies have not always been dull, nor have the bolder ones always been inspired by minor parties. On the whole, their policies have been both less compulsive and less imaginative than those of the parties of principle. History does not give us much of an answer to how different the latter would have been in office, though the course of Social Credit in Alberta may well be typical. History does tell us however that both major parties, and especially the Liberals, have as good a record in bridging Canada's social cleavages as any significant party of principle has been known to seek.

When we look at party organization, we find that cadre parties usually involve in their activities large numbers of individuals only when there is an election to be fought. Since they are oriented toward leaders, whether these are in or out of office, it has been easy for parties with a mass organization to criticize them for their lack of intraparty democracy. Certainly in theory, if not always in practice, mass parties do involve a large body of the membership in day-to-day decisions. As a result, we can expect that participants throughout the party organization will influence the selection of issues for debate, the kinds of policies evolved, and the choice of leaders. Because of the influence of members, leaders will be particularly responsive to their wishes and liable to loss of position whenever they become out of sympathy with the membership. In actual practice, however, while the membership does have considerable influence on policy making in mass parties, and certainly more than in cadre parties, this influence is always curtailed by a number of features of organized social life. For example, a party in Parliament is frequently called on to respond to events almost immediately without time for consultation with its membership outside Parliament, and the need for rapid decision making is particularly pressing in the case of parties which form the government. Size and the dispersion of members also handicap speed of consultation and the possibilities of reaching consensus. No matter how strong the commitment to popular consultation, the assumption of leadership roles in themselves will contribute to an unwillingness to give up these roles. While Michels' "iron law of oligarchy" may be an exaggeration, there is unquestionably some resistance to relinquishing leadership in all parties. As a consequence, and for other reasons as well, a mass organization party may not manifest significantly more membership participation than a cadre one. This is more likely to be the case after the party has existed for some time, and its members have lost their initial messianic fervour.[3] Yet in democratic theory, the active, politically involved citizen is considered the ideal. At the same time, however, studies of political behaviour in a number of countries have called into question the widespread existence of such citizens and, more important from the point of view of our discussion, have expressed doubt that large-scale political participation beyond voting is a healthy symptom of political stability. For example, after isolating three kinds of political orientation —participant, subject, and parochial[4]—in five countries, Almond and

CONCLUSION

Verba indicate that even where there is an emphasis on participant orientation, the resulting political culture is generally a mixed one, with subject and parochial aspects. Moreover, they see this mixture as playing a positive role in maintaining a democratic political culture, whereby, for example, the persistence of primary affiliations makes the individual's political attitudes "less intense and divisive."[5]

We can now face the question: what has been the relative effectiveness in Canada of parties with cadre and mass types of organization? The former have generally been the successful ones, and thus in a position to provide governmental leaders. We have stated that there are limits to the responsiveness of these leaders to participating party members, though the most clearly successful mass party, the Saskatchewan CCF, has always maintained some of this responsiveness. But if the mass party leader is to keep himself responsive to the party members, it is expected that the cadre party leader will keep himself responsive to the voters. In practice, this means that he will be replaced if he fails to "produce" at the polls. Here again, there are limits to this kind of responsiveness. Laurier and Diefenbaker are the two major national leaders who refused to relinquish their posts—under very different circumstances—in the face of repeated electoral failure.

In regard to decisions, the mass party seeks, in theory at least, to prepare these with the participation of members acting through resolution-passing conventions, while the cadre party, again in theory, arrives at decisions in an exchange between parliamentary leader and caucus. In practice, the attainment of governmental responsibility has caused mass parties to adapt to the latter mode, not only in Canadian provinces, but also—and more importantly—in the case of the British Labour Party. As long as policy-making remains a partially professionalized function—which it may remain until the Greek calends—the cadre party's mode of decision making will prevail as parties, no matter how organized, improve their relative standing within the polity.

The cadre organization, with its dependence on a small leadership echelon supported by experts, would seem to be both less cumbersome and more efficient than the mass organization with full scale lay partici-

---

[3] For a discussion of such transformations in the CCF, see Frederick C. Engelmann, "Membership Participation in the CCF," *Canadian Journal of Economics and Political Science*, XXII (1956), 161-73; Leo Zakuta, *A Protest Movement Becalmed: A Study of Change in the CCF* (Toronto: University of Toronto Press, 1964). Member participation in more cadre-type parties does not necessarily accompany influence on decision making either, and active participants frequently display loss of idealism in this regard. Samuel J. Eldersveld, *Political Parties: A Behavioral Analysis* (Chicago: Rand McNally, 1964).

[4] For a discussion of these concepts, see Gabriel A. Almond and Sidney Verba, *The Civic Culture* (Princeton: Princeton University Press, 1963), pp. 17-26. Briefly, participant orientations and the associated political culture emphasize rational activism. In subject orientations, there is a more passive relationship to the seats of government, though subjects do have some feelings toward them. In the parochial orientations and cultures, there is little recognition of a differentiated political system nor of a need to develop some relations with it.

[5] Almond and Verba, *The Civic Culture*, p. 475.

pation. In Canada, as in other countries with similar political systems, the most successful parties, measuring success in terms of governmental experience, have been cadre.

However, in Canada, unsuccessful cadre parties have been less significant than unsuccessful mass parties. It appears that a party oriented to principle cannot make a consistent appeal for support or operate at a high level of militancy for any length of time unless it also involves its supporters as participating members. But this combination of principle and mass organization frequently precludes winning support from a broad spectrum of voters. As a result, such parties are almost guaranteed to lose in the competition for votes.

We need say little about the relative effectiveness, in Canada, of parties with broad and restricted support bases. The success of a party with a restricted base in providing either leadership or decisions is predicated on a truncated social structure. Despite its cultural diversity, and especially the French-English division, Canada does not have subcultural cleavages that have never been bridged by political parties. It is significant that the Union Nationale has never entered federal politics, and that the Créditistes appear to have little chance of becoming the party of Quebec in Ottawa. It is even more significant that—except for the non-election years of 1942 and 1943—1965 is the only year in which the CCF/NDP showed significant signs of becoming the party of the Canadian worker. To date, the parties with broad support bases have been by far the more effective in providing leadership. In regard to policy decisions, the role of parties with restricted bases has been similar to that of parties of principle.

Our evaluation of the effectiveness of party types in Canada, inconclusive though it remains in some aspects, has by implication accounted for those categories in Chart 12-1 that have no occupant. What remains to be done is to spell out some of the implications of what has been said for the competitive conditions under which Canadian parties interact.

We said at the outset that parties form a bridge between society and government. Their nature will depend, therefore, on the kind of society and the kind of government we have. We have identified the major social cleavages of political importance in Canada as regional-ethnic (French-English) and regional-economic (Prairie agricultural-industrial East). The vote in 1965 shows that the formation of the NDP may be turning into a belated success, and that a politically relevant class cleavage may be developing. Looking at government, we find a highly centripetal, decision-oriented cabinet system in uneasy interaction with a—possibly increasingly—centrifugal federal system.

What do these factors mean in terms of party success at the polls? These factors reveal little, so far at least, that would give hope to parties of principle, mass parties, and parties with restricted bases. French Canada, the Prairies, and even the Pacific Coast, have their own parties; but these divert their energies, for the most part, to where a restricted base—speaking in nation-wide terms—gives them a chance: the provincial level. Nationally, on balance, the Liberals continue to satisfy French Canada, and Diefenbaker Conservatives have done especially well in satisfying the

Prairies. With the aid of a strong "withinput" (Easton's term for a demand stemming from the governmental structure itself) from the cabinet system, which calls for parliamentary majorities, the two major, broad-based, cadre-type, success-oriented parties have maintained a dominant position.

But at least four factors prevent us from being as sanguine about the prevailing two-party system as we would have been in 1914, or even in 1949 or 1958. (1) The support ratio between the major parties is now unbalanced not only in Quebec, but also in the Prairies. (2) CCF/NDP support has shifted from the socially declining agricultural West to labour in the Canadian heartland. (3) Federal developments have been increasingly centripetal; not only has Quebec become less "comme les autres," but the others have become more "comme le Québec." (4) Various circumstances, including the competitive balance between Liberals and Conservatives, have given Canada minority governments in four of the last five elections. It is these factors that lend some credence to Meisel's reference to the Canadian party system as "the stalled omnibus."[6] They bring into question the adequacy of both the leadership and the decisions that the two major parties can provide for Canada. For Quebec, the alternative is not Liberal or Conservative, but, as Pinard shows,[7] Liberal or something else. For the Prairies, the alternative is not Conservative or Liberal, but Conservative or something else. The industrial worker of the East appears to trisect his vote, and to cast it more strongly for the NDP. Minor parties maintain their strongholds in some of the provincial capitals, and major-party governments there flaunt their independence from Ottawa. At the seat of the national government, minority governments and strong oppositions fight each other with obstruction and allegations of scandal, with the governing party occasionally unable to provide decisions and both parties, according to many, saddled with dysfunctional but not easily removable leaders.

But what about the competitive capabilities of the parties? Is any party with a restricted base and an appeal to principle likely to be able to replace one of the major parties, as it did in the United Kingdom in the twenties? The exigencies of life in Canada impress us with the difficulties of developing broadly-appealing principles. At the most, we can only expect unifying principles to be short-lived, though this need not detract from their importance. In the long run, however, it is more likely that the myriad interests and loyalties that divide people will break up such a party unless it switches its focus to the attainment of office as an end in itself. We make a similar forecast in regard to restricted base. The number of Canadians in manual occupations is declining. Even if the class

---

[6] John Meisel, "The Stalled Omnibus," *Social Research*, XXX (1963), 367-90. The metaphor comes from G. V. Ferguson, who called the two major parties "great, nation-wide, easy going omnibus vehicles, whose occupants often have difficulty in recognizing their fellow passengers or in understanding why the driver of the bus let them in" (*Ibid.*, p. 367).

[7] Maurice Pinard, "The Rise of A Third Party" (Unpublished Ph.D. Dissertation, John Hopkins University, 1967).

vote were to increase sharply, a workers' party could attain major-party status only if it succeeded in broadening its support base to include considerable segments of white-collar employees, farmers, small business-men, or professionals, or any combination of these.

But if we see little likelihood that any minor party as now constituted will replace one of the major parties as prime competitor for office, we also see little likelihood of a return to a pure two-party system. The modified two-party system Canada now has arises from the existing polit-ically relevant fissures. It is not dysfunctional vis-à-vis the society. If it is dysfunctional, it is so vis-à-vis the system of government. If Meisel is correct in forecasting that minority governments will alternate with those enjoying fairly substantial majorities—and he may err in estimating the size of the majorities—the outputs of Canadian parties regarding both leadership and decisions may be curtailed increasingly. But society and parties are not the only variables in the polity; an additional one is the system of government. Should the omnibus break down more and more often, Canadians may have to ponder Lipset's suggestion of more than a decade ago:

. . . the peculiarities of Canadian politics . . . must be seen as the failure of the British parliamentary system to work in a society with complex internal divisions.[8]

---

[8] S. M. Lipset, "Democracy in Alberta," *Canadian Forum*, XXXIV (1954), 198.

CONCLUSION

Bibliography

•

1. CANADIAN SOCIETY

Alford, Robert R. *Party and Society: The Anglo-American Democracies*. Chicago: Rand McNally & Company, 1963.

Blishen, Bernard R., Jones, Frank E., Naegele, Kaspar D., and Porter, John. *Canadian Society*. Rev. ed. Toronto: The Macmillan Company of Canada, Limited, 1964.

Bonenfant, J. C. and Falardeau, J. C. "Cultural and Political Implications of French Canadian Nationalism." *Canadian Historical Association Annual Report*. Ottawa, 1946.

Brady, Alexander. *Democracy in the Dominions*. 3rd. ed. Toronto: University of Toronto Press, 1958.

——. "Quebec and Canadian Federalism." *The Canadian Journal of Economics and Political Science*, XXV (1959), 259-70.

Brebner, J. B. *Canada, a Modern History*. Ann Arbor: University of Michigan Press, 1960.

Brunet, M. *Canadians et Canadiens. Études sur l'histoire et la pensée de deux Canadas*. Montréal, Paris: Fides, 1955.

——. *La présence ainglaise et les Canadiens, études sur l'histoire et la pensée des deux Canadas*. Montréal: Librairie Beauchemin, 1958.

Canada. Department of Labour. Economics and Research Branch. *Skilled and Professional Manpower in Canada, 1945-55*. Royal Commission on Canada's Economic Prospects. Ottawa: July 1957.

——. Department of Labour. *Labour Organization in Canada*. Ottawa: The Queen's Printer and Controller of Stationery, 1966.

——. Dominion Bureau of Statistics. *The Canadian Balance of International*

---

*This bibliography is restricted to items on Canada. References to other items used in this book may be found in footnotes.

The categories of this bibliography do not purport to contain all of the writings on the subject categories, but rather items directly relevant to the present volume.

Payments, 1961 and 1962 and the International Investment Position. Ottawa: The Queen's Printer, August 1964.

Canada. *A Preliminary Report of the Royal Commission on Bilingualism and Biculturalism.* Ottawa: The Queen's Printer, 1965.

Clark, S. D. *Church and Sect in Canada.* Toronto: University of Toronto Press, 1948.

————. *The Developing Canadian Community.* Toronto: University of Toronto Press, 1962.

Cook, Ramsay. "The French Canadian Question." *Political Quarterly,* XXXVI (1965), 5-19.

Creighton, Donald C. *Dominion of the North.* New ed. Toronto: The Macmillan Company of Canada, Limited, 1957.

Dawson, Robert MacGregor. *The Conscription Crisis of 1944.* Toronto: University of Toronto Press, 1961.

Dion, Gérard, et O'Neill, Louis. *Le Chrétien et les élections.* Montréal: Editions de l'Homme, 1960.

Dooley, D. J. "Quebec and the Future of Canada." *Review of Politics,* XXVII (1965), 17-31.

Dziuban, Stanley. *Military Relations Between the United States and Canada, 1939-1945.* Washington: Office of the Chief of Military History, Dept. of the Army, 1959.

Easterbrook, W. T. and Aitken, H. G. J. *Canadian Economic History.* Toronto: The Macmillan Company of Canada, Limited, 1956.

Eayrs, J. "Canadian Policy and Opinion during the Suez Crisis." *International Journal,* XII (1957), 97-108.

Falardeau, Jean-Charles (ed.). *Essais sur le Québec contemporain.* Québec: Les Presses de l'Université Laval, 1953.

Filley, Walter O. "Social Structure and Canadian Political Parties: The Quebec Case." *Western Political Quarterly,* IX (1956), 900-914.

Garigue, Philippe. *Études sur le Canada Français.* Montréal: Faculté des Sciences sociales, Université de Montréal, 1958.

Gordon, Scott. *The Economists Versus the Bank of Canada.* Toronto: The Ryerson Press. 1961.

Grant, George. *Lament for a Nation, The Defeat of Canadian Nationalism.* Toronto: McClelland & Stewart, Limited, 1965.

Gzowski, Peter. "This is the True Strength of Separatism." *Maclean's* (November 2, 1963), 13-18.

Hartz, Louis. *The Founding of New Societies.* New York: Harcourt, Brace & World, 1964.

Hughes, Everett C. *French Canada in Transition.* Chicago: The University of Chicago Press, 1943.

Jamieson, Stuart. *Industrial Relations in Canada.* Toronto: The Macmillan Company of Canada, Limited, 1957.

Johnson, Harry G. *The Canadian Quandry.* Toronto: McGraw-Hill Company of Canada, Limited, 1963.

————. "The Economics of the 'Brain Drain': The Canadian Case." *Minerva,* III (Spring 1965), 299-311.

————. "Problems of Canadian Nationalism." *International Journal,* XVI (1961), 238-49.

Laurendeau, André. *La crise de la conscription.* Montréal: Editions du Jour, 1962.

Lipset, S. M. *Agrarian Socialism.* Berkeley: University of California Press, 1950.

————. *The First New Nation*. New York: Basic Books, 1964.

————. "Canada and the United States—A Comparative View." *Canadian Review of Sociology and Anthropoloy*, I (1964), 173-92.

McInnis, E. *Canada, A Political and Social History*. Revised and enlarged edition. New York: Rinehart & Company, Inc. 1959.

Morton, W. L. *The Canadian Identity*. Madison: University of Wisconsin Press, 1961.

Munro, William Bennett. *American Influences on Canadian Government*. Toronto: The Macmillan Company of Canada, Limited, 1929.

Newman, Peter C. "The Ottawa Establishment." *Maclean's*. (August 22, 1964). pp. 7-9, 33-38.

Oliver, Michael. "Quebec and Canadian Democracy." *The Canadian Journal of Economics and Political Science*, XXIII (1957), 504-15.

Porter, John. *The Vertical Mosaic: An Analysis of Social Class and Power in Canada*. Toronto: University of Toronto Press, 1965.

Reid, Escott M. "Canadian Political Parties: A Study of the Economic and Racial Bases of Conservatism and Liberalism in 1930." *Contributions to Canadian Economics*, VI (1933), 7-39.

————. "The Effects of the Depression on Canadian Politics." *The American Political Science Review*, XXVII (1933), 455-65.

Rioux, Marcel and Martin, Yves. *French-Canadian Society*, I. Toronto: McClelland & Stewart, Limited, Carleton Library No. 18, 1964.

Rotstein, Abraham. (ed.). *The Prospect of Change*. Toronto: McGraw-Hill Company of Canada, Limited, 1965.

Russell, Peter (ed.). *Nationalism in Canada*. Toronto: McGraw-Hill Company of Canada, Limited, 1966.

Schmeiser, D. A. *Civil Liberties In Canada*. London: Oxford University Press, 1964.

Schwartz, Mildred A. *Public Opinion and Canadian Identity*. Berkeley & Los Angeles: University of California Press, 1967.

Scott, Frank and Oliver, Michael (eds.). *Quebec States Her Case*. Toronto: The Macmillan Company of Canada, Limited, 1964.

Sharp, P. F. *The Agrarian Revolt in Western Canada: A Survey Showing American Parallels*. Minneapolis: University of Minnesota Press, 1948.

Siegfried, A. *The Race Question in Canada*. London: Nash, 1907.

Tansill, C. C. *Canadian American Relations, 1875-1903*. Toronto: The Ryerson Press, 1943.

Taylor, Charles. "Nationalism and the Political Intelligentsia: A Case Study." *Queen's Quarterly*, LXXII (1965), 150-68.

Trudeau, Pierre-Elliott (ed.). *La Grève de l'amiante: une étape de la révolution industrielle au Québec*. Montréal: Editions Cité Libre, 1956.

————. "Some Obstacles to Democracy in Quebec." *The Canadian Journal of Economics and Political Science*, XXIV (1958), 297-311.

Vallee, Frank G., Schwartz, Mildred, and Darknell, Frank. "Ethnic Assimilation and Differentiation in Canada." *The Canadian Journal of Economics and Political Science*, XXIII (1957), 540-49.

Wade, Mason (ed.). *Canadian Dualism: Studies of French-English Relations*. Toronto: University of Toronto Press, 1960.

————. *The French-Canadian Outlook, A Brief Account of the Unknown North Americans*. New York: The Viking Press, 1946.

————. *The French Canadians, 1760-1945*. Toronto: The Macmillan Company of Canada, Limited, 1955.

Waite, P. B. *The Life and Times of Confederation, 1864-1867*. Toronto: University of Toronto Press, 1962.

Wilson, George W., Gordon, Scott, Judek, Stanislaw, and Breton, Albert. *Canada: An Appraisal of its Needs and Resources*. Toronto: University of Toronto Press, The Twentieth Century Fund, 1965.

Woods, H. D. and Ostry, Sylvia. *Labour Policy and Labour Economics in Canada*. Toronto: The Macmillan Company of Canada, Limited, 1962.

●

2. INTEREST GROUPS AND MASS MEDIA

Clark, S. D. *The Canadian Manufacturers' Association: A Study in Collective Bargaining and Political Pressure*. Toronto: University of Toronto Press, 1939.

Cook, Ramsay. *The Politics of John W. Dafoe and the Free Press*. Toronto: University of Toronto Press, 1963.

Dawson, Helen Jones. "The Consumers Association of Canada." *Canadian Public Administration*, VI (1963) , 92-118.

————. "An Interest Group: The Canadian Federation of Agriculture." *Canadian Public Administration*, III (1960) , 134-49.

Ferguson, G. V. and Underhill, F. H. *Press and Party in Canada: Issues of Freedom*. Toronto: The Ryerson Press, 1955.

Fox, Paul. *Politics: Canada*. 2nd. ed. Toronto: McGraw-Hill Company of Canada, Limited, 1966.

Logan, H. A. *Trade Unions in Canada*. Toronto: The Macmillan Company of Canada, Limited, 1948.

Taylor, Malcolm G. "The Role of the Medical Profession in the Formulation and Execution of Public Policy." *The Canadian Journal of Economics and Political Science*, XXVI (1960) , 108-27.

Thorburn, Hugh G., "Pressure Groups in Canadian Politics—Recent Revisions of the Anti-Combines Legislation." *The Canadian Journal of Economics and Political Science*, XXX (1964) , 157-74.

●

3. THE SYSTEM OF GOVERNMENT

Aitchison, J. H. (ed.). *The Political Process in Canada: Essays in Honour of R. MacGregor Dawson*. Toronto: University of Toronto Press, 1963.

Beck, J. M. *The Government of Nova Scotia*. Toronto: University of Toronto Press, 1957.

Brady, Alexander. *Democracy in the Dominions*. See CANADIAN SOCIETY.

Clokie, H. McD. *Canadian Government and Politics*. Toronto: Longmans, Green & Company, 1944.

Corry, J. A. and Hodgetts, J. E. *Democratic Government and Politics*. 3rd. ed. rev. Toronto: University of Toronto Press, 1959.

Dawson, Robert MacGregor. *Constitutional Issues in Canada, 1900-1931*. London: Humphrey Milford, Oxford University Press, 1933.

————. *The Government of Canada*. 3rd. ed. rev. Toronto: University of Toronto Press, 1957.

————. *The Government of Canada*. 4th ed. rev. by N. Ward. Toronto: University of Toronto Press, 1963.

Donnelly, M. S. *The Government of Manitoba*. Toronto: University of Toronto Press, 1962.

Forsey, Eugene A. "The Problem of Minority Government in Canada." *The Canadian Journal of Economics and Political Science*, XXX (1964), 1-11.

——. *The Royal Power of Dissolution of Parliament in the British Commonwealth*. Toronto: Oxford University Press, 1943.

Fox, Paul. *Politics: Canada*. See INTEREST GROUPS AND MASS MEDIA.

Gwyn, R. *The Shape of Scandal, A Study of a Government in Crisis*. Toronto: Clarke, Irwin & Company, Limited, 1965.

Kornberg, Allan "Caucus and Cohesion in Canadian Parliamentary Parties." *The American Political Science Review*, LX (1966), 83-92.

——. "The Religious Factor in Canadian Attitudes toward Bi-culturalism." *The Western Political Quarterly*, XVIII (1965), 285-91.

——. "The Rules of the Game in the Canadian House of Commons." *The Journal of Politics*, XXVI (1964), 358-80.

——. "The Social Bases of Leadership in a Canadian House of Commons." *The Australian Journal of Politics and History*, XI (1965), 324-34.

—— and Thomas, Norman. "Representative Democracy and Political Elites in Canada and the United States." *Parliamentary Affairs*, XIX (1965-66), 91-102.

Laponce, Jean A. "The Religious Background of Canadian M.P.'s." *Political Studies*, VI (1958), 253-58.

Lederle, John W. "Party Forms in the Senate." *Queen's Quarterly*, LVII (1950), 21-32.

MacKinnon, Frank. *The Government of Prince Edward Island*. Toronto: University of Toronto Press, 1951.

MacQuarrie, Heath N. "The Formation of Borden's First Cabinet." *The Canadian Journal of Economics and Political Science*, XXIII (1957), 90-104.

Muller, Steven. "Federalism and the Party System in Canada." Prepared for Delivery at the 1961 Annual Meeting of the American Political Science Association, St. Louis, Missouri, September 6-9, 1961.

Scarrow, Howard A. "Federal-Provincial Voting Patterns in Canada." *The Canadian Journal of Economics and Political Science*, XXVI (1960), 289-98.

Thorburn, Hugh G. "Parliament and Policy-making: The Case of the Trans-Canada Gas Pipeline." *The Canadian Journal of Economics and Political Science*, XXIII (1957), 516-31.

Ward, Norman. *The Canadian House of Commons: Representation*. 2nd. ed. Toronto: University of Toronto Press, 1963.

——. "Parliamentary Bilingualism in Canada." *Parliamentary Affairs*, X (1957), 155-64.

——. *The Public Purse: A Study in Canadian Democracy*. Toronto: University of Toronto Press, 1962.

•

4. PARTY ORGANIZATION AND LEADERSHIP

Beck, J. M. and Dooley, D. J. "Labour Parties New and Old." *Dalhousie Review*, XL (1960), 323-28.

Bergeron, G. "Political Parties in Quebec." *University of Toronto Quarterly*, XXVII (1958), 352-68.

Borden, H. (ed.). *Robert Laird Borden: His Memoirs*. New York: The Macmillan Company, 1938.

Brady, Alexander. *Democracy in the Dominions*. See CANADIAN SOCIETY.

Careless, J. M. S. *Brown of the Globe*. Vol. I: *The Voice of Upper Canada, 1818-1859*. Toronto: The Macmillan Company of Canada, Limited, 1959; Vol. II: *Statesman of Confederation, 1860-1880*. Toronto: The Macmillan Company of Canada, Limited, 1963.

Carter, Gwendolen M. "The Commonwealth Overseas: Variations on a British Theme," *Modern Political Parties*, ed. Sigmund Neumann. Chicago: The University of Chicago Press, 1956, pp. 58-105.

Clokie, H. McD. *Canadian Government and Politics*. See THE SYSTEM OF GOVERNMENT.

Comeau, Paul-André. "La transformation du parti liberal québecois." *The Canadian Journal of Economics and Political Science*. XXXI (1965), 358-67.

Cornell, Paul G. *The Alignment of Political Groups in Canada, 1841-1867*. Toronto: University of Toronto Press, 1962.

Corry, J. A. and Hodgetts, J. E. *Democratic Government and Politics*. See THE SYSTEM OF GOVERNMENT.

Creighton, Donald C. *John A. Macdonald*. Vol. I: *The Young Politician*. Toronto: The Macmillan Company of Canada, Limited, 1952; Vol. II: *The Old Chieftain*. Toronto: The Macmillan Company of Canada, Limited, 1955.

Dafoe, J. W. *Laurier, A Study in Canadian Politics*. Toronto: McClelland and Stewart, Limited, 1963.

Dawson, Robert MacGregor. *Constitutional Issues in Canada, 1900-1931*. See THE SYSTEM OF GOVERNMENT.

————. *The Government of Canada*. See THE SYSTEM OF GOVERNMENT.

————. *William Lyon Mackenzie King: A Political Biography*. Vol. I: *1874-1923*. Toronto: University of Toronto Press, 1958.

Engelmann, Frederick C. "Membership Participation in Policy-Making in the C.C.F." *The Canadian Journal of Economics and Political Science*, XXII (1956), 161-73.

Epstein, Leon D. "A Comparative Study of Canadian Parties." *The American Political Science Review*, LVIII (1964), 46-60.

Ferns, H. S. and Ostry, B. *The Age of Mackenzie King: the Rise of the Leader*. London: Heinemann, 1955.

Filley, Walter O. "Social Structure and Canadian Political Parties: The Quebec Case." See CANADIAN SOCIETY.

Foster, W. A. *Canada First: A Memorial of the Late William A. Foster, Q.C.* Toronto: Hunter Rose Company Limited, 1890.

Graham, Roger. *Arthur Meighen*. Vol. I: *The Door of Opportunity*. Toronto: Clarke, Irwin & Company, Limited, 1960; Vol. II: *And Fortune Fled*. Toronto: Clarke, Irwin & Company, Limited, 1963; Vol. III: *No Surrender*. Toronto: Clarke, Irwin & Company, Limited, 1965.

Hoffman, David. "Intra-Party Democracy: A Case Study." *The Canadian Journal of Economics and Political Science*, XXVII (1961), 223-35.

Hougham, G. M. "Canada First: a Minor Party in Microcosm." *The Canadian Journal of Economics and Political Science*, XIX (1953), 174-84.

Hutchison, Bruce. *The Incredible Canadian: A Candid Portrait of Mackenzie King, His Works, His Times, and His Nation*. Toronto, New York: Longmans, Green & Company, 1952.

————. *Mr. Prime Minister*. Toronto: Hunter Rose Company Limited, 1964.

Irving, John A. *The Social Credit Movement in Alberta*. Toronto: University of Toronto Press, 1959.

Laporte, Pierre. *The True Face of Duplessis*. Montreal: Harvest House, 1960.

Lederle, John W. "Liberal Convention of 1893." *The Canadian Journal of Economics and Political Science*, XVI (1950), 42-52.

——. "The Liberal Convention of 1919 and the Selection of Mackenzie King." *Dalhousie Review*, XXVII (1947-48), 85-92.

Lipset, S. M. *Agrarian Socialism*. See. CANADIAN SOCIETY.

McGregor, F. A. *The Rise and Fall of Mackenzie King: 1911-1919*. Toronto: The Macmillan Company of Canada, Limited, 1962.

McHenry, Dean E. *The Third Force in Canada: The Cooperative Commonwealth Federation, 1932-1948*. Berkeley: University of California Press, 1950.

McNaught, Kenneth W. "CCF: Town and Country." *Queen's Quarterly*, LXI (1954), 213-19.

——. *A Prophet in Politics*. Toronto: University of Toronto Press, 1959.

Macpherson, C. B. *Democracy in Alberta: the Theory and Practice of a Quasi-Party System*. Toronto: University of Toronto Press, 1953.

MacQuarrie, Heath N. "Robert Borden and the Election of 1911." *The Canadian Journal of Economics and Political Science*, XXV (1959), 271-86.

Morton, W. L. *The Progressive Party in Canada*. Toronto: University of Toronto Press, 1950.

Neatby, H. Blair. *William Lyon Mackenzie King, 1924-1932: The Lonely Heights*. Toronto: University of Toronto Press, 1963.

—— and Saywell, John T. "Chapleau and the Conservative Party in Quebec." *The Canadian Historical Review*, XXXVII (1956), 1-22.

Newman, Peter C. *Renegade in Power, The Diefenbaker Years*. Toronto: McClelland and Stewart Limited, 1963.

Ostry, Bernard. "Conservatives, Liberals, and Labor in the 1880's." *The Canadian Journal of Economics and Political Science*, XXVII (1961), 141-61.

Paltiel, K. Z. "Federalism and Party Finance." Prepared for Delivery to the 1966 Annual Meeting of the Canadian Political Science Association, Sherbrooke, Quebec, June 8, 1966.

Pickersgill, John W. *The Mackenzie King Record*. Toronto: University of Toronto Press, 1960.

Quinn, Herbert F. "Third National Convention of the Liberal Party." *The Canadian Journal of Economics and Political Science*, XVII (1951), 228-33.

——. *The Union Nationale: A Study in Quebec Nationalism*. Toronto: University of Toronto Press, 1963.

Regenstreif, Peter. "Ideology and Leadership in the Canadian Party System." Prepared for Delivery at the 1964 Annual Meeting of the American Political Science Association, Chicago, Illinois, September 9-12, 1964.

Reid, Escott M. "Canadian Political Parties: A Study of the Economic and Racial Bases of Conservatism and Liberalism in 1930." See CANADIAN SOCIETY.

——. "The Effects of the Depression on Canadian Politics." See CANADIAN SOCIETY.

Roberts, Leslie. *The Chief: A Political Biography of Maurice Duplessis*. Toronto: Clarke, Irwin & Company, Limited, 1963.

——. *The Life and Times of C. D. Howe*. Toronto: Clarke, Irwin & Company Limited, 1957.

Schultz, H. J. "Portrait of a Premier: William Aberhart." *The Canadian Historical Review*, XLV (1964), 185-211.

Sévigny, Pierre. *This Game of Politics*. Toronto: McClelland and Stewart, Limited, 1965.

Sherman, P. *Bennett*. Toronto: McClelland and Stewart, Limited, 1966.

Skelton, O. D. *Life and Letters of Sir Wilfred Laurier*. London: The Century Company, 1921.

Thomas, Lewis G. *The Liberal Party in Alberta: A History of Politics in the Province of Alberta, 1905-1921*. Toronto: University of Toronto Press, 1959.

Thomson, Dale C. *Alexander Mackenzie: Clear Grit*. Toronto: The Macmillan Company of Canada, Limited, 1960.

Thorburn, Hugh G. (ed.). *Party Politics in Canada*. 1st. and 2nd. eds. Toronto: Prentice-Hall of Canada, Limited, 1963, 1967.

————. *Politics in New Brunswick*. Toronto: University of Toronto Press, 1961.

Underhill, Frank H. *Canadian Political Parties*. Canadian Historical Association booklet No. 8, Ottawa, 1957.

Williams, John R. *The Conservative Party of Canada, 1920-1949*. Durham, N.C.: Duke University Press, 1956.

•

5. PARTY PROGRAMS AND IDEOLOGY

Beck, J. M. "Socialist or Democratic Party?" *Dalhousie Review*, XLI (1961), 387-93.

Buck, Tim. *Canada: The Communist Viewpoint*. Toronto: Progress Books, 1948.

Caouette, Réal. *Réal Caouette vous parle*. Montréal: Les éditions du Caroussel, 1962.

Chaput, Marcel. *Why I am a Separatist*. Toronto: The Ryerson Press, 1962.

Dawson, Robert MacGregor. *The Conscription Crisis of 1944*. See CANADIAN SOCIETY.

Fox, Paul. *Politics: Canada*. See INTEREST GROUPS AND MASS MEDIA.

Hogan, George. *The Conservative in Canada*. Toronto: McClelland and Stewart, Limited, 1963.

Horowitz, Gad. "Conservatism, Liberalism, and Socialism in Canada: an Interpretation." *The Canadian Journal of Economics and Political Science*, XXXII (1966), 143-71.

Irving, John A. *The Social Credit Movement in Alberta*. See PARTY ORGANIZATION AND LEADERSHIP.

Kirkconnell, W. *Seven Pillars of Freedom*. 2nd. ed. rev. Toronto: Burns and MacEachern, Limited, 1952.

Knowles, Stanley. *The New Party*. Toronto: McClelland and Stewart, Limited, 1961.

League for Social Reconstruction. *Social Planning for Canada*. Toronto: Nelson, 1935.

Lewis, David and Scott, Frank. *Make this Your Canada: A Review of C.C.F. History and Policy*. Toronto: Central Canada Publishing Company, 1943.

Lipset, S. M. *Agrarian Socialism*. See CANADIAN SOCIETY.

Macdonnell, J. M. "Amateurs in Politics: Port Hope Conference." *Queen's Quarterly*, XLIX (1942), 385-93.

McGuigan, M. and Lloyd, T. *Liberalism and Socialism*. Toronto: Exchange for Political Ideas in Canada, 1964.

McHenry, Dean E. *The Third Force in Canada: The Cooperative Commonwealth Federation, 1932-1948*. See PARTY ORGANIZATION AND LEADERSHIP.

Macpherson, C. B. *Democracy in Alberta: The Theory and Practice of a Quasi-Party System*. See PARTY ORGANIZATION AND LEADERSHIP.

MacQuarrie, Heath. *The Conservative Party*. Toronto: McClelland and Stewart, Limited, 1962.

Meisel, John. "Formulation of Liberal and Conservative Programs in the 1957

Canadian General Election." *The Canadian Journal of Economics and Political Science*, XXVI (1960), 565-74.

Oliver, Michael (ed.). *Social Purpose for Canada*. Toronto: University of Toronto Press, 1961.

Pickersgill, John W. *The Liberal Party*. Toronto: McClelland and Stewart, Limited, 1962.

Regenstreif, Peter. "Ideology and Leadership in the Canadian Party System." See PARTY ORGANIZATION AND LEADERSHIP.

Smiley, Donald V. "Canada's Poujadists: A New Look at Social Credit." *Canadian Forum*, XLII (Sept. 1962). 121-23.

Thompson, Robert N. *Canadians, It's Time You Knew*. Ottawa: The Aavangen Press, 1961.

Thorburn, Hugh G. (ed.). *Party Politics in Canada*. See PARTY ORGANIZATION AND LEADERSHIP.

Underhill, Frank H. *In Search of Canadian Liberalism*. Toronto: The Macmillan Company of Canada, Limited, 1960.

————. "The Revival of Conservatism in North America." *Transactions of the Royal Society of Canada*, LII Series 3 (1958), Section II, 1-19.

Zakuta, Leo. *A Protest Movement Becalmed: A Study of Change in the C.C.F.* Toronto: University of Toronto Press, 1964.

•

6. ELECTIONS

Blair, R. S. "Electoral Competition in the Canadian Provinces." Prepared for Delivery to the 1966 Annual Meeting of the Canadian Political Science Association, Sherbrooke, Quebec, June 10, 1966.

Dean, E. P. "How Canada Has Voted: 1867 to 1945." *The Canadian Historical Review*, XXX (1949), 227-48.

Dion, Gérard et O'Neill, Louis. *Le Chrétien et les élections*. See CANADIAN SOCIETY.

Eayrs, J. "Canadian Policy and Opinion during the Suez Crisis." See CANADIAN SOCIETY.

Fox, Paul W. "Canada's Most Decisive Federal Election." *Parliamentary Affairs*, II (1958), 287-94.

Hamelin, Jean et Marcel. *Les Moeurs électorales dans le Québec de 1791 à nos jours*. Montréal: Les Éditions du Jour, 1962.

Land, Brian. *Eglinton, The Election Study of a Federal Constituency*. Toronto: Peter Martin Associates, 1965.

Laponce, J. A. "Non-Voting and Non-Voters: A Typology," *The Canadian Journal of Economics and Political Science*, XXXIII (February 1967), 75-87.

Laporte, Pierre. "Les élections ne se font pas avec des prières." *Le Devoir* (1 oct. —7 déc. 1956).

MacQuarrie, Heath N. "Robert Borden and the Election of 1911." See PARTY ORGANIZATION AND LEADERSHIP.

Meisel, John. *The Canadian General Election of 1957*. Toronto: University of Toronto Press, 1962.

————. "The June 1962 Election: Break-up of Our Party System." *Queen's Quarterly*, LXIX (1962), 329-46.

————. (ed.). *Papers on the 1962 Election*. Toronto: University of Toronto Press, 1964.

Scarrow, Howard A. "By-Elections and Public Opinion in Canada." *Public Opinion Quarterly*, XXV (1961), 79-91.

Scarrow, Howard A. *Canada Votes: A Handbook of Federal and Provincial Election Data*. New Orleans: The Hauser Press, 1962.

——. "Federal-Provincial Voting Patterns in Canada." *The Canadian Journal of Economics and Political Science*, XXVI (1960), 289-98.

——. "Patterns of Voter Turnout in Canada." *Midwest Journal of Political Science*, V (1961), 351-64.

——. "Voting Patterns and the New Party." *Political Science*, XIV (1962).

Thorburn, Hugh G. *Politics in New Brunswick*. See PARTY ORGANIZATION AND LEADERSHIP.

Wrong, Denis H. "Ontario Provincial Elections, 1934-1955: A Preliminary Survey of Voting." *The Canadian Journal of Economics and Political Science*, XXIII (1957), 395-403.

——. "Parties and Voting in Canada: A Backward and Forward Glance in the Light of the Last Election." *Political Science Quarterly*, LXXIII (1958), 397-412.

——. "The Pattern of Party Voting in Canada." *Public Opinion Quarterly*, XXI (1957), 252-64.

Young, Walter D. "The Peterborough By-Election: The Success of a Party Image." *Dalhousie Review*, XL (1961), 505-17.

•

7. PUBLIC OPINION AND ELECTORAL BEHAVIOUR

Alford, Robert R. *Party and Society: The Anglo-American Democracies*. See CANADIAN SOCIETY.

Anderson, Grace M. "Voting Behaviour and the Ethnic Variable: A Study of a Federal Election in Hamilton, Ontario." *The Canadian Journal of Economics and Political Science*, XXXII (1966), 27-37.

Beck, J. M. "The Electoral Behaviour of Nova Scotia in 1965." *Dalhousie Review*, XLIII (1966), 29-38.

Blair, R. S. "Electoral Competition in the Canadian Provinces." See ELECTIONS.

Cervin, V. "Some Correlates of Voting Behaviour in the 1952 Quebec Elections: A Pilot Study." *The Canadian Journal of Economics and Political Science*, XXI (1955), 370-73.

Cliche, Paul. "Les élections provinciales dans le Québec de 1927 à 1956." *Récherches sociographiques*, II (1961).

Davis, Morris. "Ballot Behaviour in Halifax Revisited." *The Canadian Journal of Economics and Political Science*, XXX (1964), 538-58.

Engelmann, Frederick C. and Gilsdorf, Robert R. "Recent Behavioural Political Science in Canada: An Assessment of Voting Behaviour Studies." Prepared for Delivery to the 1966 Annual Meeting of the Canadian Political Science Association, Sherbrooke, Quebec, June 8, 1966.

Fox Paul W. "A Study of One Constituency in the Canadian Federal Election of 1957." *The Canadian Journal of Economics and Political Science*, XXIV (1958), 230-40.

Grossman, L. A. " 'Safe' Seats: The Rural-Urban Pattern in Ontario." *The Canadian Journal of Economics and Political Science*, XXIX (1963), 367-71.

Groupe de Récherches Sociales. *Les électeurs Québecois*. Montréal: Groupe de Récherches Sociales, 1960.

Gzowski, Peter. "This Is the True Strength of Separatism." See CANADIAN SOCIETY.

Hamelin, Jean, Letarte, Jacques, and Hamelin, Marcel. "Les élections provinciales dans le Québec." *Cahiers de Géographie de Québec*, IV (1959-60), 5-207.

Havel, J. E. *Les citoyens de Sudbury et la politique.* Sudbury: Laurentian University Press, 1966.

Jewett, Pauline. "Voting in the 1960 Federal By-Elections at Peterborough and Niagara Falls: Who Voted New Party and Why?" *The Canadian Journal of Economics and Political Science*, XXVIII (1962), 35-53.

Johnpoll, Bernard K. "Two Aspects of Voter Behaviour in Saskatchewan." Prepared for Delivery to the 1966 Annual Meeting of the Canadian Political Science Association, Sherbrooke, Quebec, June 8, 1966.

Kamin, Leon J. "Ethnic and Party Affiliations of Candidates as Determinants of Voting." *Introductory Readings in Political Behaviour.* ed. S. Sidney Ulmer. Chicago: Rand McNally & Company, 1961, 65-73.

Laponce, J. A. "Non-Voting and Non-Voters: A Typology. See ELECTIONS.

Lemieux, Vincent. "Les dimensions sociologiques du vote créditiste au Québec." *Récherches Sociographiques*, VI (1965).

Meisel, John (ed.). *Papers on the 1962 Election. See* ELECTIONS.

————. "Religious Affiliation and Electoral Behaviour." *The Canadian Journal of Economics and Political Science*, XXII (1956), 481-96.

Pinard, Maurice. "Political Factors in the Rise of Social Credit in Quebec." Prepared for Delivery to the 1964 Annual Meeting of the Canadian Political Science Association, Charlottetown, June 1964.

Regenstreif, Peter. "The Canadian General Election of 1958." *Western Political Quarterly*, XIII (1960), 349-73.

————. *The Diefenbaker Interlude: Parties and Voting in Canada.* Toronto: Longmans Canada Limited, 1965.

————. "Some Aspects of National Party Support in Canada." *The Canadian Journal of Economics and Political Science*, XXIX (1963), 59-74.

Robin, M. "The Social Basis of Party Politics in British Columbia." *Queen's Quarterly*, LXXII (1965), 675-90.

Schwartz. Mildred A. *Public Opinion and Canadian Identity.* See CANADIAN SOCIETY.

•

8. THE CANADIAN PARTY SYSTEM: INTERPRETATION

Heasman, D. J. "The Fragmentation of Canadian Politics." *Parliamentary Affairs*, XVII (1963-64), 77-86.

————. "Political Alignments in Canada." *Parliamentary Affairs*, XVI (1962-63), 419-27.

Lipset, S. M. "Democracy in Alberta." *Canadian Forum*, XXXIV (1954), 175-77, 196-98.

Macpherson, C. B. *Democracy in Alberta: the Theory and Practice of a Quasi-Party System.* See PARTY ORGANIZATION AND LEADERSHIP.

Meisel, John. "The June 1962 Election: Break-up of Our Party System." See ELECTIONS.

————. "The Stalled Omnibus: Canadian Parties in the 1960's." *Social Research*, XXX (1963), 367-90.

Muller, Steven. "Federalism and the Party System in Canada." See THE SYSTEM OF GOVERNMENT.

————. "Massive Alternation in Canadian Politics." *Foreign Affairs*, XXXVI (1958), 633-44.

Regenstreif, Peter. "Ideology and Leadership in the Canadian Party System." See PARTY ORGANIZATION AND LEADERSHIP.

Scarrow, Howard A. "Distinguishing Between Political Parties—the Case of Canada." *Midwest Journal of Political Science,* IX (1965) , 61-76.

Smiley, Donald V. "Consensus, Conflict and the Canadian Party System." *Canadian Forum,* XL (Jan. 1961) , 223-24.

———. "One-Partyism and Canadian Democracy." *Canadian Forum,* XXXVIII (July 1958) , 79-80.

———. "The Two-Party System and One-party Dominance in the Liberal Democratic State." *The Canadian Journal of Economics and Political Science,* XXIV (1958) , 312-22.

Wrong, Denis H. "Canadian Politics in the Sixties." *Political Science Quarterly,* LXXVIII (1963) , 1-12.

Index

•

267

Federal system, political parties and, 124-30, 142-43, 145, 157-58, 197-202
Federal system, interest groups and, 94
Fielding, W. S., 194
Financing elections, 176-79
Financing parties, 135, 137-38, 147
Fiscal aspects of federalism, 127-28
"Five-cent" Speech, 199
Fleming, Donald, 84, 175
Foster, George, 89n
Fox, Paul, 89n
Franchise, 171-72
Francophobism, 105
Fredericton Conference of 1964, 139
Free Press, Winnipeg, 154
French Canadianism, 130, 136, 153, 244-45
Froman, L. A., Jr., 219n
Frost, Leslie, 196
Fulton, E. Davie, 112, 164

•

G

Gardiner, J. G., 46, 102-3
Gaudet, Hazel, 5, 77n
"Gerrymander," 123
Goldwater, Barry, 247
Globe and Mail, Toronto, 154
Gordon, Scott, 31n, 85n
Gordon, Walter, 108, 196
Gosnell, H. F., 15n
Governing party, 9-10
Government:
  operation of, as party output, 20-21
  parties and, 115-19, 183-86
  system of, Canadian, 115-32, 140-45, 254
Governmental experience, parties and, 246-47
Governmental structures, 18
Governor-General, 117, 183, 193
Graham, Roger, 121n
Greene, John J., 235
Grosart, Allister, 74
Gwyn, Richard, 75n

•

H

Hamilton, Alvin, 46, 149, 155, 175
Hannam, H. H., 103
Hanson, R. B., 193-94
Harkness, Douglas, 66
Harrill, E. E., 73n, 177
Harrold, G. L., 100
Hart, Ezekial, 60
Headquarters, party, 173, 180, 188
Health Insurance, Royal Commission on, 100

Hees, George, 164
Hepburn, Mitchell, 50, 51, 129, 198, 201
Hermens, F. A., 123n
Herring, Pendleton, 224
Hitler, Adolf, 138
Hodgetts, J. E., 148n, 225n
Home, Earl of, 193
Horowitz, Gad, 51n, 245n
Howe, C. D., 100, 102, 156
Hughes, E. C., 31n
Hugill, John W., 126
Hutchinson, Bruce, 121n, 201n

•

I

Ideological elite, 78-79
Ideology, 149-50, 153-54, 187, 244-45
  party structure and, 135-36
Immigration, growth through, 25-27
Imperial Order Daughters of The Empire, 95
Income, regional inequalities in, 29-30
Independent candidates, 142, 166
Independent Labour Party, 226
Indirect party, 136-37
Infant mortality, regional differences in, 30-31
Inputs, of political systems, 15
Intellectual elite, 139, 153-54
  opinion leadership, role of, 80-81
Interest aggregation, 93-94, 98, 107-10
Interest articulation, 92-94, 107, 150-53
Interest groups, 16-18
  access to parties of, 109-13
  accommodation of, 43-46
  influence of, 90
  organizational characteristics, 96-97
  party structure and, 136-38
  representation of, 67
  and splinter parties, 54
  taxonomy, 94-96
Internal consensus, and party influence, 206-11 (*See also* Cleavages, intraparty)
Internal issues, and party influence, 207-14
Intra-governmental party origin, 143
Intra-governmental party structure, 144-45, 168-69, 173, 182, 189
Intraparty democracy, 250
"Iron law of oligarchy," 250
Issues, policy, partisan, 155-57, 167-71

•

J

Jackson, Ernest, 197
Jamieson, Stuart, 57
Jewett, Pauline, 108, 139